MW01600649

Annals of Entrepreneurship Education and Pedagogy – 2016

ANNALS IN ENTREPRENEURSHIP EDUCATION

Series Editor: *The United States Association for Small Business and Entrepreneurship, USA*

The *Annals in Entrepreneurship Education* chronicles the state of the art in entrepreneurship education and pedagogy, both in terms of research and practice. This comprehensive source provides a focused review of top contributions delivered at USASBE's annual conference and allied activities. Invited contributions are included from scholars in the field who provide critical perspectives on methodological approaches, practices and future directions. Scholars, educators, practitioners and policy makers will find this publication to be an invaluable resource for thought leadership in entrepreneurial education.

The *Annals in Entrepreneurship Education* curates the latest and best thinking. Original material includes outcomes assessment and its impact on learning and teaching, experiential methods of learning, and methodologies that use emerging and digital tools and platforms in the classroom. This is a 'must-read' for those involved and passionate about the transformation of entrepreneurship education. Please visit the website for more information about the launch of this invaluable addition to the entrepreneurship education library: www.usasbe.org.

Titles in the series include:

Annals of Entrepreneurship Education and Pedagogy – 2014
Edited by Michael H. Morris

Annals of Entrepreneurship Education and Pedagogy – 2016
Edited by Michael H. Morris and Eric Liguori

Annals of Entrepreneurship Education and Pedagogy – 2016

Edited by

Michael H. Morris

James W. Walter Eminent Scholar Chair, University of Florida, USA

Eric Liguori

Assistant Professor of Entrepreneurship, University of Tampa, USA

ANNALS IN ENTREPRENEURSHIP EDUCATION

Edward Elgar
PUBLISHING

Cheltenham, UK • Northampton, MA, USA

Published by
Edward Elgar Publishing Limited
The Lypiatts
15 Lansdown Road
Cheltenham
Glos GL50 2JA
UK

Edward Elgar Publishing, Inc.
William Pratt House
9 Dewey Court
Northampton
Massachusetts 01060
USA

A catalogue record for this book
is available from the British Library

Library of Congress Control Number: 2016949888

This book is available electronically in the **Elgar**online
Business subject collection
DOI 10.4337/9781784719166

ISBN 978 1 78471 915 9 (cased)
ISBN 978 1 78471 916 6 (eBook)

Typeset by Servis Filmsetting Ltd, Stockport, Cheshire
Printed and bound in Great Britain by TJ International Ltd, Padstow, Cornwall

Contents

Editorial review board

Contributors

Carlos Albornoz is a Professor of Entrepreneurship at the Institute of Entrepreneurship, Universidad del Desarrollo, Chile.

Kathleen R. Allen is Emeritus Professor of Entrepreneurship and Founding Director of the Marshall Center for Technology Commercialization at the University of Southern California, USA.

José E. Amorós is Professor of Entrepreneurship, EGADE Business School, Tecnológico de Monterrey, Mexico and Adjunct Researcher, Universidad del Desarrollo, Chile.

Joseph Aniello is an Associate Professor of Management at Francis Marion University, USA.

Kendall Artz is a Professor, Chair of the Department of Entrepreneurship, and Director of the Entrepreneurship Program at Baylor University, USA.

Alex Bruton is President of The Innographer.

António Caetano is Full Professor of Organizational Behavior and Human Resources, Instituto Universitário de Lisboa (ISCTE-IUL), Portugal.

Margaret Cichosz-Grzyb is Coordinator at Bridging Entrepreneurs to Students (BETS) Program, University of Waterloo, Canada and Co-founder of Apartmint Inc.

R. Wilburn Clouse is a Research Professor in the College of Education at Middle Tennessee State University, USA.

Sara L. Cochran is a Ph.D. student in education at the University of Missouri, USA.

Silvia Fernandes Costa is a Postdoctoral Research Associate at Northeastern University, USA.

Birton Cowden is an Instructor and Associate Director, Berthiaume Center for Entrepreneurship, Isenberg School of Management, University of Massachusetts at Amherst, USA.

Martin Croteau is Director of Academic Entrepreneurship at the Ontario Centres of Excellence, Canada.

Clay Dibrell is an Associate Professor of Management in the School of Business Administration at the University of Mississippi, USA.

Donovan Dill is Youth Entrepreneurship Manager at Centennial College, Canada.

Thomas N. Duening is Team Lead and Associate Professor, Management as well as Director, Center for Entrepreneurship and the El Pomar Chair of Business and Entrepreneurship at the University of Colorado Colorado Springs, USA.

Nathalie Duval-Couetil is an Associate Professor of Technology, Leadership and Innovation, Director, Certificate in Entrepreneurship and Innovation Program, and Associate Director, Burton D. Morgan Center for Entrepreneurship, Purdue University, USA.

Jerome S. Engel is Founding Executive Director at the Lester Center for Entrepreneurship and Innovation and Adjunct Emeritus Professor at the University of California, Berkeley, USA.

Elana Fine is Managing Director of the Dingman Center for Entrepreneurship in the Robert H. Smith School of Business at the University of Maryland, USA.

Helen Fogg is the Head of Business Engagement at the Management School at Lancaster University, UK.

Valerie Fox is the Co-founder and was the Executive Director of the Digital Media Zone at Ryerson University, Canada.

Richard J. Gentry is an Assistant Professor of Management in the School of Business Administration at the University of Mississippi, USA.

Terry Goodin is an Associate Professor in the College of Education at Middle Tennessee State University, USA.

Elissa Grossman is an Associate Professor of Clinical Entrepreneurship in the Marshall School of Business at the University of Southern California, USA.

Eleanor Hamilton is Emeritus Professor of Entrepreneurship in the Department of Entrepreneurship Strategy and Innovation at the Management School at Lancaster University, UK.

Jim Hart is Director of Arts Entrepreneurship and Assistant Professor of Practice in the Meadows School of the Arts at Southern Methodist University, USA.

Justin Heacock is a Program Coordinator of the Student Innovation Incubator at the University of South Florida, USA.

Diana M. Hechavarria is an Assistant Professor of Entrepreneurship in the College of Business Administration at the University of South Florida, USA.

Giles Hertz is an Associate Professor of Business Law and Entrepreneurship at the University of Tampa, USA.

Amy Ingram is an Assistant Professor in the College of Business and Behavioral Science at Clemson University, USA.

Sarah L. Jack is Professor at the Management School at Lancaster University, UK.

Kirk Kern is Instructor/Director, Dallas–Hamilton Center for Entrepreneurial Leadership at Bowling Green State University, USA.

Eric Liguori is an Assistant Professor of Entrepreneurship in the Lowth Entrepreneurship Center at the University of Tampa, USA.

Erik Markin is a Ph.D. student in entrepreneurship in the School of Business Administration at the University of Mississippi, USA.

Annette Markvoort is an Entrepreneurial Animator at Fanshawe College in London, Canada.

Alexander McKelvie is the Chair of the Department of Entrepreneurship and Emerging Enterprises and an Associate Professor of Entrepreneurship at Syracuse University, USA.

Matthew M. Metzger is Assistant Professor of Innovation and Entrepreneurship at the University of Colorado Colorado Springs, USA.

Sam Miller is Director of the Gigot Center for Entrepreneurship and Concurrent Associate Professional Specialist at the University of Notre Dame, USA.

Kevin Moore is Director of Operations in the Entrepreneurship Center, College of Business, University of Tampa, USA.

Leigh Morland is Senior Lecturer in the Department of Leadership and Management, University of Huddersfield, UK.

Michael H. Morris holds the James W. Walter Eminent Scholar Chair and serves as the Academic Director of Entrepreneurship, Warrington College of Business Administration, University of Florida, USA.

Heidi M. Neck is the Jeffry A. Timmons Professor of Entrepreneurial Studies at Babson College, USA.

Xaver Neumeyer is Assistant Professor and Burwell Chair of Entrepreneurship at the University of North Dakota, USA.

Gene Poor is the Hamilton Endowed Professor of Entrepreneurship at Bowling Green State University, USA.

Christopher Pryor is an Instructor of Entrepreneurship in the Warrington College of Business Administration at the University of Florida, USA.

David W. Rosenthal is Emeritus Professor of Marketing, Miami University, USA.

Bill Rossi is an Emeritus Clinical Professor of Entrepreneurship at the University of Florida, USA.

Susana C. Santos is a Post-doctoral Fellow in the Center for Entrepreneurship and Innovation, University of Florida, USA.

Susan Scherreik is the Founding Director, Center for Entrepreneurial Studies, Seton Hall University, USA.

Minet Schindehutte is an Associate Professor of Entrepreneurship in the Department of Entrepreneurship at the Whitman School of Management, Syracuse University, USA.

Francine Schlosser is University of Windsor Golden Jubilee Professor in Business and Director, Research and Interdisciplinary Learning, Entrepreneurship, Practice, and Innovation Centre (EPICentre), University of Windsor, Canada.

Stuart A. Schulman is a Professor of Management in the Zicklin School of Business at Baruch College, City University of New York, USA.

Fionnuala Schultz is Business Consultancy Fellow at the Management School at Lancaster University, UK.

Ray Smilor is Emeritus Professor of Professional Practice at the Neeley School of Business, Texas Christian University, USA.

Jeffrey Stamp is the Founder and Chief Storyteller at Bold Thinking, LLC.

Kris Taylor is an Instructor in Entrepreneurship at Purdue University, USA and a Consultant to a wide variety of companies.

John Thompson is Emeritus Professor of Entrepreneurship in the Department of Leadership and Management, University of Huddersfield, UK.

John M. Torrens is a Professor at the Department of Entrepreneurship and Emerging Enterprises at Syracuse University, USA.

Edgar E. Troudt is an Assistant Professor in Tourism and Hospitality at CUNY's Kingsborough Community College, USA.

Jeff Vanevenhoven is an Associate Professor of Management at the University of Wisconsin–Whitewater, USA.

Rebecca White is a Professor of Entrepreneurship, holds the James W. Walter Distinguished Chair of Entrepreneurship, and is the Director of the Entrepreneurship Center, University of Tampa, USA.

Doan Winkel is an Assistant Professor of Entrepreneurship in the College of Business at Illinois State University, USA.

Christoph Winkler is an Assistant Professor of Entrepreneurship in the Zicklin School of Business at Baruch College, City University of New York, USA.

Preface: Teaching reason and the unreasonable

Michael H. Morris and Eric Liguori

FROM EMERGENCE TO INSTITUTIONALIZATION

As we publish the second volume of the *Annals of Entrepreneurship Education and Pedagogy*, levels of innovation in how entrepreneurship is taught, and what is taught, are unprecedented. The emergence of entrepreneurship within universities over the past 30 years has been breathtaking (Greene and Rice, 2007; Hills, 1988; Kuratko, 2005; Neck and Greene, 2011). It is not unusual at major institutions to find formal degree programs at the undergraduate and graduate levels (i.e., entrepreneurship majors, minors, concentrations, certificates, master's degrees and Ph.D. programs), a curriculum with 20 or more courses, a portfolio of co-curricular programming, and a broad mix of community engagement initiatives (Katz, 2003; Morris et al., 2013a). From a handful of programs three decades ago, today there are more than 3000 institutions offering entrepreneurship programs. The growth is likely to continue in the coming decades, as across the globe we find the twenty-first century to be the century of the entrepreneur.

Patterns in the emergence of entrepreneurship education are summarized in Table I.1. We see dramatic change as a formal discipline has taken shape, a considerable volume of high-quality research has appeared, and diverse and innovative programs of study have been established. Entrepreneurship's position within the university has been "institutionalized" as structures have been modified to include not only institutes and centers, but also academic co-departments, departments and schools of entrepreneurship. Universities are employing tenure-track faculty in entrepreneurship, and these faculty members are able to focus exclusively on teaching, researching and performing service in entrepreneurship. Meanwhile, the scope of these programs has been extended across the campus, into the community and across the globe. Program leaders are introducing novel approaches to staffing, funding, and economic engagement with the society (Morris et al., 2013a). In the process, they are able to

Table I.1   Emergence of entrepreneurship education

Relative emphasis: sidelight ➔ sub-area ➔ area ➔ major discipline

Curriculum: courses ➔ structured curriculum ➔ undergraduate degrees ➔ graduate degrees

Structure: based in existing academic unit ➔ based in center or institute ➔ creation of co-department of entrepreneurship ➔ creation of separate departments and schools of entrepreneurship

Funding model: cost center ➔ revenue center ➔ profit center

Outreach: campus-based events ➔ community and campus events ➔ integration of curriculum and outreach

Assurance of learning: course evaluations ➔ venture metrics ➔ competencies ➔ integrative model

Faculty: adjuncts ➔ shared faculty ➔ dedicated faculty ➔ joint appointments

Research: little scholarly activity ➔ core faculty publishing ➔ stimulation of interdisciplinary research agendas

Focal market: business school ➔ local community ➔ campus ➔ region ➔ nation/globe

Purpose: fill a gap ➔ develop area of study ➔ empower students and create ventures ➔ transform campuses and communities

Philosophy: help students learn about venture creation ➔ create ventures ➔ think and act entrepreneurially

---

Source: Adapted from Morris et al. (2013a).

generate significant resources for universities, while also playing a central role in a movement toward establishing the "entrepreneurial university" (Clark, 2004; Gibb and Hannon, 2006).

It could be argued that this growth and expansion has exposed tens of thousands of students to entrepreneurial possibilities, given young entrepreneurs a set of tools and concepts that can enhance their likelihood of success, and encouraged the development of ecosystems to support an entrepreneurial community, while fostering (an unclear level of) start-up activity. Yet the case could also be made that the emergence of entrepreneurship education has occurred so rapidly that it has out-paced our understanding of what should be taught by entrepreneurship educators, how it should be taught and how outcomes should be assessed.

WHERE ARE THE GAPS?

A gap exists between a growing demand for and the available supply of entrepreneurship education. On the supply side, we also confront gaps in our understanding regarding how best to design and deliver these educational programs. Examples of some of the major issues include:

- defining the field's core content or substance and its boundaries;
- the structure and flow of an entrepreneurship degree program;
- teaching techniques that are most effective for various content elements;
- best practices in classroom innovation;
- the role and extent of experiential learning and deliberate practice in an entrepreneurship program;
- the relative effectiveness of differing educational delivery mechanisms;
- implications of different learning approaches for how entrepreneur-ship is taught;
- appropriate learning outcomes and standards; and
- relevant assurance of learning measures when it comes to entrepreneurship.

Although scholarly research in entrepreneurship has been greatly expanded, the volume of substantive research focused on issues related to education and pedagogy has been limited (Katz, 2003; Morris, 2014). Similarly, few attempts have been made to document effective and ineffective practices in the classroom, or measure the relationship between course or program design and delivery approaches and tangible outcomes from entrepreneurship programs (Solomon et al., 2002).

It is also possible that these gaps will get greater. Entrepreneurship education is not static. It represents a moving target, with continuous additions to both the depth and the breadth of the content of the discipline (DeTienne and Chandler, 2004; Gorman et al., 1997). Meanwhile, entrepreneurship programs are emerging as innovation platforms (Honig, 2004). They are continually spinning off a fascinating array of new courses, pedagogies, student support programs and outreach initiatives. Further, new learning platforms, technologies and vehicles are appearing for enhancing how entrepreneurship is taught. In addition, the student audience for entrepreneurship education is global, and not only continues to grow in size but also is becoming more diverse, as reflected in the age, gender, life stage, ethnicity, professional background, motives and contexts of those wishing to better understand entrepreneurship in all of its manifestations.

WHAT SHOULD WE BE TEACHING?

Part of the challenge in establishing what is taught in the entrepreneurship classroom concerns who is doing the teaching and where the teaching is taking place. Courses today are being taught by full-time dedicated faculty members (some with degrees in entrepreneurship and most with degrees in other disciplines), faculty who primarily teach in other disciplines but find themselves teaching an entrepreneurship course, professors of practice and adjunct faculty who have strong commercial backgrounds, and others. This tendency alone can lead to wide differences in knowledge, beliefs and attitudes regarding what should be taught. Courses are taught both inside and outside business schools, which can also influence content.

The focus of entrepreneurship education would seem to include three general areas of emphasis, as summarized in Table I.2. The first area might be labeled "business basics," or how the different functional areas of business apply in an early stage venture context. One might question the extent to which entrepreneurship, approached as business basics, represents a unique discipline with its own defined content, as opposed to a field of study that relies on teaching borrowed content from such fields as management, psychology, sociology, anthropology, physics and ecology. The second area of focus might be termed "entrepreneurship basics," where core content from the emerging discipline is emphasized. Examples of topical issues here include the entrepreneurial process, innovative business models, lean start-ups, entrepreneurial orientation and entrepreneurial cognition, among others. The third focal area is the entrepreneurial mindset and its associated mix of entrepreneurial competencies. Here, educators focus on helping students develop their abilities in such areas as opportunity recognition and assessment, conveying a compelling vision, leveraging resources, mitigating risks, and engaging in guerrilla behavior (Morris et al., 2013b).

Arguably, the greatest promise lies within columns two and three in Table I.2. Business schools already teach business basics, effectively lessening the need for this type of entrepreneurship education. Approached as business basics, new ventures simply represent another context for managerial action, as opposed to a distinct discipline with a unique subject

Table I.2   What should be the focus of our teaching?

Business basics	Entrepreneurship basics	Entrepreneurial mindset and competencies
Setting up the books	Entrepreneurship defined	Opportunity alertness
How to sell	Entrepreneurial process	Risk mitigation
Hiring of staff	Characteristics of	Resource leveraging
Forms of enterprise	entrepreneurs	Conveying a
Cash flow management	Types of entrepreneurs	compelling vision
Formulating strategy	Contexts for entrepreneurship	Value innovation
Market analysis	Innovative business models	Passion
Setting up operations	Entrepreneurial cognition	Persistence and tenacity
Pricing	Nature of opportunity	Creative
Promotion and	Opportunity discovery	problem-solving
advertising	or creation	Guerrilla behavior
Financial statements	Seed and venture capital	Optimism
Franchising	Lean start-up	Learning from failure
Management control	Entrepreneurial orientation	Implementing change
Cost analysis	Entrepreneurship and	Adaptation
Protecting intellectual	society	Resilience
property	Exit strategies	Building and using
	Ethical challenges in	networks
	entrepreneurship	

matter. Entrepreneurship education must involve more than the mechanics of business start-up. The real potential lies in uncovering ways to promulgate the entrepreneurial mindset, and foster understanding regarding how to recognize and exploit opportunity in a wide variety of contexts.

TEACHING THE UNREASONABLE

The core precept guiding our pedagogical approaches should be the idea that entrepreneurship is about empowerment and transformation. We are encouraging students to create their own futures and futures for those around them. We want them to transform markets, industries, communities and economies. We are teaching them to be somewhat unreasonable, challenge norms and be disruptive. Yet, as we teach students to challenge assumptions, think in bold innovative terms, identify and leverage the resources of others, and persist in creatively overcoming obstacles, we must also teach them to approach entrepreneurial action from a perspective of structure, rigor, logic and realism. In this sense then, entrepreneurship education represents the confluence of unreasonable thinking and focused discipline.

Accordingly, educators are engaged in a balancing act. They must provide the tools and perspectives that enable students to think in bigger terms and challenge them to imagine truly novel value propositions that lead customers, create markets and transform the competitive landscape. Yet they must be vigilant in teaching and applying the frameworks and principles that bring rigor, logic and realism to student thinking and acting.

Achievement of this balance can be facilitated by pedagogical approaches built around three pillars: content-based education, competency-based education and experientially based education. With regard to content, there is a rich and growing knowledge base surrounding the entrepreneurial process and the requirements for entrepreneurial action available for educators (column two in Table I.2). Yet available teaching resources, including textbooks, tend to emphasize business basics (column one in Table I.2). In terms of competencies, Morris and colleagues (2013b) have generated a set of 13 core entrepreneurial competencies, together with guidance in how to teach and measure progress on each of them (see also DeTienne and Chandler, 2004; Fiet, 2001). Finally, a large percentage (perhaps as much as 60 percent) of the education program should center on experiential learning, or what Neck et al. (2014) label "deliberate practice." More than just case studies or business plans, the experiential dimension of education places students into their discomfort zones, forces them to think and act under conditions of ambiguity, introduces vexing obstacles, includes real elements of risk and rewards tenacity, adaptation and creative problem-solving (see also Solomon et al., 2002).

ORGANIZATION OF THE *ANNALS*

The *Annals of Entrepreneurship Education and Pedagogy*, published in partnership with the United States Association for Small Business and Entrepreneurship (USASBE), aims to identify and revisit some of the most important and provocative work generated through USASBE's annual conference and associated programs. Specifically, the editorial board of the *Annals* is charged with systematically identifying the most important papers, presentations and workshops that have appeared at USASBE during the past 30 years, and then contacting and working with the authors and presenters of this work to produce updated perspectives. The intent is that they capture the richest insights and best practices in teaching entrepreneurship, building entrepreneurship curricula, and developing educational programs.

The *Annals* is organized into three parts. In Part I, we open with perspectives from five master educators regarding what each has learned from teaching entrepreneurship for at least a decade (Chapter 1). This is then followed by 14 research chapters that reflect some of the "big issues" in entrepreneurship education. The lead chapter by Jeffrey Stamp (Chapter 2) explores how to teach creativity, a topic woven throughout most entrepreneurship programs, and often featured as a stand-alone course. Albornoz and Amorós (Chapter 3) then empirically assess the effects of entrepreneurship education, including its role in changing intentions versus developing competencies within students. The need to move toward a more competency-based approach to education is stressed by White, Hertz and Moore (Chapter 6). Grossman (Chapter 5) examines the huge popularity of the lean start-up methodology among entrepreneurship educators, while also raising some potential concerns. Rosenthal (Chapter 7) provides rich insights on using the case method when teaching entrepreneurship. Issues in experiential learning are the themes of a number of chapters. Schindehutte and Morris (Chapter 8) discuss the value of having students build experience portfolios; Morland and Thompson (Chapter 10) explore the implications for various stakeholders of degree programs centered on actual venture creation; Clouse and colleagues (Chapter 12) report on an applied research curriculum design to infuse entrepreneurial thinking into authentic problem-based learning environments across disciplines; and Pryor (Chapter 11) investigates the challenges of incorporating experiential learning when teaching large mass sections. In a related vein, Bruton (Chapter 9) provides a lens on the importance of critique and self-assessment in product and business design processes, proposing a model for articulating and framing the skills students require to successfully come up with viable ideas. How the student thinks is the concern of Santos and colleagues (Chapter 4) in their examination of the research on entrepreneurial cognition and its implications for educational efforts. Tools for use in entrepreneurship-related courses also receive attention. Morris (Chapter 13) introduces a framework that can used at the front end, or analytical stage, of consulting courses, while Markin and colleagues (Chapter 14) explain how the Architecture, Governance, Entrepreneurship and Stewardship (A-GES) framework can be used in a family business course. At a more macro level, Hechavarria and colleagues (Chapter 15) note the growing interest in entrepreneurial ecosystems, assessing the role universities can and should be playing in their development.

Part II of the *Annals* features five model academic programs in entrepreneurship: the University of Southern California (Chapter 16), Lancaster University (Chapter 17), Baylor University (Chapter 18), the University of Maryland (Chapter 19) and Syracuse University (Chapter 20). These schools were selected based on the recognition they have received from various sources, most notably the National Model Entrepreneurship Program Awards coordinated by USASBE each year. We have prioritized programs that we believe have had a significant impact on the advancing entrepreneurship education at the tertiary level. Programs were also selected to provide a representation of different types of university environments. Importantly, while each program is outlined in fairly comprehensive terms, the reader will detect a unique theme or focal aspect embedded in the programs of each of these five universities.

In Part III, we provide a collection of 11 leading edge examples of teaching innovations, unique approaches to experiential learning, and high-impact community engagement initiatives. Many of these initiatives have also won awards or recognition both from USASBE and from other prominent organizations and groups. Each of them has been selected based not only on its innovativeness and the proven results it has produced, but also because of its potential for replication and adaptation at other institutions. Moreover, the initiatives that are featured reflect innovations at both the undergraduate and graduate levels, inside and outside the business school, on-campus and off-campus, and that emphasize economic and social outcomes.

Entrepreneurship is experiencing growing pains as it continues to emerge and becomes a mainstay in the modern university. We believe the discipline is uniquely positioned not only to empower and transform students, but to empower and transform higher education. Entrepreneurship educators are poised to shed new light on interdisciplinary approaches to teaching, uncover entirely new methods for experiential learning and the design of curricula around experiences, and create new ways for universities to engage society and connect such engagement to the learning process. A key to fulfilling this promise is that we learn much more about how entrepreneurship should be taught and how educational programs should be designed. We hope this second volume of the *Annals* makes a contribution to bridging the significant gaps in our understanding that remain.

Michael H. Morris, University of Florida, USA
Eric Liguori, University of Tampa, USA

REFERENCES

Clark, B.R. (2004), Delineating the character of the entrepreneurial university, *Higher Education Policy*, **17**(4), 355–370.

DeTienne, D.R. and Chandler, G.N. (2004), The role of gender in opportunity identification, *Entrepreneurship Theory and Practice*, **31**(3), 365–386.

Fiet, J.O. (2001), The pedagogical side of entrepreneurship theory, *Journal of Business Venturing*, **16**(2), 101–117.

Gibb, A. and Hannon, P. (2006), Towards the entrepreneurial university, *International Journal of Entrepreneurship Education*, **4**(1), 73–110.

Gorman, G., Hanlon, D. and King, W. (1997), Some research perspectives on entrepreneurship education, enterprise education, and education for small business management: a ten-year literature review, *International Small Business Journal*, **15**, 56–77.

Greene, P.G. and Rice, M.P. (2007), *Entrepreneurship Education*, Cheltenham, UK and Northampton, MA, USA: Edward Elgar.

Hills, G.E. (1988), Variations in university entrepreneurship education: an empirical study of an evolving field, *Journal of Business Venturing*, **3**, 109–122.

Honig, B. (2004), Entrepreneurship education: toward a model of contingency-based business planning, *Academy of Management Learning and Education*, **3**(3), 258–273.

Katz, J.A. (2003), The chronology and intellectual trajectory of American entrepreneurship education, *Journal of Business Venturing*, **18**(2), 283–300.

Kuratko, D.F. (2005), The emergence of entrepreneurship education: development, trends, challenges, *Entrepreneurship Theory and Practice*, **29**(3), 577–598.

Morris, M.H. (ed.) (2014), *Annals of Entrepreneurship Education and Pedagogy – 2014*, Cheltenham, UK and Northampton, MA, USA: Edward Elgar.

Morris, M.H., Kuratko, D.F. and Cornwall, J.R. (2013a), *Entrepreneurship Programs and the Modern University*, Cheltenham, UK and Northampton, MA, USA: Edward Elgar.

Morris, M.H., Webb, J.W., Fu, J. and Singhal, S. (2013b), A competency-based perspective on entrepreneurship education: conceptual and empirical insights, *Journal of Small Business Management*, **51**(3), 352–369.

Neck, H.M. and Greene, P.G. (2011), Entrepreneurship education: known worlds and new frontiers, *Journal of Small Business Management*, **49**(1), 55–70.

Neck, H., Greene, P. and Brush, C. (2014), Practice-based entrepreneurship education using actionable theory, in M.H. Morris (ed.), *Annals of Entrepreneurship Education and Pedagogy*, Cheltenham, UK and Northampton, MA, USA: Edward Elgar, pp. 3–20.

Solomon, G.T., Duffy, S. and Tarabishy, A. (2002), The state of entrepreneurship education in the United States: a nationwide survey and analysis, *International Journal of Entrepreneurship Education*, **1**(1), 65–86.

PART I

Leading edge research perspectives

1. What I have learned about teaching entrepreneurship: perspectives of five master educators

Jerome S. Engel, Minet Schindehutte, Heidi M. Neck, Ray Smilor and Bill Rossi

INTRODUCTION

The editors of this volume asked five leading educators what they have learned about teaching entrepreneurship. We reached out to faculty members acknowledged by their peers, leading academic organizations, their institutions and their students to be among the very best in entrepreneurship education. Each of these individuals has over a decade of experience in the entrepreneurship classroom, and has witnessed the rapid evolution of a very dynamic discipline. In the pages that follow, they provide unique perspectives on what is taught and how it is taught. The opening piece captures a bit of the trajectory of entrepreneurship education and the contemporary challenge, while the four that follow provide personal insights on teaching entrepreneurship in ways that meet that challenge.

Jerome S. Engel

We have made great progress in entrepreneurship education. When I first came to Berkeley in 1991 after a successful career in industry, fundamental challenges to the role of entrepreneurship in education were open and raw. One would frequently be asked:

- Can entrepreneurship be taught?
- Does entrepreneurship belong in the university?

Thanks to educators like the contributors to this volume and their predecessors, these basic challenges have been laid to rest. It is understood that entrepreneurship is a life skill with broad applicability. It is important and helpful to many beyond those who choose to pursue entrepreneurship

3

as a career. Like mathematics, it is broadly relevant and not limited just to those who choose to become mathematicians.

It is now our turn to ask:

- What are entrepreneurship education's best practices?
- How can we best utilize entrepreneurship education to mobilize the resources and talents to create value for our students and their stakeholders, for our communities and for society as a whole?

Reflecting on my experience as an entrepreneurship educator over the last 25 years, I believe that we clearly have made great progress in developing the educational curriculum and experiential methods to help our students build successful entrepreneurial ventures and careers. I will focus here on three big challenges that we now face as we broaden our influence and impact:

1. the importance of entrepreneurship education to corporate innovation strategy broadly;
2. the importance of entrepreneurship education to university education writ large;
3. the importance of entrepreneurship education to the creation of healthy innovation communities and economies, for example clusters of innovation.

LET ME SHARE A HISTORICAL PERSPECTIVE

In the beginning, entrepreneurship education was the domain of the business school.

In the 1980s . . .

When we thought of entrepreneurship education, if we thought of it at all, we thought of "Small Business" – SMEs. Entrepreneurship was often a stand-alone cross-disciplinary capstone course where students built business plans and integrated the skills they had learned in their marketing, finance and management courses. Case studies were the new pedagogical innovation, and experiential learning was limited to internships or student projects for smaller firms.

In the 1990s . . .

We discovered the startup. Especially with the arrival of the internet, the opportunity for any student to start his or her own business became evident. Business plan competitions grew like mushrooms. When we founded our competition at Berkeley in the mid 1990s it was still considered an innovation, though we were following in the well-worn path of Moot Corp (University of Texas at Austin) and others. We still taught entrepreneurship with case studies and business plans. In fact, the common philosophy was that technology startups were just *smaller versions* of big businesses. With their potential for explosive growth they were exciting opportunities – and we focused on teaching the articulation of the business plan for the management of rapid growth. We had not yet recognized and isolated for analysis and teaching the very special attribute of a startup, that it was a temporary state meant for experimentation to discover and validate a business model, which could then be executed with greater certainty and justifiably greater capital. This insight would have to await the next major disruption looming on the horizon.

The Turn of the Century Brought a New Reality . . .

On March 10, 2000 the NASDAQ index reached a peak of $5048. By October 9, 2002 it had collapsed to $1114, and it would not start a sustained recovery until November 2008, a full nine years after the bust. With the bursting of the internet bubble, some questioned the value and durability of the entrepreneurial revolution. A leading Silicon Valley venture capital firm published a briefing on internet enterprises for its limited partners headlined with a tombstone engraved R.I.P. – Rest in Peace!

The hiatus of the excesses of the bubble, and the subsequent rebirth of the technology startup opportunity, not only yielded Google and many other global success stories, but also supplied new approaches to discovering opportunity by using less capital and more experimentation. Out of the necessity of the capital crunch of the post-bubble period came the first instances of the entrepreneurial *management* practices we now know as "Lean" – the Lean Startup or the Lean LaunchPad.

2010 Onward . . .

In the last decade we have seen these methods become well understood and broadly promulgated. We have built new tools. The triad of the business model canvas, customer discovery and the minimum viable product has become ubiquitous. We have developed a new pedagogy. We no longer teach that a startup is a smaller version of a big business; rather we now teach that a startup is a temporary organization whose purpose is to *discover* a viable and scalable business model. We teach evidence-based entrepreneurship. The business plan – while still a valuable management tool – is understood as an execution tool, a tool to be used once the startup is ready to scale. The capstone case study is no longer about someone else's business, but the student's own venture. The professor is no longer the source of all wisdom, but rather a guide who provides an enriched environment for the student's own research and experimentation.

WHAT ARE THE CHALLENGES OF THE NEXT DECADE?

Three challenges loom.

The *first* challenge is increasing the impact of what we have learned by accelerating corporate innovation, taking what we have learned about accelerating innovation using the entrepreneurial startup model to the larger stage. Again history is our guide. The modern corporation was the innovation engine of the mid-twentieth century. With massive corporate R&D labs doing some of the best basic research, the modern twentieth-century corporation was a vertically integrated technology commercialization machine. But that model is long gone. With the focus on execution forced on top management by the public financial markets, research departments have been spun off or devolved to product development. True research has been relegated to the university, and innovative new market creation and disruptive innovation outsourced to the startup.

For some, open innovation has simply meant scouting for and acquiring promising startups. The challenge of the next decade for the leaders of entrepreneurship education will be to help the more progressive major corporations go beyond such "open innovation" to become true ambidextrous organizations: organizations that simultaneously execute and experiment. This evolution has already started. Many major corporations are trying in different ways to adopt entrepreneurial business model experimentation. It will be our job to aid them, study the results and synthesize the best practices so we can bring them back to the classroom. That classroom may not initially be the traditional college venue – at first it may well be more suitable for executive education. But those are the experiments that are in our future.

Our *second* challenge involves entrepreneurship education's role in the entire university. Entrepreneurship education has long left the exclusive purview of the business school. Its relevance to engineering and the sciences has never been clearer. Many engineering programs have embraced entrepreneurship, establishing their own faculties and curriculum. Further, the U.S. federal government is embarked on an ambitious program, the *National Science Foundation's Innovation Corps (I-Corps)*, of which I have the privilege to be the National Faculty Director. It is embedding the Lean LaunchPad, an intense 10-week entrepreneurship experiential immersion, into the very core of technology commercialization funding. In just four years since its inception, this program has already trained over 1500 NSF-funded scientists and is now expanding across the technology commercialization efforts of the National Institutes of Health, the Department of Energy and other federal agencies. Beyond these direct efforts, it is having a fundamental ripple effect, impacting entrepreneurship education at universities across the country.

Going beyond its bedrock constituents in business, engineering and the sciences, entrepreneurship education is penetrating and adding value to the pursuit of the arts and the professions, such as journalism, medicine and law. Over 10 years ago when Wake Forrest, a top quality liberal arts college in North Carolina, established the first entrepreneurship curriculum focused on the arts, it was considered extraordinary. Now not only has entrepreneurship education spread into new fields, but the corollary is also true – more and more diverse fields are influencing the advancement of entrepreneurial studies. I need only cite the impact of "design thinking" to make my case.

Now let's turn to our *third*, and perhaps most impactful, challenge: the role of the university in creating clusters of innovation. Just as entrepreneurship has established itself on campus, the critical contribution of the university in fostering healthy innovation communities has received broader recognition. The university has long been recognized as a provider of the seed corn of knowledge and technology. What is new is the awakening of new pathways for social contribution, through commercialization driven by entrepreneurial ventures. As this effect has become more profound in scale and scope, so the role of the university in fostering and enabling this process has deepened. The university's contribution is important not just for academic relevancy, but for effective public policy as well.

Five years ago, a dozen scholars gathered to raise the question: "What is the role of the university in the creation of an innovation society?" I was gratified that the group chose to anchor their analysis on a framework I had created that extended the work of Michael Porter of Harvard, Henry Etzkowitz of Stanford and other great contributors before them. That framework, which the group came to call the Cluster of Innovation Framework, went beyond its predecessors' focus on the components of a cluster – namely industry concentration, venture capital and such – and placed equal or even greater focus on the soft factors of *behaviors*, such as the mobility of people, money and technology, the propensity for risk taking, acceptance of failure as a learning process, and *structures* that create *alignment of interests*, engender teamwork and foster win–win scenarios, such as broad-based equity compensation. Elaborating the Cluster of Innovation Framework led to an important insight – that clusters of innovation did not have to be restricted by *physical boundaries*. Communities that shared these propensities, these behaviors and these structures could extend beyond physical borders and align with other like communities around the world, forming a new "silk road," a global network of clusters of innovation.

What is the relevance of global clusters of innovation to entrepreneurship education? The active protagonists in these communities are our students! Properly educated, they are better prepared to succeed in today's innovation economy – an economy that is characterized by the rapid emergence, dominance and sunset of technologies, business models, and the businesses that give them life.

The role of the university is central in this new world, and it is undergoing a major make-over, reaching beyond the technical contribution of modern science and engineering and the training of a qualified workforce. The modern university contributes a new resource – the entrepreneurial team – which is at the center of the innovation process.

Entrepreneurship educators stand on the cusp of a new day and new challenges:

- taking what we have learned about innovation from the entrepreneurial model into the broader corporate enterprise, enabling the creation of new *management practices* that support the ambidextrous organization, one that can both execute and innovate;
- embracing the entire university in entrepreneurship and innovation education, informing and being informed by the contributions of others;
- undertaking our mission as cornerstones in the creation of clusters of innovation in our communities, and as academics using our special access to foster collaboration with other partners around the world so our communities can benefit from the synergies of the global network of clusters of innovation.

These goals may seem audacious – too grand and ambitious – but, if I may borrow liberally from a biblical scholar, *if not us, then who*? Who else is better situated, or better prepared? These opportunities are at our doorstep.

Minet Schindehutte

Five discoveries have shaped my professional life as an entrepreneurship educator. These five lessons came from many encounters on my journey – from students in the United States, South Africa and India, from entrepreneurs across the world, and from other teachers who are passionate about entrepreneurship. I share these insights with the hope that one (or more) of them will resonate with others engaged in the lives of students in an entrepreneurship classroom.

1.   BE INSPIRED

Entrepreneurship is in everything we do, but it is also in between those things. It is a mashup of the three main modes of thinking: philosophy (as the creation of new concepts), art (as the creation of new experiences) and science (as the creation of new functions). Entrepreneurship as art, as science and as philosophy – or rather where the boundaries between art, science and philosophy are transgressed – requires that we recognize its power to transform, that is, to create difference and divergence, rather than to encourage imitation and conformity. Thus, we should *not* view entrepreneurship as a discipline – something that we can define and know. Rather, we should view entrepreneurship in terms of what it might be able *to do*: in terms of its potentiality, a becoming for the sake of change itself. Teaching entrepreneurship as a philosophy for life – *not* an occupation – goes beyond facts, and involves a principles-based approach. This set of principles is distilled from experiences that provide guidance on how to live an entrepreneurial life.

Gilles Deleuze, a French philosopher, is my muse. For Deleuze (1990), life is difference, the power to think differently, to become different and to create differences. I did not fully understand what "difference" meant until I encountered Deleuze's philosophy of becoming. Reading Deleuze enriched my life with radically new perspectives on everything. For the first time, I saw potential everywhere. Whereas educators think about the start and end of the course (as learning outcomes), students are always in the middle: on their way to *becoming-other* – full of infinite potential. I encourage students to write a manifesto for how to lead an entrepreneurial life. Rather than provide them with training materials for an occupation, these personalized principles can guide their everyday choices: an operating system working in the background, reminding them to be inspired and to inspire others.

2.   BE RELEVANT

Most of the students in my classroom have no intention of starting a business after graduation (or perhaps ever). They are would-be accountants, marketers, entrepreneurs, scientists, industrial designers and engineers – but they are also authors, musicians, photographers, painters, poets, hobbyists, foodies and sports fans. The one thing they all share is a deep uncertainty about who they are and what they want to do. The lesson I have learned from my students is that most of them are looking for "something" – something that is impossible to articulate, yet something (often particular to the individual) that they know they have not yet discovered, and something they will need in whatever they choose to do next. Being a student in the age of uncertainty means learning *for* entrepreneurship – not *about* entrepreneurship. In short, "the student's being in the world is more important for her learning than her interests in developing knowledge and understanding in a particular field" (Barnett, 2007, p. 6).

Consequently, I encourage students to approach entrepreneurship (and life!) as an act of creation. Regardless of a chosen professional career, students are creators of their lives – connecting to their true potential is a birthright. Unfortunately, information about how to create the future cannot be found in a textbook. Staying abreast of all new developments, technological advances and entrepreneurs' endeavors is an immensely time-consuming process, but it is a necessary process if one believes that learning is *for life,* and that teaching entrepreneurship should provide opportunities for students to experience the joy of creating, to flex their "entrepreneurial muscle" and to exceed their *own* expectations (not strive to meet mine or those of their parents). This belief translates into crafting assessment tools that involve invention – creating something new – rather than regurgitation. It can take the shape of a DIY exam or something more experiential, but in all instances students are challenged to rethink the information they considered as "fact," and to glimpse reality with their imaginations and even their hopes. To a certain extent then, I am a (life) coach rather than a teacher. My role is to create the conditions for behavior change, that is, self-directed learning through self-discovery, self-acceptance and self-expression in which learning is a search for (lifelong) meaning, and learning entrepreneurship is part of a student's way-finding.

3.   BE ADVENTUROUS

Students do not become more entrepreneurial by reading *about* entrepreneurship; they have to *live* it – not one day in the future, but now, and every day.

I believe the role of the entrepreneurship educator is to challenge, provoke, disrupt, reinvent and be out in front. It requires a willingness to experiment and try new things, to model the innovative behavior required of students. This means setting the entrepreneurship classroom apart from others, making it clear that this is where entrepreneurship *happens*. Students learn *how* to think and act entrepreneurially, not *what* to learn about entrepreneurship. They do not have to start businesses or do internships in high growth businesses to experience entrepreneurship. It can be simulated through transformational experiences – both inside and outside the classroom – with the potential to make a real difference in students' lives, often in unpredictable ways. In the words of Shoshana Felman, "if teaching does not hit upon some sort of crisis, if it does not encounter either the vulnerability or the explosiveness of a (explicit or implicit) critical and unpredictable dimension, it has perhaps *not truly taught*" (1992, p. 53, italics in original).

In an *experience-first* approach to teaching entrepreneurship, the "test" precedes the "lesson." I simply create a platform for students – a set of facilitative conditions, rather than constraining rules – and then set them free. Students are invited to participate (with others) in a variety of unconventional activities, from exploratory to symbolic, learning collaboratively and supporting each other, rather than competing for grades. This alternative to one-size-fits-all pedagogies challenges, and indeed resists, education-as-usual and all its associated assumptions, assessments and procedures.

4. BE INQUISITIVE

Entrepreneurship is often taught in a problem–solution approach – the predefined problem is associated with an opportunity that is transformed into a venture (the "right answer" to the problem). Unfortunately, the ability to problematize, to linger in that dynamic, generative space in between problems and solutions that remains *unresolved*, is sometimes neglected. Becoming proficient at intellectual exploration through inquiry – reflexively and relationally, following unexpected detours rather than looking for specific answers – is an important transferable skill, especially when students experience first-hand how moments of insight pierce through the veil of uncertainty.

The message to my students, in the words of the German poet Rainer Maria Rilke, is as follows:

> Be patient toward all that is unsolved in your heart and try to love the questions themselves, like locked rooms and like books that are now written in a very

foreign tongue. Do not now seek the answers, which cannot be given you because you would not be able to live them. And the point is, to live everything. Live the questions now. Perhaps you will then gradually, without noticing it, live along some distant day into the answer. (1993, p. 35)

An inquiry-based approach in which students are encouraged to love the questions themselves – not the-end-of-textbook-chapter questions, but questions that are intrinsically motivated by a *wondering-about*, questions *students* ask at a perspective-changing level – can be one of the most valuable tools for entrepreneurship education.

Concomitantly, students are encouraged to become more introspective and contemplative by journaling about their learning experiences (becoming their own sounding board) and to derive relevant principles from the "so what" questions. Apart from taking pride in what they have created, students develop a more personal relationship with course content – making connections between self, entrepreneurship and world. I use student e-portfolios to support critical reflection, as well as for assessing experiential competencies. This shifts the purpose of the e-portfolio from an employer focus (portfolio as a hiring or career tool) to a student focus (portfolio as a platform for learning).

5. BE AUTHENTIC

This is the final (and most important) lesson. As a beginner entrepreneurship educator, I often wished that I could teach like one of the "masters." It wasn't until I developed my own teaching style – one that was distinctly different from that of my colleagues – that I realized the importance of being true to oneself. It seems so obvious after the fact, but it was not apparent during the early days, especially given the importance attached to student evaluations. The classroom as a space for exploration, questioning and meaning-making is not without challenges. For the teacher it means taking risks, being comfortable with unpredictable outcomes, and letting the reins go in order to find the sweet spot between chaos and order. For the student, it is fraught with ambiguity. Not every student enjoys the "messiness" of an experimental, improvisational classroom in which unexpected possibilities exist. Some students prefer (or rather demand) the familiarity and efficiency of a lecture-based or case-based pedagogy – either because they are uncomfortable with ambiguity and uncertainty, or because they simply resist change. Students' differing responses to *how* I teach entrepreneurship in an inverted classroom increase the complexity of managing class sessions, especially when class sizes exceed 40 students (which is typical).

Source: https://www.facebook.com/gapingvoidgallery/posts/1010285655697107.

Unanticipated events invariably unsettle even my most painstakingly planned and well-intended efforts.

Unlike some educators, I find that I am still *becoming-teacher* – learning *with*, and *from*, my students. As in the case of becoming an entrepreneur, these lessons cannot be learned in a book or in a classroom. They are derived from teaching experiences, and after making innumerable mistakes. However, an intense period of failure is often the source of critical insight. Moreover, it almost always prompts re-evaluation of my own, as well as contemporary, pedagogical options. And, although I often cringe in retrospect, I sincerely believe you have to do something that scares you: to feel the fear and do it anyway. *Why not?* Isn't that what we expect of our entrepreneurship students?

Heidi M. Neck

When asked to contribute to this chapter of the *Annals* I was thrilled to be in the company of so many educators that I admire. The challenge to reflect on what I've learned about teaching entrepreneurship was both exciting and terrifying. I was excited to have an excuse to intentionally and purposefully reflect on my teaching over the past 15 years yet terrified that I would not have anything of impact to say to those reading this volume – presumably other entrepreneurship educators. There were many days where I said to myself, "I will get this short section done today!" On those same days I sat looking at a blank screen experiencing a sort of writer's block regarding the one thing I love most – teaching entrepreneurship. Frustration set in, which only exacerbated my writer's block!

I decided to seek out inspiration. I keep many "teaching files" on my computer and even in hard-copy form in my office. I have files for my student opinion surveys (Babson's version of student ratings of professors), files for new course ideas, files for new exercises to try, files with video links, files with inspirational quotes, files with all types of articles on teaching, and even emails and other correspondence from current and past students. In this latter file I found an article that I had saved from the *Babson Magazine* (2013). In the Spring issue a few graduates were asked to recall professors or classes that made an impact. To my surprise and delight I was mentioned by a former MBA student, Chet:

> Professor Heidi Neck's introductory entrepreneurship course always reminded me of the Elvis lyric, "A little less conversation, a little more action please." She pushed us to stop theorizing and just experiment. She preached about the importance of failure in the creative process, and then facilitated an environment in which it was safe to fall flat on your face. Plenty of students can tell you about a professor who helped them succeed, but it's rare to speak so highly of a professor who helped you fail.[1]

Chet became my inspiration! The lightbulb went off! The "aha moment" struck! I was finally free of that irritating writer's block. What was the idea? Drum roll, please . . .

I decided *not to* write about what I had learned about teaching entrepreneurship, assuming my audience for this volume is educators. I decided *to* write an open letter to my students, past and present, about what they had taught me about teaching entrepreneurship. If you "hear" in my writing how I talk to students, perhaps you can understand my teaching philosophy. This letter is dedicated to Chet and so many others who participated in my courses as I learned how to teach:

Dear Student,

I want to thank you for being a part of my life, because you have shaped who I am as an educator. I can never stop learning how to teach. If or when I do, I cease being an effective teacher. Every student who enters my classroom has taught me something about teaching, and I want to share these lessons that now form my teaching philosophy.

You have helped me learn what works, how to keep you engaged, and how much I can push. I understand the importance of looking you in the eye, reading your body language, and listening – really listening. I anticipate and leverage those unexpected teaching moments that are uncomfortable yet unforgettable. These moments bind us.

I strive to practice what I preach. I demand that you think and act entre-preneurially, which requires you to develop creative solutions, take early action, accept and learn from small losses, and improvise when things do not go according to plan. I have to do the same. Teaching entrepreneurship requires continuous innovation, fearless experimentation and structured chaos.

I have learned that I must teach to excite, inspire, motivate and even shock you. I strive to create the unexpected in order to capture attention and spark enthusiasm for entrepreneurship – the necessary antecedents to learning. I have extremely high expectations with little tolerance for mediocrity and apathy, yet the culture of my classroom is open, playful and respectful. A class plan is necessary for organization and preparedness but not sufficient for student learning. Flexibility, humor, reactivity and improvisation are pillars of my philosophy.

Most importantly my approach to teaching is action-based. It has to be. In order to learn entrepreneurship one must do entrepreneurship. I have worked tirelessly to ensure you are able to practice aspects of entrepreneur-ship rather than be passive learners. Every day I strive to create a learning laboratory for experimentation and practice. You have taught me that action-based learning creates a sense of shared ownership in the learning process.

I encourage all students to use their voice – to debate, push back, and challenge me and their peers. I've developed the confidence to do the same. But I'll admit that the little things bother me. I have zero tolerance for unprofessional behavior. Arriving to class late, using smartphones and laptops inappropriately, and disrespecting me or other students have no place in my classroom. I will not hesitate to stop class, solve a particular issue and then restart class. You have taught me that ignoring bad behavior only perpetuates that behavior. And that behavior can become a cancer that spreads unless it is detected and stopped early. On the other hand *patterns* of negative behavior are 100 percent my fault. If half the class is con-sumed by their phones or computers then I am doing something wrong. If students are constantly arriving late or leaving during class to go [*fill in the blank*], I am doing something wrong. I am failing to engage; therefore, I must change my approach immediately.

The fact that I have no tolerance for unprofessional behavior does not mean I want a staid atmosphere. This would be the antithesis of entrepreneurship. I know that my courses need to be alive, exciting, relevant, challenging, creative, innovative and even playful and joyful. A community of learning and engagement must be omnipresent if we are going to transcend our preconceived notions of what entrepreneurship is and its importance in the world today. In other words, you have a huge responsibility as a nascent or practicing entrepreneur to create something of economic and social value to you and others.

I also have an enormous responsibility. Entrepreneurship is a complex phenomenon, chaotic, and lacking any notion of linearity. As an educator I have the responsibility to develop your discovery, thinking, reasoning, experimentation, and implementation skills so you may lead, manage, innovate and excel in highly uncertain entrepreneurial environments. These skills enhance the likelihood that you will identify and capture the right opportunity at the right time for the right reason. Entrepreneurs of all kinds impact the world, so entrepreneurship education is a necessary and formidable change agent. I really want you to do something great, take action and change your world! I will do everything I can to help facilitate your journey.

Keep entrepreneuring!

Ray Smilor

In my approach to teaching, I see myself as a guide. I lead students on a journey of self-discovery, a journey that reflects the entrepreneurial process itself – experiential throughout, surprising and unexpected at times, quite ambiguous now and then, intense on occasion, challenging and demanding most of the time, personally revealing, and potentially highly rewarding.

As a guide, I point direction but never dictate it. I warn of hazards but never prevent them. I don't predict but I do challenge. I debrief success and recognize the power of failure. I recognize talent but reward hard work. I encourage hope and bet on potential.

My philosophy is that each and every student is an entrepreneur capable of creative thinking and effective action. Interestingly, many students don't see themselves as either creative or entrepreneurial when they start my entrepreneurship courses. By the end, however, they are convinced that they are. How does this transformation happen?

FIVE LESSONS

Having taught entrepreneurship at all levels in many countries over the last 35 years, I have learned five key lessons that shape what I teach and how I teach it.

1.   Create a Truly Different Learning Environment

From the first moment of the first class, I want students to be bolted into believing that this class is really different from all others. Thus I learn the name of each student *before* they come into class and call them by name. That gets their attention! Then, before I introduce myself or discuss the syllabus, I conduct an experiential exercise that forces them to think unconventionally. For example, in my Opportunity Recognition class, I ask them "What is half of 13?" The first response is always 6.5. But I continue to ask over and over, "What is half of 13?" Eventually, we get to an incredibly wide range of answers that include 1, 2, 3, 6, 11, thir and teen, and many others, demonstrating that there is never just one right answer, that there is always more than one alternative, if one is daring enough to consider them.

In another class, I will introduce myself with a "bag resume." This presents a bisociative connection between a brown grocery store bag and the traditional paper resume. I pull six items out of the bag, each representing something that helped shape who I am as a person. It's unexpected, emotional and concrete. Then, in the next class, I have each student present their own bag resume as a way to demonstrate their own creativity and resourcefulness.

Even my syllabi are different. In my EMBA class on Innovation and Entrepreneurship, for example, I intersperse quotes, starting with Apple's 1997 "Think Different" commercial about crazies and genius, and end with Arthur Ashe's comment about the importance of one's reputation. I even include a cartoon about the entrepreneurial mindset.

If I can make each class really different from any other, then I can set high expectations, build enthusiasm and get the best out of each student.

2.   Instill an Entrepreneurial Attitude

What does it mean to have an entrepreneurial attitude? For me, three elements are essential: a willingness to be wrong, a desire to make connections, and a belief that it is okay to fail. To instill these elements in students, I set up opportunities for them to test each element.

Sir Ken Robinson, the noted scholar on creativity, has pointed out that to be creative one must be willing to be wrong. In my classroom, this sometimes translates into the courage to look ridiculous. For example, I've required students to take dance lessons from a professor of classical dance. Once they do that they tend not to be afraid of anything! And they are much more willing to test out their own crazy ideas by ignoring the criticism of others!

Students too often believe that they must come up with an idea that no one ever thought about before to be successful. And yet real innovation often comes by making connections between things that people have thought a lot about before but never combined: a phenomenon that historian Arthur Koestler called bisociation – the ability to relate two seemingly unrelated things, to take two wildly different things and put them together. So, in my New Venture Development course, I utilize exercises that force unusual connections leading to business concepts that link apparently unrelated things – not only fun but practically useful.

I help students realize that successful entrepreneurs fail all the time. Through case studies, guest speakers, hands-on activities and their own efforts in class, they come to realize that mistakes demonstrate what is not working and needs fixing. The key is how we label failure. How we think about something affects how we feel about it and influences how we act towards it. In my classes, failure is not an end but another type of learning experience.

3.   Require Active Involvement and Engagement

In my career, I have learned that, if one never speaks up, it is assumed that one has nothing to say. Thus I require that students speak up, and I grade them on their active involvement in each class on a 0 to 4 scale (a technique that I learned from case teacher Dave Rosenthal). Zero means a student has said nothing. Four means the student has made an important contribution to the discussion at hand. So, when we analyze a case or critique a business plan, my emphasis is not on the quantity of participation but the quality. I provide continual feedback to students on their participation. Because I know each student personally, they take this feedback constructively and come to class prepared to be engaged.

My focus is on both attitudes and behaviors. By requiring involvement and engagement, I not only look for thoughtful discussion but also expect students to participate in experiential exercises with an open mind, a positive approach, and a willingness to take some risk. Through interactive debriefs of class activities, and sometimes written "experience memos," I take time for each student to reflect on his or her own learning. Students thus must consider what they have experienced, identify their take-aways, and assess what specifically applies to their own behavior. Self-reflection thus becomes a kind of cement for the learning process.

4.   Promote "Yes, and" Behavior

Entrepreneurs improvise. They have to make things up as they go along and often must operate in ambiguous circumstances. How do we help students get more comfortable in this type of environment? I believe lessons from improvisation are important here: to listen actively, to eliminate "no" and "but," and to stay in the moment. These are skills that students can learn and hone.

For me, "Yes, and" has been the key to my success, and I believe it is essential for the pursuit of opportunity. For example, when I have students interview an entrepreneur, I require that they explain what they have discovered that they did not set out to discover. This requires active listening and asking probing questions, important attributes in understanding and responding to the needs of others. In working in teams to generate ideas, they must avoid "no" and "but" and instead first communicate that they have understood the idea presented ("Yes") and then add something to expand or improve it ("and"). Lastly, to hone their "Yes, and" behavior, they must stay in the moment, that is, not jump ahead to push their own agenda but learn to focus on the person in front of them.

I help develop these skills with movie clips and experiential exercises. For example, I love the clip from *Apollo 13* about the "Square Peg in a Round Hole," in which engineers have limited resources and limited time to solve an oxygen problem in the space craft. Thus I developed the Flying Device Game to simulate this situation. Students have to build a flying device from limited materials in a limited time that flies the farthest and the straightest – an exercise that emphasizes the "Yes, and" approach by dealing with problem-solving, team communication and innovation – and it's great fun.

5. Address All Learning Styles

We all learn differently. That is, we have different learning preferences. In my classes, I structure each session to address each style. As the Kolb Learning Style Inventory (which I have students complete) shows, there are four major learning styles of feeling (concrete experience), watching (reflective observation), thinking (abstract conceptualization) and doing (active experimentation). If I can structure a class to touch on all four, then I am more likely to keep their attention and bring out their best thinking and action. For students with a feeling orientation, I can use simulations, consulting projects and elevator pitches; for those with a watching orientation, I can utilize movies, demonstrations, guest speakers, and interviews with entrepreneurs; for those with a thinking orientation, I can include interactive lectures, case studies and special readings; for those with a doing orientation, I can bring in business plan development, company evaluations and hands-on experiences.

MY RESPONSIBILITY

For me, entrepreneurship is not about starting a business, though that may be one outcome. It is about leading a more fulfilling life. It is about making the world a better place by finding one's purpose and then applying it to something personally meaningful. It is a mindset in which one pursues opportunity, creates values, communicates a compelling vision and maximizes limited resources in whatever career one chooses. So a person can be entrepreneurial in launching a startup venture, leading a growth enterprise, serving as an intrapreneur in a corporation, directing a government agency or even building an academic program.

I have taught at every level – elementary, secondary, undergraduate, graduate and executive education. And I've observed this: people learn what they want to learn. I want them to come out of my classes feeling as though the classes are the most useful, pertinent and engaging learning experience that they have ever had. For this to happen, I must address my responsibilities as a teacher: to prepare fully for each class, to give my best thinking and effort to every session, and to treat each student and his or her own hopes and aspirations with respect and dignity.

In each class, I must perform at my best. I use the term "perform" purposefully. Performance combines substance (real content) and form (genuine interest). Both are essential. If I am not deeply engaged and personally enthused, and visibly show these by my performance, then why should my students be? By performing at my best, maybe I can inspire and not just tally grades. For a teacher, there is joy in that.

To teach and to be taught by entrepreneurial students is a privilege. Every time I walk into my classroom, I remind myself of something: I don't have to do this; I *get* to do this. I *get* to make students aware of how creative and entrepreneurial they are. I *get* to share my experience and passion. I *get* to inspire. I *get* to teach entrepreneurship. What a deal!

Bill Rossi

Most effective professors report that they had a mentor, and that the mentor helped importantly to shape their style and teaching philosophy. When I began teaching entrepreneurship, I had no mentor. I had to find my own way. So I talked with students to identify who were their favorite teachers. I then watched the teachers at work by observing their classes. Each of these educators seemed to have a unique style, so identifying the best style to adopt seemed arbitrary. I concluded that I had to find my own comfort zone in developing a style that would reflect who I am rather than what I did, and a teaching objective that reflected what I wanted to accomplish. These two elements would have to then be guided by an overall teaching philosophy that reflected my personal values.

TEACHING STYLE

Story Telling

I began by trying to teach the concepts embodied in the entrepreneurial process, and met with limited initial success. My students were neither embracing these concepts nor seeing them as an overall process. Frustrated, I examined my approach and realized that the concepts were too ambiguous, and their relevance to students as individual concepts wasn't clear. Students could repeat them, but the concepts weren't being internalized or seen in the context of an overall entrepreneurship process.

While we teach that failure can be a good thing, for me it was not an option. Recalling that my favorite TED talks all featured stories, I crafted and incorporated stories from my personal entrepreneurial background that highlighted every concept in the entrepreneurial process. Success! Stories work; students love them. I'm a story teller now. Stories breathe life into entrepreneurial concepts, allowing them to be seen as an overall process.

Teach Frameworks

We are visual learners. Entrepreneurship is a discipline, replete with many concepts, but fundamentally it's a process, and every element of that process can be defined by a framework. I began by trying to teach concepts, but it's hard. Students failed to see the relationship between related concepts. The result was that they reverted to memorization, which precluded them from ever understanding entrepreneurship as a mindset. Frameworks define every major element of the entrepreneurship process, and teaching frameworks provide that visual reference. Frameworks enhance understanding of concepts, the relationship between them, and how ultimately the concepts all coalesce into a process that becomes the entrepreneurial mindset.

Deliberate Practice

Great pianists became great through intense practice. The same can be said of great football and basketball players. People learn most things through repeated practice. In particular, learning and internalizing the elements of the entrepreneurial process are best done through practice. As a strong proponent of experiential learning, every class day I teach some content, but then supplement this with repeated, deliberate practice of the concepts embodied in entrepreneurial competencies.

Risk Taking

We teach risk mitigation as an entrepreneurial competency, but I haven't encountered many good ways of experientially illustrating risk taking. So, a few years ago, I tried to incorporate risk in an entrepreneurship course. I proposed that the final exam be optional. If taken, there would be only two possible grades. Solid performance would result in a letter grade increase in course grade; poor performance would result in a letter grade reduction in course grade. Simple: a B pre-final could become either an A . . . or a C. The result was a colossal failure. Pre-final grades ranged from A– to C–. Every student in the class elected not to take a final exam. Apart from Dr. K's Spine Sweat course (which I don't personally have the risk posture to adopt), I still haven't found a good tool to teach risk, but feel strongly that one should be incorporated in teaching entrepreneurship.

Enthusiasm

I'm extremely enthusiastic teaching entrepreneurship; I even get excited. I think this draws students into class and gets them involved. My demeanor might be called a performance, although it is not. I'm simply tremendously enthusiastic about entrepreneurship as a discipline and its empowering and transformative nature, and I'm sincerely anxious to get my students to see it in the same light. Most students interpret my enthusiasm as passion for entrepreneurship, and my faculty evaluations reflect that.

Compelling Presentations in the Classroom

These are every bit as important as conveying a compelling vision for an entrepreneur. They're not dry nor given by a talking head, but are vibrant, full of enthusiasm, structurally logical, easily understood and delivered by someone who exudes passion for the topic. I practice core presentation skills:

1. Move around. (With a pedometer as my tool, my objective is 4000 steps per class. As they watch me move around, students are listening to me, and that's my objective.)

2. Hand and body motions and vocal inflections make you animated, even entertaining. Without them you're a talking head and difficult to listen to for more than five minutes.
3. Direct eye contact. When you look at someone directly in the eye, you connect with that person. From then on, the person feels you are talking directly to him or her, no matter where you face.

TEACHING OBJECTIVE

My teaching objective is to train students to think, act and do in an entrepreneurial way in every aspect of their life. I want to inspire those that can be leaders, whether in business or other pursuits, to understand and embrace the entrepreneurial approach as a way of thinking. I want to instill in the others the sincere belief that contributors are just as important as leaders, but only if they too are entrepreneurial in their approach and become the very best that they can be in the way they've chosen to contribute.

TEACHING PHILOSOPHY

My teaching philosophy reflects my values, beliefs and passion for teaching entrepreneurship. Three tenets form that philosophy:

1. The best teachers are themselves students. Having practiced entrepreneurship for an entire career, I'm comfortable with my domain expertise. Scholarly research though regularly features new entrepreneurial concepts and sheds light on new applications of existing concepts. I'm a student of this research. My purpose is to challenge students, not only with the traditional concepts but with the newest cutting edge thinking about entrepreneurship. I work to be the perpetual student, to learn and then create an active learning environment where students will be challenged and inspired and will flourish.
2. Learning is facilitated by teachers who are respected by students. I've taught long enough now to have many students who have graduated and are well along in their careers. Some, and from many parts of the world, have started their own businesses and still stay in contact with me. Having thought a lot about this, I've come to believe these students stay in contact with me because they respected me, and now are seeking my respect. This to me illustrates the power of inspiration born of respect.

I work hard to earn respect from every student, and the way I earn respect is to give respect. I respect every student as an individual and cater to his or her unique needs. I strive to find a shared perspective with each student. While this takes a lot of personal interaction, I find that students believe that I care for them as individuals. This creates respect for me, facilitating my ability to influence them through course content.

I respect their time. My office hours are any time, and include weekends.

Finally, I respect their efforts. Encouragement drives effort, so I easily complement clear thinking and solid effort. Challenge and encouragement are inseparable and are key elements in inspiring students' interest in entrepreneurship and their desire to learn more.

3. Substantial learning occurs outside of the classroom, where students review and discuss feedback and assessment of their deliverables. I believe that the learning process and permanent learning are advanced by providing substantive feedback for every deliverable, both constructive criticism and praise. This gives the student another opportunity to learn. Providing such extensive feedback is not without cost – a lot of time. But it's also not without value. Students regularly comment to me that they rarely receive such in-depth commentary on their work, and wished they did.

In summary, teaching entrepreneurship is not a job; it's a privilege. The style used to teach it I think has to be unique, and reflects one's comfort zone in terms of how one interacts with students. It is not something that can be observed in others and emulated. Teaching objectives can be similar among teachers. One's teaching philosophy I feel must also be unique, as it reflects one's values, beliefs and passion for teaching entrepreneurship.

NOTE

1. "Reflections from graduating students," *Babson Magazine*, Spring 2013, http://www.babson.edu/news-events/babson-magazine/spring-2013/babson-beyond/Pages/reflections-from-graduating-students.aspx.

REFERENCES

Barnett, R. (2007), *Will to Learn: Being a Student in an Age of Uncertainty*, New York: Open University Press.

Deleuze, G. (1990), *The Logic of Sense*, trans. M. Lester and C. Stivale, New York: Columbia University Press.

Felman, S. (1992), Education and crisis, or the vicissitudes of teaching, in S. Felman and D. Laub (eds.), *Testimony: Crises of Witnessing in Literature, Psychoanalysis, and History*, New York: Routledge, pp. 1–56.

Rilke, R.M. (1993), *Letters to a Young Poet*, trans. M.D. Herter, New York: Norton.

2. What entrepreneurship educators do not understand about creativity and how to teach it

Jeffrey Stamp

Central to entrepreneurship is the notion that entrepreneurs *create* value. Hence, educators often focus on describing what value is, how value is found, and what defines value in an entrepreneurial context. Yet the entrepreneur is often more concerned at the early stages of the entrepreneurial journey with the personal attributes of actually how to be creative, to be innovative, and how to capture value from the creative experience. So the gap between knowing about and experiencing creativity and recognizing the outcomes from creative expressions or the creative experience is what this chapter will attempt to bridge. This is important because entrepreneurs are increasingly relying on their own creative expression and efforts as part of the knowledge economy. Yes, sweat equity has now become creative equity.

For entrepreneurship students, the allure of using their creative ability to discover and exploit opportunity is a major draw in these programs. Yet, in my exposure to entrepreneurship students worldwide and the faculty who guide them, I routinely get asked "Why do college students underperform when asked to be creative?" This question isn't limited to the entrepreneurship classroom. In my experience with many different groups, organizations and individuals, this same sentence could be universally applied with: Why do ___ underperform when (asked, required) to be creative?

My answer to this question is framed from observations of creative individuals and groups, combined with the analysis of the thousands of outcomes of the creative process in my years working with diverse groups as a creativity consultant and educator. The bottom line is that there is no simple answer. Creativity isn't a single skill or aptitude conducted by the human mind. Rather, creativity is a complex systems thinking approach that engages in searching for meaning where one is trying to develop a choice-filled decision-making engine that produces superior outcomes.

A productive illustration of this involves one of the pioneers of creativity research – E. Paul Torrance. In 1951, having just completed his Ph.D. on the role of self-concept in the educational success of college freshmen, Torrance diverted from the expected role of taking a position as a junior faculty member at a university to accepting a research challenge that deeply intrigued him at the U.S. Air Force Survival School.

The Survival School had been established because of the data that revealed that a high percentage of the bomber crews shot down in World War II survived the bailout but didn't survive on the ground. During his six years of conducting research on the psychology of survival, Torrance discovered that the major underlying factor critical to survival was creativity. This formed the basis for his survival definition of creativity: "when one is faced with a problem for which there is no practiced or learned solution, some degree of creativity is required" (Millar, 1995). This new awareness of the importance of thinking abilities beyond retrieval of memorized knowledge is still used in military survival training today. Torrance's early definition of creativity can be equally applied to the survival skills required of the nascent entrepreneur.

DIVERGENT AND CONVERGENT THINKING

Creativity is an essential and natural part of the human experience. Every moment of our lives we are confronted with a complex combination of sensory perceptions that we need to make meaning from. Each of these moments as they are perceived can be considered as another problem-solving moment we are required to navigate. During cognitive periods of high focus when we recognize the problem and additionally have a satisfactory memory of a high probability outcome, we exercise convergent thinking behavior and select a single response that forms our next behavior (Gelernter, 2016). This sort of convergent cognitive behavior derived from memory recall of existent knowledge is often defined as uncreative thinking.

However, during those perceptual moments where the stimulus is not familiar or a solution is currently non-obvious, then we could choose a divergent thinking behavior to produce a set of alternative choices from which emerges a selected choice response that forms our next behavior (Vincent et al., 2002). This sort of divergent cognitive behavior, which results in an emergent process of choice creation, assembly and selection, is often defined as a form of creative thinking.

These two simplified scenarios describe activities related to human cognitive performance. We either make decision choices from knowledge we currently have at our recall or generate new knowledge from which useful future choices will be selected.

Or do we? Is it that simple? Might the processes of convergent and divergent thinking be more integrated in everyday experience? If so, how can we leverage them better to produce superior experience outcomes?

CREATIVITY AS AN APTITUDE

Historically, studies on human cognition have focused on what is believed to be fundamental mental properties and cognitive processing such as intelligence, memory, judgment, logical reasoning and attention. Yet, despite the overwhelming evidence of the economic value of the outputs of the highest levels of human performance (e.g., genius), invention, talent and creativity at the everyday level have nonetheless yielded far less scholarly attention and study and even less in the classroom. One contextual perspective utilized in the study of creativity focuses on three vantage points, namely the personality approach, the cognitive approach and the sociocultural approach (Sawyer, 2012).

The personality approach is focused on studying the personalities of exceptional creators and has been described as "Big C" creativity. This domain is reserved for identifying those characteristics that lead to eminent works of creative output. The early focus on the Big C event helped to fuel the already-standing myth that people either have or do not have creativity, with no capacity for improvement. This myth is still widely believed by the public and teachers alike even though there is considerable research over the last 30 years that strongly refutes it (Amabile, 1983; Sawyer, 2012). In addition, the Big C focus has fostered a second myth, namely that creative ideas suddenly appear in a moment of insight or mysteriously from the unconscious. While everyone has had an "Aha!" experience, it isn't mysterious. When an idea suddenly enters the conscious mind, it has been shown in numerous studies that these insights follow from bits of previously held knowledge that are carried forward on a trajectory of new meaning assembled by the creator (Gelernter, 2016).

The cognitive approach based in cognitive psychology, is focused on what is described as "little c" creativity, and illuminates the internal mental processes that are leveraged by the individual engaged in creative behavior to assemble new knowledge structures. Despite the mountains of research conducted on well-defined themes to the contrary (Smith et al., 1995; Sternberg, 2003), there is still the lingering pervasive stereotype of the creative individual as the loner, the dreamer, the nonconformist, or the disruptive malcontent always trying to change things. These stereotypes continue to fuel the view in both the public and scholarly circles that creativity is a soft psychology rather than a viable thinking paradigm.

In reality, creativity can be developed and enhanced. It is an aptitude and not a trait. Sadly, many professors still think that some people are and some people are not creative. A variety of researchers have shown that creative thinking processes at the individual level such as divergent thinking, cognitive flexibility, analogical reasoning and situational memory skills can be enhanced with practice and formulated into observable creative ability (e.g., Plucker et al., 2006; Torrance, 1972; Vincent et al., 2002). Improvements in both the ability to create ideas and the quality of those ideas have also been shown in both individual and group creative abilities through the use of intentional practice (Mitchell et al., 2015). In addition, there are many popular creative skill training programs such as lateral thinking (de Bono, 1970), mindmapping (Wycoff, 1991) and creative thinking exercises (Michalko, 1991) that are widely used to foster a creative attitude and mindset that bring conscious awareness to the process of generating new ideas.

The sociocultural approach considers the effects of various social and environmental factors on the acceptance of new things as produced by individuals or groups but ultimately accepted or agreed upon from a usability perspective by the surrounding societal group. At the individual level, a creative outcome is one that is both new and novel. However, when the creative process is employed by a group or the outcomes are engaged in the wider society, then not only do additional perspectives of the newness and novelty define the creative work but there is also a necessity for the creative work to be useful. Hence, an outcome can be more or less creative. Researchers have developed valuable methods such as the Creative Assessment Technique (Getzels and Csikszentmihalyi, 1976; Kaufman and Beghetto, 2009) that emphasize the evaluation of the output of creativity against expert norms.

The impact of new creative ideas that are produced by a group or organization is often labeled innovation (Amabile, 1996). In this case, there are two separate viewpoints from which to consider the effectiveness of the creative moment – the intrinsic motivation of the individual within the group and the assessment of the creative outcomes as appropriate to the social group.

CREATIVITY AND ENTREPRENEURSHIP: THE IMPORTANCE OF EXPERIENCING

The awareness of creativity as a strategic way of thinking or as a problem-solving process should be inherently interesting to the entrepreneur. The link between creativity and entrepreneurship has been implied, expressed and considered for quite some time (Beattie, 1999; Dimov, 2007; Drucker, 1985; McMullen and Shepherd, 2006; Mitchell et al., 2004; Morris et al., 2003; Whiting, 1988; Zahra, 2005). Creativity and entrepreneurship have both been subjected to confusion and argument in their respective and combined scholarly literatures over definitional and process orientations as well as legitimacy as a field of study. This can be seen in the inclusion of creativity in the definitional identity of entrepreneurship, and some have even posited that entrepreneurship is simply a sub-field of creativity (McMullan and Kenworthy, 2015).

Notwithstanding the debate in ordering the interaction between creativity and entrepreneurship, the value of creativity research in the context of entrepreneurship should yield valuable results. Both creative and entrepreneurial activities often exist in a domain of ill-defined problems where there are few solutions and ambiguity. In both cases, characteristics of autonomy, flexibility, openness to experience, risk tolerance, self-efficacy and intrinsic motivation have been identified as beneficial at the individual level in practice. Yet what of their value in the entrepreneurial classroom? Given the inherent lack of structure in these pursuits independently, how can creativity blended into the entrepreneurial classroom yield meaningful learning moments that translate into real-world practice and experience?

Experiencing creativity will help entrepreneurs identify and realize their unique creative talents. From a pedagogical perspective, the constructivist approach (Savery and Duffy, 1995) to learning and teaching is valuable here. It stresses the role of knowledge creation as opposed to knowledge transmission in yielding greater capability among entrepreneurship students in the control of the creative process. Further, it emphasizes the unique societal and environmental influences on creativity that will be vital to both the emergence of the nascent entrepreneur and the critical act of entrepreneurship as experience that will benefit the entrepreneur in the venture development process (Morris et al., 2012).

In addition, experiencing creativity will help entrepreneurs become better problem solvers who can utilize creative reasoning to solve important problems that they face in both a market and a societal context and not just divergent thinking or creative method awareness. Creativity is best achieved when flexible, exploratory, non-predetermined paths of discovery are possible (Amabile, 1983), so it is important to provide nascent entrepreneurs with an environment of safe experience from which to test out new ways of thinking. Moreover, experiencing creativity will help entrepreneurs become more effective leaders addressing even more pressing issues facing our ever-changing, fast-moving society. Creativity is also viewed as a central element in problem solving, and there are a number of ways in which creative thinking can facilitate decision making (Sternberg, 2003).

For entrepreneurship educators, experiencing creativity can enable them to teach more effectively. Over the past 20 years of teaching creativity at the college level, I've certainly learned from constant innovation in the classroom and from helping and guiding others to use creativity more in the classroom. The role of the instructor changes when creativity is being experienced because the role shifts from the sage on the stage to an active side-by-side participant or guide to the creative process. This is an uncomfortable position to be in because creativity is a searching experience that depends more on questions than on answers.

OVERCOMING MYTHS AND MISPERCEPTIONS

It's hard to think of any breakthrough product or service launched by an entrepreneur that didn't involve some level of creativity along the way. In the entrepreneurship classroom, there is always a palpable feeling that somewhere in the herd of gray matter inhabits the next big idea that will lead to a blockbuster IPO. So why then are college business plans still crowded with the next new bar, textbook reseller, dorm furniture storage, or food delivery service ideas? The key lies in the constant competing behavioral actions between familiar, habitual actions and seldom-exercised creative ones. In the dual pressures of daily life and the totality of college course work, many students operate from the easily accessible domain of the knowledge and experiences they hold from their current vantage point. This too is compounded by the natural constraints of a one-semester course that requires perhaps an entire business plan to be created such that any focus on creative processes is often confined to a few lectures at the beginning of a semester. Add in the trepidation by entrepreneurship faculty to guide or manage a seemingly fuzzy process such as creativity, and it can lead to a variety of perceptions and behaviors that actually inhibit the creative process. In my journey as a professional creative I have seen many groups of corporate professionals full of the appropriate aspiration and motivation to succeed creatively, but they struggle with producing novel and useful concepts. In the classroom these same behaviors that inhibit creativity need to be identified and then practical ways found to foster new creative behaviors that can produce superior creative outcomes. Here is my list of the 10 most common creativity inhibitors and practical ways to integrate creativity into any entrepreneurship classroom.

1. Starting Too Big

There is a lot of value in motivating students to do their best work. Yet again, when it comes to the creative process, it's a separate issue to set the bar too high, too early. In practice, beginning a semester emphasizing the importance of coming up with big Aha! moments for their projects isn't a request with a high probability of success. It isn't that students can't come up with the next Facebook or Uber; rather it's a matter of proficiency in creative cognition. As I've guided countless corporate creative teams that struggle with their sole professional task of creating breakthrough innovations that change the world, I'm aware of the low probabilities at play in these efforts. So it is important to distinguish between "Big C" and "little c" creativity in practice.

What does it mean to be creative? This question gets the same level of impressions and suggestions as does the question of what it means to be entrepreneurial. As with entrepreneurship, a standard definition of creativity has been lacking in the field. Plucker et al. (2004) did a comprehensive literature review of 90 different articles that had the word "creativity" in the title from peer-reviewed business, education and psychology journals over a three-year period. Only 38 percent of the peer-reviewed papers analyzed explicitly defined what creativity was. This lack of structural terminology only aids in the continued propagation of the myths of what creativity is. Plucker et al.'s (2004) work provides a synthesized framework of creativity from the combined literature that now forms a widely accepted definition: "Creativity is the interaction among aptitude, process, and environment by which an individual or group produces a perceptible product that is both novel and useful as defined within a social context" (p. 90).

Gardner defines the "creative individual" as "a person who regularly solves problems, fashions products, or defines new questions in a domain in a way that is initially considered novel but that ultimately becomes accepted practice in a particular cultural setting" (Gardner, 1993, p. 35). Gardner then defines creative works as "the small subset" of works in a domain that are ever deemed to be "highly novel, yet appropriate for the domain" (p. 38); these works "actually cause a refashioning of the domain." Those great minds such as Freud, Einstein or Picasso were eminent examples of domain innovators or disruptors that ultimately refashioned their domains, but refashioning was deemed valuable not only by the producers of the new knowledge but also by the sociocultural definitions of what is valuable.

But what about the rest of us? Kaufman and Beghetto (2009), in their 4-C Model of Creativity, expand on the traditional conceptions of the creative output to include "mini-c," which is the creativity inherent in the learning process. Fostering motivation to learn in students has a direct positive effect on creative ability (Plucker et al., 2006). In addition to defining who and what is considered creative, there also is a need to include student exposure to the factors that lead individuals to undertake creative actions intentionally. The continual experience of these types of cognitive skills in the creative process can be important to seeding the necessary entrepreneurial scripts that can be used in future entrepreneurial behavior (Mitchell et al., 2009).

In my view, the key in the creativity classroom while decidedly constructivist in orientation (Novak, 2002) is purposed on exposing students to new ways of information processing that can lead to more desirable cognitive habits that enhance their ability to think creatively. Welling (2007) identified four mental operations that account for a large proportion of creative cognition: application, analogy, combination and abstraction. Of these, abstraction, which is defined as the discovery of any structure, regularity, pattern or organization that is present in some different perceptions, is of key importance in the entrepreneurial context that can be experienced and practiced in the classroom as a precursor to opportunity identification.

Exercise – "frame it report"
The key for seeding new creative scripts in students is to start by breaking the creative process into discernible steps that can be recognized as different ways of processing information and observing the world around them. It is also valuable to reflect on any newly practiced mindfulness and awareness activity through a creative journal that captures their experiences of thinking. Engage the students to look purposefully for their own or observed behavior to process. One of the important roles of the teacher is to set the frame by which the focus of the behavior is observed to give the students a place to start. This exercise is designed to bring intention to three everyday frames (Goffman, 1974) from which to observe everyday mental tasks: the negative frame – "bug report" of things or situations that proved inadequate to a satisfactory experience; the positive frame – "possibility report" of what else something can do; or the neutral frame – "causality report" of open discovery of how things work or operate and identifying what is missing or gaps in knowledge to others. The overt exercise helps to seed discovering thinking and brings awareness to the non-obviousness in the world around the student. This dynamic framing exercise is straightforward, spawns considerable discussion in the classroom and often reveals ideas for new ventures. The key is guiding the students to expand the frames from which they view behavior and get them to recognize that discovery often begins with a question.

The bug report is the easiest to start with. Simply look for something that bugs you and then discover a new way to overcome the bug. For example, a team of students were rock climbing enthusiasts. They were dissatisfied with the lack of options in rock climbing holds for the gym that mimicked real rock formations. So they discovered a way to make 3D measurements of famous rock climb segments and then reproduce them on a 3D printer to recreate indoor practice climbs that matched their real outdoor surfaces.

The possibility report will produce an extension of a current idea or a cross-over into a new domain. For example, a team of students noticed that a popular brand of casual Crocs® clogs didn't have accessories, so they fashioned prototypes of insulated clogs that could be worn in winter conditions.

The causality report is often the more challenging exercise because it does require more domain specific knowledge to find new uses or identify missing information that students can discover on their own. For example, a student wanted to find new opportunities in green, sustainable materials and, after helping his father install new fiberglass insulation in the attic, searched for green materials that could act as affordable, viable insulation alternatives.

2. Not Honoring the Process of Questioning

Entrepreneurs often operate at the edge of what they do not know (Hill and Levenhagen, 1995). In the entrepreneurial creativity context, awareness of sensemaking processes is a valuable practice to develop in students. In the classroom, I have noticed there is still an over-reliance on students asking questions and teachers providing the answers. I have learned that simply answering a question, while expedient, can inhibit the process of discovery and creative exploration by the student. Therefore, I focus my internal dialog to remind myself that I want to solve students' questions not by giving them the answers but by providing a path for them to develop stronger sensemaking skills and available problem-solving scripts. To do this, we employ the universal open question process of answering any question with the phrase "it depends" and then defining the contextual frame from which discovery can reveal satisfactory answers.

Individuals continually engage in sensemaking processes that reflect the synergistic interaction of information seeking, meaning ascription, and action (Ford, N., 1999). I find that exercising these three processes can significantly increase both curiosity and intrinsic motivation to search ever-widening contextual frames. This is one of my favorite activities, as it brings a collective sense of discovery to the entire class as students push for bringing their Aha! moments to share.

Exercise – question behind the question
Get students to ask a question that interests them and is a novel new question to them. Then require them to answer the question by seeing how many "it depends" questions it can spawn. Example: how many jeans do they sell at a local mall? The students pick a store and spend time watching customers and develop an answer. Then they use that experience to pose deeper questions: Where do the jeans come from? Where does a particular brand source its cotton for the jeans? How many total miles does it take for jeans to end up in this mall? Is the practice of stone-washing jeans a sustainable practice? How many gallons of water does it take to raise and produce one pair of jeans? Are there fair trade systems in place for cotton growers in developing economies as with coffee? Evaluate on both the breadth and the thoughtfulness of these questions. Often this will lead to interesting new venture ideas.

3.   Lack of Practice, Practice, Practice

The majority of the formal education experience is structured around the acquisition and retention of explicit knowledge. This knowledge acquisition and memorized structure develops a set of habitual actions that students perfect over time and recognize as the behaviors that are rewarded. Thus, when faced with a new challenge they tend to utilize a best-fit approach to previously held knowledge as a problem-solving strategy. Even in circumstances that favor some sort of creative action, students will likely choose familiar memory-recalled behavior options that are relatively more attractive based on their past success, relative ease, and certainty (Ford, N., 1999). Teachers also foster these memorized behaviors, because it is easier to develop grading rubrics for explicit information and to fit it into a well-defined syllabus. Thus, when it comes time to incorporate creativity-based activities it is seldom more than a single lecture or two in an entire semester.

The eminent creativity researcher E. Paul Torrance was one of the first proponents of adding creativity methods in the classroom with the development of an instructional model for facilitating suprarational thinking, defined as thinking beyond the rational thinking process (Torrance, 1972). His model specifies stages of heightening anticipation, encountering the expected and unexpected, and going beyond. The key cognitive behaviors that are experienced in the creative process embody the tension of anticipation and expectation. Torrance had as a goal to help students develop a metacognitive awareness of how they positioned their thinking when addressing creative challenges.

I certainly agree with Torrance that creative teaching isn't a guarantee of miracles in the classroom. That said, it has been shown that, with diligent practice, students will grow creatively and will solve many learning problems that otherwise defy solution (Torrance, 1972). I have confirmed this finding in the entrepreneurship classroom and have many students carry these metacognitive techniques with them in professional practice. The first step is to develop an awareness of how the mind is processing information and recognizing the role of continued memory reliance in both helping and inhibiting the quest for developing new connections that lead to novel ideas. In the Torrance Test of Creativity (TTC), this is measured as ideational fluency that asks students to come up with alternative uses for a common object (e.g., describe as many uses as you can for a brick). This seemingly simple instruction is often in itself a hurdle to many students because they are over-reliant on memory of those explicit uses already memorized for the utility of a brick (e.g., a house, a dog house, a wall, a sidewalk, a road based on common themes) and conscious of the traditional educational expectation of succeeding in finding the "right" answer to this challenge.

The emphasis on divergent thinking processes in the TTC is but one of many creative cognition processes that students need to master to achieve superior creative outcomes. In addition to fluency (the number of ideas created in the responses), the TTC also looks at flexibility (i.e., the number of different categories of uses identified in the responses), originality (i.e., a statistical measure of novelty of the responses) and elaboration (i.e., the amount of elaboration in the responses) (Torrance, 1972). In exploring ways to train students that result in improved TTC scores over a semester, I have found that training students with metacognitive exercises that seed for both fluency and flexibility builds skill in learning how to process creative stimulus. This measure is defined as fluidity and evaluates the ability of intentional shifts between explicit and implicit thinking.

Exercise – "What do you see?"

One approach to improving the core of ideational fluency is experiential practice with creative stimulus. There are two kinds of stimulus: related or unrelated to the task or problem. Stimulus can be used in any sensory form, including visual, sound, taste, smell, tactile or proprioception (Stamp, 2000). I've found the easiest is with picture-based stimulus (i.e., a picture is worth a thousand words). The most accessible pictures from which sensory imagery can be processed are those with action (e.g., a surfer on a wave, a horse and rider jumping a barrier, a ballerina, or a bowling ball rolling down a lane). Select a picture and then ask: "What do you see?" Have the students write down as many words that describe the picture as possible in 15 seconds. What you will get in the first attempt are words that relate explicit information about the picture (e.g., surfer on a wave: water, surfboard, wave, blue, sunshine, California, beach, vacation, wipeout, etc.). Then ask the students to read aloud the responses and collectively as a class compare the breadth of the words expressed. Generally, over 90 percent of the words will be in ever-more specific reference to what is explicitly in the picture. This is because they are using habitual memory processing to look at the picture and interpret correct responses to the original question.

Next, have the students do this again and coax them into increasingly implicit interpretations of the picture (e.g., surfer on a wave: wipeout, vacation, fun, whoa!, hang 10, life of a start-up venture, taking an exam). Again, have the students share their words and link the interpretations through metaphor (e.g., a new venture as a surfer on a wave). This collective sharing of implicit viewpoints shows the students that the origins come from the ability to derive new meaning and sense-giving to the images. The key learning moment with the students is that, while each individual implicit view of picture stimulus is unique to the student, it is identifiable to each student once aware.

Finally, allow the students to repeat the exercise for an additional 15 seconds with the same prompt, "What do you see?" Awareness of the freedom to freely associate the picture to any implicit meaning as long as they can communicate its meaning fulfills the mental construct as a viable creative idea (i.e., it is new to them, it is useful to the individual in that it fulfills the problem statement, and it is useful to the group to add to their meaning). I do this same basic exercise for many weeks each semester, and this can be used in a testing format as well. As the students gain fluidity skill, they can easily record 20 or more explicit words or phrases and 20 implicit words or phrases in the same 15-second period. Once they have achieved this level of fluidity in developing new and useful mental models to stimulus they have an increased likelihood of creating bigger ideas when searching for new venture opportunities.

4.   Providing Examples

Showing examples in class is great. In my new venture class, I love to show students examples of new business ideas gleaned from social media or other online sources. While it is both stimulating and exciting to share the latest new app or newest breakthrough idea recently funded by Silicon Valley VCs and generates ample discussion in the classroom, it's a win/win at the expense of creativity. Showing examples, I've found, can inhibit creativity in a couple of subtle ways. Firstly, showing an example is a suggestive behavior on my part as leader in the discussion. This example is then interpreted by the students as the best or an ideal way to approach the problem, and they generally accept this as the preferred solution, since I represent the expert view in the room. This often results in causing creative blocks or "me-too" derivative ideas in the classroom as students use this example as their basis for comparison. This suggestive effect isn't confined to the entrepreneurship classroom. I have seen this effect in corporate brainstorming sessions countless times. When someone of authority gives an example up front before work on a creative challenge is started, the social standard of the group shifts toward that example. This effect has been demonstrated in research. Beaty and Silvia (2012) confirmed other research that ideas in a divergent thinking task tend to get more creative across time. They also showed that, as intelligence increased, this disrupted the normal serial effect in idea generation, concluding that individuals use executive process to converge on more productive solutions. Thus, when an intelligent example is presented, students actively revert to convergent thinking strategies rather than explore new idea spaces.

Secondly, an example, and in particular an elegant or novel solution to a creative challenge, can intimidate students still trying to assimilate the idea in their own knowledge structures. This effect is even more pronounced when bringing up "latest trend" conversations in the classroom, as students who are particularly aware of a category or well versed in trends tend to share examples they have memorized from other sources, which inhibits the other students in the class who sense they have less to contribute.

To stimulate and provide an environment for the creative process to flourish, instead of offering an example up front, I better define the context for which the original creative problem existed and then guide them into the creative space to explore their new knowledge generation. I only use the example then to show as an endpoint comparison. For example, I like to use the opportunity space of "tech-active sports gear." This market category is a familiar conceptual space to college students and is also particularly active commercially. To get them started, I share some of the work of Boden (2004), who contextualizes the creative space into three perspectives: new combinations, new explorations and new transformations. Then I have the students put these perspectives to use. In this example, one viable conceptual space for sports gear is the backpack. One example of a new combination is to combine sensors with backpacks. A new exploration of the backpack concept space is to re-envision the backpack as not only a device to carry items but also one that re-charges the electronic items you carry. A new transformation of the backpack could be to combine solar panels so that the backpack can provide a heated interior of the backpack to keep your electronics from freezing in cold outdoor climates for hikers, explorers, the military or students in cold climates. In each of these cases, the students can develop new backpack concepts and then compare them to commercial examples to evaluate their creativity on novelty, utility, and acceptability to a particular customer target. Examples have their role after the creative process. Eliminating examples altogether also inhibits the creative process, as students will often hesitate, not knowing where to begin as their minds resort to memory-based behaviors searching for the correct answer. The key is to balance the use of examples as an evaluative comparison tool and not as a creative tool.

Exercise – "What if?"
This is a re-envisioning of the standard divergent thinking alternate uses exercise in the Torrance Test of Creativity. The idea here is, when students ask for guidance or suggestions related to a concept idea that they are working on, to resist the temptation simply to provide an example. The goal of the creative process is to provide more choices from which to choose in making a decision about a conceptual idea or product. Instead, provide them a new context from which to view their task. Often this is a process of deconstructing assumptions and then forcing a new combination of elements to change the opportunity space.

Here's what to do. Take an everyday object and have the students create new concept ideas to repurpose or find new uses for the object (e.g., a pen, a plastic drinking cup, a ping-pong paddle, a Pringles® can, etc.). Then set up the task in an entrepreneurial context by having the students proto-type their concept after the creative process, test the idea with a targeted customer, and produce a rough estimate of costs and pricing to establish viability. The key here is to help them re-envision the problem space by deconstructing the item and asking questions: What is it made of? What physical utility does it have? What is it used for? What benefit does it provide the user? What could be added to this to transform its utility or benefit? How could this be used in a different way for a different customer?

One of my favorite new product concepts for this exercise was a team of students who came up with a new use for a Pringles® can that took the properties of volume, structural rigidity, and the observed Aha! moment that it could fit into a car cup holder to develop a concept for a pet store that utilized the can as a storage structure to transport fish home. The idea was cleverly simple. The can would be sold to pet stores with a plastic bag, twist tie and pre-printed stickers that gave care and feeding instructions to customers on their new pet. Now transporting that new goldfish home from the pet store is safe for both the owner and the fish. The prototype concept was so well received by pet store owners that the students spent a summer sourcing supplies and developing the idea, which they eventually sold to a local pet store.

5.   Relying on Demonstration

I will never forget the first time I saw a demonstration in a class. I was in first-grade math and the teacher was showing how to solve single digit addition problems using a number line. I was hooked. However, I saw a different way to perceive the process of adding two numbers by reinterpreting the origin of the problem and how it affected the count on the number line. This of course was one of my first indications that I had a natural curiosity to question explicit knowledge structures. The teacher, however, simply called me stubborn. The teacher was interested in showing us the "what and how" of addition, and I wanted to know the "why."

Yet demonstrations remain a central part of the teaching classroom. When I use a demonstration, I am mimicking and suggesting the "right" way to do something. The classic study of monkey see, monkey do behavior in humans shows that a demonstration is a powerful way to imitate desired future behavior (Millgram et al., 1969). However, a demonstration has also the power to inhibit creative thinking, because in showing the "right" way I have effectively circumvented what students might have conceived had they been allowed an opportunity to view the process from a fresh, unbiased perspective.

A common example in the entrepreneurship classroom is in demonstrating customer experience usage assumptions as explicit knowledge versus allowing the students the freedom of deconstructing potential customer needs and then formulating their creative concept of a business, transaction or usage model. While I'm a big proponent of design thinking or human factor design as a framework for creating new ideas, it is important to keep in mind that filling up a wall with Post-it® notes isn't creative until a value-focused concept is captured from that process and validated with potential customers for acceptability.

Exercise – "I spy"

In this exercise, instead of demonstrating the user experience of an app or a website or the buying experience of a product or service, I let the students set up experience gathering sessions. They even have to determine how many observations they are motivated to gather to make and support user trends or conclusions. One of my favorites is to utilize video technology to capture user behavior or to conduct user stories or conversations. For example, students will go into a grocery store and, while they are shopping, engage with shoppers in unassuming conversation to ask why they are buying or using a certain product. Then the students are required to create new usages or applications, combinations, transformations, customizations or aftermarket add-ons. While this is a familiar variation of the focus group or consumer surveys, it is purposefully unstructured so that the students experience first-hand the value of consumer-centered inquiry. For example, a team of students went to a car oil change location and investigated customer stories around dealing with long wait times for car service. The students, then realizing the value of a consistent pool of captive customers, proposed new concepts in customer service and new revenue streams to fill the repair wait opportunity.

6.   Creative Freedom

This question always comes up sooner or later – how much freedom do people need in order to be creative? I have a love, hate relationship with this question. Many creative practitioners will point to the seminal work of Alex Osborn (1963) in his book *Applied Imagination* as interpreting the creative process as one without constraints – that creativity needs to have maximum freedom to increase ideational efficiency. However, in professional practice I have found that, if there is too much freedom without a particular focus, then the individual or group involved in the creative exercise will revert to habitual thinking practices in search of readily available ideas or familiar ideas with high probability (i.e., "low-hanging fruit" ideas). What Osborn actually said was that, to improve ideational efficacy, two factors were required: 1) go for quantity; and 2) defer judgment. Many have treated deferring judgment as a proxy for freedom to say any idea that comes to mind. Deferring judgment or withholding criticism is important for allowing individuals to feel free to offer unusual or unconventional ideas, but this is different from freedom or release from a focused goal orientation.

The real issue is the interpretation of the term "freedom" as it relates to the context of the creative process experienced by the individual, which if unresolved can inhibit the creative process. At the individual level, the freedom issue can range from mild concern to fearful apprehension by individuals who wonder where or when new creative ideas will appear. This is initiated by the myth held by both students and teachers requiring creativity to include the necessity of experiencing a flash of insight (Sawyer, 2012). This misconception can often be traced from students as a misunderstanding of the role and value of incubation used in their creative experience.

Many teachers and practicing creatives utilize the historic four-stage creative process model proposed by Wallas (1926) of preparation, incubation, illumination and verification. This has been a useful conceptual foundation for creativity researchers as well (Sadler-Smith, 2015). Perhaps the most intriguing of the steps to put into practice is the step of incubation – often defined as that stage of creative problem solving where the problem is temporarily set aside after a period of initial work (Smith and Dodds, 1999). However, the challenge centers on how incubation is practiced – is it exclusively accidental or can it be practiced intentionally? Even in Wallas's book he doesn't make an explicit distinction between when to use conscious thought and when to use unconscious thought but does encourage two techniques for incubation as either conscious work on other problems (i.e., a distraction) or relaxation from all mental work (Sadler-Smith, 2015).

Gelernter (2016) describes a variable of human consciousness that operates along a spectrum from high focus to low focus many times during the day. At high focus, the mind works in a convergent manner. It identifies specific problems and tasks. It calls on the memory for data, patterns and instructions necessary to answer the questions and perform the job at hand. In times of high focus the mind is busy thinking on purpose. By comparison along this continuum, the mind at low focus may drift and even seem to go blank. At lowest focus, when the body is asleep, the dreaming mind turns up images and memories in an attempt to pursue meaning by inventing stories, not according to a rational blueprint, that we sense as dreams. A logical argument and a story are two ways of putting fragments in proper relationship (Lakoff and Johnson, 1980). This approach according to Gelernter can place the range of creative production from scientists to poets on the same spectrum. Others have argued and shown empirically that incubation effects are the brain's active forgetting process of eliminating inappropriate mental sets, which allows for new combinations to become favored.

This brings us back to the most often used method of creative focus, the brainstorming group. To Osborn's credit, in the early 1960s when he proposed his method, it was touted as a way to double the number of ideas created to address a problem (Osborn, 1963). Brainstorming was created in an information-sparse environment and was a method to gather a group of people to collectively focus on a problem space. At that time, communication of ideas occurred fastest and was best done in the same room at the same time. In effect, the early brainstorming group was its own private knowledge network. This strategic gathering of a carefully selected network of explicit knowledge holders could produce unique combinations of that knowledge quickly and efficiently to provide new concepts. However, in today's highly connected world, how people access information has changed. It is now harder to "think outside the box," when search engines have expanded the size of the box exponentially and almost instantly. With the cost of knowledge fast approaching zero, it changes the entire role of the brainstorming group and how we engage others in the creative process (Altman et al., 2015). Therefore the brainstorming process whether individually or in a group needs to evolve from a practice of high focus to one where low-focus approaches can be used to actively foster incubation of the vast knowledge choices into manageable superior creative outcomes (Mitchell et al., 2015).

Exercise – hatching eggs

In this exercise I encourage the students to discover active incubation strategies that help them prepare for the process of individual or group brainstorming effectiveness. The idea is very simple and designed to help active incubation by providing alternative stimuli not related to the task in an active attempt to use both the incubation tactics and distraction and relaxation to a strategic advantage. The use of stimulus helps the unconscious processes in the mind make new combinations that may become conscious at a later time and hatch unexpected but novel ideas. Students can do this exercise either alone or in groups, but I require them at least to hold one brainstorming group as part of the exercise so that they can experience group thinking around a creative problem. The key is to allow the student to explore secondary free knowledge sources that may spark new knowledge.

Here's what to do. Assign a creative challenge. One of my favorites is to have students or teams create new board games. In the Wallas (1926) structure, in the Preparation Phase, there is complete design freedom here to define what is a board game, define what is the concept of play, explore how games are played, and explore who is the intended target audience for the game. However, the final prototype must be a game (i.e., contain true gaming elements: fun, competition, scoring, winners and rules). Then in the Incubation Phase students must identify and utilize a non-game stimulus to help provide conscious awareness of design elements relevant to the creative challenge. One of the suggestions I give them is to go to a bookstore or newsstand and pick out 10 random magazines without judgment and then utilize the visual images to spark ideas for their games. Then they are asked to go for a walk-about in a social meeting place and see how humans engage in play. Some students have gone to the mall, park, playground, subway station, hospital waiting area, or even a zoo (i.e., animals play too). The key here is to watch others and let the mind actively perceive the stimulus without regard to its immediate application. Then the students are asked to set aside the problem until the next day, when they hold another brainstorming group or proceed individually to develop novel game concepts. The concepts are evaluated for play value and fit to the expected consumer target, and the students submit their favorite three game concepts with rules and play descriptions. The topic concept is prototyped, and the students must record on video actual user interaction with the game and conduct enough trials to establish verification of their initial concept assumptions.

It is interesting to read in the students' creativity journals when the ideas become conscious to them. Part of the obvious revelation that occurs is the students' determination of the goals and limitations of their newly formed ideas. In addition, when students develop improved metacognitive awareness of their internal creativity ability they demonstrate a greater ability when performing creative tasks (Puryear, 2015).

7. Not Encouraging Ownership of Ideas

I love to hear live music. Not only is it a source for experiencing a type of creative expression, but it also is a source of creative inspiration. When listening to a musician play a set on stage, it is often very easy to distinguish a song written by someone else that the artist is covering versus a song that the artist wrote. There is a discernible difference that comes out into what I term the "ownership sound." This distinctive sound of ownership in the expression of the music performed seems to be a real-life example of the intrinsic motivation principle of creativity, which states that people are most creative when they feel motivated primarily by the interest, enjoyment, satisfaction and challenge of the work itself – and not by extrinsic or outside motivators (Amabile, 1983). Intrinsic motivation is one of four factors of the componential theory of creativity, which in essence is a comprehensive model of the social and psychological components necessary for an individual to produce creative work and includes high domain expertise and high skill in creative thinking, and works in an environment high in support for creativity. Taken together, in the proper social environment creativity flourishes. This explains in some part the viral nature of some cover versions of otherwise famous songs that have been re-envisioned, reworked, deconstructed, sampled or reinterpreted by a new performer and then hit the popular music charts. It reinforces in the entrepreneur classroom that I shouldn't be describing a breakthrough innovation but rather how this breakthrough innovation breaks away from the commonplace standard in its category. We all work on the shoulders of those who create before us, but more than simply borrow inspiration we need to own it in order that the next stage of improvement can truly emerge.

Exercise – word hack

In this exercise I want to simulate a real-world test of Amabile's componential theory of creativity. For this to be universal to everyone in the class in some experience domain where they could generally participate with equal expertise, I decided to leverage the everyday use of language and explore word innovation in the English language. English is a language that has a very malleable structure. There are hundreds of examples of hybrid words that are in common use in our culture, such as television (tele = at a distance, vision = to see). Popular products also inherit hybrid names that are used to set them apart from the competition, such as NyQuil® (Ny = night time, Quil = tranquility). The word hack exercise when utilized in a supportive creative environment in the classroom works amazingly well as an exercise because creating new language sparks a natural intrinsic motivation to own what is created, as it finds immediate social usefulness and fits the criteria for a creative work because it is also novel, and I require that the word be tested in social media for acceptance by others. In addition, it fulfills the componential theory's other two tenets in that expertise in spoken language is fairly uniform at the college level (even if English is not the first language) and the exercise emphasizes the development of expertise in the important creative skill of bisociation (Koestler, 1964), itself a hybrid word that means to connect two things that come from two different contexts into one.

Here's how it works. This exercise can be done individually or in groups. First, the most efficient source of stimulus is any newspaper that obviously has numerous sections and is full of words. Then have the students work to identify by visual inspection about 20 multi-syllable words and write them on a separate piece of paper. From the collected words, draw a vertical line between the natural syllable splits in the words and then combine by random or visual experimentation syllables from two words and make a new word. The exercise can be used in any allowed time frame, but the key is to allow for the assembly of a few new word options from which a preferred creation is identified. The exercise is completed by creating, in addition to the word, a definition and an example of the new word used in a sentence (see Stamp, 2015 for an illustration). A few examples of words created by students in real classroom sessions were: demonstrate + achieving = demichieving – only getting half of one's work done but always getting full credit in the eyes of the boss or teacher; saliva + explosive = salivosive – a food that is so desirable it causes someone to drool excessively at the mere thought of it; fun + anniversary = funversary – if you have to work on a defined national holiday, your employer allows you to specify a different paid holiday that you identify as your personal funversary; beverage + emergency = bevmergency – a meeting that is so boring that only an adult beverage can make the situation tolerable.

The final task in this exercise is to test the newly created words in a real social context. For this, the students use the words in any online social media form they wish with the goal to see how much reach and re-use they can effect. In this portion, it is also expected that the creator define and measure what is termed reach. This sparks a new creative task to see how much ownership of the words a student will take and where these words will end up. Some created words have ended up on nationally syndicated blogs or even on the local television station used by a host in a news report.

8.   Forcing Traditional Grading

I get asked this question a lot – how do you grade creative assignments? I often think this question is asked because there are a lot of people who still secretly believe you cannot grade the output of creative efforts and use this as a clever ploy to convince me that there is no way to grade creative efforts. I couldn't disagree more. This is very similar to the ongoing debate within and around entrepreneurship – you can't teach entrepreneurship. In both cases, the research literature is proving this is no longer a debate. Both creative and entrepreneurial ability can be nurtured and improved with practice. However, if I grade on a traditional normative standard without providing appropriate guidance and feedback in improving creative awareness then I can inhibit student creative self-efficacy. Instead, I have become a big fan of longitudinal approaches to assessing creative ability, and these methods have direct utility in the experiential entrepreneurial classroom.

In the entrepreneurial domain, the creation and writing of a business plan is considered both an essential part of the curriculum and a vital skill that translates to critical steps in the creation of a venture. From a pedagogical perspective considerable effort has been advanced to develop effective models for teaching the craft of business plan writing and analysis. One way to assess the ability of a student to grasp the essential knowledge structures and skill to construct a business plan is to use an experience-based tool that qualitatively assesses investment criteria that are important to venture capitalists. White et al. (2011) demonstrated using a situated and community practice approach for 13 business plan criteria evaluated by students and a panel of three expert evaluators that a high level of internal consistency between students and experts could be achieved. This indicates that using a business plan as an experiential template prepares students to understand the structure, meaning and importance of concepts, behaviors and skills necessary in the practice of entrepreneurship. Others have taken a behavioral approach to measuring longitudinal growth in entrepreneurial intentions throughout the entrepreneurship education process (Fayolle, 2004).

In the creativity domain, similar methods have evolved over time to assess creativity and creative ability in students. One of the most effective is the Consensual Assessment Technique (CAT) first articulated by Amabile

(1982). In the CAT, a product or concept is deemed creative to the extent that appropriate observers agree that it is creative. This method too as it has been developed over time has shown reliability and construct validity in the assessment (Hennessey, 1994). The only issue that arises is the criteria used and the form of the creative product. The CAT is used to assess a variety of outputs, such as a form of literature (e.g., poem or story), an art creation (e.g., collage or drawing) or a product (e.g., inventions or science-based experiments) evaluated from a defined beginning framework such as a theme or word prompts. Another approach is to borrow the time-honored practice in art and design of the critique. Researchers have adapted this highly experiential methodology and practice from the design studio to the creativity classroom with great success in measuring growth in creative abilities (Hokanson, 2012). In the behavioral domain, researchers have developed metacognitive awareness assessments to build student creative self-efficacy and intention (Puryear, 2015).

In the intersection between creativity and entrepreneurship, I have found that one of the best ways to evaluate creative output is to blend a literary form with a product form and blend it into an essential part of the entrepreneurial process, the concept. A concept in this context is a written and often visual treatment of the core attributes and description of the value proposition that the entrepreneur is attempting to transact with the desired consumer. The development of a successful value proposition, business model and consumer desired attributes are a critical first step in the early stages of business plan development. Using a word-based concept (e.g., in paper or web landing page format) as an assessment to evaluate both creativity and entrepreneurial abilities in students works particularly well in the classroom because it both is time efficient and can be done before significant resources are committed to building prototypes or models. In addition, a concept is a very usable framework to identify both value-creating elements essential to entrepreneurs (e.g., consumer benefits) and awareness of the creative process (e.g., novelty, utility and social acceptance). Part of the learning process as well comes not only from learning to produce a concept but also in critically evaluating and interpreting concepts created by others.

Exercise – three stars
This exercise is one that I use multiple times during the semester in a testing environment to provide a longitudinal measure of student growth in creative ability. The test exercise has three parts. It starts with a carefully selected visual image (see the exercise "What do you see?"). Part one asks students to provide 10 words that describe what they see in the picture on a continuum from explicit to implicit knowledge. The key here is to evaluate

students' command of their mental fluidity and evaluate their ability to recognize what is explicit versus implicit knowledge and interpret how they visually perceived the objects in the picture.

Part two asks the students to use the picture as a primary source of stimulus and create three seed ideas where this image could be used effectively as an image in an advertisement (e.g., traditional print or landing page). A seed concept (30 words or less) is a simple description of the idea, the target consumer and the main consumer benefit. Then the student is asked to qualitatively (as opposed to subjectively) rate their seed ideas from 1 (best) to 3 (least) in terms of benefit preference and fit to the consumer target.

Part three then asks the students to write an expanded concept of their preferred idea in an advertisement format of no more than 100 words. A concept in advertisement format includes a picture, positioning language and attribute description to communicate a consumer-focused offering that has been validated in the literature to represent an accurate medium to estimate consumer trial (Kahle et al., 1997). This format is most effective when the information in the written concept mirrors the information consumers have when they decide what to purchase. An advertising directed concept to test consumer trial purchase of a product or service is similar to using a business plan to test investor trial investment in an entrepreneur.

The exercise is evaluated and scored without student names attached by myself and a panel of three former students who serve as creative process experts. A scoring rubric is defined for each part. In part one, each of the 10 words on the continuum from explicit (left-side anchor) to implicit (right-side anchor) is awarded for accuracy (if it actually exists in the picture it counts and is on the left side of the continuum) and originality (it exists on the right side of the continuum and can be inferred from the level of sophistication in word choice and its connection to the picture).

Part two is evaluated and a weighted average score of the order ranking of the three seed concepts of the student's ranking is compared to the panel's. Maximum points are given if the student ranking compares to the expert panel ranking. This is an effective grading because it requires students to demonstrate they understand value creation in a concept and how to make it attractive to a perceived consumer rather than simply picking the concept they personally like or find appealing. One of my best resources for expert panelists is former students from my creativity class who volunteer to be raters in order to keep their creativity skills fresh.

Part three rates the concept as described in the CAT for written creative tasks (Amabile, 1982). The CAT has been validated for the three predictive factors of creativity, style and technical correctness. For consumer concepts, creativity is evaluated by the expert judges for attention-getting relevance, fit to consumer mindset, and ability to draw the consumer in. Style is interpreted in writing skill, appropriateness and structure. Technical correctness is the ability to communicate effectively overt consumer benefit, reason to believe, and new and different scales.

I have used this exercise format since 1999 and have found it to have a couple of surprising outcomes. First, students don't see this as a test as much as they perceive this exercise as a way to showcase or demonstrate their newly developed creative skills. Students grow at different rates as their creativity awareness and practical skill emerge. When students see this improvement it builds their intrinsic motivation to try increasingly challenging creative problems. In fact, over time I've added a qualitative assessment of ambition in order to award extra credit to students who take on impressive depth in their concepts and excel at a higher level. Second, students are generally proud of their work in this exercise (testing) format. I've had many students tell me they have kept these tests for years after college to remember the creative processes we experienced in class and applied it to professional challenges. In addition, I've had students who have proudly shown these tests in a job interview when recruiters ask what differentiates them from other candidates, because corporate recruiters recognize the concept format and can compare it to professional competency, and love to hire students with a mature entrepreneurial mindset who can adequately communicate ideas.

9.   Requiring Success

During the course of any creative project, there are bound to be both roadblocks that appear in internal cognitive processing and external design obstacles that arise during the course of information acquisition or knowledge development. It is one thing to provide a supportive environment in the classroom but that doesn't always result in the individual personalities in the classroom overcoming these blocks. It is vital to the learning process within creativity to develop schemas and heuristics for overcoming roadblocks and failures that arise to successfully persist to an acceptable outcome.

C. Ford (1996) suggested that sensemaking is guided by schemas that construct meaning and structure on information and can positively influence creativity. When students perceive a negative outcome in their own creative processes or receive negative feedback from a teacher these events could result in schemas that inhibit the creative process. Of course, each person when receiving negative feedback responds emotionally in different ways, and ability to persist or use intrinsic motivation to overcome these obstacles can vary greatly. What is considered negative feedback by one student can be simply a suggestion to try something different to another. Researchers have not yet found a solid link between failure feedback and future levels of creativity, but others have found that the ability to carefully manage goal orientation can moderate positive effects of negative feedback to create successful creative outcomes (He et al., 2016).

Since having a strong goal orientation increases intrinsic motivation for positive outcomes to the effort, it is important to understanding and experiencing failure in the creative process. In the classroom, mastering the skill of asking open-ended questions (see the exercise "question behind the question") is a practice that helps students work through creative obstacles as they encounter them. It is also important that the classroom develops a culture of the class time as a forum of open conversation for creative reaction to failure or roadblock resolution that moves issues forward.

The creative process is designed as an idea generating process that results in more solution choices for ill-defined problems. But often, in the active working of problems that take an extended time, students in response to challenging ill-defined problems resort to familiar behaviors of habitual convergent thinking and search for the single right answer. This problem-solving strategy is often at odds with the prescribed challenge, and students experience feedback from the experience that is perceived as negative when the results are less than satisfactory. This effect is particularly pronounced in entrepreneurship problems because of the inherent ambiguity involved in working on innovation type problems such as business model invention. Even the task of specifying the goal in entrepreneurship problems can lead students to struggle at creative tasks to solve those problems. In this case, it is often concluded by the teacher that the creative ability of the students must be lacking when in many cases it is an issue of prescribing the outcome goal expectations with better clarity.

Creativity researchers also debate the role of creativity in solving problems. The literature for many years has continued a lively debate on whether better creative outcomes are derived from general creativity knowledge (Plucker, 1998) or domain specific or event task specific knowledge (Baer, 1998). The argument persists because many divergent thinking assessments ask for specific creative outcomes (e.g., uses for a brick) from a general creative process (e.g., create as many uses as possible without regard to the utility or success implied by the instruction). While numerous studies show that more ideas are produced when there is greater domain specificity to the required task, it has been shown that, when people are presented with a specific creative task such as writing a poem, a higher level of creative performance is exhibited by someone with domain expertise in writing than someone with equivalent domain expertise in say mathematics (Baer, 1998). This has also been shown to be true in task specific problems like making a collage, which has greater creative outcomes by those with more graphic design domain experience as compared to those without. Whether or not these empirical results are research design and analysis artifacts is still hotly debated (Plucker, 1998).

This goal or process ambiguity can easily happen in the entrepreneurship classroom. One of the favorite creative problems posed in a venture initiation class is to create a new business model for an established business. I've seen this problem pose negative feedback perceptions throughout the creative problem-solving process. Part of this is lack of domain specific expertise, and part of this is a lack of specific goal orientation. Even the entrepreneurship literature debates a common definition of a business model (Morris et al., 2005). Then couple this with the confounding goal orientation of working through the development choices for which goal – value for the firm, value for a targeted customer, firm-level competitive advantage, firm positioning in the marketplace, economic model or resource combination effects – can inhibit the creative process and the students revert quickly from divergent process to convergent identification of "What is the correct answer the teacher is looking for within all these factors?"

In my experience, the hurdle to creativity in solving this problem is caused by two inhibitory factors: 1) the assignment isn't personally meaningful to the student, with little ownership, so there is little intrinsic motivation that can help the student persevere when business model design obstacles appear; and 2) the assignment specifies a general problem (create a new business model) with a specific expectation (that it is novel and economically viable, i.e., it works) rather than asking for options for a specific problem (create a new transaction model) with a general expectation (does the new invention make money for the firm?). This allows the student to shift the locus of the intrinsic motivation to a learning goal orientation that strengthens the creative process through the problem design obstacles to achieve new and different knowledge with a searched and identified cause and effect basis. It is unreasonable for the teacher to have an expectation of protecting entrepreneurs from making mistakes either in the classroom or in the real world, but we can help seed the important entrepreneurial traits of perseverance when faced with ambiguity.

Exercise – pivot proof
In this exercise have the students select a product or service and pivot it to a completely different market category (e.g., profit to non-profit, or taking something from a traditional business model and pivoting to the shared economy model). Another way to conduct this exercise is to select a vacant building in your community and ask the class to create an ideal business for

this location. The choice can be any space from a well-defined open space in a popular mall or prime retail location to a long-empty building that has seen better economic prosperity. In this creative challenge there are two parts: 1) creation of three possible concepts for the space; and 2) evaluation of the business model assumptions for concepts to be economically competitive in that space. Have the students present the three concepts and their findings to establish which is the best concept for the space and why the other two are less successful. Often any or all of the concepts need to pivot during the evaluation phase as new information is discovered for the concept to become competitive. Many students will experience many iterations of creativity and evaluation before they decide on which concept produces the best simultaneous creative and economic outcome. This exercise accomplishes a shift from high-risk failure in achieving successful domain specific solutions (a correct answer) to a low-risk failure general creative process experience that seeds useful schemas and heuristics for overcoming design obstacles that can be utilized when addressing future specific problems.

10. Watching the Clock

I am a big fan of allowing the creative process to take its course. Despite all the practice, skill attainment and creative cognitive awareness, time is one of the best resources to spawn creativity. I'm always amazed at the expectations people have for the creative process. I once had a senior-level human resources executive with a Fortune 100 company designate within the schedule of a two-day national sales meeting with 55 participants a time slot of 23 minutes for my creative session for novel marketing ideas for the next year. When I inquired into both the amount of time scheduled and the unique value of 23 minutes, the response I received was "Well, that should be enough time for you to come up with something, don't you think?" I've faced a lot of creative constraints in many projects, and with a skilled team constraints don't kill creativity as is widely assumed. Even the literature shows a movement on this issue. Where some theorists have described the ideal creative process as unstructured, open-ended, and free of external limitations, others have found that creative individuals and teams can benefit from constraints (Rosso, 2014).

The key to working with constraints is to be highly prepared for the creative process, be skilled in mental fluidity as discussed earlier (see the exercise "What do you see?") and have a mindset of the creative constraints as a focus that point to where ideas will emerge rather than as a line that can't be crossed (Mitchell et al., 2015).

The classroom itself can be a constraint to students in many ways. There is the physical reality that a 55-minute time slot can evaporate very quickly for students who are just acquiring new creative skill sets and adapting to group creative activities. In the case of teams who are very skilled and whose scope of work is clearly defined and focused, 55 minutes can yield dozens of ideas that can be achieved compared to the same time period for student groups. In addition, the classroom holds perceptual constraints. I have observed from extensive interviews of both students and professionals in a group creative setting that approximately 50 percent of the ideas that are generated are never shared with the group. The three main factors that are related time and time again for this holding behavior are: 1) fear of saying something that is perceived as wrong or unintelligent; 2) fear that if they share in the larger group they won't receive proper credit for their contribution; and 3) fear that, if the group likes the idea and upon further effort it is determined that the idea isn't novel or unique, the individual praise from the group is annulled.

To overcome this I am a big fan of scheduling the class as a lab format that combines the three 55-minute lectures into one three-hour lab. Then structure the class in a flipped or inverted format where explicit knowledge acquisition from readings, videos or slide decks can be done outside of the classroom and the classroom utilized as an implicit knowledge processing lab. In this way, the class acquires a discovery atmosphere that changes the mindset of the students and increases group participation and sharing. I am also in favor of designating and formalizing a co-work space for the students to meet for team assignments so that they develop a sense of space and discipline for the creative process, giving them a space to integrate design thinking or other visually intensive processes into their creative activities. This can also be done for students who want to do projects independently. Developing a personal environment and process of personal creativity is also an excellent assignment for students to develop reflections that should be included in their creative journaling and shared in class.

Exercise – video PSA
This exercise is a free-form creative problem that blends creative thinking with the added ingredient of humor. Koestler (1964) first identified the link between creativity and humor as having the same structure as science or art in its discovery of hidden similarities. Humor works on the social level by leveraging an unexpected change in the angle of the optics of reality, as does science or art. Since the creation and production of humor is a form of opportunity recognition (i.e., it is implied that the customer here will have some level of appreciation for the humor) where the payoff is laughter or a new insight or appreciation rather than an economic one, this exercise is easily incorporated into the classroom. In this exercise the

student or teams are required to create a short three-minute or less public service announcement (PSA) on their favorite or invented cause. The goal is to blend a creative new approach to communicating the main benefit of the cause with humor as a vehicle for attention and reception of the benefit message. The big risk of this exercise to both the student and the teacher is the extent of the appropriateness and boundaries used in the humor portion of the challenge. The students create the videos outside of the classroom, and the class time is used for showing and discussion of the creative product. Grading is done on a weighted-average score of my critique and that of a student panel of former students from my class who volunteer as raters as an estimator of social acceptance. Some of my favorite PSAs were spots entitled "The emerging epidemic in America: how the government uses cat videos for spying on us," "Look both ways: your guide to one-way streets" and "Good vegetarian hunting," which created a new vision on the topic of animal protection by substituting the hunting of large game vegetables such as watermelons or heirloom tomatoes. The two students dressed in camouflage and proceeded to stalk and hunt vegetables in the wild. While the video received a high humor score, the classroom critique generated a lively discussion on the merits of hunting in general, animal rights and the concept of vegetable rights. Video projects in general also carry with them a high degree of intrinsic motivation to the students. The two students actually used the vegetarian hunting video as part of their job interview process with great success as a demonstration of their creative skill.

CONCLUSIONS

One of the defining, widely accepted moments in the development of the field of creativity was the 1950 address by J.P. Guilford at the annual American Psychology Association meeting in which he stated that less than 2 percent of the books and articles included in the *Psychological Abstracts* for the preceding quarter of a century were focused on some aspect of creativity. As history would have it, Guilford was able to give another "state of the field" address 20 years later and reflect on the publication of almost as many studies on creativity topics in each year thereafter as there were for the entire 25 years prior to his address (Guilford, 1970).

At the interface between creativity and entrepreneurship are the students who desire to acquire the cognitive abilities to be successful in their chosen area of the entrepreneurial experience, be it their own venture, corporate venturing, social, public or academic. In any of these, creativity will be a core competency that demands mastery. The entrepreneurship–creativity connection is more than just the creation of a new business; it occupies a central place as one of the most important decision-making systems at the entrepreneur's disposal. One of my favorite quotes, with which I begin each semester of my new venture initiation class, is this one that sets the framework for the entrepreneurial experience:

> Entrepreneurship is a dynamic process of vision, change, and creation. It requires an application of energy and passion towards the creation and implementation of new ideas and creative solutions. Essential ingredients include the willingness to take calculated risks in terms of time, equity, or career; the ability to formulate an effective venture team; the creative skill to marshal needed resources; the fundamental skill of building solid business plan; and finally, the vision to recognize opportunity where others see chaos, contradiction, and confusion. (Kuratko and Hodgetts, 2004, p. 30)

I utilize this quote as a launching-off point for emphasizing the importance and undeniable connection between the creative thinking process and the entrepreneurial thinking process. The creative process yields ideas; the entrepreneurial process requires creative ideas and, when combined with the creative process, is vital to the "big bang" of the entrepreneur's universe – the vision to recognize opportunity.

Every idea has a context and a consequence. Our job as entrepreneurship educators is to provide the necessary creative aptitude skills and environment to help the students develop the proper connections in between. The key is recognizing that even in the scope of a semester the growth in creative self-efficacy and proficiency in practice is the point of the process, independent of creating the next disruptive innovation. I see continued opportunity in education research on the early creative components of entrepreneurship of what I term protoentrepreneurial ability: developing a sense of insight, recognizing that what one perceives can change, awareness that there are conscious choices in how to perceive the world, and the conation to turn perceptions into facts that form a concept that can be used to influence meaning for others. This form of situated cognition vital to the beginning behaviors of entrepreneurs is analogous to the protoimperative pointing used by children as a spatial language before they learn formal language behaviors (Jackendoff and Landau, 1992). Each cohort of students will have a different aggregate level of creative aptitude. Our task in the classroom is to transform their practiced, learned solution methods of habitual thinking and give them the awareness of both when to use creative thinking and how to utilize creative thinking processes in the scope of everyday use to achieve superior decision outcomes.

REFERENCES

Altman, E.J., Nagle, F. and Tushman, M.L. (2015), *Innovation without Information Constraints: Organizations, Communities, and Innovation When Information Costs Approach Zero*, in C. Shalley, M.A. Hitt and J. Zhou (eds.), *The Oxford Handbook of Creativity, Innovation, and Entrepreneurship*, New York: Oxford University Press, pp. 353–378.

Amabile, T.M. (1982), Social psychology of creativity: a consensual assessment technique, *Journal of Personality and Social Psychology*, **43**, 997–1013.

Amabile, T.M. (1983), *The Social Psychology of Creativity*, New York: Springer Verlag.

Amabile, T.M. (1996), *Creativity in Context: Update to the Social Psychology of Creativity*, Boulder, CO: Westview Press.

Baer, J. (1998), The case for domain specificity of creativity, *Creativity Research Journal*, **11**(2), 173–177.

Beattie, R.E. (1999), The creative entrepreneur: a study of the entrepreneur's creative processes, Doctoral dissertation, University of Abertay Dundee.

Beaty, R.E. and Silvia, P.J. (2012), Why do ideas get more creative across time? An executive interpretation of the serial order effect in divergent thinking tasks, *Psychology of Aesthetics, Creativity, and the Arts*, **6**(4), 309–319.

Boden, M.A. (2004), *The Creative Mind: Myths and Mechanisms*, 2nd edn., London: Routledge.

Bono, E. de (1970), *Lateral Thinking: Creativity Step by Step*, New York: Harper & Row.

Dimov, D. (2007), Beyond the single-person, single-insight attribution in understanding entrepreneurial opportunities, *Entrepreneurship Theory and Practice*, **31**(5), 713–731.

Drucker, P.F. (1985), *Innovation and Entrepreneurship: Practice and Principles*, New York: Harper & Row.

Fayolle, A. (2004), Evaluation of entrepreneurship education: behavior performing or intention increasing? *International Journal of Entrepreneurship and Small Business*, **2**(1), 89–98.

Ford, C.M. (1996), A theory of individual creative action in multiple social domains, *Academy of Management Review*, **21**(4), 1112–1142.

Ford, N. (1999), Information retrieval and creativity: towards support for the original thinker, *Journal of Documentation*, **55**(5), 528–542.

Gardner, H. (1993), *Creating Minds*, New York: Basic Books.

Gelernter, D. (2016), *The Tides of Mind: Uncovering the Spectrum of Consciousness*, New York: Liveright Publications.

Getzels, J.W. and Csikszentmihalyi, M. (1976), *The Creative Vision: A Longitudinal Study of Problem-Finding in Art*, New York: Wiley Interscience.

Goffman, E. (1974), *Frame Analysis: An Essay on the Organization of Experience*, Boston, MA: Northeastern University Press.

Guilford, J.P. (1970), Creativity: retrospect and prospect, *Journal of Creative Behavior*, **4**(3), 149–168.

He, Y., Yao, X., Wang, S. and Caughron, J. (2016), Linking failure feedback to individual creativity: the moderation role of goal orientation, *Creativity Research Journal*, **28**(1), 52–59.

Hennessey, B.A. (1994), The consensual assessment technique: an examination of the relationship between ratings of product and process creativity, *Creativity Research Journal*, **7**(2), 193–208.

Hill, R.C. and Levenhagen, M. (1995), Metaphors and mental models: sense-making and sensegiving in innovative and entrepreneurial activities, *Journal of Management*, **21**(6), 1057–1074.

Hokanson, B. (2012), The design critique as a model for distributed learning, in L. Moller and J.B. Huett (eds.), *The Next Generation of Distance Education: Unconstrained Learning*, New York: Springer Science + Business, pp. 71–83.

Jackendoff, R. and Landau, B. (1992), Spatial language and spatial cognition, in R. Jackendoff, *Languages of the Mind*, Cambridge, MA: MIT Press, pp. 99–124.

Kahle, L.R., Hall, D.B. and Kosinski, M.J. (1997), The real-time response survey in new product research: it's about time, *Journal of Consumer Marketing*, **14**(2), 234–248.

Kaufman, J.C. and Beghetto, R.A. (2009), Beyond big and little: the four c model of creativity, *Review of General Psychology*, **13**(1), 1–12.

Koestler, A. (1964), *The Act of Creation*, New York: Macmillan.

Kuratko, D.F. and Hodgetts, R.M. (2004), *Entrepreneurship: Theory, Process, Practice*, Mason, OH; South-Western Publishers.

Lakoff, G. and Johnson, M. (1980), *Metaphors We Live By*, Chicago, IL: University of Chicago Press.

McMullan, W.E. and Kenworthy, T.P. (2015), *Creativity and Entrepreneurial Performance: A General Scientific Theory*, Cham, Switzerland: Springer International.

McMullen, J.S. and Shepherd, D.A. (2006), Entrepreneurial action and the role of uncertainty in the theory of the entrepreneur, *Academy of Management Review*, **31**(1), 132–152.

Michalko, M. (1991), *Thinkertoys*, New York: Berkley Books.

Millar, G.W. (1995), *E. Paul Torrance: The Creativity Man*, Norwood, NJ: Ablex.

Millgram, S., Bickman, L. and Berkowitz, L. (1969), Note on the drawing power of crowds of different size, *Journal of Personality and Social Psychology*, **13**(2), 79–82.

Mitchell, R.K., Busenitz, L., Lant, T., McDougall, P.P., Morse, E.A. and Smith, J.B. (2004), The distinctive and inclusive domain of entrepreneurial cognition research, *Entrepreneurship Theory and Practice*, **28**(6), 505–518.

Mitchell, R.K., Mitchell, B.T. and Mitchell, J.R. (2009), Entrepreneurial scripts and entrepreneurial expertise: the information processing perspective, in A.L. Carsrud and M. Brannback (eds.), *Understanding the Entrepreneurial Mind*, New York: Springer Science + Business, pp. 97–137.

Mitchell, R.K., Smith, B.J., Stamp, J.A. and Carlson, J. (2015), Organizing creativity: lessons from the *Eureka! Ranch* experience, in C. Shalley, M.A. Hitt and J. Zhou (eds.), *The Oxford Handbook of Creativity, Innovation, and Entrepreneurship*, New York: Oxford University Press, pp. 301–337.

Morris, M.H., Schindehutte, M. and LaForge, R.W. (2003), Entrepreneurial marketing: a construct for integrating emerging entrepreneurship and marketing perspectives, *Journal of Marketing Theory and Practice*, **10**(4), 1–19.

Morris, M., Schindehutte, M. and Allen, J. (2005), The entrepreneur's business model: toward a unified perspective, *Journal of Business Research*, **58**(6), 726–735.

Morris, M.H., Pryor, C.G. and Schindehutte, M. (2012), *Entrepreneurship as*

Experience: How Events Create Ventures and Ventures Create Entrepreneurs, Cheltenham, UK and Northampton, MA, USA: Edward Elgar.

Novak, J.D. (2002), Meaningful learning: the essential factor for conceptual change in limited or inappropriate propositional hierarchies leading to empowerment of learners, *Science Education*, **86**(4), 548–571.

Osborn, A.F. (1963), *Applied Imagination*, 3rd edn., New York: Charles Scribner.

Plucker, J.A. (1998), Beware of simple conclusions: the case for content generality in creativity, *Creativity Research Journal*, **11**(2), 179–182.

Plucker, J.A., Beghetto, R.A. and Dow, G. (2004), Why isn't creativity more important to educational psychologists? Potentials, pitfalls, and future directions, *Educational Psychologist*, **39**(2), 83–96.

Plucker, J.A., Runco, M. and Lim, W. (2006), Predicting ideational behavior from divergent thinking and discretionary time on task, *Creativity Research Journal*, **18**(1), 55–63.

Puryear, J.S. (2015), Metacognition as a moderator of creative ideation and creative production, *Creativity Research Journal*, **27**(4), 334–341.

Rosso, B.D. (2014), Creativity and constraints: exploring the role of constraints in the creative processes of research and development teams, *Organization Studies*, **35**(4), 551–585.

Sadler-Smith, E. (2015), Wallas' four-stage model of the creative process: more than meets the eye? *Creativity Research Journal*, **27**(4), 342–352.

Savery, J.R. and Duffy, T.M. (1995), Problem based learning: An instruction model and its constructivist framework, in B.G. Wilson (ed.), *Constructivist Learning Environments: Case Studies in Instructional Design*, Englewood Cliffs, NJ: Educational Technology Publications, pp. 135–148.

Sawyer, R.K. (2012), *Explaining Creativity: The Science of Human Innovation*, New York: Oxford University Press.

Smith, S.M. and Dodds, R.A. (1999), Incubation, in M.A. Runco and S.R. Pritzker (eds.), *Encyclopedia of Creativity*, Vol. 2, New York: Academic Press, pp. 39–43.

Smith, S.M., Ward, T.B. and Finke, R.A. (1995), *The Creative Cognition Approach*, Cambridge, MA: MIT Press.

Stamp, J.A. (2000), Eureka! Unleashing great ideas, *Chemical Business*, **28**(6), 46–52.

Stamp, J.A. (2015, November 7), *What an Idea Needs to Survive* [video file], TEDx Normal, retrieved from https://www.youtube.com/watch?v=b4R6Z1sw8kw.

Sternberg, R.J. (2003), *Wisdom, Intelligence, and Creativity Synthesized*, New York: Cambridge University Press.

Torrance, E.P. (1972), Can we teach children to think creatively? *Journal of Creative Behavior*, **6**, 114–143.

Vincent, P.H., Decker, B.P. and Mumford, M.D. (2002), Divergent thinking, intelligence and expertise: a test of alternative models, *Creativity Research Journal*, **14**(2), 163–178.

Wallas, G. (1926), *The Art of Thought*, London: J. Cape.

Welling, H. (2007), Four mental operations in creative cognition: the importance of abstraction, *Creativity Research Journal*, **19**(2–3), 163–177.

White, R., Hertz, G. and D'Souza, R. (2011), Teach a craft – enhancing entrepreneurship pedagogy, *Small Business Institute Journal*, **7**(2), 1–14.

Whiting, B.G. (1988), Creativity and entrepreneurship: how do they relate? *Journal of Creative Behavior*, **22**(3), 178–183.

Wycoff, J. (1991), *Mindmapping: Your Personal Guide to Exploring Creativity and Problem Solving*, New York: Berkley Books.

Zahra, S.A. (2005), Entrepreneurship and disciplinary scholarship: return to the fountainhead, in Z.J. Acs and D.B. Audretsch (eds.), *Handbook of Entrepreneurship Research*, New York: Springer, pp. 253–268.

3. Does entrepreneurship education change minds? A multinational analysis of mandatory and voluntary entrepreneurial training

Carlos Albornoz and José E. Amorós

THE RELEVANCE OF ENTREPRENEURSHIP EDUCATION

Along with the accumulation of evidence supporting the role of entrepreneurship in economic development and job creation (Acs and Armington, 2006; Kuratko, 2005; Reynolds, 2007), governments persist in encouraging people to become entrepreneurs (Ács and Stough, 2008; Carsrud et al., 2008). These efforts attempt to reproduce the conditions under which opportunity entrepreneurship emerges. Opportunity-based entrepreneurship refers to individuals who discover a new business opportunity and undertake a series of actions to exploit this opportunity and convert it into a new venture (Reynolds et al., 2005; Shane and Venkataraman, 2000). We agree with the literature that higher rates of opportunity-based entrepreneurship are preferable to higher rates of necessity-based entrepreneurship (Ács and Varga, 2005; Acs et al., 2005). Necessity-motivated entrepreneurs are individuals who are pushed into entrepreneurship because they do not have better job options. Reynolds et al. (2005) define necessity-based entrepreneurs as individuals who "cannot find a suitable role in the world of work," where "creating a new business is their best available option" (p. 217).

It is important to distinguish between opportunity- and necessity-based entrepreneurship because the conditions under which the two types emerge are radically different (Shane, 2008). In order to promote opportunity entrepreneurship, one condition to which governments have begun paying attention is the level of entrepreneurial skills among the population. A troubling economy, rapidly changing technology and constantly evolving business models created a new context for business (Gibb, 2002). On the one hand, there has been a pressing need from policy makers to provide an education that empowers citizens to deal with uncertainty and globalization (Fiet and Pankaj, 2008; Klimoski, 2007; Van Auken et al., 2009). On the other hand, because of the permanent potential for economic crisis, entrepreneurship and entrepreneurship education have more relevance today than ever (Neck and Greene, 2010).

Researchers are making increasing efforts to understand how individuals and teams learn to successfully start a business (Kyrö, 2015). The growing number of entrepreneurship courses and extracurricular activities begs for research about what to do when teaching entrepreneurship. Further, the literature exploring entrepreneurial programs has not distinguished whether entrepreneurship education at the university and high school levels should be voluntary or compulsory, especially given that compulsory experiences have considerably more variation in the motivations of those enrolled (Oosterbeek et al., 2010). The answer here is pursuant to more basic questions such as whether new business creation has a positive effect on the economy, and whether entrepreneurship education positively affects the quantity and quality of available entrepreneurs.

The purpose of this chapter is to explore the relationship between entrepreneurship education and entrepreneurial actions, exploring the three stages of the entrepreneurial process, and distinguishing between voluntary and compulsory training in order to differentiate the effect on individuals who enroll voluntarily versus those who are obligated to enroll. We are interested in exploring this effect within the Latin American (LATAM) region. LATAM is an interesting context for our research for three reasons. First, the region has been experiencing rapid growth in the past two decades coupled with substantial improvements at the social and institutional levels. Even as political, social and economic problems persist, many countries in the region present dynamic environments for new business creation (Singer et al., 2015; WEF, 2015). Second, changes in the business environment have compelled most governments in LATAM to respond to more global, hyper-connected, competitive and fast-paced ways of doing business (Chesbrough et al., 2006; Duderstadt, 2010; Gibb, 2002; Klimoski, 2007). For these reasons, entrepreneurship in general and entrepreneurship education in particular have received high priority in many policy agendas in LATAM. Entrepreneurship is believed to positively affect the economy through innovation and relocation of talent. Third, in recent years many colleges and universities in Latin America have been making entrepreneurship education programs mandatory for all students (e.g., Universidad del Desarrollo, Chile, Tecnológico de Monterrey, Mexico and Universidad de los Andes, Colombia, among others).

For our empirical approach, we used the Global Entrepreneurship

Monitor (GEM) database related to the special report on entrepreneurship education and training (Coduras et al., 2010). This is a uniquely large dataset (n>10 000) that has information about the nature of entrepreneurship education received by LATAM´s entrepreneurs. We examine the relationship between entrepreneurial training and three stages of the venture creation process: 1) intention; 2) early entrepreneurial activity; and 3) an established business. In this study, we focus on opportunity entrepreneurs and not on necessity entrepreneurs.

DEFINING ENTREPRENEURSHIP: IMPLICATIONS FOR PEDAGOGY

For this research, we adopt a definition of entrepreneurship related specifically with new business creation (Reynolds et al., 2005). We used Reynolds et al.'s (2005) definition because it allows a measurable aspect in the creation of a business: paying salaries. Reynolds (2007) distinguishes three stages within the entrepreneurial process. The first stage is related to the intention to start a business in the next three years. The second stage starts with the first concrete actions to create the new firm and ends when the business has been in place for 3.5 years. The second stage considers the early-stage entrepreneurial activity and starts after the entrepreneur has paid three consecutive months of salaries and ends at 3.5 years. The third stage starts after the business has accomplished more than 3.5 years' running and is considered an established firm.

The first stage does not include actions, just giving serious thought. This is relevant in order to think about *entrepreneurship education and training* (EET). Should training programs aim to develop intentions or improve performance, or both? The intention to start a business is an internal process, a perception of the future, an attitude toward a type of activity in which one will be involved, a desire to be an entrepreneur. The curriculum needed to develop positive attitudes toward business venturing has to be different from what is needed to perform the behaviors that allow success in the second stage. Different behaviors can be considered the boundary between the first (thinking about) and second stages (e.g., searching for information, registration, opening, housing, personnel, inventory, first customer, first cash flow). Among researchers, a widely accepted point of transition between the first and the second stages is the payment of wages for more than three months (founders' wages are also considered wages). The second stage involves actually doing something to create the business. Individuals in this stage are considered nascent entrepreneurs. If an individual has paid salaries for more than three months he/she has overcome the intention stage (first stage) and entered the early entrepreneurial activity stage (second stage). Individuals who have paid salaries and wages for more than 3.5 years are considered established business owners (third stage). This definition of firm establishment is relatively straightforward and can be applied across a range of countries and economic sectors (Reynolds et al., 2005).

ENTREPRENEURIAL INTENTIONS AND ACTIONS

The link between entrepreneurship education programs and the intention to become an entrepreneur has been explored using Ajzen's (1987) theory of planned behavior (TPB). This theory assumes that social behavior can be reasoned, controlled and planned. Therefore, higher intentions to express a specific behavior will increase the likelihood that the behavior emerges. Intention is the single best predictor of planned behavior (Ajzen, 1991). The intention to start a business then requires the same attitudinal antecedents as any other behavior: 1) the desire to perform the action, that is, start the business; and 2) the conviction that success is possible, that is, feasibility (Galloway and Brown, 2002; Lüthje and Franke, 2003; Zhao et al., 2005). Anchored on TPB, authors (Brazeal and Krueger, 1994; Krueger et al., 2000) have argued that perceived feasibility and perceived desirability are the two main factors underlying the formation of entrepreneurial intentions. Brazeal and Krueger (1994) have argued that a subjective norm is not always a predictor of intentions.

Among other factors that would influence an individual's becoming an entrepreneur are personal attributes, traits, background, experience and disposition. A personal attribute that seems especially important is entrepreneurial self-efficacy (ESE). According to social cognitive theory (SCT), an individual's sense of self-efficacy can be influenced through four processes: 1) enactive mastery; 2) role modelling and vicarious experience; 3) social persuasion; and 4) judgments of one's own physiological states, such as arousal and anxiety (Bandura, 1977). Self-efficacy is the basis for believing that success is possible. In theory, individuals should not develop the intention to do something if they believe failure is highly probable. Individuals need to believe there is a chance of success. By increasing self-efficacy, EET positively affects entrepreneurial attitude. However, entrepreneurial intention also requires positive attitudes toward the behaviors to be exhibited. If the individual does not like to perform the behaviors requested, most probably he/she will not develop the intention. Related to entrepreneurial intentions, in theory, if someone does not like uncertainty, managing resources, speaking in public or controlling others' performance, that person probably will not engage in entrepreneurship.

Since entrepreneurial intention needs both desirability and feasibility, a training program may increase feasibility and reduce desirability. This is more likely to happen if the training is mandatory, because a proportion of the students taking the training will not like behaving as entrepreneurs. Oosterbeek et al. (2010) study the impact of entrepreneurship education in a mandatory course. Their results showed that the effect on students' self-assessed entrepreneurial skills was insignificant. Additionally, the effect of the course on entrepreneurial intentions was significantly negative. In another study, von Graevenitz et al. (2010) investigated 357 students enrolled in a business planning course in the Munich School of Management. Von Graevenitz et al. (2010) found that, after an obligatory business planning course, intentions to become entrepreneurs declined, while having a significant positive effect on students' self-assessment of their entrepreneurial skills.

Based on the entrepreneurial intention model, EET seems a logical instrument to increase the number of people trying to start a business. However, the effectiveness of EET in creating more entrepreneurs needs to be analyzed in detail. Although the positive relationship between EET and entrepreneurial intention is seemingly intuitive, the relationship is not always positive. Empirical research supports this idea (Levie et al., 2009). Some authors have found a positive relationship between EET and entrepreneurial intention (Coduras et al., 2010; Kwon and Arenius, 2010; Levie and Autio, 2008), while others argue that the relationship is non-existent, suggesting instead that the positive effect is in fact self-selection (Hamidi et al., 2008). Von Graevenitz et al. (2010) showed that intentions could decrease after an entrepreneurship course.

We analyzed mandatory versus voluntary entrepreneurship training programs in order to explore whether the reason behind the differences in the effect of EET could be related to the students' interest in the topic. If there is a genuine desire by the individuals to start a new firm, voluntary EET should have a positive effect in terms of the three stages of entrepreneurship, while mandatory EET should have no effect in the first stages (intentions) and a positive effect in the second (early actions) and third stages (established). This is because intentions cannot be forced to change, while learning may be forced. People can learn something even though they do not want to. In fact, this is true for many mandatory courses in formal education. If the student does not fail the course, knowledge has to move forward after training despite the attitude toward the behavior. However, knowing more about a topic does not mean you will like the topic more. For instance, someone could have a bad attitude toward the activity of gardening but be obligated to attend a course on how to plant tulips. He/she will learn something or at least remain with the same amount of knowledge, but it is very difficult to come out of the course knowing less than before taking the (approved) course.

Contrary to mandatory courses, in voluntary EET most students are likely to have positive attitudes toward entrepreneurship; otherwise they would not be taking the course. Voluntary students may be seeking out further knowledge on the subject owing to their involvement in entrepreneurial activity. While some are likely just to be curious about entrepreneurship, many students in entrepreneurship training programs are interested in starting a venture at some point in their lives and therefore search for learning opportunities regarding entrepreneurship. The learning need may also positively influence the attention and amount of time allocated to the class sessions, potentially contributing to the development of self-efficacy, at least relative to those without such learning needs. The effect of EET in voluntary courses could be positive.

Based on this discussion we propose the following hypotheses:

H1a: Voluntary entrepreneurship education has a positive effect on entrepreneurship intentions.

H1b: Mandatory entrepreneurship education has a negative effect on entrepreneurship intentions.

H2a: Voluntary entrepreneurship education has a positive effect on early-stage entrepreneurial actions.

H2b: Mandatory entrepreneurship education has a negative effect on early-stage entrepreneurial actions.

H3a: Voluntary entrepreneurship education has a positive effect on business creation.

H3b: Mandatory entrepreneurship education has a negative effect on business creation.

METHODOLOGY

In 2008, the Global Entrepreneurship Monitor consortium introduced a set of additional questions in the Adult Population Survey in order to measure the effect of entrepreneurship education on the different stages of the entrepreneurship process and to capture specific information about the general population and the relationship with different types of entrepreneurship education (for more details see Coduras et al., 2010). The training types were business or enterprise training at school, college or university, placements in small or medium-sized businesses whilst at school, college or university, or in government programs, online or by oneself. Following the GEM methodology, we divided the adults who were involved in any kind of entrepreneurial activities into categories: 1) individuals who manifest their intentions to be entrepreneurs; 2) nascent entrepreneurs (early-stage entrepreneurship activity); and 3) established business owners. The data include almost 15000 adults aged 18 to 64 across some LATAM countries.

Because very few individuals over the age of 45 had ever taken part in mandatory business or enterprise training, adults over 45 were dropped, because we wanted to test voluntary and mandatory training. It has been in the past two decades that scholars and policy makers have really focused on entrepreneurship education as a possible strategy to create jobs and boost competitiveness within Latin American countries. For example, in Chile, the oldest entrepreneurship course is from 1998. Therefore, we decided to keep individuals between 18 and 45, aiming to compare more similar generations of people in terms of the business environment they dealt with and the type of training they could have received.

We argue that entrepreneurship educators want to produce successful opportunity entrepreneurs. Opportunity-motivated entrepreneurs are also the group that policy makers seek to foster in LATAM, as the impact on economic growth of necessity entrepreneurs is low. In LATAM, the rate of necessity-motivated entrepreneurs is higher than in Europe or the United States, and many of those entrepreneurs operate in the informal sector (Naudé, 2007). In order to make our results more comparable to those of other global regions, we focused our analysis on opportunity entrepreneurs. Therefore, all individuals who reported having started their business for reasons other than opportunity were dropped from the dataset. The final sample kept those who were not entrepreneurs and those who were involved in opportunity entrepreneurship. Note that individuals who report an intention to start a business cannot be classified as necessity or opportunity entrepreneurs. People reporting intentions to start a business are assumed to have a personal desire to do so.

We also dropped from the dataset all individuals who had closed their businesses, because we wanted to know the effect of entrepreneurship education on individuals who classify themselves as having the intention to start a business, or performing the actions of running a business, or owning a business. Former entrepreneurs who were currently working in other contexts were not considered part of those three groups.

Our final sample included 10 672 adults living in eight South-American countries (Argentina, Bolivia, Brazil, Chile, Colombia, Ecuador, Peru and Uruguay). The sample included those who had received entrepreneurial training at some point in their life and those who had never received entrepreneurial training. In the final sample, 75.1 per cent reported not having received any kind of entrepreneurial training and 24.8 percent had received training. The survey used a stratified random sampling method to locate adults in households according to strict guidelines laid down by the GEM consortium and supervised by the GEM international data managers (Levie and Autio, 2008; Reynolds, 2007).

Description of the Participants

The average age of participants was 30.6 years (s.d. = 8.1). Of the sample cases, 45.3 percent were males and 54.7 percent females. With some variance within countries, an average of 41.6 percent of the sample had the intention to start a business, 20.6 percent were involved in entrepreneurial activity and 9.8 percent were business owners. Table 3.1 summarizes descriptive statistics for the sample.

Dependent Variables

This research focuses on the relationship between entrepreneurship education and business creation, distinguishing between compulsory and voluntary education or training. Our dependent variables were operationalized as follows: "presence or absence of the intention to start a business within the next three years," "presence or absence of specific activities to

Table 3.1   Age, gender and presence of dependent variable by country

Country	Cases	Average age	% Males	% Females	Intention		Activity		Established	
					% No	% Yes	% No	% Yes	% No	% Yes
Argentina	1 099	31	46.7	53.3	72.9	27.1	81.5	18.5	90.7	9.3
Brazil	1 425	29	48.7	51.3	72.2	27.8	86.1	13.9	87.7	12.3
Chile	1 188	30	43.1	56.9	59.6	40.4	87.6	12.4	95.6	4.4
Colombia	1 386	31	48.0	52.0	26.4	73.6	73.1	26.9	88.0	12.0
Bolivia	1 415	30	42.6	57.4	53.7	46.3	68.9	31.1	84.3	15.7
Ecuador	1 542	31	36.8	63.2	56.0	44.0	82.2	17.8	91.0	9.0
Peru	1 520	30	48.9	51.1	57.8	42.2	73.1	26.9	92.9	7.1
Uruguay	1 097	30	48.4	51.6	73.8	26.2	86.3	13.7	93.1	6.9
Total	10 672	30	45.3	54.7	58.4	41.6	79.4	20.6	90.2	9.8

create an opportunity business at the time of the interview," and "presence or absence of business ownership created after the identification of an opportunity." We used logistic regression to estimate the independent effect of entrepreneurship education on the different stages. The first model tested "intention to start a business" as the dependent variable. Intention corresponds to adults between 18 and 45 years of age who responded "yes" on the item "Are you, alone or with others, expecting to start a new business, including any type of self-employment, within the next three years?" The second model tested "total entrepreneurial activity" (TEA) as the dependent variable, and the last model tested "business ownership" as the dependent variable. TEA corresponds to the total number of adults between 18 and 45 years old involved in a nascent firm whose motivation to get involved in the firm was the identification of a business opportunity. "Established businesses" corresponds to the total number of adults between 18 and 45 years old involved in an established firm as owner and manager for which salaries or wages have been paid for more than 42 months. This group of business owners indicated they started the business because they had identified a business opportunity.

Independent Variables

Our independent variables are the two types of entrepreneurship education (voluntary and compulsory) that people may have received during their lives. We tested whether individuals who received voluntary or compulsory entrepreneurship education were more likely to become entrepreneurs. Specifically, respondents were asked: "Have you ever taken part in training on starting a business?" If the answer was "yes," then they were asked about the source of that training. Choices were "primary or secondary school," "after completed school," "finished official schooling," "during college or university," "in a local association of business people," "by a government agency" and "by a past or present employer." After each question, respondents were asked if the training was voluntary or compulsory. To run the regression, we created two dummy variables, one for people who received compulsory training and one for those receiving voluntary training. We entered the two dummies in the regression along with the other control variables. Individuals who reported having received the two types of entrepreneurship education (voluntary and compulsory) were not considered in the regression. This was, first and primarily, because the size of this group was very small (about 16 cases) and, second, because we wanted to be as specific as possible in terms of the original motivation of each group to enroll in entrepreneurial training (by personal choice or forced by their institution or program). Individuals who did not receive entrepreneurship education (either voluntary or compulsory) received a value equal to 0, while individuals who received entrepreneurship education received a value equal to 1.

Control Variables

Entrepreneurial intention and the consecutive stages included in the process of creating a business are a function of several variables. In communities where there are a large number of jobs available, the option of self-employment may not be as attractive as in communities coping with high unemployment rates. Following this argument, we included unemployment as a control variable. Each individual was assigned values corresponding to the unemployment rates of their countries in 2008.

Entrepreneurship also is related to the business, legal and political environments (Bowen and De Clercq, 2008; Grilo and Thurik, 2005; Hwang and Powell, 2005). The institutional context may have an effect on the propensity of people to start a business after they develop the entrepreneurial intention through training and education. For that reason, it was important to control for the institutional context in which entrepreneurship students exist. In order to control for the business environment, we created a variable assigning each individual a value corresponding to the score of his/her country on the Doing Business Ranking (DBR) elaborated by the World Bank. The DBR provides objective measures of business regulations and their enforcement across 183 economies. By gathering and analyzing comprehensive quantitative data to compare business regulatory environments across economies and over time, the DBR offers measurable benchmarks about regulation that affect the business climate of each country. The DBR is included as one of the control variables. Table 3.2 described DBR scores for each country in the sample in 2008.

Table 3.2   Unemployment rate and Doing Business Ranking by country

	Unemployment rate in 2008	Doing Business Ranking
Chile	7.8	33
Peru	6.4	58
Colombia	13.2	66
Uruguay	7.6	98
Argentina	7.8	109
Brazil	7.1	122
Ecuador	7.3	128
Bolivia	7.6	140

Highly educated people may choose not to become entrepreneurs if they think it will reduce their income compared to other employment opportunities (Cassar, 2006). Therefore, higher education levels could reduce the likelihood of someone starting a business. Following this argument, we included educational level as a control variable. We included three dummies: elementary school completed, high school completed, and college degree.

Demographic characteristics have been reported to influence entrepreneurial rates. In the U.S., men start 76 percent of all new firms, and people between 18 and 34 years old start 79 percent of new firms (Reynolds, 1997). Numbers are similar in South America. For instance, in Chile men create 60 percent of the new businesses, and the average age of people involved in early-stage entrepreneurial activity is 38 (GEM, 2010). Therefore, age and gender were included as control variables.

Social support, fear of failure, and attitudes toward entrepreneurship also have been viewed as predictors of entrepreneurial intentions. The variable "social support" was created from the statement "In my country, most people consider starting a new business a desirable career choice." The variable "fear of failure" was created using the statement "Fear of failure would prevent you from starting a business." The variable "entrepreneurial networking" was created using the question "Do you know someone personally who has started a business in the past two years?"

RESULTS

We formally tested our hypotheses using binomial logistic regression models. Binomial logistic regression estimates the probability of an event happening, which, in our case, is the presence or absence of entrepreneurial intention, entrepreneurial activity, or established business ownership. We ran three binomial logistic regression models: one for the group who had entrepreneurial intentions, one for the group who reported being involved in entrepreneurial activities, and one for the group who reported owning an established business. We report the Nagelkerke statistic, which indicates the variance explained by our models. In order to make the interpretation of the results easier, we also report the odds ratio for each of the predictor variables.

Before conducting a logistic regression on the sample, a list-wise correlation matrix was constructed that included all the variables to be entered in the regression (Table 3.3). Accordingly, no problems of multicollinearity appear to exist.

Tables 3.4 to 3.6 show the most parsimonious models of direct effects

Table 3.3   Correlation matrix for independent variables

	1	2	3	4	5	6	7	8	9	10
1 Doing business	1									
2 Unemployment	-0.206**	1								
3 Voluntary EE	-0.080**	0.107**	1							
4 Compulsory EE	-0.111**	0.066**	0.144**	1						
5 Elementary school	0.004	-0.097**	0.025**	-0.010	1					
6 High school	-0.144**	0.011	0.166**	0.072**	-0.287**	1				
7 College degree	-0.183**	0.074**	0.117**	0.133***	-0.224***	-0.177***	1			
8 Fear of failure	0.029***	-0.034***	-0.061***	-0.026***	-0.011	-0.029***	-0.019**	1		
9 Networks	-0.034***	-0.040***	0.175***	0.067***	0.005	0.076***	0.103***	0.054**	1	
10 Attitude	-0.094***	0.066***	0.085***	0.000	0.007	0.022**	-0.009	-0.059**	0.044**	1

Notes:
EE = entrepreneurship education.
*p<0.1; **p<0.05; ***p<0.01.

Table 3.4   Regression model results and statistics

Variable	B	Standard error	Odds ratio
(Constant)	−4.671***	0.255	0.009
Voluntary EE	0.763***	0.076	2.147
Compulsory EE	−0.331**	0.148	0.718
Elementary school completed	0.105***	0.089	1.111
High school completed	0.145	0.111	1.156
College degree	0.906	0.071	2.475
Fear of failure	0.326***	0.075	1.385
Know an entrepreneur	1.552***	0.068	4.719
Entrepreneurs have high status	1.775***	0.069	5.899
Age	−0.016***	0.004	0.984
Gender	0.178***	0.062	1.194
Doing Business Ranking	0.002***	0.001	1.002
Unemployment rate	0.250***	0.017	1.285

(Dependent variable: intention to start a business)

Adjusted R^2	Wald $\text{chi}^2(12)$	Log
24%	1238.99***	pseudolikelihood −3190.6342

Notes:
n = 6563.
EE = entrepreneurship education.
*$p<0.1$; **$p<0.05$; ***$p<0.01$.

of entrepreneurship education (where voluntary and compulsory entrepreneurship education were entered simultaneously with control demographics, attitudinal variables, and contextual variables such as unemployment rates and the Doing Business Ranking). The value assigned was 1 if the individual received the type of education tested (for instance voluntary entrepreneurship education) and 0 if he/she did not receive voluntary entrepreneurship education.

For the first model, using "intention to start a business" as a dependent variable, Nagelkerke R square was 0.24, suggesting that 24 percent of the variability is explained by the set of variables included in the model (see Table 3.4). Considering the control variables first, age and gender appear to be in the expected direction, and intention is higher in males (B=0.178, p<0.01) and younger people (B=−0.016, p<0.01). Three levels of education were included in the regression model: elementary, high school completed, and college degree. Only elementary school completed demonstrated a positive effect on entrepreneurial intentions. This positive effect can be explained following the theory of human capital. Highly educated people may not choose to become entrepreneurs if they have good employment opportunities (Cassar, 2006). On the contrary, for people with a lower level of education, entrepreneurship is certainly a permanent opportunity to make a living. The first model supports that argument.

As TPB theory suggests, the effect of attitudinal variables such as entrepreneurial networks, social status, and fear of failure positively affected entrepreneurial intention. The three variables are positive and significant. Turning to the training variables, entrepreneurship education exhibited a significant effect on intention, but only if it was voluntary (B=0.763, p<0.01). Individuals are less likely to have the intention to start a business if they have received compulsory entrepreneurship education (B=−0.331, p=<0.05). Odds ratios for voluntary entrepreneurship education were 2.14, and 0.78 for compulsory entrepreneurship education (with a negative beta).

Nagelkerke R square for the second model, using entrepreneurial activity as the dependent variable, was 0.16, suggesting that 16 percent of the variability is explained by the set of variables included in the model (see Table 3.5). The second model suggests that individuals are more likely

Table 3.5 Regression model results and statistics

Variable	B	Standard error	Odds ratio
(Constant)	−5.00***	0.003	0.005
Voluntary EE	0.278*	0.208	1.321
Compulsory EE	0.102	0.323	1.107
Elementary school completed	0.217	0.187	1.243
High school completed	0.050	0.195	1.052
College degree	0.065	0.233	1.067
Fear of failure	0.164	0.199	1.178
Know an entrepreneur	1.987***	1.158	7.294
Entrepreneurs have high status	1.617***	0.804	5.036
Age	0.015**	0.007	1.015
Gender	0.140	0.141	1.151
Doing Business Ranking	0.009***	0.002	1.009
Unemployment rate	−0.062	0.062	0.940

(Dependent variable: activities to create a business)

Adjusted R^2	Wald chi^2(12)	Log pseudolikelihood
15%	244.79***	−959.01077

Notes:
n = 4632.
EE = entrepreneurship education.
*p<0.1; **p<0.05; ***p<0.01.

to perform specific actions to create a start-up if they have received voluntary entrepreneurship education. Again, voluntary entrepreneurship education has a positive, significant effect on early entrepreneurial activity (B=0.763, p<0.01). Compulsory entrepreneurship education has no effect on early entrepreneurial activity.

The analysis of the control variables in the second model suggests that the business environment has a significant impact on people's decision to get involved in actual entrepreneurial activities. The Doing Business Ranking had a positive significant effect on early entrepreneurial activity (B=0.009, p<0.01). The unemployment rate, on the contrary, did not have an effect on early entrepreneurial activity. Table 3.5 describes the regression models including total entrepreneurial activity (TEA) as the dependent variable.

Regarding the other control variables, level of education does not increase or decrease the likelihood of people getting involved in early entrepreneurial activity. This is interesting because in developed economies having a college degree has a positive impact on entrepreneurial actions (Shane, 2003). It may be that in developing economies the type of businesses that people start are not very intensive in knowledge, and therefore having more formal education makes no difference when pursuing opportunity entrepreneurship.

Gender was not significant, while age changed direction compared to the first model. Although intention was higher in younger people, entrepreneurial activity increased as people became older. As has been suggested (Al-Laham et al., 2007), young people usually need to get more experience before performing concrete and specific actions to start a business. Therefore it is not a surprise that younger people have less likelihood of being involved in early entrepreneurial activity.

For the third model, using business ownership as the dependent variable, Nagelkerke R square was 0.23, suggesting that 23 percent of the variability can be explained by the set of variables included in the model (see Table 3.6). The effect of compulsory entrepreneurship education on individuals was found not to be significant.

Turning to the control variables, we had an interesting finding. The more formal education the individuals had, the more likely they were to own a business that was conceived to capture an opportunity. Having a high school diploma (B=−0.432, p<0.1) and having a college degree (B=0.629, p<0.01) had a positive effect on business ownership. Gender was significant (B=0.477, p<0.01), as well as age (B=0.800, p<0.01). Business ownership was higher as people became older.

The context, measured using the DBR, was significant and positive (B=0.008, p<0.01), while the unemployment rate was not significant.

Table 3.6   Regression model results and statistics

Variable	B	Standard error	Odds ratio
(Constant)	−1.017***	0.896	0.000
Voluntary EE	0.514***	0.201	1.672
Compulsory EE	0.023	0.444	1.023
Elementary school completed	−0.100	0.284	1.001
High school completed	0.432*	0.242	0.905
College degree	0.629***	0.224	1.541
Fear of failure	0.001	0.203	1.876
Know an entrepreneur	1.850***	0.207	6.360
Entrepreneurs have high status	2.089***	0.216	8.074
Age	0.079***	0.010	1.082
Gender	0.491***	0.160	1.634
Doing Business Ranking	0.019***	0.003	1.019
Unemployment rate	0.036	0.074	1.036
(Dependent variable: established business ownership)			
Adjusted R^2	Wald chi^2(11)	Log	
23%	267.22***	pseudolikelihood 601.4194	

Notes:
n = 4512.
EE = entrepreneurship education.
*p<0.1; **p<0.05; ***p<0.01.

Finally, the effects of attitudes, social norms and self-efficacy were highly related to entrepreneurial action, intentions and activity.

CONCLUSIONS AND IMPLICATIONS

We tested the effect of entrepreneurship education on the three stages of business creation (intention, action and ownership), finding that only voluntary entrepreneurship education has positive effects on entrepreneurial intentions and actions. At a first glance, this empirical evidence suggests that potential entrepreneurs seek learning opportunities. The fact that voluntary training is a good predictor of entrepreneurship intentions and actions tells us that inside our classrooms (where students learn about entrepreneurship) there are many potential future entrepreneurs. However, despite the limitations of our methods, the results indicate entrepreneurship education may not be as useful as we may believe in the changing of minds. Potential entrepreneurs actively seek learning opportunities while trying to start a business, making entrepreneurial training look highly effective. This obvious finding is a hint for business educators: voluntary entrepreneurship courses attract a good number of potential and real entrepreneurs but do not change the mind of those who plan to be employees. We can see in our first model that mandatory entrepreneurship education can even be detrimental to transforming non-entrepreneurs into entrepreneurs. However, people who attend voluntary entrepreneurship education have positive attitudes toward business and are more likely to be involved in entrepreneurship later.

Mandatory entrepreneurship education was found not to affect intentions or actions. This finding provides evidence that entrepreneurship courses do not have the power to influence intentions, or, if they do, the influence is negative. EET may increase self-efficacy while decreasing intentions or having no effect over intention. Self-efficacy could be reduced after training because of the reality check that training implies, but not because students end up having less knowledge than before the training. In this case, it should not be a difference between compulsory and mandatory in terms of intentions. The reality check should be the same for voluntary and mandatory types of training.

These findings should be considered not only when deciding on how mandatory entrepreneurial programs should be, but also when designing the content taught to voluntary students. The curriculum should be designed to make people more effective in the discipline rather than to change attitudes toward the discipline. Entrepreneurial awareness is still an important component of many entrepreneurship programs (especially in Latin America), and the findings of this research suggest that it should not be that important. This claim is consistent with Wilmoth (2016), who found that the Millennial generation (students born after 1980) are less prone to start businesses compared with Generation X (students born before 1980). In 2014, less than 2 percent of Millennials reported self-employment compared to 7.6 percent for Generation X and 8.3 percent for Baby Boomers. The Millennial generation is the most exposed generation to EET, so EET seems not to be good at producing entrepreneurs as we used to believe. If entrepreneurship courses change minds, they do so to reduce entrepreneurial intentions and chase people away from starting a business.

Given that our sample for this chapter is cross-sectional, we cannot infer causality from the results. We can, however, infer that compulsory entrepreneurship education is not related to any entrepreneurial stage and can even be detrimental for intention. Two possible explanations can be elaborated for the null and negative effect of compulsory entrepreneurship education on business intentions, actions and ownership. One explanation centers around the idea that career paths are hard to change. If individuals are obligated to take courses in entrepreneurship they may learn more but not necessarily change their career path to develop a new career as entrepreneurs. It seems that compulsory entrepreneurship education does not make people more prone to accept entrepreneurship as a viable form of work.

Alternatively, people who receive compulsory entrepreneurship education increase their human capital, gaining access to better job offers, which in turn reduces their likelihood of becoming entrepreneurs. Since people with a naturally high propensity toward entrepreneurship will seek entrepreneurial knowledge anyhow, ceteris paribus people without a natural propensity toward entrepreneurship will have a reduced likelihood of becoming entrepreneurs by increasing their value in the job market. This can be more notorious in developing economies because education is more expensive and the income gap between professional and non-professional workers is higher than in developed economies. In consequence, the opportunity cost to get involved in entrepreneurship is higher for professionals in developing economies.

Finally, an explanation for the negative effect of mandatory entrepreneurship education on intention can be elaborated considering the awareness that individuals may achieve during entrepreneurial training. It may be that people adjust their view about what is involved when pursuing an entrepreneurial career. After entrepreneurial training, students receive a reality check from experienced entrepreneurs who tell them how hard it is to survive as business owners. The result is people moving away from entrepreneurship rather than moving closer. Still this is a positive outcome, because starting a business implies energy and resources that need a deep commitment from the entrepreneur. It is a good outcome to chase away those who are not ready to go into self-employment. It is possible that people who receive compulsory entrepreneurship education will avoid big failures by desisting before they occur. Without compulsory training, more people would be exposed to the possibility of losing time and money doing something they do not really like or do not have the skills for.

In Latin America, there are many educational programs in colleges and high schools that make entrepreneurship compulsory for all students. The effect of entrepreneurship education in Latin America has to be analyzed with care. In Latin America, the larger proportion of college students come from the richest segment of the society, and the income gap between those who graduate from college and those who never went to college is very large. Wu and Wu (2008) found that people with a high level of education within high-income economies are less likely to become entrepreneurs than people with comparable educational levels in lower-income countries.

FUTURE RESEARCH

Previous research in entrepreneurship education has demonstrated that training in entrepreneurial intention does not always have the same effect (Coduras et al., 2010; Kwon and Arenius, 2010; Levie and Autio, 2008). Sometimes it increases intentions and sometimes reduces it. This chapter provides evidence to suggest that mandatory entrepreneurship education has a negative effect on intentions. A reason for the negative influence of mandatory EET on intentions could be related to education levels. Mandatory courses are common in business schools that teach in cohorts, and those students may have better work opportunities after they graduate. Better opportunities can be detrimental for entrepreneurial intentions because of the opportunity cost of not accepting a good job. Well-educated people are also well paid in LATAM and have less incentive to start their own businesses.

Another type of explanation could be the effect of mandatory EET on the attitudes and self-efficacy of people (related to entrepreneurship). The theory of planned behavior proposes that, in order to develop entrepreneurial intentions, individuals' self-efficacy and attitudes need to be positive. In theory, EET affects entrepreneurial intentions by developing positive attitudes and self-efficacy toward entrepreneurial actions. If someone receives training, the self-perception about his/her own capabilities in the field should be positive after the training, unless the self-perception is adjusted based on the training, providing a reality check on what it really takes to launch a venture successfully. If you receive training on how to prepare spaghetti, after the training you perceive yourself as more capable of preparing spaghetti.

The database used for this research allows us to examine whether a cross-sectional sample of students appear to react in the same manner after receiving mandatory EET. Some students may have a positive or neutral attitude toward entrepreneurship and develop a negative attitude after knowing more about the topic (entrepreneurship). Other students may have a high self-efficacy and reduce this self-perception after the training. Note that only mandatory EET resulted in a negative effect on intentions, and this indicates that something happens with mandatory courses that does not happen with voluntary ones. An angle for future research is to understand how self-selection relates to self-efficacy, attitudes and exposure to training. Why does mandatory EET produce negative attitudes while voluntary EET does not? The reality check's argument should have the same effect in voluntary and mandatory students unless we assume voluntary students have a more precise self-perception of their skills. Are voluntary students not affected by the reality check of training compared to students obligated to take the entrepreneurship course? Future research may explore this by identifying students' attitudes and self-efficacy toward entrepreneurship before they enter training and observing the evolution of those patterns through the training process. It may be that students with negative or neutral attitudes toward entrepreneurship are those who will reduce their intentions after the training while those with positive attitudes will not.

LIMITATIONS

A major limitation of this study concerns the ability to assign the same level of importance to any type of education regardless of whether it was received in high school, college or a chamber of commerce and regardless of the hours involved in the training. We understand that different types of entrepreneurship education could be treated differently, but we choose this limitation instead of selecting a subgroup and dealing with a complex tree of decisions (going to college, taking entrepreneurship education, deciding to start a business). We did so because the goal of this research was to explore the effect of compulsory and voluntary entrepreneurship education regardless of the source.

Another important limitation relates to the quality of the entrepreneurship education received by the individuals included in this study. We are assuming all subjects received a similar quality and type of education. It might be that compulsory entrepreneurship education had no effect because of the effectiveness of the training.

We understand that appropriate content of entrepreneurial education continues to emerge, and hence entrepreneurship education means different things in different places. While other disciplines, such as law or medicine, tend to have an agreed-upon body of knowledge, within entrepreneurship we cannot assume uniformity. In fact, different teaching methods are likely to have different impacts on entrepreneurial intentions and actions. Entrepreneurship educators can pursue different teaching goals, such as informing students about the role of entrepreneurs in society, the characteristics of entrepreneurs, and the nature of successful business ideas, among many other foci. Education can also include tools, frameworks, and different approaches to the challenges of developing novel business models or acquiring external funding. In spite of these major differences, there is not much debate, driven by research, about the expected outcomes of entrepreneurship education. Part of the purpose of this chapter was to open the discussion about the benefit of compulsory entrepreneurship education as well as to challenge the idea that entrepreneurship education develops in students a positive attitude toward entrepreneurship. It may be that preventing people from investing time and resources in creating a business is a good way to contribute to economic growth. We need to think about how good entrepreneurial content can better prepare potential entrepreneurs for failure. As we know, most businesses fail, but many entrepreneurship courses fail to help potential entrepreneurs recognize this issue, reduce the likelihood of failing, or prepare people to deal with failure when it happens.

REFERENCES

Acs, Z. and Armington, C. (2006), *Entrepreneurship, Geography, and American Economic Growth*, New York: Cambridge University Press.

Ács, Z.J. and Stough, R. (2008), *Public Policy in an Entrepreneurial Economy: Creating the Conditions for Business Growth*, New York: Springer.

Ács, Z.J. and Varga, A. (2005), Entrepreneurship, agglomeration and technological change, *Small Business Economics*, **24**(3), 323–334.

Acs, Z.J., Arenius, P., Hay, M. and Minniti, M. (2005), *Global Entrepreneurship Monitor: 2004 Executive Report*, Babson Park, MA and London: Babson College and London Business School.

Ajzen, I. (1987), Attitudes, traits, and actions: dispositional prediction of behavior in personality and social psychology, in L. Berkowitz (ed.), *Advances in Experimental Social Psychology*, Vol. 20, New York: Academic Press, pp. 1–63.

Ajzen, I. (1991), The theory of planned behavior, *Organizational Behavior and Human Decision Processes*, **211**, 179–211.

Al-Laham, A., Souitaris, V. and Zerbinati, S. (2007), Do entrepreneurship programmes raise entrepreneurial intention of science and engineering students? The effect of learning, inspiration and resources, *Journal of Business Venturing*, **22**(4), 566–591.

Bandura, A. (1977), *Social Learning Theory*, Englewood Cliffs, NJ: Prentice Hall.

Bowen, H.P. and De Clercq, D. (2008), Institutional context and the allocation of entrepreneurial effort, *Journal of International Business Studies*, **39**, 747–767.

Brazeal, D.V. and Krueger, N.F. (1994), Entrepreneurial potentials and potential entrepreneurs, *Entrepreneurship Theory and Practice*, **18**(3), 91–104.

Carsrud, A., Brannback, M. and Krueger, N. (2008), Challenging the triple helix model of regional innovation systems, *International Journal of Technoentrepreneurship*, **1**(3), 257–277.

Cassar, G. (2006), Entrepreneur opportunity cost and intended venture growth, *Journal of Business Venturing*, **21**, 610–632.

Chesbrough, H.W., Vanhaverbeke, W. and West, J. (2006), *Open Innovation: Researching a New Paradigm*, Oxford, UK: Oxford University Press.

Coduras, A., Levie, J., Kelley, D., Saemundsson, R. and Schott, T. (2010), *A Global Perspective on Entrepreneurship Education and Training: A Special Report of the Global Entrepreneurship Monitor*, Wellesley, MA and Santiago: Babson College and Universidad del Desarrollo.

Duderstadt, J. (2010), Engineering for a changing world, in D. Grasso and

M. Brown Burkins (eds.), *Holistic Engineering Education: Beyond Technology*, New York: Springer.

Fiet, J.O. and Pankaj, C.P. (2008), Entrepreneurial discovery as constrained, systematic search, *Small Business Economics*, **30**, 215–229.

Galloway, L. and Brown, W. (2002), Entrepreneurship education at university: a driver in the creation of high growth firms? *Education and Training*, **44**(8), 398–405.

GEM (Global Entrepreneurship Monitor) (2010), retrieved from www.gemconsortium.org/.

Gibb, A. (2002), In pursuit of a new enterprise and entrepreneurship paradigm for learning: creative destruction, new value, new ways of doing things and new combinations of knowledge, *International Journal of Management Review*, **4**(3), 233–269.

Graevenitz, G. von, Harhoff, D. and Weber, R. (2010), The effects of entrepreneurship education, *Journal of Economic Behavior and Organization*, **76**(1), 90–112.

Grilo, I. and Thurik, R. (2005), Entrepreneurial engagement levels in the European Union, *International Journal of Entrepreneurship Education*, **3**(2), 143–168.

Hamidi, D., Wennberg, K. and Berglund, H. (2008), Creativity in entrepreneurship education, *Journal of Small Business and Enterprise Development*, **15**(2), 304–320.

Hwang, H. and Powell, W.W. (2005), Institutions and entrepreneurship, in S. Alvarez, R. Agarwal and O. Sorenson (eds.), *Handbook of Entrepreneurship Research: Disciplinary Perspectives*, New York: Springer, pp. 201–232.

Klimoski, R.J. (2007), From the editor: becoming a prophet in our own land, *Academy of Management Learning and Education*, **6**, 433–438.

Krueger, N.F., Reilly, M.D. and Carsrud, A.L. (2000), Entrepreneurial intentions: a competing models approach, *Journal of Business Venturing*, **15**(5), 411–432.

Kuratko, D.F. (2005), The emergence of entrepreneurship education: development, trends, and challenges, *Entrepreneurship Theory and Practice*, **29**(5), 577–598.

Kwon, S.W. and Arenius, P. (2010), Nations of entrepreneurs: a social capital perspective, *Journal of Business Venturing*, **25**(3), 315–330.

Kyrö, P. (2015), The conceptual contribution of education to research on entrepreneurship education, *Entrepreneurship and Regional Development*, **27**(9–10), 599–618.

Levie, J. and Autio, E. (2008), A theoretical grounding and test of the GEM model, *Small Business Economics*, **31**(3), 235–263.

Levie, J., Hart, M. and Anyadike-Danes, M. (2009), The effect of business or enterprise training on opportunity recognition and entrepreneurial skills of graduates and non-graduates in the UK, *Frontiers of Entrepreneurship Research*, **29**(23), 1–11.

Lüthje, C. and Franke, N. (2003), The "making" of an entrepreneur: testing a model of entrepreneurial intent among engineering students at MIT, *R&D Management*, **33**(2), 135–147.

Naudé, W.A. (2007), *Peace, Prosperity, and Pro-growth Entrepreneurship*, WIDER Research Paper 2007/02, Helsinki: UNU WIDER.

Neck, H. and Greene, P. (2010), Entrepreneurship education: known worlds and new frontiers, *Journal of Small Business Management*, **49**(1), 55–70.

Oosterbeek, H., van Praag, M. and Ijsselstein, A. (2010), The impact of entrepreneurship education on entrepreneurship skills and motivation, *European Economic Review*, **54**, 442–454.

Reynolds, P.D. (1997), Who starts new firms? Preliminary explorations of firms-in-gestation, *Small Business Economics*, **9**(5), 449–462.

Reynolds, P. (2007), *Entrepreneurship in the United States: The Future Is Now*, New York: Springer.

Reynolds, P., Bosma, N., Autio, E., Hunt, S., De Bono, N., Servais, I., Lopez-Garcia, P. and Chin, N. (2005), Global Entrepreneurship Monitor: data collection design and implementation 1998–2003, *Small Business Economics*, **24**(3), 205–231.

Shane, S. (2003), *A General Theory of Entrepreneurship*, Cheltenham, UK and Northampton, MA, USA: Edward Elgar.

Shane, S.A. (2008), *The Illusions of Entrepreneurship: The Costly Myths That Entrepreneurs, Investors, and Policy Makers Live By*, New Haven, CT: Yale University Press.

Shane, S. and Venkataraman, S. (2000), The promise of entrepreneurship as a field of research, *Academy of Management Review*, **25**(1), 217–226.

Singer, S., Amorós, J.E. and Moska, D. (2015), *Global Entrepreneurship Monitor: 2014 Global Report*, Wellesley, MA: Babson College, Universidad del Desarrollo, Universiti Tun Abdul Razak, and Tecnológico de Monterrey.

Van Auken, S., Wells, L.G. and Borgia, D. (2009), A comparison of Western business instruction in China with US instruction: a case study of perceived program emphases and satisfaction levels, *Journal of Teaching in International Business*, **20**(3), 208–229.

WEF (World Economic Forum) (2015), *Global Competitive Index*, retrieved from http://reports.weforum.org/global-competitiveness-report-2015-2016/.

Wilmoth, D. (2016), The missing millennial entrepreneurs, Economic Research Series, US Small Business Administration, retrieved May 2016 from https://www.sba.gov/sites/default/files/advocacy/Millenial_IB.pdf.

Wu, S. and Wu, L. (2008), The impact of higher education on entrepreneurial intentions of university students in China, *Journal of Small Business and Enterprise Development*, **15**(4), 752–774.

Zhao, H., Seibert, S. and Hills, G. (2005), The mediating role of self efficacy in the development of entrepreneurial intentions, *Journal of Applied Psychology*, **90**(6), 1265–1272.

4. Bridging entrepreneurial cognition research and entrepreneurship education: what and how

Susana C. Santos, Silvia Fernandes Costa, Xaver Neumeyer and António Caetano

Entrepreneurial cognition perspectives have contributed decisively to the progress of research and practice in entrepreneurship. Grounding their research in social cognitive theory, scholars found that entrepreneurs' distinctive characteristics are not based on their personality traits (Gartner, 1989), but are more related to the specific information-processing systems they develop over time within their experiences (e.g., Corbett and Hmieleski, 2005). However, despite the fact that the aim of entrepreneurial cognition research is to understand how entrepreneurs think and act, these developments have yet to catch on in entrepreneurship education.

The main goal of entrepreneurship education is to facilitate the acquisition of knowledge structures and to shape and change them (Glaser, 1984). It also involves gaining and developing a number of skills that are specific to entrepreneurial behavior. And, as entrepreneurial behavior is primarily related to a unique set of knowledge structures (both heuristic and scripted) and to decision-making processes (assessment and judgment), understanding the interplay between entrepreneurial cognition and entrepreneurship education is crucial to enhancing entrepreneurial learning. We suggest that entrepreneurship education targeting cognitive development and based on entrepreneurial cognition principles can be a powerful and effective approach for empowering and igniting students' entrepreneurial mindsets and behavior. Additionally, an evidence-based teaching approach can contribute towards instilling and disseminating entrepreneurial awareness among students using theoretically and empirically well-grounded perspectives on entrepreneurship.

As educators, we first need to define *what* to teach and then *how* to teach it. In this chapter, we intend to contribute to this debate about *what* and *how* entrepreneurship should be taught (e.g., Fayolle, 2013; Kuratko, 2005). First, we analyze the literature and provide an approach that incorporates the insights of entrepreneurial cognition research in entrepreneurship education. Based on this, we introduce *cognitive entrepreneurship education* as the answer to the *what* question. Second, we propose that experiential learning is the most adequate method for *how* entrepreneurship should be taught. These two building blocks constitute the foundations for developing students' mindsets and awareness of entrepreneurship.

ENTREPRENEURIAL COGNITION

Entrepreneurial cognition refers to "the knowledge structures that people use to make assessments, judgments or decisions involving opportunity evaluation and venture creation and growth" (Mitchell et al., 2002a, p. 97). Entrepreneurial cognition borrows theories, empirical evidence and concepts from cognitive psychology and social cognition literature and has been focusing on explaining the development of the mental mechanisms and structures of entrepreneurs that are responsible for entrepreneurial behavior and thinking.

During the last decade, findings from cognition research provided considerable insight into how entrepreneurs think and make decisions. These can be categorized as follows: 1) heuristic-based logic; 2) perceptual processes; 3) entrepreneurial expertise; and 4) effectuation (in Mitchell et al., 2007).

Heuristics are simple and automated strategies that individuals use to make decisions in contexts characterized by high complexity and information density (e.g., Gigerenzer and Gaissmaier, 2011; Gilovich et al., 2002; Tversky and Kahneman, 1974). Heuristics are characterized by two principles: 1) the accuracy of heuristics depends on the complexity and structure of the environment; and 2) the effective use of heuristics is learnable and based on sufficient experience and specialized knowledge (Gigerenzer and Gaissmaier, 2011). The use of heuristics is especially relevant for entrepreneurs who have to make time-sensitive decisions in uncertain environments. Thus, this heuristic-based logic allows entrepreneurs to process uncertain and complex situations with superior sense-giving, and to make more expeditious decisions. For example, entrepreneurs are more overconfident (overvaluing the probability of being right) and use more representative strategies (the tendency to generalize from a few characteristics or attributes) than managers (Busenitz and Barney, 1997), but their use is a function of individual and contextual factors (Forbes, 2005). In short, heuristics are automatic perceptive mechanisms that can be learned and used effectively when explored in an experiential learning way. Because experience is crucial for the use of heuristics, helping students to effectively transform their experiences into knowledge through entrepreneurship education will enable them to use heuristics more effectively in an uncertain situation, especially with regard to recognizing and evaluating opportunities (Bryant, 2007).

The second category of entrepreneurial cognition research relates to perceptual processes. Entrepreneurs employ unique perceptual processes that allow them to perceive and interpret information at key stages of the entrepreneurial process (e.g., Grégoire et al., 2010a). There are two main perceptual processes that previous research on entrepreneurial cognition has identified: entrepreneurial alertness and business opportunity prototype. Entrepreneurial alertness is defined as a distinctive set of perceptive and information-processing skills, and is a critical engine for driving opportunity identification processes (Gaglio and Katz, 2001; Kirzner, 1973). It comprises three dimensions: scanning and searching for information; connecting previously disparate information; and making evaluations about the existence of profitable business opportunities (Tang et al., 2012). Second, entrepreneurs exhibit unique mental prototypes that not only allow them to recognize patterns among perceived changes in the environment but also help them see new opportunities (Baron, 2006; Baron and Ensley, 2006). Specifically, research has found that business opportunities share prototypical features: 1) solving a customer's problems; 2) the ability to generate a positive cash flow; 3) manageable risk; 4) superiority of the product or service; and 5) potential to change the industry (Baron and Ensley, 2006; Costa et al., 2016; Santos et al., 2015). In short, entrepreneurial alertness and business opportunity prototype constitute perceptual processes that are specific to entrepreneurs and that contribute to the recognition and pursuit of entrepreneurial opportunities. Including these notions of cognitive perception in entrepreneurship education is key to enhancing entrepreneurial awareness from an evidence-based perspective. Understanding the basic perceptive mechanisms of entrepreneurs allows potential entrepreneurs such as students, for example, to be alert to the same type of information during their entrepreneurial experiences.

Yet another category of work on entrepreneurial cognition concerns entrepreneurial expertise. Expertise theory (Ericsson, 2006) postulates that scripts are grounded and developed in a specific area of activity, and that they allow complex situations and problem solving to be dealt with efficiently. Expertise is defined as the accumulation of knowledge and extensive professional experience, which leads to superior expert performance (Ericsson, 1990). Entrepreneurial expertise is built on entrepreneurs' unique knowledge structures and information-processing systems related to their entrepreneurial activities (Mitchell et al., 2000). Entrepreneurs' expertise comprises cognitive scripts that enable them to be more effective in new venture creation decisions, entrepreneurial activities and tasks (Mitchell, 2005). The cognitive scripts of new venture creation include arrangement scripts, willingness scripts and ability scripts (Mitchell et al., 2000). Arrangement scripts are knowledge structures that support superior expert performance, and they refer to resource possession and leveraging, network utilization, patent protection, and venture network accessibility (Mitchell et al., 2000). Willingness scripts are knowledge structures related to commitment and receptiveness to starting a venture, for example opportunity seeking, risk and action orientation, investment values and orientation, and openness to possibilities (Mitchell et al., 2000). Ability scripts are knowledge structures referring to individuals' knowledge, capabilities, skills, and attitudes towards venture creation, such as time investment criteria, venture versus business knowledge base, and success attribution (Mitchell et al., 2000). All in all, this set of expert scripts characterizes the entrepreneurial mindset (Mitchell et al., 2002b). Including entrepreneurial expertise in entrepreneurship education is important, as it allows students to understand the foundations of entrepreneurs' expert performance, how entrepreneurs think, and their cognitive architecture.

The final category of cognition research refers to effectuation, which is a particular aspect of entrepreneurial expertise. Effectuation theory was developed by Sarasvathy (2001, 2008) as a form of reasoning which "take[s] a set of means as given and focus[es] on selecting between possible effects that can be created with that set of means" (Sarasvathy, 2001, p. 245). Effectual logic is consistent with emergent and unpredictable strategies and occurs under uncertain conditions where planning is limited. According to effectuation theory, entrepreneurs are not able to decide the best course of action, but they have to deal with the contingencies, be flexible, use experimentation and be disposed towards taking a set of means or tools and selecting the possible effects that can be built with them. Sarasvathy (2001, 2008) further suggested that entrepreneurs engaged in the effectuation approach use the results of their decisions as a new information source to change an action, work with the resources at their disposal and develop any necessary adjustments. Effectuation is then a special case of expertise that leads to superior expert performance in entrepreneurship activities. Once again, the role of experience is crucial in the development of effective entrepreneurial strategies and behaviors. Bringing effectuation into the educational setting is also central to successfully training potential entrepreneurs.

On the whole, these streams of research have been able to demonstrate that entrepreneurs develop an idiosyncratic way of thinking and behaving (Mitchell et al., 2007). It is important to stress, however, that, despite the fact that entrepreneurs draw on unique cognitive structures and processes, these very structures and processes are not stable. They change over time during the entrepreneurs' unique life experiences (Gielnik et al., 2014), as well as their entrepreneurial experience (Morris et al., 2012). Furthermore, entrepreneurial cognition is dependent on the characteristics of a specific environment. Cognition and perceptual processes are not formal operations, but rather are situated where the individual plays the main, active role in these processes (Anderson, M., 2003). Entrepreneurial cognition is thus developed within the unique experiences that individuals carry out. Therefore, it is important to bring to entrepreneurship education those notions of entrepreneurial cognition that relate to how entrepreneurs think and act. This will enable students to make sense of their own experiences within this entrepreneurial framework and develop an entrepreneurial mindset. We suggest that the main principles of entrepreneurial cognition should be integrated in entrepreneurship education efforts, following the evidence-based teaching and learning approach. In the next section, we present the main perspectives on the literature about entrepreneurship education.

EVIDENCE-BASED ENTREPRENEURSHIP EDUCATION

Entrepreneurship education came about because of the assumption that entrepreneurship is a discipline (Drucker, 1985) and, like all disciplines, can be learned (Kuratko, 2005). Entrepreneurship education is broadly defined as all the activities that aim to foster entrepreneurial mindsets, attitudes and skills, which cover a variety of aspects such as idea generation, start-up, growth and innovation (e.g., Fayolle and Gailly, 2008). Evidence-based education builds on a set of previous principles and practices for enhancing the educational policies and practices (Davies, 1999) of a specific scientific field. Entrepreneurship education benefits from the empirical and conceptual principles that have been established and from evidence-based entrepreneurship (Frese et al., 2014).

Entrepreneurship education literature is broad, and can be organized under three general topics. First, there is the need to point out that teaching entrepreneurship requires several specificities that differentiate it from teaching other subjects (e.g., Jack and Anderson, 1999; Neck and Greene, 2011). Entrepreneurship started being taught as a part of management programs, mainly inspired by traditional disciplines focused on entrepreneurship, such as management and economics (e.g. Landström and Benner, 2010). Nowadays, it is clear that entrepreneurship goes beyond the boundaries of management and business schools (Kuratko, 2005), is present across campuses and permeates all the disciplines (Kuratko and Morris, forthcoming). Moreover, the literature shows that entrepreneurship requires specific teaching and learning approaches, which cannot be achieved using traditional pedagogical methods (Anderson, A. and Jack, 2008; Jack and Anderson, 1999; Neck and Greene, 2011). In line with this trend, Kuratko (2005) argued that entrepreneurship not only goes beyond mere venture creation and is not depleted by the number of businesses created, but is a much wider and transversal phenomenon, with diverse types of expressions and outcomes. Thus, entrepreneurship education must take into consideration all the aspects of the entrepreneurial process such as opportunity recognition, evaluation, exploitation, risk taking and how to bring ideas to fruition (Kuratko, 2005).

Second, there has also been concern to include individual-centered approaches and learning styles in entrepreneurship education (e.g., Béchard and Grégoire, 2005). These would involve background factors (Wang and Wong, 2004), personality traits (Lüthje and Franke, 2003), motivations (DeMartino and Barbato, 2003), experience (Kyrö, 2008) and entrepreneurial competencies (Morris et al., 2013). This body of research highlights that entrepreneurship education involves individuals' unique significant experiences (Morris et al., 2012). Accordingly, entrepreneurial experiences and the knowledge acquired from them are two critical aspects of entrepreneurship education (Politis, 2005). Research on entrepreneurial experience suggests that entrepreneurship can be learned by engaging in significant experiences which are then transformed into knowledge (Morris et al., 2012).

Third, academics have also been discussing *what* should be taught in entrepreneurship and *how*, with the focus on systematizing entrepreneurship education (e.g., Béchard and Grégoire, 2005; Kuratko, 2005; Pittaway and Cope, 2007). Regarding *what* should be taught in entrepreneurship, Kuratko (2005) listed the main topics which are frequently related to entrepreneurs and new venture creation. The topics listed by Kuratko (2005) can be summarized into four major categories (Costa, 2015): 1) contents focused at the individual level (psychological variables of entrepreneurship; entrepreneurial awareness/spirit; risks and trade-offs of the entrepreneurial journey); 2) contents regarding the organizational level (entrepreneurial and managerial domains; venture financing; corporate entrepreneurship; entrepreneurial strategies); 3) contents regarding the societal level of entrepreneurship (women and minorities; economic and social contributions); and 4) contents regarding other topics related to research purposes (ethics and entrepreneurship; predictors of success). Despite the seminal work of Kuratko (2005) on entrepreneurship education, agreement has yet to be reached among entrepreneurship scholars on what the topics are that should be taught in entrepreneurship education. This might be also due to the fact that each of these topics is relevant and useful for different purposes and at diverse stages of the development of a student's entrepreneurial mindset. Another line of research addresses the notion that entrepreneurship education should focus on the promotion of attitudes and affective variables towards entrepreneurship, rather than be centered mostly in knowledge acquisition (Fayolle and Gailly, 2015; Shepherd, 2004). Beyond the debate on *what* to teach in entrepreneurship, Fayolle (2013) expresses his concerns regarding the fact that the field of entrepreneurship education needs to be grounded in solid and proven theories and principles capable of strengthening entrepreneurship programs and thus contributing to narrowing the gap between research and practice (Edelman et al., 2008; Frese et al., 2014).

Regarding *how* entrepreneurship should be taught, there is a consensus that universities are privileged environments for entrepreneurship education (Block et al., 2011; Neck and Greene, 2011), that entrepreneurship happens across campuses (Kuratko and Morris, forthcoming), and that higher education itself is a predictor of entrepreneurial activity (e.g., Rasmussen and Sørheim, 2006). Additionally, Neck and Greene (2011) proposed that entrepreneurship education should be viewed as a method, and as a practice (Neck et al., 2015). With regard to entrepreneurship education as a method, Neck and Greene (2011) focus primarily on entrepreneurship as a way of thinking, where students are given the opportunity to develop a portfolio of entrepreneurial competencies based on their critical experiences. Entrepreneurship education as a practice involves five domains: the practice of creation; the practice of experimentation; the practice of play; the practice of empathy; and the practice of reflection (Neck et al., 2015). Despite agreement on the relevance that practice, hands-on approach and experience have for entrepreneurship education, it is not yet empirically established which methods are more efficient in entrepreneurship education. Nevertheless, it is always crucial that researchers and educators deeply and critically reflect on their practices (Fayolle, 2013).

As summarized, there has been remarkable growth in entrepreneurship education over the last 30 years (Kuratko, 2005). However, we keep looking for answers to the two fundamental questions regarding entrepreneurship education: *what* contents entrepreneurship education should be focusing on, and *how* entrepreneurship education can be taught. We suggest that one relevant contribution towards answering these two questions resides in teaching the principles of entrepreneurial cognition, and using experiential learning methods.

COGNITIVE ENTREPRENEURSHIP EDUCATION

As discussed previously, *what* should be taught in entrepreneurship education is still one of the fundamental questions in the literature. The current conversation on entrepreneurship education acknowledges that the focus should go beyond new venture creation and the start-up processes (Kuratko, 2005; Morris et al., 2013). In fact, entrepreneurship education programs first have to target changes in attitudes and mindsets, focus on raising entrepreneurial awareness, and develop a *way of thinking* before focusing on *how to do it* (Fayolle et al., 2006). In other words, the principles of entrepreneurship education are centered on teaching and learning a way of thinking and analyzing the world, in order to raise students' awareness of entrepreneurship as a mindset that embraces several dimensions of their life.

Conceiving entrepreneurship education as primarily targeting a way of thinking emphasizes the role of entrepreneurial cognition. However, cognitive approaches in entrepreneurship education are still scarce in the literature (Béchard and Grégoire, 2005). Building on these assumptions, we suggest that entrepreneurship education should be designed to provide students with the opportunity to learn the *entrepreneurial way of thinking* and the *cognitive principles* that promote entrepreneurship. Thus, the foremost concern of entrepreneurship education should be to imbue students with entrepreneurial cognition frameworks and processes, taking an evidence-based teaching approach. This can be achieved by using the most established principles of previous research as subjects to be incorporated in their education.

Cognitive entrepreneurship education emerges from where entrepreneurial cognition, evidence-based teaching and entrepreneurship education intersect, as depicted in Figure 4.1. On the basis of this intersection, we define cognitive entrepreneurship education as *those activities which, based on available evidence, aim to foster the knowledge structures that individuals use to make assessments, judgments or decisions involving opportunity evaluation, and venture creation and growth*. Cognitive entrepreneurship education focuses on the development of individual knowledge structures and reasoning processes, and recognizes the potential of each individual to learn how to think entrepreneurially and make decisions within entrepreneurial settings (Neck and Greene, 2011).

Cognitive entrepreneurship education is based on the assumption that, by teaching our students the characteristics, patterns and processes of thinking related to entrepreneurship, it is possible to shape their thinking patterns accordingly. Heuristic-based reasoning (e.g., Simon et al., 2000), perceptual processes (e.g., Grégoire et al., 2010a), entrepreneurial scripts

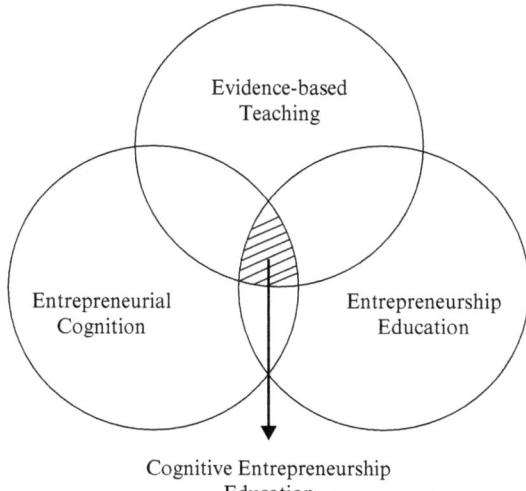

Figure 4.1   The intersection of cognition, education and evidence-based teaching: cognitive entrepreneurship education

(e.g., Mitchell et al., 2000) and effectuation principles (Sarasvathy, 2008) can be learned and, together with a desire to become an entrepreneur, can contribute positively to enhancing entrepreneurship education. What is more, the relevance of taking a cognitive perspective towards entrepreneurship education recognizes how important the mind and reasoning processes are for entrepreneurial activities.

In this way, cognitive entrepreneurship education answers the question of *what* in entrepreneurship education, as it specifies that entrepreneurship education should be teaching the available principles of entrepreneurial cognition, decision-making and reasoning strategies, and knowledge structures. It is relevant to stress that cognitive entrepreneurship education is also a response to the area of research on entrepreneurship that focused on traits, looking for the stable and predisposition characteristics of entrepreneurs (Cope, 2005; Palich and Bagby, 1995). Despite the relevance of personality traits (Brandstätter, 2011), they do not distinguish all the determinants of entrepreneurial behavior, and the trait perspective has been widely questioned (Gartner, 1989). Thus, approaches to entrepreneurship education and techniques have to go beyond personality traits and have to include the teaching of thinking processes, knowledge structures and competencies because they represent the flexible, learnable and dynamic criteria required of entrepreneurship activity.

Cognitive theory has been contributing to identifying the idiosyncrasies underlying entrepreneurial behavior and thinking. From the cognitive point of view, everything individuals do depends on mental processes, and it is certainly no different with regard to entrepreneurship-related activities. Individuals perceive information from the environment and they categorize and analyze the information within the mental frameworks they have constructed during their life experience (e.g., Anderson, J., 1980). For example, based on human cognition research in general, and on cognitive frameworks in particular, Baron (2004, 2006) suggested that individuals perceive business opportunities as they perceive connections between apparently unrelated events or trends – for example changes in technology, demographics, markets or government policies – as a meaningful pattern. Beyond the structure of these events, the trends and changes are objective for the individuals – they can identify them in the environment; and the process of *connecting the dots* between them to generate a meaningful pattern is the result of a subjective process, based on perception mechanisms and shaped by the individual's prior knowledge, experience and interests. This means that the process of opportunity recognition stems from objective pieces of information (i.e., events, trends, changes) that students can learn to recognize, and that merge into subjective perceptions which form opportunity patterns that can be learned (e.g., Grégoire et al., 2010b). As an example, from the same group of changes perceived in the environment, each student can recognize unique patterns, which can be further associated with opportunities, and later developed as business concepts. In order to be recognized as an opportunity, the pattern that is revealed will be compared to the business opportunity prototype that the individual has in his or her cognitive structure. The business opportunity prototype, or any other expert script, can be dissected and broken down into its key components, and be taught in the classroom context as a comprehensive framework that can then be applied in examples and real-time experiences. Specifically, we can teach our students that opportunities share five prototypical dimensions, as outlined by Baron and Ensley (2006): 1) solving a customer's problems; 2) ability to generate a positive cash flow; 3) manageable risk; 4) superiority of the product/service; and 5) potential to change the industry. We can then show students how to use this framework to analyze their own opportunities. This is an example of entrepreneurship processes and knowledge structures that can be included in entrepreneurship education programs aimed at raising awareness in entrepreneurship and changing ways of thinking (Fayolle, 2013). Metaphorically speaking, using cognitive frameworks to identify, transform and shape information is analogous to developing a muscle. The more our students train the muscle of entrepreneurial cognitive frameworks, the more likely they are to use them effectively when needed. Table 4.1 describes the

Table 4.1   *Cognitive entrepreneurship education subjects: principles and processes*

Concept	Definition	Suggestions of application in education
Heuristics	Baron (1998); Busenitz and Barney (1997); Tversky and Kahneman (1973, 1974). Entrepreneurial heuristics are defined as "thumb-rules guiding the management decisions involved in the start-up and management of a new venture" (Manimala, 1992, p. 477). These are simplifying strategies that individuals use to make decisions. They are subjective, depend on informal processes and experience and are influenced by internal beliefs. Entrepreneurs are more likely to effectively use heuristics than managers (e.g., Baron, 1998; Busenitz and Barney, 1997).	Overconfidence and representativeness (Busenitz and Barney, 1997) are two examples of heuristics that can be trained in the classroom, using hypothetical decision-making scenarios, for the different stages of the entrepreneurship process. Students can be exposed to different entrepreneurial scenarios that include manipulation of the amount of information and risk involved. The decision-making process based on the available information can be developed individually and in teams. Students can reflect to what extent they are using overconfidence and representativeness heuristics, as well as other cognitive shortcuts that can bias decision making.
Entrepreneurial cognitive scripts Arrangement scripts	Mitchell et al. (2000). ". . . knowledge structures individuals have about the use of the specific arrangements that support their own performance and expert-level mastery in a given domain" (Mitchell et al., 2000, p. 977), "particularly about funding and financial resources, asset and idea protection, and contacts/networks necessary to new value-creating economic relationships" (Seawright et al., 2011/2013, p. 206).	Students can be exposed to the different entrepreneurial cognitive scripts, by presenting their general framework. Then students can be introduced to the three types of scripts: arrangement, willingness and opportunity–ability. Each type of script has a discretionary list of features which can then be used in hypothetical scenarios or case discussion. Students are asked to identify examples of arrangement, willingness and

Table 4.1   (continued)

Concept	Definition	Suggestions of application in education
	Arrangement scripts include resource possession, people and asset networks, network utilization, patent protection, venture versus general skill set, and venture network accessibility (Mitchell et al., 2000).	opportunity–ability scripts in entrepreneurial cases. At a more complex level, students are asked to develop and use the arrangement, willingness and opportunity–ability scripts in their own entrepreneurial project. Team and class discussion follows.
Willingness scripts	Knowledge structures that underline commitment to venturing and receptivity to the idea of starting a venture, and explore economic possibilities, urgency, and risk-taking motivation (Mitchell et al., 2000; Seawright et al., 2011/2013). Willingness scripts include comfort in new or familiar situations, action orientation, openness to possibilities or settled, action orientation, risk orientation, time values, commitment values, investment values and investment orientation (Mitchell et al., 2000).	
Opportunity–ability scripts	". . . knowledge structures that individuals have about new venture scenarios and patterns, new venture situations, the needed orientation towards success, and opportunity-recognition" (Seawright et al., 2011/2013, p. 206). Ability scripts include normative knowledge bases, success attribution, opportunity recognition, problem recognition, venture success scripts, time investment criteria, locus of investment	

Table 4.1   (continued)

Concept	Definition	Suggestions of application in education
	criteria, venture versus business knowledge bases, diagnosis from specific situations, delineation of knowledge bases, awareness or venture situations (Mitchell et al., 2000). Mitchell et al. (2009) reviewed the structure and content of entrepreneurs' scripts (pp. 120–124). The authors list a set of script cues categorized by individual attributes, experiences, resources, prior training and organizational characteristics that can be used as a self-assessment tool for students' reflection about their entrepreneurial scripts (Mitchell et al., 2009).	
Business opportunity prototype	Baron (2006); Baron and Ensley (2006).	
	Cognitive frameworks with which newly perceived patterns are compared in order to determine whether they constitute opportunities, and that are characterized by 10 dimensions: 1) solving a customer's problems; 2) the ability to generate a positive cash flow; 3) manageable risk; 4) superiority of the product or service; 5) potential to change the industry; 6) a favorable financial model; 7) positive assessment or advice from others (friends, financial advisors and industry experts); 8) the novelty of the idea; 9) a large untapped market; and 10) intuition or gut feeling.	The 10 dimensions that are part of the business opportunity prototype (Baron and Ensley, 2006) can be used as a tool to monitor and evaluate (self- and peer evaluation) potential business opportunities. Students can apply this cognitive framework by ranking and assessing a generated pool of potential business opportunities.

Table 4.1   (continued)

Concept	Definition	Suggestions of application in education
Entrepreneurial alertness	Gaglio and Katz (2001); Kirzner (1973); Tang et al. (2012). "... distinctive set of perceptual and cognitive processing skills that direct the opportunity identification process" (Gaglio and Katz, 2001, p. 96), and that is "consisting of three distinct elements: scanning and searching for information, connecting previously-disparate information, and making evaluations on the existence of profitable business opportunities" (Tang et al., 2012, p. 77). Entrepreneurial alertness is composed of three dimensions that can be taught and applied in entrepreneurship education: the search effort (scanning and searching for information); the content combination effort (connecting previously disparate information); and the profitable evaluation effort (making evaluations on the existence of profitable business opportunities) (Gaglio and Winter, 2009).	Entrepreneurship education can explicitly train students: to develop their abilities to scan their environment, using deliberate search and effortless discovery; to have some awareness of how they use their mental models, and develop diverse iterations on connecting the dots among information acquired; and to define the viability of entrepreneurial opportunities in terms of future goods and services, and in terms of new ventures.
Effectuation	Decision-making strategy is based on the following: "Effectuation processes take a set of means as given and focus on selecting between possible effects that can be created with that set of means" (Sarasvathy, 2001, p. 245).	Effectuation in the classroom can be developed by a set of exercises, case studies, diagnostic tools, and simulations that are available for entrepreneurship education online (for more information visit http://www.effectuation.org/teach). Overall, these exercises lead students to take the resources and means at their disposal at a given moment and derive diverse possible solutions and effects.

Table 4.1   (continued)

Concept	Definition	Suggestions of application in education
		The effectuation principles (starting with your own means; focus on the downside risk; leverage contingencies; form partnerships; and control versus predict) can be trained and used as a logic of thinking in different possible scenarios and situations. Effectual logic can be taught using entrepreneurship-related information, but also using daily situations, objects and changes perceived in the environment.

central entrepreneurial cognition principles and processes that could be introduced as subjects in cognitive entrepreneurship education programs.

As described in Table 4.1, another example of entrepreneurial cognition principles that can be integrated into entrepreneurship education is effectuation (Sarasvathy, 2001, 2008). The identification and development of a decision model involving effectual reasoning processes were found to be common to entrepreneurs and critical among them. The effectuation theory has influenced and shaped the course of entrepreneurship research, mainly with regard to business opportunity emergence and entrepreneurial decision-making processes (Sarasvathy, 2001, 2008). Teaching effectuation principles has also been on the agenda, and Sarasvathy (2008) describes a toolbox and exercises that promote effectual reasoning. This toolbox is primarily based on experiential learning principles and is also aligned with the conceptualization of an entrepreneurial method, analogous to the scientific method, as the necessary mechanism behind what makes someone an enterprising person (Venkataraman et al., 2012). The entrepreneurial method allows a systematic approach to entrepreneurship, and can thus enhance the growth of entrepreneurship education from the very outset of the school curriculum, by wagering on the development of cognitive frameworks and processes. In the next section, we focus on experiential learning and put our case for why this could be a relevant and effective method to teach cognitive entrepreneurship education.

EXPERIENTIAL LEARNING FOR COGNITIVE ENTREPRENEURSHIP EDUCATION

After the identification of *what* some of the primary subjects are that entrepreneurship education should focus on, the next critical question is *how* to teach cognitive entrepreneurship education. There is a consensus that entrepreneurship is best learned from contact with examples, cases and hands-on exercises and by engaging effectively with the experiential perspective (Morris et al., 2012), since as a result of the actual learning process this can be more effective in modifying and shaping knowledge structures (e.g., Corbett, 2007; Fayolle and Gailly, 2015; Neck and Greene, 2011; Shepherd, 2004).

Specifically, cognitive frameworks are live structures, and they develop within the significant and relevant experiences of individuals. Thus, all activities that can involve experiencing will positively contribute to effectively acquiring and changing cognitive frameworks and knowledge structures. Experiential learning, therefore, is an adequate method for the inception of entrepreneurial thinking. What is more, experiential learning can actually result in learning how to identify, categorize and transform information, knowledge and processes that are perceived in the environment. Nevertheless, it is important to stress that entrepreneurial experiences have to go beyond mere contact with examples or inspirational role models (Corbett, 2005). Developing cognitive structures and processes occurs with the transference and transformation of these experiences into significant knowledge. Thus, individuals play an active role in this learning process, with the conversion of experiences into knowledge being dependent on their active engagement in the entrepreneurial learning process. Doing, feeling, living and experiencing aspects related to entrepreneurship are critical to igniting the entrepreneurial awareness of each individual. On the basis of these principles, we propose that experiential learning is an effective way of making the "thinking–doing" link in entrepreneurship education, and can contribute to the development of an expert mindset (Krueger, 2007).

Previous research has demonstrated that developing the perceptions and entrepreneurial intentions of students can be positively influenced by particular teaching methods such as experimenting with solutions to problems, learning by doing, critically reflecting on theories and engaging in real-life situations (Pittaway and Cope, 2007; Rasmussen and Sørheim, 2006). This is the underlying assumption of experiential learning which was developed based on the pioneering work of Kolb (Kolb, A. and Kolb, 2005; Kolb, D., 1984). The experiential learning theory provides a holistic model of the learning process consistent with what we know about how people learn, grow and develop (Kolb, D., 2014). And it is characterized as a holistic process of adaptation to a world that requires the resolution of conflicts and contradicting models, and which involves transactions between the individual and the environment (Kolb, D., 1984). In short, learning is "the process whereby knowledge is created through the transformation of experience" (Kolb, D., 1984, p. 38).

The experiential learning model of Kolb (Corbett, 2005, 2007; Kolb, D. 1984) describes a process whereby knowledge is created through the transformation of experience, and which integrates four learning styles or preferences based on the four-stage learning cycle (Figure 4.2): concrete experience (feeling); reflective observation (watching); abstract conceptualization (thinking); and active experimentation (doing). These four learning styles vary on the processing continuum (how we do things) and on the perception continuum (how we think about things). The processing continuum (along the horizontal axis), refers to how the learning processes are approached, and it ranges from active experimentation, involving actually doing things, to reflexive observation, which refers to watching. This processing continuum entails the two dimensions of transforming experience: transformation via extension, which means that people learn through actively testing real ideas and experiences; and transformation

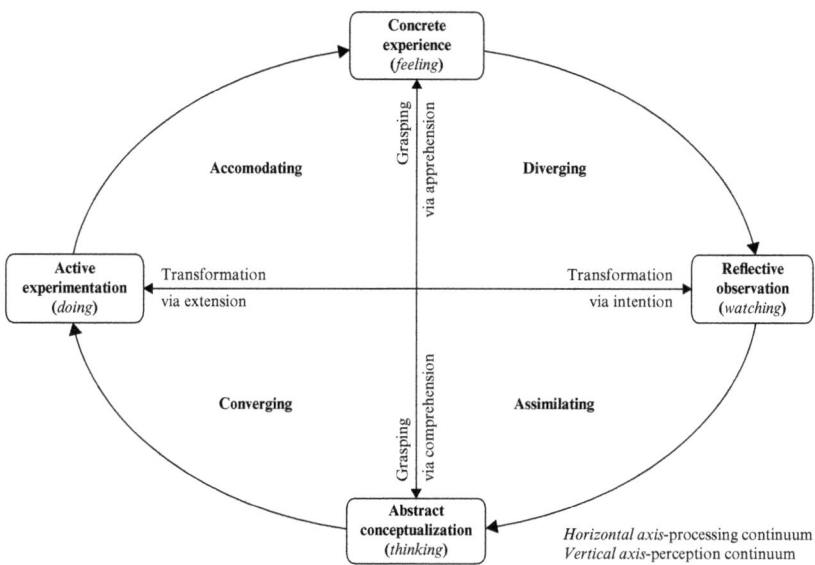

Source: Adapted from Corbett (2005).

Figure 4.2   A view of Kolb's model of experiential learning

via intention, which means that they internally reflect upon the different characteristics of their experiences and ideas. Both of the processes are relevant, and they can be used in the classroom through particular exercises that stimulate more active experimentation (doing) or reflective observation (watching). The perception continuum (the vertical axis) refers to the emotional response that individuals can adopt during their learning process. It ranges from the concrete experience, focused on the feelings involved in the situation, to the abstract conceptualization, characterized by conceptual thinking (Kolb, D., 1984). These two continuums define four quadrants that correspond to the four styles of learning: accommodating (feeling and doing), diverging (feeling and watching), converging (thinking and doing) and assimilating (thinking and watching) (Kolb, D., 1984). How individuals acquire and transform information will determine the processes in which individuals prefer to engage.

Experiential learning has been emphasized as an adequate cognitive training method (Kolb, A. and Kolb, 2009), for addressing cognitive frameworks (Fenwick, 2000), cognitive and experiential search (Gavetti and Levinthal, 2000), and acquisition of knowledge (Armstrong and Mahmud, 2008). Specifically in the entrepreneurship field, experiential learning is acknowledged to be key to learning opportunity recognition (Corbett, 2005), as all learning styles are involved in the process of opportunity recognition. Experiential learning is also described as a preeminent method for developing entrepreneurial thinking (Krueger, 2007), entrepreneurs' attitudes towards failure (Politis and Gabrielsson, 2009), and the ability to engage in real-life opportunity recognition (e.g., Pittaway and Cope, 2007).

Based on the previous findings that experiential learning is an adequate method for achieving change and transformation in cognitive structures and processes, we suggest that experiential learning is the preferable method for cognitive entrepreneurship education.

Adapting the four experiential learning styles (Kolb, D., 1984) to cognitive entrepreneurship education is a challenge that needs to be tackled. The suggested subjects of cognitive entrepreneurship education described in Table 4.1 can be taught using the four experiential learning styles depicted in Figure 4.3. Students can be trained in heuristic decision making through the use of real experiences in scenarios. This would elicit watching, and consequent active thinking, to generate decisions based on the use of different heuristics, and is an example of using assimilation (thinking and watching) for learning heuristic decision making. Entrepreneurial cognitive scripts, in particular, can be learned by converging (thinking and doing). Knowledge structures like entrepreneurial cognitive scripts require reasoning and solving problems to find solutions to practical issues and, as a cognitive

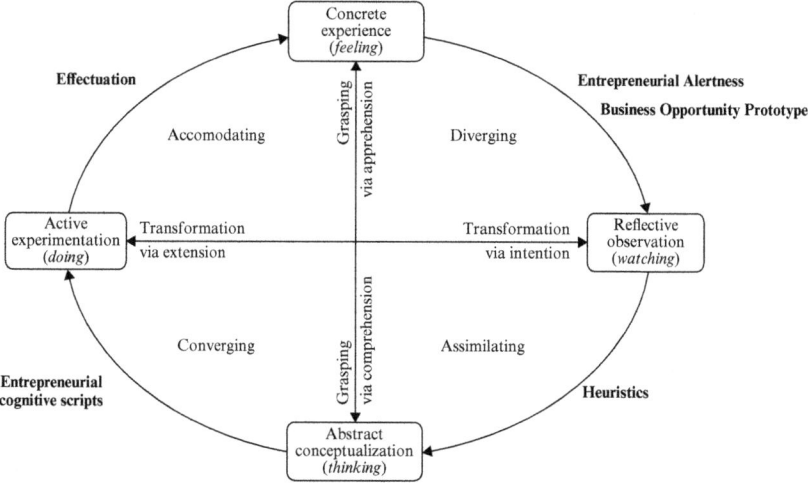

Source: Adapted from Corbett (2005).

Figure 4.3   Cognitive entrepreneurship education subjects based on Kolb's four experiential learning styles

and technical ability, scripts are less concerned with interpersonal aspects. Converging via arrangement, willingness and opportunity–ability scripts, for example, is the best learning style for subjects that require finding active experimentation and abstract conceptualization. The business opportunity prototype and entrepreneurial alertness can both be learned by a hands-on method, using the diverging style (feeling and watching). Entrepreneurial alertness entails observation, watching, tending to gather information and using imagination to solve problems. Diverging is an adequate method for viewing concrete situations from different perspectives, scanning and searching for information and making connections. Entrepreneurial alertness entails giving the students the opportunity to feel and watch different iterations based on connecting the dots between information. Using the business opportunity prototype framework as a tool to monitor and evaluate potential business opportunities can be taught by involving the students in observing the environment, looking for patterns, and feeling the pressure points and needs that they are trying to solve. Effectuation is traditionally a content that is deliverable through a hands-on approach, following a practical and highly experiential strategy, based on doing and feeling. The accommodation learning style, aligned with the principles of effectuation, requires doing with the means available, and acting based more usually on instinct rather than predictive analysis. Simulations, cases and toolbox kits are methods that elicit an accommodation learning style that calls for doing and feeling.

Besides the examples suggested above, cognitive entrepreneurship education subjects involve the four experiential learning styles and will benefit from diverging, assimilating, accommodating and converging. This is particularly relevant owing to the experiencing and living nature of entrepreneurial activities. Entrepreneurship is not delivered in a handbook; it is not based on deliberate knowledge; it is a philosophy of life, a way of thinking about the self and the world. Entrepreneurship education is about attitudes, thinking modes and behaviors, and these are the most challenging contents of education, since they require engagement in doing, experiencing and feeling the educational content. The "thinking–doing" link in cognitive entrepreneurship education demands to be addressed through the experiential learning method.

CONCLUSION

In this chapter, we proposed cognitive entrepreneurship education as a valuable framework to promoting entrepreneurship awareness among students across the university. We defined cognitive entrepreneurship education as being at the intersection of entrepreneurial cognition and entrepreneurship education, based on teaching evidence-based principles (see Goodman and O'Brien, 2012). Entrepreneurial cognition aims to understand how entrepreneurs act and think in a given situation and context (Mitchell et al., 2002b). Cognitive entrepreneurship education aims to develop the unique knowledge structures that individuals use to make assessments, judgments or decisions involving venture creation and growth. Based on a literature review, we proposed that there are five major subjects in cognitive entrepreneurship education: heuristics; entrepreneurial cognitive scripts; business opportunity prototype; entrepreneurial alertness; and effectuation.

Moreover, we contend that experiential learning is the most adequate teaching method for cognitive entrepreneurship education, as it is more effective for learning and changing knowledge structures and reasoning processes. Deep experiential learning contributes to shaping ways to perceive, transform and elaborate information, and thus is an adequate method to achieve deep cognitive change. We stressed that proper experiential learning is required to make a difference in knowledge structures and cognitive processes that establish the entrepreneurial mindset. Using the experiential learning model of D. Kolb (1984) we suggested that the five subjects of cognitive entrepreneurship education can be delivered using a specific learning style: assimilating is specifically appropriate for learning heuristics; converging is particularly appropriate for learning entrepreneurial cognitive scripts; diverging is adequate for learning business opportunity prototype and entrepreneurial alertness; and accommodating is suitable for learning effectuation. However, we also acknowledged that all four learning styles are relevant for cognitive entrepreneurship education.

Despite the fact that we advocate that entrepreneurial programs should focus less on purely theoretical content about entrepreneurship, and instead focus further on developing the entrepreneurial mindset, it is not our purpose to eliminate other perspectives and disciplines in entrepreneurship education. On the contrary, we acknowledge that entrepreneurship education should include a diverse set of approaches, methods and perspectives, and that they are not mutually exclusive. Nevertheless, we stress that entrepreneurial cognition is a key content to be included in entrepreneurship education, particularly in the early stage of education, where the aim is to call students' attention to entrepreneurship and to start changing the knowledge and cognitive structures that constitute the entrepreneurial mindset. Additionally, it is important to highlight that cognitive entrepreneurship education programs are strongly grounded in established theories and previous research findings that are translated to the classroom using the experiential learning approach, and follow evidence-based teaching principles.

Entrepreneurship education aims to develop an entrepreneurial way of thinking by raising awareness of entrepreneurship and through developing a student's entrepreneurial mindset. The entrepreneurial way of thinking involves imagination processes, critical and divergent thinking and constantly seeking opportunities for improvement. Cognitive entrepreneurship education aims to promote this entrepreneurial way of thinking and living by driving deep cognitive change. While cognitive entrepreneurship education attributes the main role in the learning process to the individual and his or her experiences, educators also have a responsibility to promote the settings where these experiences are transformed into knowledge. This is why it is so important that entrepreneurship education practices are well grounded in solid theoretical and empirical foundations, and that a connection to practice is highly stimulated at the same time. We argue that cognitive entrepreneurship education can bring these educational and learning goals together and can drive actual attitudinal, behavioral and mindset change among students.

REFERENCES

Anderson, A.R. and Jack, S.L. (2008), Role typologies for enterprising education; the professional artisan, *Journal of Small Business and Enterprise Development*, **15**(2), 259–273.

Anderson, J.R. (1980), *Cognitive Psychology and Its Implications*, San Francisco: Freeman.

Anderson, M.L. (2003), Embodied cognition: a field guide, *Artificial Intelligence*, **149**(1), 91–130.

Armstrong, S.J. and Mahmud, A. (2008), Experiential learning and the acquisition of managerial tacit knowledge, *Academy of Management Learning and Education*, **7**(2), 189–208.

Baron, R.A. (1998), Cognitive mechanisms in entrepreneurship: why and when entrepreneurs think differently than other persons, *Journal of Business Venturing*, **13**(4), 275–294.

Baron, R.A. (2004), Opportunity recognition: insights from a cognitive perspective, in J. Butler (ed.), *Opportunity Identification and Entrepreneurship Behaviour*, Greenwich, CT: Information Age Publishers, pp. 47–73.

Baron, R.A. (2006), Opportunity recognition as pattern recognition: how entrepreneurs "connect the dots" to identify new business opportunities, *Academy of Management Perspectives*, **20**(1), 104–119.

Baron, R.A. and Ensley, M.D. (2006), Opportunity recognition as the detection of meaningful patterns: evidence from comparisons of novice and experienced entrepreneurs, *Management Science*, **52**(9), 1331–1344.

Béchard, J.-P. and Grégoire, D.A. (2005), Entrepreneurship education research revisited: the case of higher education, *Academy of Management Learning and Education*, **4**(1), 22–43.

Block, J.H., Hoogerheide, L. and Thurik, R. (2011), Education and entrepreneurial choice: an instrumental variable analysis, *International Small Business Journal*, **31**(1), 23–33.

Brandstätter, H. (2011), Personality aspects of entrepreneurship: a look at five meta-analyses, *Personality and Individual Differences*, **51**(3), 222–230.

Bryant, P. (2007), Self-regulation and decision heuristics in entrepreneurial opportunity evaluation and exploitation, *Management Decision*, **45**(4), 732–748.

Busenitz, L.W. and Barney, J.B. (1997), Differences between entrepreneurs and managers in large organizations: biases and heuristics in strategic decision-making, *Journal of Business Venturing*, **12**(1), 9–30.

Cope, J. (2005), Toward a dynamic learning perspective of entrepreneurship, *Entrepreneurship Theory and Practice*, **29**, 373–397.

Corbett, A.C. (2005), Experiential learning within the process of opportunity identification and exploitation, *Entrepreneurship Theory and Practice*, **29**(4), 473–491.

Corbett, A.C. (2007), Learning asymmetries and the discovery of entrepreneurial opportunities, *Journal of Business Venturing*, **22**(1), 97–118.

Corbett, A.C. and Hmieleski, K.M. (2005), How corporate entrepreneurs think: cognition, context, and entrepreneurial scripts, in K.M. Weaver (ed.), *Academy of Management Best Paper Proceedings*, August.

Costa, S.F. (2015), Uncovering the business opportunity prototype: cognitive and learning aspects of entrepreneurial opportunity recognition in higher education,

Doctoral thesis, Instituto Universitário de Lisboa, ISCTE-IUL, retrieved from http://hdl.handle.net/10071/9020.

Costa, S.F., Ehrenhard, M.L., Caetano, A. and Santos, S.C. (2016), The role of different opportunities in the activation and use of the business opportunity prototype, *Creativity and Innovation Management*, **25**(1), 58–72.

Davies, P.T. (1999), Teaching evidence-based health care, in M.G. Dawes, P.T. Davies, A. Gray, J. Mant, K. Seers and R. Snowball, *Evidence-based Practice: A Primer for Health Professionals*, Edinburgh: Churchill Livingstone.

DeMartino, R. and Barbato, R. (2003), Differences between women and men MBA entrepreneurs: exploring family flexibility and wealth creation as career motivators, *Journal of Business Venturing*, **18**, 815–832.

Drucker, P. (1985), *Innovation and Entrepreneurship*, Oxford, UK: Butterworth-Heinemann.

Edelman, L.F., Brush, C. and Manolova, T.S. (2008), Entrepreneurship education: correspondence between practices of nascent entrepreneurs and textbook prescriptions for success, *Academy of Management Learning and Education*, **7**(1), 56–70.

Ericsson, K.A. (1990), The scientific study of expert levels of performance: general implications for optimal learning and creativity, *High Ability Studies*, **9**, 75–100.

Ericsson, K.A. (2006), The influence of experience and deliberate practice on the development of superior expert performance, in K.A. Ericsson, N. Charness, P. Feltovich and R.R. Hoffman (eds.), *The Cambridge Handbook of Expertise and Expert Performance*, Cambridge, UK: Cambridge University Press, pp. 685–706.

Fayolle, A. (2013), Personal views on the future of entrepreneurship education, *Entrepreneurship and Regional Development*, **25**(7–8), 692–701.

Fayolle, A. and Gailly, B. (2008), From craft to science: teaching models and learning processes in entrepreneurship education, *Journal of European Industrial Training*, **32**(7), 569–593.

Fayolle, A. and Gailly, B. (2015), The impact of entrepreneurship education on entrepreneurial attitudes and intention: hysteresis and persistence, *Journal of Small Business Management*, **53**, 75–93.

Fayolle, A., Gailly, B. and Lassas-Clerc, N. (2006), Assessing the impact of entrepreneurship education programmes: a new methodology, *Journal of European Industrial Training*, **30**(9), 701–720.

Fenwick, T.J. (2000), Expanding conceptions of experiential learning: a review of the five contemporary perspectives on cognition, *Adult Education Quarterly*, **50**(4), 243–272.

Forbes, D.P. (2005), Are some entrepreneurs more overconfident than others? *Journal of Business Venturing*, **20**(5), 623–640.

Frese, M., Rousseau, D.M. and Wiklund, J. (2014), The emergence of evidence-based entrepreneurship, *Entrepreneurship Theory and Practice*, **38**(2), 209–216.

Gaglio, C.M. and Katz, J.A. (2001), The psychological basis of opportunity identification: entrepreneurial alertness, *Small Business Economics*, **16**(2), 95–111.

Gaglio, C.M. and Winter, S. (2009), Entrepreneurial alertness and opportunity identification: where are we now?, in A.L. Carsrud and M. Brännback (eds.), *Understanding the Entrepreneurial Mind: Opening the Black Box*, New York: Springer, pp. 305–325.

Gartner, W.B. (1989), "Who is an entrepreneur?" is the wrong question, *Entrepreneurship Theory and Practice*, **13**(4), 47–68.

Gavetti, G. and Levinthal, D. (2000), Looking forward and looking backward:

cognitive and experiential search, *Administrative Science Quarterly*, **45**(1), 113–137.

Gielnik, M.M., Krämer, A.-C., Kappel, B. and Frese, M. (2014), Antecedents of business opportunity identification and innovation: investigating the interplay of information processing and information acquisition, *Applied Psychology: An International Review*, **63**(2), 344–381.

Gigerenzer, G. and Gaissmaier, W. (2011), Heuristic decision making, *Annual Review of Psychology*, **62**, 451–482.

Gilovich, T., Griffin, D. and Kahneman, D. (2002), *Heuristics and Biases: The Psychology of Intuitive Judgement*, Cambridge, UK: Cambridge University Press.

Glaser, R. (1984), Education and thinking: the role of knowledge, *American Psychologist*, **39**(2), 93–104.

Goodman, J.S. and O'Brien, J. (2012), Teaching and learning using evidence-based principles, in D.M. Rousseau (ed.), *Oxford Handbook of Evidence-based Management*, Oxford, UK: Oxford University Press, pp. 309–336.

Grégoire, D.A., Barr, P.S. and Shepherd, D.A. (2010a), Cognitive processes of opportunity recognition, *Organization Science*, **21**(2), 413–431.

Grégoire, D.A., Shepherd, D.A. and Lambert, L.S. (2010b), Measuring opportunity recognition beliefs, *Organizational Research Methods*, **13**(1), 114–145.

Jack, S.L. and Anderson, A.R. (1999), Entrepreneurship education within the enterprise culture: producing reflective practitioners, *International Journal of Entrepreneurial Behaviour and Research*, **5**(3), 110–125.

Kirzner, I.M. (1973), *Competition and Entrepreneurship*, Chicago, IL: University of Chicago Press.

Kolb, A.Y. and Kolb, D.A. (2005), Learning styles and learning spaces: enhancing experiential learning in higher education, *Academy of Management Learning and Education*, **4**(2), 193–212.

Kolb, A. and Kolb, D.A. (2009), The learning way: meta-cognitive aspects of experiential learning, *Simulation Gaming*, **40**, 297–327.

Kolb, D.A. (1984), *Experiential Learning: Experience as the Source of Learning and Development*, Englewood Cliffs, NJ: Prentice Hall.

Kolb, D.A. (2014), *Experiential Learning: Experience as the Source of Learning and Development*, Upper Saddle River, NJ: Pearson Education.

Krueger, N. F. (2007), What lies beneath? The experiential essence of entrepreneurial thinking, *Entrepreneurship Theory and Practice*, **31**(1), 123–138.

Kuratko, D.F. and Morris, M.H. (forthcoming), If entrepreneurship is now everywhere then what is its future trajectory? *Journal of Small Business Management*.

Kuratko, D.F. (2005), The emergence of entrepreneurship education: development, trends, and challenges, *Entrepreneurship Theory and Practice*, **29**(5), 577–598.

Kyrö, P. (2008), A theoretical framework for teaching and learning entrepreneurship, *International Journal of Business and Globalisation*, **2**(1), 39–55.

Landström, H. and Benner, M. (2010), Entrepreneurship research: a history of scholarly migration, in H. Landström and F. Lohrke (eds.), *Historical Foundations of Entrepreneurship Research*, Cheltenham, UK and Northampton, MA, USA: Edward Elgar, pp. 15–45.

Lüthje, C. and Franke, N. (2003), The "making" of an entrepreneur: testing a model of entrepreneurial intent among engineering students at MIT, *R&D Management*, **33**, 135–147.

Manimala, M.J. (1992), Entrepreneurial innovation: beyond Schumpeter, *Creativity and Innovation Management*, **1**, 46–55.

Mitchell, R.K. (2005), Tuning up the global value creation engine: the road to excellence in international entrepreneurship education, in Dean A. Shepherd and Jerome A. Katz (eds.), *International Entrepreneurship*, Advances in Entrepreneurship, Firm Emergence and Growth, Vol. 8, Bingley, UK: Emerald Group Publishing, pp. 185–248.

Mitchell, R.K., Smith, J.B., Seawright, K.W. and Morse, E.A. (2000), Cross-cultural cognitions and the venture creation decision, *Academy of Management Journal*, **43**(5), 974–993.

Mitchell, R.K., Busenitz, L., Lant, T., McDougall, P.P., Morse, E.A. and Smith, J.B. (2002a), Entrepreneurial cognition theory: rethinking the people side of entrepreneurship research, *Entrepreneurship Theory and Practice*, **27**(2), Winter, 93–104.

Mitchell, R.K., Smith, J.B., Morse, E.A., Seawright, K.K., Peredo, A.M. and McKenzie, B. (2002b), Are entrepreneurial cognitions universal? Assessing entrepreneurial cognitions across cultures, *Entrepreneurship Theory and Practice*, **26**(4), 9–32.

Mitchell, R.K., Busenitz, L.W., Bird, B., Marie Gaglio, C., McMullen, J.S., Morse, E.A. and Smith, J.B. (2007), The central question in entrepreneurial cognition research 2007, *Entrepreneurship Theory and Practice*, **31**, 1–27.

Mitchell, R.K., Mitchell, B.T. and Mitchell, J.R. (2009), Entrepreneurial scripts and entrepreneurial expertise: the information processing perspective, in A.L. Carsrud and M. Brännback (eds.), *Understanding the Entrepreneurial Mind: Opening the Black Box*, New York: Springer, pp. 97–140.

Morris, M.H., Kuratko, D.F., Schindehutte, M. and Spivack, A.J. (2012), Framing the entrepreneurial experience, *Entrepreneurship Theory and Practice*, **36**, 11–40.

Morris, M.H., Webb, J.W., Fu, J. and Singhal, S. (2013), A competency-based perspective on entrepreneurship education: conceptual and empirical insights, *Journal of Small Business Management*, **51**, 352–369.

Neck, H.M. and Greene, P.G. (2011), Entrepreneurship education: known worlds and new frontiers, *Journal of Small Business Management*, **49**(1), 55–70.

Neck, H.M., Greene, P.G. and Brush, C.G. (2015), *Teaching Entrepreneurship: A Practice-based Approach*, Cheltenham, UK and Northampton, MA, USA: Edward Elgar.

Palich, L.E. and Bagby, D.R. (1995), Using cognitive theory to explain entrepreneurial risk-taking: challenging conventional wisdom, *Journal of Business Venturing*, **10**(6), 425–438.

Pittaway, L. and Cope, J. (2007), Entrepreneurship education: a systematic review of the evidence, *International Small Business Journal*, **25**(5), 479–510.

Politis, D. (2005), The process of entrepreneurial learning: a conceptual framework, *Entrepreneurship Theory and Practice*, **29**(4), 399–424.

Politis, D. and Gabrielsson, J. (2009), Entrepreneurs' attitudes towards failure: an experiential learning approach, *International Journal of Entrepreneurial Behavior and Research*, **15**(4), 364–383.

Rasmussen, E.A. and Sørheim, R. (2006), Action-based entrepreneurship education, *Technovation*, **26**(2), 185–194.

Santos, S.C., Caetano, A., Baron, R.A. and Curral, L. (2015), Prototype models of opportunity recognition and the decision to launch a new venture: identifying the basic dimensions, *International Journal of Entrepreneurial Behaviour and Research*, **21**(4), 510–538.

Sarasvathy, S. (2001), Causation and effectuation: toward a theoretical shift from economic inevitability to entrepreneurial contingency, *Academy of Management Review*, **26**(2), 243–263.

Sarasvathy, S.D. (2008), *Effectuation: Elements of Entrepreneurial Expertise*, New Horizons in Entrepreneurship Research, Cheltenham, UK and Northampton, MA, USA: Edward Elgar.

Seawright, K.W., Smith, I., Mitchell, R.K. and McClendon, R.J. (2013), Exploring entrepreneurial cognition in franchisees: a knowledge-structure approach, *Entrepreneurship Theory and Practice*, **37**, 201–227 (Pre-publication version 2011).

Shepherd, D.A. (2004), Educating entrepreneurship students about emotion and learning from failure, *Academy of Management Learning and Education*, **3**(3), 274–287.

Simon, M., Houghton, S.M. and Aquino, K. (2000), Cognitive biases, risk perception, and venture formation: how individuals decide to start companies, *Journal of Business Venturing*, **15**(2), 113–134.

Tang, J., Kacmar, M. and Busenitz, L. (2012), Alertness in the pursuit of new opportunities, *Journal of Business Venturing*, **27**(1), 77–94.

Tversky, A. and Kahneman, D. (1973), Availability: a heuristic for judging frequency and probability, *Cognitive Psychology*, **5**(2), 207–232.

Tversky, A. and Kahneman, D. (1974), Judgment under uncertainty: heuristics and biases, *Science*, **185**, 1124–1130.

Venkataraman, S., Sarasvathy, S.D., Dew, N. and Forster, W.R. (2012), Reflections on the 2010 AMR decade award: Whither the promise? Moving forward with entrepreneurship as a science of the artificial, *Academy of Management Review*, **37**(1), 21–33.

Wang, C.K. and Wong, P.K. (2004), Entrepreneurial interest of university students, *Technovation*, **24**, 163–172.

5. Weighing in: reflections on a steady diet of Lean Startup

Elissa Grossman

When entrepreneurship educators today refer to "Lean Startup," they are often describing a real-world, customer-centric approach to early concept development and innovation that 1) begins with a search for product–market fit; 2) progresses through cycles of hypothesis testing across the various building blocks of a potential business model; and 3) reaches a provisional "end of the beginning" with a launched startup poised for rapid growth. As deployed in a classroom, Lean Startup describes a set of teachable tools and methods that can, instructors tell their students, help adapt and validate new business concepts, reducing risk and minimizing the chances of failure. As described by its progenitors, Lean Startup represents a "movement" that has allowed founders, corporate innovators and even those in more traditional corporate roles to become more flexible, more agile and more successful.

That Lean Startup represents some sort of movement, here defined as something much more than just a portfolio of techniques for researching and advancing business concepts, seems clear. The language of lean (e.g., pivots, minimum viable products or MVPs, customer discovery, traction) has become integrally linked not solely to the vacuous flash and dazzle of so-called "Startup Culture," but also to the more serious discussions held in VC conference rooms, angel meetings, Fortune 500 hallways and Lean Startup conferences. The books of Lean Startup have sold in the hundreds of thousands (if not millions). At this author's most recent count, Lean Startup Meetups numbered more than 3300, and Lean Startup Circle groups had started in 94 cities across 17 countries around the world. A Lean Startup curriculum is used within the National Science Foundation's Innovation Corps (or iCorps), a program that has directed many millions of dollars into regional, university-based nodes and, indirectly, into hundreds of university-based teams working to commercialize inventions. Indeed, most top-ranked schools now use the lexicon and specific component parts of the approach in teaching at least a subset of their classes, in supporting a variety of co-curricular activities, and in marketing their entrepreneurship programs.

In the past five years, however, as Lean Startup has grown explosively, there has been very little in the way of accompanying research – about its unique points of difference relative to the tools and techniques taught prior to its emergence, about its perceived versus real utility in launching new ventures, about its generalizability beyond the software-focused firms for which it was first proposed, and about its effectiveness within startup versus established companies. It is the goal of this chapter to consider what we know and what we do not know across each of these areas – to ask some perhaps tough questions, to provide some speculative answers or observations, and to propose a research agenda that might allow us to better understand Lean Startup's contributions in an academic context. Importantly, it is *not* the goal of this chapter to "take down" Lean Startup. It is clear that the approach is philosophically and practically aligned with much of what entrepreneurs and entrepreneurship educators do and have done – and that it has provided an immense number of people a clear process and a shared lexicon for describing, planning, researching and evolving new venture concepts. That said, with so little truly known about such a pervasive phenomenon, there is good reason to view it with a little caution, and to begin understanding how and where its concepts fit into the larger set of tools, methods, perspectives and theories, long-lived and new, that populate a truly comprehensive educational portfolio.

In its current iteration, Lean Startup describes an approach that merges three key components: 1) the Customer Development process, introduced by Steve Blank in the 2001 book *The Four Steps to the Epiphany*; 2) the Lean Startup label, introduced by Eric Ries in a 2008 blog post with that phrase in its title; and 3) the Business Model Canvas, introduced by Alexander Osterwalder and Yves Pigneur in their book *Business Model Generation* (2010), elaborating and amending work completed by Osterwalder in his 2004 dissertation.[1] It is perhaps unsurprising that Lean Startup merged with Customer Development: Ries was a student in Blank's first course on the latter, at UC Berkeley, subsequently becoming a recurrent guest speaker in Blank's classes. It was during one of those visiting sessions, within a joint Berkeley–Columbia executive MBA program, that the two discussed how lean or agile development techniques might be paired with customer development techniques for effective startup use. Thereafter (one day later, to be more exact), Ries introduced, via his blog, the term "lean startup." Broadscale embrace and momentum, however, required, as Ries has noted, an organizing "front-end" framework; that emerged with the publication of Osterwalder and Pigneur's book (2010).

A comprehensive understanding of the aggregate Lean Startup approach arguably requires, first, some disaggregation – as the contribution of each component is aligned, but different. The remainder of this chapter is thus structured to describe and consider the Customer Development process, Lean Startup nomenclature, and Business Model Canvas individually, with an eye to understanding them collectively. The chapter will conclude with some suggestions for further research and discussion.

THE CUSTOMER DEVELOPMENT PROCESS

In Steve Blank's book *The Four Steps to the Epiphany* (2001), he first introduced a four-stage startup process that he labeled Customer Development. He described this process as involving: 1) Customer Discovery (when entrepreneurs seek to confirm, through hypothesis testing, that they have identified a valuable and hence saleable solution to a problem shared by a clearly defined target customer); 2) Customer Validation (when entrepreneurs scaffold their early findings with additional research to support construction of a viable business model); 3) Customer Creation (when entrepreneurs convert prospective customers into real customers); and 4) Company Building (when entrepreneurs spend more of their time on execution than on "learning and discovery," and begin to establish more formal business systems). Of the stages, Customer Discovery and Customer Validation arguably secured the most attention, by virtue of their focus on crafting falsifiable hypotheses, testing those hypotheses, and then allowing results to shape subsequent steps forwards or backwards. Blank's process was thus iterative rather than inherently linear, involving pre-launch experimentation, learning and adaptation.

Blank described Customer Development as "the path that is hidden in plain sight" (2001, p. 1), suggesting that startup success followed those who walked the path and startup failure followed those who did not. More specifically, he emphasized that Customer Development represented a previously invisible but essential process run in tandem with the traditional Product Development process – the latter of which he described as a relentlessly linear "waterfall" model in which product specifications are first developed, then built, and finally sold (successfully or unsuccessfully). In his view, Product Development was flawed in that it limited or prevented customer input at the earliest stages, when such input was most critical. He thus positioned Customer Development and Product Development as "siblings," giving the former favored child status.

From the very first page of his book, however, even before he began to describe Customer Development, Blank made a strong claim – that, while the details of each startup's journey might vary considerably, the "outline" of each journey was the same. He espoused the view that others can circumvent much of the risk traditionally associated with a startup by recognizing and embracing this similarity as providing a more assured path to success:

> Most entrepreneurs travel down the startup path without a roadmap and believe no model or template could apply to their new venture. They are wrong. For the path of a startup is well worn and well understood . . . [T]here is a true and repeatable path to success, a path that eliminates or mitigates the most egregious risks and allows the company to grow into a large, successful enterprise.

In essence, Blank overturned the conventional wisdom of entrepreneurship as individualistic and idiosyncratic by placing that variation into a larger, formula-driven context. Where Santayana observed that "[t]hose who cannot remember the past are condemned to repeat it," Blank offered a twist: those who remember the past can flourish by repeating it. He addressed this point directly and immediately, noting that *all* successful startups have *invented* the process he describes, "through trial and error, hiring and firing . . . [E]ach and every startup that succeeds recapitulates it, knowingly or not" (Blank, 2001, p. 1). It is not the purpose of this chapter to question the veracity of this claim; while not definitively provable, it seems likely to be true. All new organizations grow by trial and error, and all organizations hire and fire. It is difficult to imagine a startup that would grow in any other way.

What's also true, however, is the fact that, in parallel with characterizing startups as "inventing" the process, Blank claimed he was offering a first-of-its-kind, formalized articulation of that process. He noted: "the path of a startup is well worn and well understood. The secret is that no one has written it down" (2001, p. 1). Almost a decade later, he and co-author Bob Dorf, in a subsequent book, echoed and amplified this claim, describing the approach as providing "the first management tools specifically for startups" (2012). Objectively, these statements are inaccurate. Abundant work in the more than three decades of entrepreneurship education and research pre-dating Blank's introduction of Customer Development covered similar ground. Therein lies an initial critique: that Blank's examination of the past was (and remains) selective, encompassing startups, but excluding (knowingly or otherwise) prior research and instruction about or relevant to startups.

A cursory review of the work published prior to Blank's *Epiphany* reveals an extant literature replete with similar exhortations to research new business concepts and affirm the reality of opportunities prior to crafting a business plan or launching a business. Van Slyke and Stevenson (1985), for example, reminded readers that a business plan's underlying "thoughts and assumptions" were often more critical than the plan itself, as a plan tends to detail a "situation at a moment in time" (p. 1); quality, they emphasized, was driven by early ("pre-start") research and analysis across an array of business components, including, notably, customers. They addressed this latter directly, observing: "[T]he creation of real value depends on our ability to offer products and services that satisfy some real need among the customers" (p. 6). That same year, in a published discussion of new venture planning, Block and MacMillan (1985) observed a sequential but iterative process whose first step (or "milestone") was "Completion of Concept and Product Testing." This pairing of concept and product was very much like Blank's reference to sibling customer and product development processes, with concept testing framed in terms of customer interviews. In describing the emergence of a word processing venture in the 1970s, for example, the authors observed that interview-based prospective user research was initiated "long before starting [product] development work" (p. 179).

Others to characterize new venture emergence as involving a clear process were Hamel and Prahalad (1990). Though their units of study were existing organizations, their research involved the pursuit of new opportunities in potentially new markets; their focus was therefore clearly entrepreneurial in nature. They opened by expressing their data-driven belief in a "logical process through which companies unleash corporate imagination" (p. 83), subsequently elaborating on the need to "escape the tyranny of the served market" (a corporate construct that can be readily re-conceptualized in new venture terms as consistent with a flexible search for product–market fit). They also emphasized the importance of "getting out in front of customers" (i.e., of asking and listening, in lieu of deploying traditional market research techniques) – an instruction much like an oft-repeated Customer Development refrain to "get out of the building." Still others to publish work focused on some aspect of early analysis, customer-prioritized research, and/or experimentation and testing. These included McGrath and MacMillan (1995) on "discovery-driven planning" and Sull (2002) on "a strategy to meet the challenges of entrepreneurship."

It seems clear that much of the path Blank described as "hidden in plain sight" was not truly hidden. That said, the path also wasn't in plain sight. Though the discussed papers were printed in the *Harvard Business Review* and similar outlets, their reach was limited by the technology, the trends, and the nature of entrepreneurship education at the time: no internet, no dotcom boom and bust, no Google or Facebook, no social media, no "Shark Tank" feeding frenzy, and countless business school courses focused exclusively on business plan development. Indeed, the phrase "business model" was largely a product of the dotcom era – growing in prevalence during and thereafter, but not (or almost never) before. A student might, for example, take an entrepreneurship course in a business school and be asked to consider the topics addressed within the discussed works, but that student might not be asked to pursue a project with substantive real-world components. Further, it seems likely that few non-students were looking at the early publications for guidance, particularly if they were aspiring entrepreneurs; *HBR* and its ilk were targeted at, for the most part, those in more established and traditional companies. In fact, one explanation for the current enthusiasm about Blank's approach could be the "right time, right place, available channels" story. But that feels simplistic. A more comprehensive argument for the success of Customer Development seems essential.

While Blank's generalized approach is not new, there are features of the Customer Development process that do differ from that which was described by his predecessors. First, as its name suggests, the process puts customers on a pedestal, under a spotlight, in a way that others did not. While others acknowledged customers as critical, they typically did so within a very long list of other topics meriting early attention (e.g., financial resources, revenue model, product feasibility, management team); even when they referenced customers as the first point of contact in a thoughtful pre-start review, their consideration of the topic was often limited and brief. Second, in part because he focused almost exclusively on customers in the early stages, Blank offered greater clarity (and practical instruction) than predecessors regarding how customer data might be aggregated and used, with particular emphasis placed on the notion that early business concepts not only could change, but should change; his work emphasized the centrality of the "pivots" necessary for achieving product–market fit. Though others framed their research as guiding changes, most placed comparatively less emphasis on change than on sourcing data to populate a business plan. Third, Blank's approach was about taking immediate action, outside of the classroom environment, to beget effective decisions and new venture success. Despite the fact that others emphasized similar research to support decision-making and next steps, their discussion was often placed into a more passive, academic context, using more traditional research techniques (e.g., survey research, as prioritized over long interviews). In aggregate, Blank's laser-like focus on customers, plus the approach's inherent action-orientation, might also have helped drive adoption. The Customer Development process clearly addresses the question "Where do I start?"

At some level, as much time as has just been dedicated to proving that Blank's approach may not be entirely new, that fact feels irrelevant in the context of its popular embrace and perceived utility. What seems relevant is whether or not Blank's approach is truly effective. Is perceived utility also real utility? It could be argued (and has been argued) that the wide-scale adoption of Customer Development is a proxy for effectiveness;

anecdotally, various successful ventures now claim to have deployed Customer Development techniques, in whole or in full, when starting, to affirm its value (e.g., Dropbox). But therein lies a set of additional questions. Isn't it likely that an untold number of failed startups also followed the outline that Blank provides? Taking it one step further, might it be the case that, if all successes followed this process, all failures did too? There is also a broader question: how does one separate process from product? In other words, to what extent has the underlying quality of each successful company's founding team or even initial business concept driven success, rather than application of the approach itself? The challenge in answering these questions is clear: the data have not been aggregated, crunched, and made available publicly. We simply cannot know – yet – if the proposed approach is truly as effective as claimed. That is the critical next step.

THE LEAN STARTUP, NOW THE *"LEAN STARTUP"*

The "Lean Startup" label was introduced by Eric Ries in a 2008 blog post (aptly titled "The lean startup," 2008b), and popularized thereafter by publication of a 2011 book (with the same name) (Ries, 2011a). An experienced software engineer who had co-founded multiple software companies, some failed and some successful, Ries described the label quite specifically, as capturing his views on the most effective means of identifying and developing new, software startups. He emphasized that the use of "lean" was meant to 1) convey the centrality of "low-burn" methods in new venturing (i.e., techniques designed to "reduce waste" in expended startup development money and development time), and 2) pay homage to existing work on "Lean Thinking" and "Lean Software Development." Within his inaugural public post on the topic, Ries observed that his phraseology and perspective reflected ongoing trends in software development – encompassing the use of: 1) open source, free platforms; 2) agile development methods; and 3) "ferocious customer-centric iteration." That the last two of these three trends sounded much like Steve Blank's Customer Development approach was intentional; that's what Ries was indirectly describing. Arguably, in fact, the first of the cited trends also reflected Blank's Customer Development approach. Open source, free platforms represented a central mechanism by which to build a testable software product with a "minimum feature set" (what Ries and Blank later began to call the "Minimum Viable Product" or MVP) and deliver on the Lean Startup's waste reduction promise (i.e., increasing production speed and lowering production cost).

Though Ries did not directly blog about Customer Development in his first post on Lean Startup, he had mentioned it the day earlier – noting that Blank and he had, a day prior to that, in Blank's Berkeley–Columbia class, first "tried to do an overview of a software engineering methodology that integrates practices from agile software development with Steve's method of Customer Development" (Ries, 2008a). While this phrasing suggests that Lean Startup was an effort to add dimension to Blank's extant Customer Development work, it is not clear that "agile development" was in fact a new companion piece. Within even the first chapter of *The Four Steps to the Epiphany*, published seven years earlier, Blank had cast his approach as entirely aligned with "agile development" – even while not using the term itself. From the outset, his work had repeatedly referenced the inadequacy of "waterfall" product development processes, and the attendant need for very early stage, incremental and repeated iteration. Arguably, thus, Ries and Blank's "first" overview of a methodology described as coupling agile development to Customer Development was not truly new; it was a re-positioning that 1) acknowledged the existing prevalence and pervasive use of agile development (whose core concepts emerged as early as 1970, in the work of Winston Royce), while 2) more clearly defining Customer Development as unique and differentiated from more traditional approaches, as based in part on 3) a more definitive consideration of the MVP (a term used first not by Ries or Blank, but by its trademark owner, Frank Robinson, in 2003; Furr and Dyer, 2014). In other words, Lean Startup could be viewed, at a fundamental level, even from the term's first published use, as a re-launch of Steve Blank's early work. Whether intentional or not, it represented a branding effort, and an immensely successful one at that; it allowed Customer Development (and the MVP) to become the star of the show.

Initially, Ries seemed circumspect about Lean Startup's generalizability. He noted that the first presentation on the topic (then called "Customer Development Engineering") motivated questions about the methodology's utility beyond software startups (Ries, 2008b), and also acknowledged that he had not run a business with a hardware component. He offered, however, what he felt might be an indicator of the approach's broader relevance: automotive manufacturing. If cars can be made using similar techniques, he conjectured, so too might those techniques "add agility and flexibility to any product development process." As sound as that argument might appear (i.e., car production clearly benefited from lean techniques), Ries was describing "lean manufacturing" – a process encompassing agile development, but not Customer Development. Though Ries has since referenced the importance of early internal customer or "user" stories as inputs to agile development, he and Blank have always positioned Customer Development as inherently distinct. His speculation thus did not obviously include what made his (and Blank's) proposed approach feel different – the fact that agile techniques were being coupled to early and frequent customer interaction, with the intent of reducing waste and maximizing success. (To be fair, this speculation was not unreasonable; it was offered in the context of the Lean Startup label's first, brief public appearance, and Ries had no reason to believe that a blog post might become a global business movement or be subjected, years later, to deeper analysis.)

Since its first mention, the Lean Startup story has changed dramatically – not in terms of its directive or prescriptive content, but in terms of both its described benefits and its claimed applicability. Customer Development was reframed as one part of a larger Build–Measure–Learn loop, a shift that allowed additional attention to be paid to the types of "actionable" metrics that might help guide rapid product and business iteration. Further, Ries (2011b) determined that reduced costs did not represent a focal benefit of Lean Startup ("The . . . method is not about cost, it is about speed"). Of course, too, the blog post attracted a following, which motivated a best-seller that garnered devotees and top spots on many business book lists. Today, the utility of Lean Startup is suggested indirectly by its extensive sales, but also, explicitly, by the many high-profile individuals who have provided book jacket and other endorsements; that a subset of these testimonials come from leaders of large, established companies (e.g., General Electric) reveals the extent to which the book has been embraced as offering relevant guidance beyond the realm of its early focus (i.e., the software startup). As Ries noted recently, in his foreword to one in a series of Lean Startup books authored by others,

> A startup includes any human enterprise designed to create a new product or service under conditions of extreme uncertainty, and an entrepreneur is anyone tasked with ushering in that change. Whether they're building a company in their garage, working for a VC-backed startup, or trying to drive innovation at an enterprise or nonprofit, what all entrepreneurs share is the need for a process that converts the raw materials of innovation into real-world success. (Alvarez, 2014)

Though Ries's use of words was here quite general (i.e., referencing *a* process, rather than *the* Lean Startup process in particular), his intent was clearly to reinforce the power of Lean Startup. And the implication is quite grand – namely, that Lean Startup is an approach that can help in a multitude of business environments; the qualifying criterion for utility is no longer the new software venture, but the dual criteria of newness (for almost any product or service, in almost any organizational context) and *extreme* [my emphasis] uncertainty. It is not clear how the leap from

software to everything was made, but the leap has clearly happened nonetheless. Ries has noted in his talks, to give a further example, that Lean
Startup has "nothing to do with size of company, sector of the economy,
or industry" (e.g., Ries, 2011b). Those sorts of claims raise questions. For
example, how might "extreme" be defined or operationalized? Given that
almost all ventures face uncertainty (including, notably, uncertainty about
what customers want), what is the minimum threshold at which a venture
is "extreme" enough to warrant the use of Lean Startup techniques? (And
why are these techniques *not* useful in less extreme environments?) More
broadly, how do those within established organizations suddenly learn to
be lean and act on lean principles? Perhaps most importantly, on what
basis, using more than anecdotal data, might the much more comprehensive statement of Lean Startup's utility be proven? In fact, even if Lean
Startup techniques are more narrowly re-focused on just those ventures in
the "startup space," what data exist to confirm generalizability encompassing all or moving beyond software? (As earlier, these latter questions are
not meant to suggest that generalizability can't be proven; they are meant
only to suggest that broad utility has not yet been proven. They also imply
that a claim of partial or customized utility might improve the precision or
accuracy of the current claims.)

When entrepreneurship educators teach about new venture initiation,
they rarely limit their instruction to just the software startups that Ries
was first describing (and that are the focus, so often, of public fascina-
tion and venture capitalist interest). They teach about all businesses – in
part because high-growth startups represent only about 2 percent of the
total number of businesses out there (U.S. Bureau of Labor Statistics,
2013), and in part because most students, no matter how interested in
entrepreneurship they might be, will spend at least some of their earliest
post-graduate years working in more traditional organizations. An estimated 33 percent of all new entrepreneurs have college degrees, but only a
fraction of them founded a startup straight out of college – as seen in the
fact that, of all new founders in 2014, just 24.7 percent were aged 20–34
(Fairlie et al., 2015). In an environment where it is known that only a very
small number of students will become immediate entrepreneurs, educators
define outcomes in terms of more than just startup numbers; they seek
to 1) provide entrepreneurial tools and develop entrepreneurial skills that
will be useful across an array of organizations, at different points in those
organizations' life cycles, and 2) instill an entrepreneurial mindset (i.e., the
ability to value and enact individual flexibility, adaptability and decision-
making under conditions of uncertainty). Most would likely agree that the
principles of Lean Startup seem entirely (and perhaps even powerfully)
consistent with the educational goal of developing an entrepreneurial

mindset. It is not clear, however, that the *techniques* of Lean Startup are equivalently consistent.

At the heart of Lean Startup's guidance to exploring product–market fit (i.e., at the heart of early stage Customer Development and the Build–Measure–Learn loop) is the MVP – as coupled to quantifiable, "action metrics" (i.e., measures that provide direct insight to shape decision-making). Ries (2009) defines the MVP as "that version of a new product which allows a team to collect the maximum amount of validated learning about customers, with the least effort." In a software context, an MVP seems comparatively easy to build (and test) – assuming one can find a talented coder. The same might be said in a hardware context, or in the case of a tangible consumer product. But ... what is an MVP if your desired product or service is a restaurant? How does one stress-test, for rapid progression, an entire menu, a diner experience, or a combination of the two? Alternatively, what does it mean for a new event-planning firm? Given the inherent variability of customer demands in an event context, what can be tested as an MVP – beyond the generalized concept, branding, and customer–client processes of the proposed venture? Even further, what constitutes "validated" learning in these sorts of scenarios, when tangible MVPs are unavailable? Yes, an aspiring chef or restaurateur can try a pop-up evening or an at-home taste testing. A future wedding planner can get a first client, to see how the experience works out. But both of these feel like poor proxies for the sort of MVP described by the Lean Startup.

To address the sorts of critiques that point out the difficulty in building a tangible MVP, it has been suggested that entrepreneurs focus on various experiments (e.g. "smoke tests") that involve basic websites, sample Google AdWord campaigns and the like. But those, too, are weak proxies for MVPs. Though minimal and viable, they are not products (or services); they are conceptual representations that allow for some testing, but are rarely meaningful enough to provide the same sort of robust customer learning available through the mechanisms associated with something *real*. If the MVP is the primary tool by which experimentation (or Customer Discovery and Validation) can be deployed, it remains unclear how those unable to build a meaningful MVP can adopt the approach. How are MVPs useful to those pursuing lifestyle ventures or international social enterprises, for example? How is an MVP useful to the roughly 20 percent of entrepreneurs who start up from necessity and not by virtue of choice, inspiration or positive opportunity? If Lean Startup is to be truly useful in these contexts, its progenitors and proponents arguably need to do more than just pay lip service to their claims of generalizability. There is a need for the discussion to clarify how the most unique aspects of Lean Startup contribute new dimensions to these other types of businesses – beyond the value already contributed by existing agile development and market research techniques.

THE BUSINESS MODEL CANVAS

It seems doubtful that Alexander Osterwalder and Yves Pigneur were paying close attention to Steve Blank and Eric Ries when writing *Business Model Generation* (2010). The book makes no reference to Blank or Ries, and does not include the lexicon of Customer Development or Lean Startup (never using, for example, the words "pivot," "customer discovery," "minimum viable product," or "hypothesis"). And yet, today, the Business Model Canvas introduced within that book has become the most visible tool in the Lean Startup kit – the template most often used in entrepreneurship classrooms (and elsewhere) to support hypothesis identification and experiment design for the purpose of launching new products or services. Blank has acknowledged (2013) that the Business Model Canvas "provided . . . a much-needed front end to organize all of a startup's hypotheses into a simple framework that serves as a baseline and a scorecard for teams as they move through Customer Development" (p. ix). It might be argued, similarly, that Customer Development and Lean Startup provided the Business Model Canvas a much-needed back end, helping to clarify the Canvas's utility as more than just a largely blank form into which new venture descriptions could be placed (i.e., the core principles of Blank and Ries's work helped provide a more robust foundation upon which to take Osterwalder and Pigneur's Canvas beyond the Business Model and into Generation).

Even before *Business Model Generation* was published, others had 1) critiqued "business model" as a managerial construct discussed frequently and imprecisely, and 2) made associated efforts to provide it a useful definition. Though the term itself seems to have first appeared in academic publications as early as 1957, its usage was then quite different than it is today; only in the 1990s and thereafter has the phrase, as it is currently used, emerged as a part of academic and popular discourse (DaSilva and Trkman, 2013). Just five published papers in total included the phrase before 1990 (Osterwalder et al., 2005). By 2000, at least 20 papers – each year – included the phrase (in the title alone); by 2010, that titular annual number had reached about 90 (DaSilva and Trkman, 2013). Over those same years, a shared view seemed to emerge around the basic notions that business models were important and often composed of more than one component part. Hamermesh et al. (2002), defined it, for example, "as *a summation of the core business decisions and trade-offs employed by a company to earn a profit*," as organized across the four categories of: 1) revenue sources; 2) key expenses; 3) investment size; and 4) critical success factors (p. 1). Later that same year, in a well-received explanation of "Why Business Models Matter," Magretta (2002) described business models as stories that identify: 1) the customer; 2) what that customer values; and 3) how the business will profitably deliver that value. Eisenmann (2011) has described business models as composed of four slightly different (and broader) categories: 1) customer value proposition; 2) technology and operations management; 3) go-to-market plan; and 4) profit formula. His and the others' categories are all encompassed within the model of Osterwalder and Pigneur (minus the specificity of Hamermesh et al.'s "investment size").

According to *Business Model Generation*, business models are composed of nine "building blocks" whose characteristics collectively describe the underlying logic guiding business strategy decisions, business success, and profit. The building blocks are: 1) customer segments; 2) value proposition; 3) channels; 4) customer relationships; 5) revenue streams; 6) key resources; 7) key activities; 8) key partnerships; and 9) cost structure. Of these, the book's authors note the comparative importance of customers (the "heart" of a business), value proposition ("the reason customers turn to one company over another," p. 22), and revenue model (the "arteries" of the business) – three categories that map, almost perfectly, to Magretta's earlier work (and that are highly aligned with the other above-mentioned work as well). The Business Model Canvas is a visual representation of these nine components, on a single piece of paper. In describing how to interpret the Canvas, Osterwalder and Pigneur observed that the items on its right side (i.e., building blocks 1 through 5) emphasize value, while the items on its left side (i.e., building blocks 6 through 9) emphasize efficiency – much as the right brain is said to manage emotion and the left brain is said to manage logic. They further noted that innovations tend to derive from one or more of the building blocks describing finances, resources, value, or customers. Left unarticulated in the book were clear instructions regarding how the Business Model Canvas itself could be used to provide much more than a descriptive visualization of what is or might be organizationally true.

Though Osterwalder and Pigneur described the Business Model Canvas as providing a mechanism by which entrepreneurs might, in effect, build and share a "paper prototype" of a provisional or real business model, they did little to directly bridge the gap between the innovation or new venture creation process and the Canvas's populated contents at any given point in that process. It could be argued, in fact, that beyond the Business Model Canvas itself they offered comparatively little that was new; their discussion of business model generation and innovation sounded much like similar discussions found in a multitude of forums elsewhere, over many years – including references to design thinking, ideation (using techniques such as brainstorming), SWOT analysis, Four Actions analysis, counterfactual argumentation, and storytelling. This observation is not meant to be an overwhelming critique; the simplicity, organization and one-pagedness of the Canvas clearly enhanced users' ability to present and discuss business models – as did the Canvas's ability to simultaneously showcase the whole and its parts. But the Canvas did not, at least initially or obviously, offer much more than that. Its creators built a communication tool (i.e., a "conceptual map," a "visual language with corresponding grammar," p. 272), which has evolved – owing to Blank and Ries's approach – into a foundational tool of process management. In pairing the Canvas with Lean Startup and Customer Development, the Canvas took on new meaning. Now, instead of simply describing what the business model was or might be, each building block could be positioned as describing a "hypothesis" that merited further testing. In *The Four Steps to the Epiphany*, Blank had developed worksheets on which individuals could craft testable hypotheses – across many of the same components represented by Osterwalder and Pigneur's building blocks. In bringing the work of all four men together, the collective (and, thus, the work of each) became more resonant.

In the time since the Business Model Canvas has been introduced, many have questioned its generalizability – in much the same way that they have questioned the generalizability of Lean Startup. Some have even "iterated" on the Canvas (even while continuing to champion the original), to provide what they believe to be helpful, context-driven alternatives (as, for example, with Ash Maurya's (2012) Lean Canvas, designed for particular use in startup environments). To the extent that more substantial critiques have been levied at the Canvas, they tend to fall into two categories. First, it has been observed that the simplicity of the Canvas is such that the true complexity of most business models and businesses is left unaddressed; it is not clear how to visualize or interpret the interactions that must exist between building blocks (and no method by which the inclusion of redundancies across blocks might be addressed). Second, while a business model might be the sum of many parts, the Canvas is largely mute with respect to helping its users identify which parts matter most; no mechanisms of isolation or prioritization exist to help guide decision-making. For entrepreneurship educators who seek to provide generalizable lessons for later application, these issues are arguably significant. While an in-progress founder might be immersed in a business model at the level of wanting to and being able to readily tease out nuance within the Canvas, students can tend to find such critical thinking to be more difficult – as they tend to be one step removed from the reality of the process, even when working on specific business concepts (i.e., because assignments, as compelling as they might be, still lack the feel of the real).

Throughout this chapter, it has been argued that Lean Startup and Customer Development's popular embrace has largely been driven by the single-minded emphasis of both (which are one) on customer engagement and feedback at the earliest stages of the startup process – as manifest in robust, in-person conversations. The implication within, at the risk of radically oversimplifying the essence of Lean Startup, is that most people understand and appreciate the method as almost exclusively focused on how a founder or organization might rapidly identify a customer who values a product or service at a sufficient level to motivate purchase (in a manner that substantially reduces the risk of failure). If this argument is extended to its natural conclusion, in the context of the Business Model Canvas, it would be the case that only a few of the building blocks are really considered by most entrepreneurs. In other words, the power of the Canvas might not lie in the gestalt, but in just those building blocks that represent the customers and the value proposition, as those define the revenue model. It is thus, perhaps, worth asking: Is the left side of the Canvas actually useful? Or, more reasonably, is the right side of the Canvas the portion truly representative of Lean Startup – and the left side of the Canvas instead an approximation of the business's operational needs? If it is the case that only the right side of the Canvas tends to be used for the purposes of Customer Delivery and Validation (i.e., the most resonant components of the research process), then the Business Model Canvas is arguably vulnerable to a critique not of excessive parsimony, but of superfluousness; the tool might be improved to the extent that it provides better focus.

CONCLUSION

It is an incontrovertible fact that Blank, Ries, Osterwalder and Pigneur's work has sold globally, in the hundreds of thousands, and has been deemed useful by a meaningful subset of those people. It is similarly true that this author has used the work of all four authors to help guide her students. There is great utility in what they address and great accessibility in the lexicon and tools that they have packaged for entrepreneurial and managerial use. While this chapter does consistently (and perhaps too persistently) address the fact that the Lean Startup Movement was not as novel or radical as some might believe, providing that broad reminder is not in fact the primary goal here. The central intent of this chapter is to raise some of the questions that seem to merit further exploration, particularly given the monumental attention and adherence that Lean Startup appears to have garnered. As the authors have justifiably claimed, their method has become a pervasive part of startup, corporate, and classroom conversations; it is also supported to the tune of millions of US government dollars. It feels, in light of this aggregated investment (measured in terms of not solely money, but also time and people), that we, in academia, might have a responsibility to better understand more.

Blank wrote (2001), "[W]hile educators and startup investors ... adapted tools and processes for *executing* a business model, there were no tools and processes to *search* for a business model" (p. ix). This statement was (and remains), objectively, incorrect. That doesn't mean that the Lean Startup approach isn't meaningful; it means that our tools and processes should be better understood to maximize effective deployment. It could be argued that almost every successful venture started lean. It could be argued that almost every successful venture had to adapt its plans upon bringing its concept to its first customers. It could also be argued that Lean Startup, while accommodating and providing some guidance with respect to what might be universal, is not effective on all fronts. It never, for example, describes how entrepreneurs should identify, acquire and manage or leverage resources. It is largely mute with respect to the role of bootstrapping in lean (assuming, quite specifically, that new ventures are not small bootstrappers, but firms capable of deploying large amounts of capital). It does not give consideration to guerrilla approaches to fact-finding, marketing, and sales, instead hewing consistently to the Customer Development path – a path that accommodates recursive loops, but is fairly resistant to non-linear detours. It also does not acknowledge existing and competing decision-making approaches within entrepreneurship (including, for example, effectuation, which emphasizes the importance of building incrementally, as based on the social capital and expertise of the founder).

It has felt, candidly, very daunting to write this chapter – as if, in merely raising questions, the content (and the author!) might be perceived as "too controversial." But popularity and true effectiveness are not the same thing – and, as entrepreneurship educators in search of real outcomes, it behooves us all to always try to shine light on the latter. The primary goal of this chapter is to acknowledge the power of the aggregated Lean Startup approach, while also highlighting some of the assumptions (or hypotheses) that we might have a collective responsibility to test. Though hundreds of companies have thus far graduated from the NSF iCorps program, researchers have only just begun aggregating and analyzing the effectiveness of that program in terms of outcomes that seem critical (e.g., number of companies founded, number of companies to reach breakeven, number of patents filed, number of technologies successfully commercialized) – and it may take many more years to have a definitive sense of the program's practical import (e.g., number of companies to survive beyond a specified age, number employed by founded companies, total profit). Of those more diffusely exposed to Lean Startup techniques – through, for example, regional training programs, college classes or conferences – it is difficult to control, in success or failure, for the many variables that might have contributed to results. In essence, we neither do know nor at this point can know if Lean Startup has driven or is driving the sorts of immense business success that its proponents claim. In fact, even if Lean Startup was the primary approach used in building a successful new venture, it is impossible to know if that was a key determinant of success. Nonetheless, it is time – even well past time – for us to begin a meaningful research effort.

NOTE

1. These dates appear to represent the first "public" emergence of each component. Each was likely referenced in various ways, across various contexts, by its originator, in the years preceding broad dissemination.

REFERENCES

Alvarez, C. (2014), *Lean Customer Development: Build Products Your Customers Will Buy*, Sebastopol, CA: O'Reilly Media.

Blank, S. (2001), *The Four Steps to the Epiphany: Successful Strategies for Products That Win*, Menlo Park, CA: K & S Ranch.

Blank, S. (2013), *The Four Steps to the Epiphany: Successful Strategies for Products That Win*, 2nd edn., Menlo Park, CA: K & S Ranch.

Blank, S. and Dorf, B. (2012), *The Startup Owner's Manual: The Step-by-step Guide for Building a Great Company*, Pescadero, CA: K & S Ranch.

Block, Z. and MacMillan, I. (1985), Milestones for success venture planning, *Harvard Business Review*, September–October, 177–191.

DaSilva, C. and Trkman, P. (2013), Business model: What it is and what it is not, *Long Range Planning*, retrieved May 8, 2016 from http://dx.doi.org/10.1016/j.lrp.2013.08.004.

Eisenmann, T. (2011), *Business Model Analysis for Entrepreneurs*, Harvard Business School Background Note 812–096.

Fairlie, R.W., Morelix, A., Reedy, E.J. and Russell, J. (2015), *The 2015 Kauffman Index: Startup Activity, Trends*, retrieved July 7, 2016 from http://www.kauffman.org/~/media/kauffman_org/research%20reports%20and%20covers/2015/05/kauffman_index_startup_activity_national_trends_2015.pdf.

Furr, N. and Dyer, J. (2014), *The Innovator's Method: Bringing the Lean Startup into Your Organization*, Boston, MA: Harvard Business Review Press.

Hamel, G. and Prahalad, C. (1990), Corporate imagination and expeditionary marketing, *Harvard Business Review*, **69**(4), 81–92.

Hamermesh, R., Marshall, P. and Pirmohamed, T. (2002), *Note on Business Model Analysis for the Entrepreneur*, Harvard Business School Background Note 802–048.

Magretta, J. (2002), Why business models matter, *Harvard Business Review*, **80**(5), 86–92.

Maurya, A. (2012), Why Lean Canvas vs Business Model Canvas?, retrieved from http://practicetrumpstheory.com/why-lean-canvas.

McGrath, R. and MacMillan, I. (1995), Discovery-driven planning: turning conventional planning on its head, *Harvard Business Review*, **73**(4), 44–54.

Osterwalder, A. (2004), The business model ontology: a proposition in a design science approach, Dissertation, University of Lausanne, Switzerland.

Osterwalder, A. and Pigneur, Y. (2010), *Business Model Generation: A Handbook for Visionaries, Game Changers, and Challengers*, Hoboken, NJ: John Wiley & Sons.

Osterwalder, A., Pigneur, Y. and Tucci, C.L. (2005), Clarifying business models: origins, present, and future of the concept, *Communications of the Association for Information Systems*, **15**(1), 751–775.

Ries, E. (2008a), Customer development engineering, *Startup Lessons Learned*, September 7, retrieved July 7, 2016 from http://www.startuplessonslearned.com/2008/09/customer-development-engineering.html.

Ries, E. (2008b), The lean startup, *Startup Lessons Learned*, September 8, retrieved July 7, 2016 from http://www.startuplessonslearned.com/2008/09/lean-startup.html.

Ries, E. (2009), Minimum viable product: a guide, *Startup Lessons Learned*, August 3, retrieved July 7, 2016 from http://www.startuplessonslearned.com/2009/08/minimum-viable-product-guide.html.

Ries, E. (2011a), *The Lean Startup: How Today's Entrepreneurs Use Continuous Innovation to Create Radically Successful Businesses*, New York: Crown Business.

Ries, E. (2011b), "The lean startup," Google Tech Talk, Presented at Google NYC, April 1, PowerPoint slides retrieved May 7, 2016 from http://www.slideshare.net/startuplessonslearned/eric-ries-the-lean-startup-google-tech-talk.

Sull, D. (2002), A strategy to meet the challenges of entrepreneurship, *Financial Times*, August 12.

U.S. Bureau of Labor Statistics (2013), High-employment-growth firms: defining and counting them, *Monthly Labor Review*, retrieved May 8, 2016 from http://www.bls.gov/opub/mlr/2013/article/clayton.htm.

Van Slyke, J. and Stevenson, H. (1985), *Pre-start Analysis: A Framework for Thinking about Business Ventures*, Harvard Business School Background Note 9-386-075.

6. Competency based education in entrepreneurship: a call to action for the discipline

Rebecca White, Giles Hertz and Kevin Moore

INTRODUCTION

Introduced by David McClelland in the early 1970s, competencies were recognized as significant predictors of employee performance and success and were traditionally more associated with training than education. More recently, competency based learning has been adopted by the State of New Hampshire's public school system,[1] the health disciplines, and other advanced education systems to develop and assess mastery of knowledge and skills. The concept and practice of using competencies to define and measure performance have been widely researched and defined. For our purposes, we use the term "competency" to describe the capability of applying or using knowledge, skills, abilities, behaviors, and personal characteristics to successfully perform in a given domain.

Competency based education (CBE) is a framework for designing and implementing education that focuses on the desired performance capabilities of the learner within this broad definitional context. While attaining a level of "competence" has long been the goal of traditional educational systems, these traditional models of curriculum design have largely been based on the delineation of intended learning objectives of instruction. Courses and curricula are then created based on these learning objectives that focus on identifying and measuring what a learner should know. Success is measured by the completion of hours in the classroom as much as by more direct measures of learning. By contrast, CBE makes the acquisition of selected competencies explicit by establishing observable and measurable performance metrics that learners must *demonstrate* to be deemed "competent." Whereas traditional education tends to focus on what and how learners are taught, CBE is focused on whether or not learners can demonstrate application of learning to solve problems, communicate effectively, perform procedures, and make appropriate decisions within a given context.

In recent years educators in the field of entrepreneurship have been seeking a model to define key learning outcomes for entrepreneurship education and to develop assessment models as a way to integrate curricular and co-curricular programs. CBE models provide a meaningful solution to these challenges. Why? First, CBE is based on competency sets of knowledge, skills, abilities, and other characteristics (KSAOs) of high performance in a particular domain. These include behaviors demonstrating abilities that then can be used to assess degrees of competency. This methodology allows for clear assessment of learning in any educational program that is experiential by design. Second, CBE allows for distinguishing between top performers and average performers; thus, there is a fit with the traditional grading models. Third, CBE allows for change over time in competencies, offering an opportunity to evaluate individual student growth in competencies. Finally, the use of CBE models to design an educational program provides an opportunity to tie models of learning directly to best practices in the field.

A few scholars have attempted to explore competencies as a way to understand entrepreneurial behavior.[2] Additionally, a small number of schools are in the early stages of attempting to apply CBE in their entrepreneurship programs. However, there is significant misunderstanding of what this application must include in order to ensure the delivery of the desired results. In early 2016, a group of scholars from 10 US universities came together to apply and extend this work based upon the principles of competency based education that have been successfully applied in other contexts and are in the early stages of application to entrepreneurship education at the University of Tampa.[3] This chapter is a call to action for entrepreneurship educators and a discussion of why a discipline-wide approach is the most effective and efficient pathway to CBE.

COMPETENCY BASED POST-SECONDARY EDUCATION

CBE models are at the root of a learning revolution which is being driven by the advancement of technology as well as a new competitive landscape that includes institutions with missions that promise to deliver education anytime, anywhere. In this new paradigm of learning, delivery options are multiple, learning products are explicitly defined and assessment is made at a new level of granularity not captured by traditional transcripts (Voorhees, 2001). However, we argue that embedded in the model of

CBE is a method to create and assess learning that can be adapted to and enhance traditional higher education models – especially in highly applied disciplines. Voorhees (2001, p. 5) describes the role of CBE as follows: "The bridge between the traditional paradigm, which depends on traditional credit hour measures of student achievement, and the learning revolution can be found in competency based approaches."

CBE is not new. These models were introduced in the early 1970s (McClelland, 1973) and have been used for the past 40 years to enhance human performance in the workplace (Ennis, 2008). The interest in applying CBE in higher education was first formalized in the US with the establishment of the National Skill Standards Board, an entity created in 1994 in the Goals 2000: Educate America Act. Since that time a number of states and institutions have adopted CBE in some form, most notably the movement toward the three-year degree programs funded by the Department of Education and instituted at Southern New Hampshire University, Grace College in Indiana, Arcadia University in Pennsylvania, and Lynn University in Florida. These programs seek to address the issues of the accelerating cost of higher education, increasing competition from non-traditional higher education and the need for an opportunity to institute curriculum innovation (Bradley et al., 2012).

The practice of using competencies to define and measure performance has been widely researched and discussed. However, as with many concepts, the term "competency" has suffered from multiple definitions both in research and in application. The definition of "competency" dominated the early CLM literature. In 1997, the Society of Industrial and Organizational Psychology (SIOP) established a task force led by Jeffery Shippmann and leading researchers and practitioners to focus on the following five questions:

1. What is a competency?
2. What is the difference between competency modeling and job analysis?
3. Why are competencies so appealing to consumers in business and industry?
4. Should competency models be validated?
5. What is the future of competency modeling?

For two years the task force investigated these questions and, based upon a comprehensive literature review, concluded that even with the most knowledgeable competency modeler or researcher there was no single agreed-upon definition of competency. However, they did agree upon a number of principles. First, a job analysis is "work focused," while competency modeling is "individual" focused, and neither is a singular approach to describing the working environment. Second, competency models should be validated using a process involving those who are in the workforce and already doing the work of interest. Finally, while there exists a significant need for further research in specific areas there is great hope for the discipline of competency modeling (Shippmann et al., 2000).

For our purposes, we define a competency as *the capability of applying or using knowledge, skills, abilities, behaviors, and personal characteristics to successfully perform in a given domain.* While admittedly broad, this definition is based on the one developed by the National Center for Public Policy and Higher Education workgroup which was funded by the US Department of Education to develop a common language for CBE (US Department of Education, 2002). Personal characteristics include the mental/intellectual/cognitive, social/emotional/attitudinal, and physical/psychomotor attributes necessary for success (Boyatzis, 1982; Dubois, 1993; Fogg, 1999; Lucia and Lepsinger, 1999), as well as internal and external constraints, environments, and relationships related to performance. These personal characteristics help explain why learners pursue different learning experiences and acquire different levels and kinds of skills, abilities, and knowledge. Motivations and perceptions of the activity and one's self or talents are also viewed as influential in competently and successfully performing in a given role (Boyatzis, 1982; Fulmer and Conger, 2004; Gangani et al., 2006; Sandberg, 2000). Therefore, competencies become the result of integrative learning experiences. It should be noted that this definition of competency is more inclusive than "knowledge and skill" and focuses on the *application* of knowledge, skill, attitude, and the ability to meet complex demands by drawing on many psychosocial resources (Mann et al., 2009; Schratz et al., 2013).

CBE is a framework that focuses on desired performance in a given context. The learner is put into a situation, given conditions, taught the rules, provided with coaching and mentoring, and allowed to practice until he or she can reach desired performance standards. For example, in the game of basketball one might argue that dribbling, passing, and shooting a basketball are three of the key abilities necessary for success. We know from experience that it is likely that, at some point in a game, a player will be fouled and be given the opportunity to shoot a foul shot. In fact, we also know that many games are won and lost with foul shots. Thus, it follows that one (among many) of the abilities that a basketball player should have is the ability to shoot a foul shot. Therefore, we might set up a performance measure that reads as follows: *Given a ball, a hoop and a foul line, a learner will practice shooting until he or she reaches the ability to shoot 10 foul shots with a success rate of 8 out of 10.* Not all learners will get to that level of mastery, but some may exceed it. Thus, CBE is customized learning, and the heart of CBE is simply the framework, which is made up of performance based learning objectives, designed by the educator, that will allow individualized learning and assessment. This framework is commonly referred to as a competency structure or model.

It is important to note here that the authors are well aware of the difference between training and education and, while CBE provides a structure that will work for either, we are advocating a structure that is education focused. A competency structure aids in the design, development and assessment of learning programs. It does not dictate how the teacher teaches these concepts. So, in the earlier example of the game of basketball, one would need to put the player into the game to observe other critical abilities, such as the ability to respond creatively to a play that is set up by the other team. The practice of basketball provides the opportunity to learn various responses, with coaching that can help a learner respond in a favorable way to unpredictable experiences on the basketball floor. This is not unlike entrepreneurship or medicine or many other fields where CBE has been applied with success. The goal of the remainder of the chapter is to describe a method for how entrepreneurship educators can begin the process of building a discipline-wide approach to CBE by applying it to the field of entrepreneurship education.

CBE AND ENTREPRENEURSHIP EDUCATION

Many of the leading educators in the discipline of entrepreneurship are advocating that entrepreneurship education is an instrument of empowerment for individuals and a tool for transforming markets, businesses, industries, economies, and communities (Morris, 2013; Timmons and Spinelli, 2008). However, educators in the field have acknowledged that traditional pedagogy is not sufficient and that teaching entrepreneurship may be considered more like the study of other "crafts" such as medicine and architecture (White et al., 2011). The result has been a new interest in CBE as a foundation for curriculum design and learning assessment.

A few scholars have attempted to explore competencies as a way to understand entrepreneurial behavior. For example, Wing Yan Man (2006) empirically explored entrepreneurial behaviors through a competency framework and identified six behavioral patterns in the entrepreneurial learning construct. More recently, Morris et al. (2013) identified 13 competencies demonstrated by successful entrepreneurs, and White and Moore (2016a) have developed a model for the application of CBE to both coursework and co-curricular learning experiences. Table 6.1 compares the three CBE models.

In late 2015, four university based entrepreneurship programs[4] came

*Table 6.1   Competency based education research in entrepreneurship –
selected models*

	White, R. and Moore, K. (2016b), Developing a competency structure for higher education, Working paper, University of Tampa. Also discussed in White, R.J. and Moore, K. (2016a), Application of competency based learning to entrepreneurship education: integrating curricular and co-curricular elements to enhance discipline mastery, in C. Wankel and W. Wankel (eds.), *Integrating Curricular and Co-curricular Endeavors to Enhance Student Outcomes.*	Morris, M.H., Webb, J., Fu, J. and Singhal, S. (2013), A competency-based perspective on entrepreneurship education: conceptual and empirical insights, *Journal of Small Business Management,* **51**(3), 352–369.	Man, T.W., Lau, T. and Chan, K.F. (2002), The competitiveness of small and medium enterprises: a conceptualization with focus on entrepreneurial competencies, *Journal of Business Venturing,* **17**, 123–142.
Definition used	The capability of applying or using knowledge, skills, abilities, behaviors and personal characteristics to successfully perform in a given domain.	A competency refers to the knowledge, skills, attitudes, values and behaviors that people need to successfully perform a particular activity or task, such as rewiring a house or performing a surgical procedure (Brophy and Kiely, 2002; Rankin, 2004).	Entrepreneurial competencies are the total ability of entrepreneurs to perform a job role successfully.
Explanation	Identified six competencies based upon feedback from more than 500 entrepreneurs from a convenience sample using Q-sort	Utilized panel survey data from 20 entrepreneurs and 20 entrepreneurship educators to identify 13 distinct competencies.	Developed from semi-structured interviews with 12 entrepreneurs, which were conducted with a focus

Table 6.1   (continued)

Explanation	Imethodology. Each competency is listed in bold below and followed by the abilities for each competency identified as critical by entrepreneurs.	Entrepreneurs had grown highly successful companies with 100 or more employees. In a two-multilevel study, panelists were asked to identify the key competencies required to lauch a new venture.	on the critical incidents in which significant learning occurred prior to and during the development of their businesses.
	Entrepreneurial competencies		
	Entrepreneurship	Opportunity recognition	Opportunity recognition and development
	Market risk awareness	Opportunity assessment	Relationship building
	Passion and drive	Risk management and mitigation	Conceptualizing
	Opportunity recognition	Conveying a compelling vision	Organizing
	Honesty and ethics	Tenacity and perseverance	Strategy formation
	Adaptability	Creative problem solving and imaginativeness	Personal commitment
	Continuous learning	Resource leveraging	
	Communication	Guerrilla skills	
	Relationship building	Value creation	
	Empathy	Maintaining focus yet adaptability	
	Interpersonal communication	Resilience	
	Written communication	Self-efficacy	
	Communicating through conflict	Building and using networks	
	Thinking		
	Situational awareness		
	Judgment		
	Creativity and innovation		
	Problem solving		
	Self-awareness		

Table 6.1   (continued)

Reflection
Professionalism
Accountability
Attitude and
appearance
Knowledge and
certification
Technology aptitude
Integrity and values
Continuous
improvement
Acting autonomously
Leadership
Business acumen
Collaboration
Sensitivity
Strategic thinking
Diversity and culture
Change management
Ethics
Developing people
Managing the work
Planning
Delegation
Establishing priority
Coordination
Measurement
Team building
Controlling

---

together at the Global Consortium of Entrepreneurship Centers' Annual Conference to present their interest in, and research on, the application of CBE in entrepreneurship education (White et al., 2015). This group identified four primary arguments for the application of CBE to entrepreneurship education.

First, the discipline is being impacted by the new learning revolution that is affecting all of higher education and has developed via advanced technology and increased competition from non-traditional educational sources. In the case of entrepreneurship, the discipline has been so successful with selling the value of entrepreneurship education that vast numbers of people and institutions from city and state governments to business leaders and service providers have created their own version of education for aspiring entrepreneurs. As in any market space where disruption is occurring, the incumbent is called upon to clearly demonstrate value to stakeholders. Moreover, if entrepreneurship education programs do not step up and define learning outcomes for themselves, those guidelines will be imposed from elsewhere. A CBE approach can provide clear measurements of learning progress and prevents the dilution of the discipline.

Second, while traditional educational programs in entrepreneurship have more than 40 years of experience in educating entrepreneurs, there is no consensus on a common nomenclature for the discipline. This has led to challenges as the discipline has moved beyond the walls of the business colleges and into disciplines such as engineering and the arts where educators have created their own versions of entrepreneurship. While across-discipline access to entrepreneurship is a necessary and valuable step in the growth of entrepreneurship, without a common language of learning outcomes "entrepreneurship everywhere can quickly transform into entrepreneurship nowhere."[5] Thus, one of the key attributes of employing a CBE model is the ability to develop a common language upon which to build student learning.

Third, many educators have faced the challenge of students succeeding as entrepreneurs while enrolled in a degree program but failing their coursework in the process. Entrepreneurship has become one of the most popular areas of study on many college campuses, with students from all disciplines interested in the field. One of the key components of these programs is their experiential nature. In fact, it can be argued that the majority of learning often takes place outside of the classroom, where students apply what they are currently learning in the classroom. Programs such as boot camps, pitch competitions, and networking events provide the opportunity for students to learn the basic skills required for success in new venture creation. To date, measuring learning in these environments has been mostly anecdotal and has not provided an avenue for longitudinal program assessment, nor the opportunity for continuous improvement based upon multiple evaluations. As suggested by White and Moore (2016a), CBE can provide a solution for this.

Finally, assessing learning in entrepreneurship has been a challenge for the discipline as well. Few studies have examined the short-term or long-term effects of entrepreneurship education on student attitudes, behaviors, and professional competencies (Duval-Couetil, 2013; Pittaway et al., 2009). To date, the literature has focused on the development of programs, with an assumption that, through the offering of well-designed courses and curricula, students will increase their knowledge and skills and that this will lead to an increased likelihood of success in the workplace and as founders of new ventures. However, few studies have tested this assumption (Dickson et al., 2008; Gorman et al., 1997). According to Duval-Couetil (2013) the assessment of entrepreneurship education programs has several unique challenges. These include that it is a young and ill-defined discipline, there is significant diversity among programs, it emphasizes practice and instructors include both academic educators and practitioners, and it is assumed that both venture creation and economic development are the primary outcomes. In order to address these unique challenges we suggest developing and implementing competency based learning models. These validated models offer the opportunity to clearly address the first three challenges and provide an avenue to expand the field beyond the narrow perspective of outcomes limited to venture creation and economic development. Thus, by applying a discipline based approach to CBE in entrepreneurship education we believe many of the current challenges can be addressed. We identify a two-step approach: 1) develop a common language; 2) use real time data and technology to create continuous feedback and improvement mechanisms.

ADOPTING A DISCIPLINE APPROACH: STEP 1 – DEVELOPING A COMMON LANGUAGE

The Competency Structure

Based upon the foregoing discussion, we suggest a discipline developed and directed CBE implementation model in entrepreneurship education. Any CBE program begins with a competency set. A competency set is those competencies and abilities that are used within a particular function or practice. Recommendations are based on a five-phase competency program development process[6] utilized at the University of Tampa (Figure 6.1) and informed by 10 shared best practice design elements identified in a 2015 study by Public Agenda and funded by the Bill and Melinda Gates Foundation.[7] The 10 best practices are outlined in Figure 6.2 and include: learner-centered; clear, cross-cutting and specialized competencies; coherent, competency-driven program and curriculum design; measurable and meaningful assessments; proficient and prepared graduates; engaged faculty and partners; flexible staffing roles and structures; enabling and aligned business processes and systems; new or adjusted business and financial models; and embedded process for continuous improvement.

The process begins with a competency identification and validation process, followed by curriculum mapping, and a pre-assessment which directs a customization process and learning path for each student,

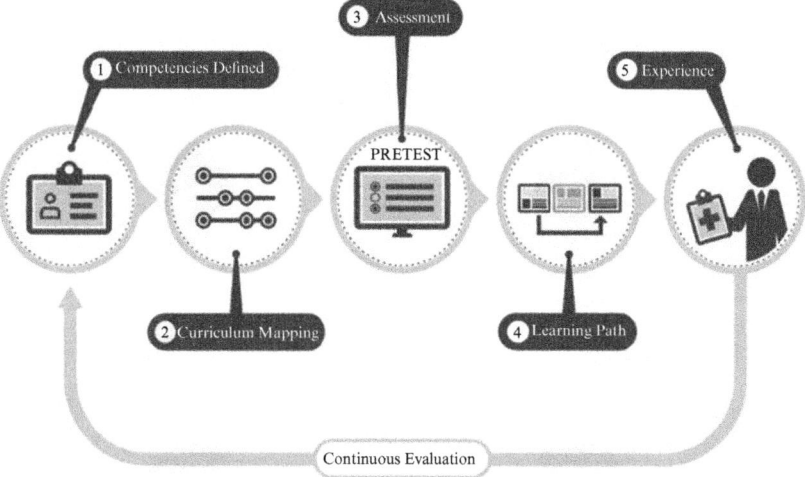

Figure 6.1   Five-phase competency program

concluding with experiences that measure performance. This process utilizes a *competency structure* as the foundation at program level.

A competency structure is the general architecture used to guide a CBE program, and includes the four levels of detail that are applied to the curriculum, course and/or learning event. These four levels include: 1) a list of well-defined competencies; 2) the abilities (well defined) necessary to achieve each competency; 3) clearly defined measurable behaviors that demonstrate each of the abilities; and 4) the performance level of each learner in each competency measured on a scale from knowledge at the lowest end to leadership at the highest level of performance. Figure 6.3 illustrates how the competency structure roughly correlates with traditional instructional models from courses to lessons to topics to assessments.

Previous attempts to apply competencies have focused primarily on using a list of desired abilities, behaviors, and attributes of a successful entrepreneur. However, the use of a competency structure offers significant benefit for both the instructor and the learner. For instructors it provides a nomenclature and implementation plan in all aspects of curriculum, course and learning event design, from the establishment of learning objectives to the development of assessments. For learners, the use of a competency structure offers the opportunity for a personalized learning path that can continue well beyond graduation.

Thus, a discipline-wide approach begins with the establishment of a competency structure that is based in practice. The first phase of the process is establishing a baseline competency structure upon which to

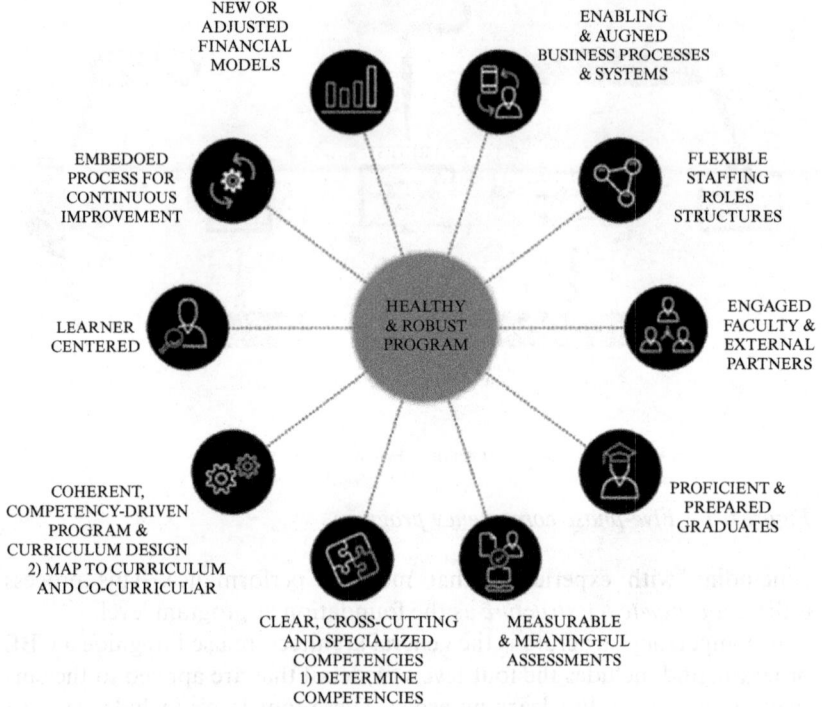

Source: Public Agenda.

Figure 6.2   Shared design elements and suggested practices of competency based education programs

build. It is important to note that the establishment of a discipline-wide, generally accepted competency model will not destroy the unique and innovative nuances of individual programs or institutions. In fact, having a common competency structure that can be applied in a wide variety of institutional settings and unique programs will enable institutions to create their own innovations in education while ensuring that agreed-upon educational outcomes are met. For example, any level of study from undergraduate to graduate can utilize the structure, and those institutions may apply the structure to a course, a curriculum, a co-curricular learning event or an entire program. For example, one institution may apply the structure only to an incubator program, while others may apply it to the entire entrepreneurship program campus-wide to provide a common language for entrepreneurs among disciplines such as engineering, the arts, and business.

The steps involved in establishing a competency structure include the

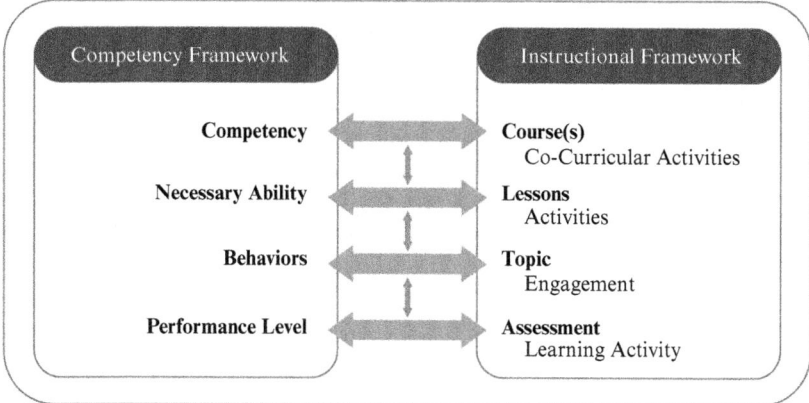

Figure 6.3   Matching competency structure to traditional instructional framework

following: 1) working with key stakeholders to define the program goals and intended use of the competency model; 2) determining the competency structure based on intended goals; and 3) creating a discipline based competency evaluation team (DBCET) that includes key leaders in the discipline (e.g., subject matter experts such as entrepreneurs, entrepreneurship educators, experts in curriculum, instructional design and competency modeling, and technical writers).

Meaningful competency statements provide enough information about expected student performances as can be used to guide assessment (Jones, 2001). This component begins with a literature review that includes looking for common themes and language to describe abilities necessary for success in the field. Once the review has been completed, a draft of competencies and the necessary abilities for each is developed and compared with other competency frameworks that use similar competencies. Once potential competencies have been identified it is important to get feedback from stakeholders, including faculty, alumni, students and prospective employers (Jones, 2001).

There are two common approaches to obtaining this feedback. The first approach is the strategy of developing a curriculum that is used for guiding the formal analysis of positions or occupations at the professional, managerial, technical, skilled, and semi-skilled levels (Norton, 1998). This process involves seeking input from practitioners by engaging them (in this case, entrepreneurs) in a process of reviewing and analyzing a list of knowledge, skills, and attitudes necessary to perform successfully in the domain (in this case, as an entrepreneur). After the list is developed it is usually validated by a second group of practitioners and experts, thus creating a "curriculum" of topics to be covered that can then be turned into competency and ability statements.

A second, research based approach is the Delphi method. This process has been used in a wide variety of higher education settings to improve communication and reach consensus (Uhl, 1971, 1983). In this case, designers solicit nominations to get the best experts to make informed judgments about the competencies necessary for success. These experts complete several rounds of surveys to identify the items with agreement and those with significant disagreement relative to a particular competency. For example, entrepreneurs, faculty, alumni, and prospective employers may be asked to rate the importance of specific skills necessary for success as an entrepreneur via a survey. An analysis of variance can be performed to identify differences in the mean responses across groups. Subsequent survey rounds then get survey participants to again rate the importance of the skills with the greatest disagreement, providing a chance to revise their earlier rating. In each subsequent round, participants are provided the mean score and given the chance to disagree in writing. The goal is to move toward agreement on the key competencies and abilities for the baseline competency structure.

It is important to consider the notion of bundling and unbundling at this stage. A single competency can be used in many different ways depending upon the discipline and context. For example, communication skills are important for all graduates regardless of major. However, the specific abilities within different contexts vary greatly. Pitching a startup to investors requires a very specific skill set that is not typically necessary for success in other fields. Therefore, it is important to consider that competencies within different contexts require different *bundles* of skills and knowledge (Voorhees, 2001). It is decisions by educators and the competency review team about the bundling and unbundling of skills and knowledge that drive CBE initiatives at this stage. Once developed, a process for involving other stakeholders in the process should be taken. The discipline may conduct focus groups and collect data from both entrepreneurs and entrepreneurship educators. The DBCET can then synthesize findings from this research and begin to conduct a larger-scale field test of the model that can ultimately lead to the competency structure.

Designing a competency structure is no trivial task. If done well, it takes time, and the resulting matrix is both broad and deep. Fortunately, the recommended process includes the broad-scale application in a wide variety of settings and thus means that designers do not have to create the perfect product immediately. By applying the use of technology, over time the application of the structure will provide data that can enhance and validate the model.

This need for a large-scale validation process is the primary reason we recommend a discipline-based approach to building CBE into entrepreneurship education programs. While many educators have already begun to try out the use of competencies in their programs or institutions, we believe the true value of a CBE model will come from wide-scale application and use across institutions and contexts.

Curriculum Mapping

A discipline-wide application begins with the curriculum mapping process at the institutional level. Curriculum mapping provides the opportunity to embed competencies across courses and other learning experiences with the intention of enhancing student learning (Jones, 2001). The process of mapping an existing curriculum is not a simple matter, as it must be thorough and continuous. Moreover, ideally the process is based on a team approach and involves all faculty members within the program. Involving the entire faculty team avoids problems later with other issues such as scheduling faculty for classes or programs, and interpretation and structure of each learning objective by instructors at the course level. However, Ervin et al. (2013) discovered the mapping process has several notable challenges: interpretation and agreed-upon definitions of competencies and skills, philosophical interpretations, difficulty determining an agreed-upon proficiency level, rater (faculty) bias, and the often intimate relationship between each competency.

The curriculum mapping process for an entrepreneurship program has four levels: 1) determining which courses and co-curricular learning events will be included in the model; 2) identifying where various competencies are covered in the curriculum and/or learning events by matching each individual course and/or learning event to the necessary abilities and behaviors of the competencies; 3) developing learning objectives for each course and/or co-curricular activity within the program based on the competency structure that has been developed; and 4) assigning performance expectations to the assessments within the courses and across the curriculum that will measure the level of competency mastery for individual learners who participate in each course or learning event.

One of the most valuable outcomes of using a competency structure model is its ability to assist with both curriculum and course or learning event design. The mapping process provides an opportunity for global discussion questions that allow for the examination of assumptions and opinions about how to define a competent entrepreneur and identifying the abilities graduates should possess. More specific to each program, discussions can examine program and curriculum gaps and redundancies, and how to make improvements at the course, event, or curriculum level. Discussions on the performance level required for each course and the type of assessment used within the learning environment can provide clarity for all instructors regarding the role of an individual course or learning event in the entire learning process for any individual student. For example, in one case during the mapping process, we identified gaps in the program that we did not account for in the regular curriculum design process. Specifically, we found that freshmen did not have the opportunity to take entrepreneurship courses until they were accepted in the business college as juniors. In order to provide an opportunity for students to engage sooner we added a freshman course for students interested in entrepreneurship. Through our discussions we also found that students often have limited opportunities to engage in programming during the late evening hours and on weekends. To remedy this, we were able to add a live and learn component by specifying a dorm for students declaring an interest or major in entrepreneurship and adding supportive programming for this group. In addition, we increased the hours of access to the entrepreneurship center by adding new space that is staffed later into the evening hours when students often do school related work. Thus, the process of mapping the curriculum to the competency model had many unintended but very positive outcomes.

ADOPTING A DISCIPLINE APPROACH: STEP 2 – USING DATA AND TECHNOLOGY

While the process of developing a common competency structure and mapping to individual programs, curricula, courses, and learning events is alone a valuable process, the power of applying CBE to learning is the ability to access, accumulate, and share data about the learning process and outcomes with instructors, learners, and other interested stakeholders. The adoption of a common platform to share information across institutions and with learners provides tremendous value and has been identified as one of the best practices among successful CBE programs (Public Agenda, 2015). Technology not only makes it possible to collect historical data that can be used to improve instruction, share outcomes and conduct research, but also provides the opportunity for using real time data to inform learners and provide customized learning paths that can follow them throughout a lifetime practice of entrepreneurship. It can also be useful to connect learners to learning opportunities outside of traditional classroom instruction.

One of the interesting dimensions of entrepreneurship education is the common practice of engaging practicing entrepreneurs and other individuals from the local, regional, state, national, and/or international entrepreneurial ecosystems. Students commonly learn not only from their professors but also from a wide variety of experiences and mentors who move in and out of the learning system on a frequent basis. The use of a common platform can allow for the engagement of these individuals in the learning process in a more meaningful way.

Another benefit from the adoption of a shared platform is the opportunity for educators to provide "nanocourses" or small bites of learning to be shared with entrepreneurship learners at any stage of their learning. Nanocourses started as crash courses in the sciences as a way to teach topics in a condensed fashion. Today, many different institutions use this term to describe the teaching of small bites of knowledge, and Udacity (online education born out of Stanford University) has trademarked the term "Nanodegree."[8] Regardless of the name, the movement toward small bites of learning is growing and could be effective as a part of the learning path in entrepreneurship. The adoption of a common language and a common technology platform can allow for a collaborative discipline-wide approach to remaining relevant among the disruption of the education industry that is being driven by organizations like Udacity.

BENEFITS OF A DISCIPLINE BASED APPROACH TO CBE

As outlined above, a discipline based approach to applying CBE to entrepreneurship education has numerous benefits to the discipline, from providing us with more meaningful measures of outcomes for entrepreneurship education to a better assessment of learning in a wide variety of learning contexts. However, there are significant benefits to individual institutions that choose to participate, including the opportunity to:

● evaluate their curriculum in a purposeful manner and align this to the practice of entrepreneurship;
● improve courses, lessons, topics and methods of assessment in meaningful ways;
● align co-curricular activities to competency and ability statements, providing legitimate linkages and assurance of learning to these activities;
● provide useful data on the entrepreneurial ecosystem and how course and co-curricular learning events align;

- provide the opportunity to modify and improve individual activities within programs;
- provide a pathway to improve mentoring and advising of learners;
- offer a way to engage with alumni and participate in their learning after graduation; and
- offer the opportunity to develop personalized learning paths for individual students.

CHALLENGES

Achieving the full benefit of the adoption of a discipline-based approach to CBE in entrepreneurship education has challenges. As mentioned earlier, the development of a competency structure and mapping the structure is not a trivial task. It will require a significant investment of time and energy from the leaders in the discipline. Moreover, as with most disruptive innovations, faculty will need to serve as champions and change agents in their institutions and perhaps fight some battles in order to enact change. However, entrepreneurship educators have served as pioneers and change agents in their institutions for the past 50 years and any review of the history of the discipline demonstrates the hard work that has been required to build its legitimacy. We believe the discipline is, without a doubt, up to the task. The most important step is the first one – to come together with a plan and get started.

NOTES

1. See Bradley et al. (2012) and Bramante and Colby (2012) for application in the State of New Hampshire.
2. For example see Morris et al. (2013) and Wing Yan Man (2006).
3. For more information on the development of the program at the University of Tampa see White and Moore (2016a).
4. The University of Tampa, University of Florida, Northern Kentucky University and University of Central Florida.
5. Adapted from the Keynote and Welcome Presentation, Donald F. Kuratko, Presentation to the United States Association for Small Business and Entrepreneurship, 2016.
6. The process was adapted from products developed commercially by Tier One Performance Solutions for Toyota Manufacturing in 1994 and later for Wright-Patterson Airforce Base.
7. Public Agenda is a nonprofit, non-partisan organization that helps diverse leaders and citizens navigate divisive, complex issues and work together to find solutions. The referenced study examined thriving CBE programs in an attempt to identify best practices. For the full report see http://www.publicagenda.org/pages/who-we-are#sthash.6KG6xj1A.dpuf.
8. For more information see https://www.udacity.com/us.

REFERENCES

Boyatzis, R.E. (1982), *The Competent Manager: A Model for Effective Performance*, New York: Wiley.

Bradley, M.J., Seidman, R.H. and Painchaud, S.R. (2012), *Saving Higher Education: The Integrated, Competency Based Three-year Degree Bachelor's Degree Program*, San Francisco: Jossey-Bass.

Bramante, F. and Colby, R. (2012), *Off the Clock: Moving Education from Time to Competency*, Thousand Oaks, CA: Corwin.

Brophy, M. and Kiely, T. (2002), Competencies: a new sector, *Journal of European Industrial Training*, **26**(2/3/4), 165–176.

Dickson, P.H., Solomon, G.T. and Weaver, K.M. (2008), Entrepreneurial selection and success: does education matter? *Journal of Small Business and Enterprise Development*, **15**(2), 239–258.

Dubois, D.D. (1993), *Competency-based Performance Improvement: A Strategy for Organizational Change*, Amherst, MA: HRD Press.

Duval-Couetil, N. (2013), Assessing the impact of entrepreneurship education programs: challenges and approaches, *Journal of Small Business Management*, **51**(3), 394–409.

Ennis, M.R. (2008), Competency models: a review of the literature and the role of the employment and training administration (ETA), Office of Policy Development and Research, Employment and Training Administration, US Department of Labor.

Ervin, L., Carter, B. and Robinson, P. (2013), Curriculum mapping: not as straightforward as it sounds, *Journal of Vocational Education and Training*, **65**(3), 309–318.

Fogg, C.D. (1999), *Implementing Your Strategic Plan: How To Turn "Intent" into Effective Action for Sustainable Change*, New York: American Management Association.

Fulmer, R.M. and Conger, J.A. (2004), Identifying talent, *Executive Excellence*, **21**(4), 11.

Gangani, N., McLean, G.N. and Braden, R.A. (2006), A competency-based human resources development strategy, *Performance Improvement Quarterly*, **19**(1), 127–139.

Gorman, G., Hanlon, D. and King, W. (1997), Some research perspectives on entrepreneurial education, enterprise education and education for small business management: a ten year review, *International Small Business Journal*, **15**(3), 56–77.

Jones, M. (2001), Critical care competencies, *Nursing in Critical Care*, **7**(3), 111–120.

Lucia, A.D. and Lepsinger, R. (1999), *Art and Science of Competency Models*, San Francisco: Jossey-Bass.

Man, T.W., Lau, T. and Chan, K.F. (2002), The competitiveness of small and medium enterprises: a conceptualization with focus on entrepreneurial competencies, *Journal of Business Venturing*, **17**, 123–142.

Mann, K., Gordon, J. and MacLeod, A. (2009), Reflection and reflective practice in health professions education: a systematic review, *Advances in Health Sciences Education*, **14**(4), 595–621.

McClelland, D.C. (1973), Testing for competence rather than for intelligence, *American Psychologist*, **28**, 1–14.

Morris, M.H. (2013), Entrepreneurship as empowerment and transformation, Presentation to the Global Consortium of Entrepreneurship Centers, Kansas City, MO.

Morris, M.H., Webb, J., Fu, J. and Singhal, S. (2013), A competency-based perspective on entrepreneurship education: conceptual and empirical insights, *Journal of Small Business Management*, **51**(3), 352–369.

Norton, R.E. (1998), Quality instruction for the high performance workplace: DACUM, Education Resources Information Center.

Pittaway, L., Hannon, P., Gibb, A. and Thompson, J. (2009), Assessment practice in enterprise education, *International Journal of Entrepreneurial Behaviour Research*, **15**(1), 71–93.

Public Agenda (2015), *A Research Brief on the Survey of the Shared Design Elements and Emerging Practices of Competency-based Education Programs*, retrieved from http://www.publicagenda.org/files/Sur veyOfSharedDesignEle-mentsAndEmergingPracticesOfCBEPrograms_PublicAgenda_2015.pdf.

Rankin, N. (2004), The new prescription for performance: the eleventh competency benchmarking survey, *Competency and Emotional Intelligence Benchmarking Supplement*, *2005*, 181–191.

Sandberg, J. (2000), Understanding human competence at work: an interpretative approach, *Academy of Management Journal*, **43**(1), 9–25.

Schratz, M. et al. (2013), *The Art and Science of Leading a School: Central5: A Central European View on Competencies for School Leaders: Final Report of the Project: International Co-operation for School Leadership Involving Austria, the Czech Republic, Hungary, Slovakia, Slovenia, Sweden, 2013*, Budapest: Tempus Public Foundation.

Shippmann, J.S., Ash, R.A., Batjtsta, M., Carr, L., Eyde, L.D., Hesketh, B., Kehoe, J., Pearlman, K., Prien, E.P. and Sanchez, J.I. (2000), The practice of competency modeling, *Personnel Psychology*, **53**(3), 703–740.

Timmons, J.A. and Spinelli, S. (2008), *New Venture Creation: Entrepreneurship for the 21st Century*, Vol. 4, Burr Ridge, IL: Irwin.

Uhl, N.P. (1971), *Encouraging Convergence of Opinion through the Use of the Delphi Technique in the Process of Identifying an Institution's Goals*, Durham, NC: Education Testing Service.

Uhl, N.P. (1983), Using the Delphi technique in institutional planning, *New Directions for Institutional Research*, **1983**(37), 81–94.

US Department of Education, National Center for Education Statistics (2002), *Defining and Assessing Learning: Exploring Competency-based Initiatives*, NCES 2002–159, prepared by Elizabeth A. Jones and Richard A. Voorhees, with Karen Paulson, for the Council of the National Postsecondary Education Cooperative Working Group on Competency-based Initiatives, Washington, DC: US Department of Education.

Voorhees, Richard A. (2001), Competency based learning models: a necessary future, in Richard A. Voorhees (ed.), *Measuring What Matters: Competency Based Learning Models in Higher Education*, New Directions for Institutional Research, No. 110, San Francisco: Jossey-Bass, pp. 5–13.

White, R.J. and Moore, K. (2016a), Application of competency based learning to entrepreneurship education: integrating curricular and co-curricular elements to enhance discipline mastery, in C. Wankel and W. Wankel (eds.), *Integrating Curricular and Co-curricular Endeavors to Enhance Student Outcomes*, Thousand Oaks, CA: Corwin, pp. 99–118.

White, R. and Moore, K. (2016b), Developing a competency structure for higher education, Working paper, University of Tampa.

White, R.J., Hertz, G.T. and D'Souza, R.D. (2011), Teaching a craft – enhancing entrepreneurship education, *Small Business Institute® Journal*, 7(2), 1–14.

White, R., Moore, K., Ford, C., D'Souza, R. and Kraft, J. (2015), Developing competency-based entrepreneurship education that works, Presentation at the International Meeting of the Global Consortium of Entrepreneurship Centers, Gainesville, FL.

Wing Yan Man, T. (2006), Exploring the behavioural patterns of entrepreneurial learning: a competency approach, *Education + Training*, **48**(5), 309–321.

7. The art of case teaching

David W. Rosenthal

It is really simple . . . if you want to have a long-lasting, important impact on the lives of your entrepreneurship students, I recommend the case method – one form of experiential learning.

Don't believe me? Here are quotes from a couple of my alumni:
Every once in a while someone comes along in your life that makes you think differently. To really understand what it means to "think." Not to memorize facts or regurgitate what others have said but actually have to solve a problem using discipline and creativity.

"Learning how to think" really means learning how to exercise some control over how and what you think. It means being conscious and aware enough to choose what you pay attention to and choosing how you construct meaning from experience.

The lessons I learned in that class sit in my brain and are called upon daily for professional and personal situations [35 years later]. That is a true living legacy. (Miami, 1980)

One of the ways that you impacted my life significantly was a time that you weren't even present. It was 1999 and I had recently been hired to run a new division of an established company. The owners had a vague vision on what they wanted this new division to sell and that was simply as far as it went. I frequently like to joke in retrospect that "They were dumb enough to hire a 24-year-old" and "I was dumb enough to go." There I sat in a quiet conference room, struggling to figure out a massive puzzle: What should we sell? To whom? What would be our differentiators? It was a massive task for someone with little experience. I fell back to my experiences with you at Miami. I pulled out the framework notes that I had built in class and started filling in the blanks. That framework was my business plan template. I built that business from nothing to about a million dollars in two years. More importantly, that experience started my confidence in being able to build organizations. Without that framework, I think things would have ended up differently. Not only did you help me build the framework that was so useful. You taught me how to think critically about the world around me. I credit those skills to much of my success.

Today, I see things differently than other people do. I dive down deeper into the scenarios and look for the root causes that you taught me to find through case studies. I push others to think and find the solutions for themselves. Instead of giving them the answers, I question their thinking and assumptions. (Miami, 1997)

What Is the Case Method?

Simply stated, the case method requires students to critically examine a situation that requires a response or action, followed by a thorough discussion of observations, opinions, interpretations, recommendations and expected outcomes. Through critique over multiple experiences students develop a structured method for problem solving.

My version of case method traces its roots to the origins of the Harvard Business School under Dean Edwin F. Gay, who identified the "problem method" as analogous to the study of case law. He referred to "visits of inspection" and "field work" in his 1908 description of the methods to be used in the new school.

Dean Gay reasoned that the development of a new discipline of business should follow the Aristotelian method of observation, followed by classification – the recognition of patterns – and then development of theory, structure and principles.

Thus, the case method involves exposing students to real business situations, in their messy natural conditions, and asking the students to interpret what they are observing, *and to develop a plan of action to deal with it*.

To repeat, case method:

- Is real – there is no substitute for reality in learning the intricacies of business. Business is by definition a *human* endeavor, and humans are complex, unpredictable and often just plain weird. By addressing real situations students learn to deal with uncertainty and develop creativity and flexibility.
- Requires skills of observation – the ability to gather data from myriad sources and points of view, and sorting fact from opinion from falsehood.
- Classifies data into meaningful groupings – which suggest relationships and permit organized thought.
- Encourages the development of theory – repeated patterns suggest underlying principles and successful approaches in application.

The Case Teacher as Coach

Another way of thinking about case method is that it puts students into a series of practice scrimmages for business where conditions are as "real world" as possible, but without the threats of bankruptcy or imprisonment.

The case teacher determines what the nature of the practice is going to be for each session, giving care to recognize the strengths and weaknesses of the players, the particular sport or discipline, the level of development of the team, the students' ability to absorb lessons and criticisms, and so on.

Most importantly, the coach must recognize that the players are the ones who will actually participate in the game, and it is the real game that counts!

Students know everything! The role of "teacher as teller" is nearly useless in twenty-first-century education. Students have the sum of all knowledge available at their fingertips. They can access lectures on any subject, books, articles or monographs on any topic, opinions, anecdotes, multiple media approaches, and varying levels of sophistication from the most mundane to the most erudite.

Question: In a world of total information what is the role of a teacher?
Answer: Coach.

The Case Method Is Robust

Cases can be used for many purposes, including:

- application of models or tools;
- discovery/theory building;
- "reinventing the wheel" – learning what others already know;
- argumentation;
- risk taking;
- analysis;
- synthesis;
- deductive reasoning;
- inductive reasoning;
- presentation skills;
- groupwork/teamwork;
- communication skills;
- organization;
- self-awareness or confidence.

The beauty of the case method is that students will take away the elements that are most meaningful to them. While one student is learning how to present a persuasive argument, the student in the next chair is learning a set of analytical tools. The key, of course, is the support of the teacher/coach in reinforcing the lessons.

Cases tend to be *effective* rather than *efficient* learning tools. Coverage of a broad range of topics in detail is better accomplished through lecture or other means. The specific lesson at the crux of the case will generally be learned and retained well, but it takes time. Thus, other topics will have to be skimmed over or even ignored.

HOW TO TEACH WITH CASES

First, Position the Course

The role of cases in education depends in part upon the nature of the course and its purpose and placement in the curriculum:

- introductory, advanced;
- elective, required;
- content, process;
- undergraduate, graduate;
- tools, capstone.

As a general rule of thumb, the more advanced the course, the more complex (and longer) the cases can be. The more process oriented (focus upon creating a learning structure), the greater the number of cases that are used, and the less directive the instructor in the discussion. The more content oriented (specific applications or concepts), the fewer the cases and the more directive the discussion leader.

"Pre" and "Post" Theory Usage of Cases

If students have already been exposed to a particular theory or model, a case will generally provide a very different learning experience than if they are ignorant of that particular theory or model. If students are asked to analyze a case *before* they have been exposed to a concept, they can be guided to "reinvent the wheel." Granted, the wheel will be lumpy and only vaguely round, but, as with their first ashtray, the students will be very proud of it. Further, they will understand and more fully appreciate the "real wheel" when they see it. They learn the "what" and "why." *After* students have studied a concept, cases can be used to allow them to apply the concept in a "real world" setting, underscoring the "hows" and the "whens," the limits of the theory. If many cases are used, the students learn structure and relationships.

- Content versus process: There are ongoing arguments regarding whether cases are appropriate for teaching technical classes, conveying content or theory. The common wisdom is that cases are best used for illustration – after the theory has been explained,

Table 7.1   The case course objective grid

	PRE	POST
FEW	Topical content application Goal: reinventing the wheel	Topical content application Goals: illustration, application
MANY	Focus on process Goals: discovery, theory building, synthesis	Focus on process Goals: application, synthesis, seeing structure and relationships

and application – to show how a tool can be used in practice. One often hears: "My colleagues expect me to cover certain things in my course" or "One has to know certain things in order to be considered educated in the field of interstellar humflubbery."

- From a practical standpoint: You have to live with your colleagues. Go slow and insert cases where you can. Examine the role of the course in the curriculum.
- From an educational standpoint: I'll bet that the students in the content courses do not *learn* the material very well *until* they practice with it. Why separate the two processes? Involve the students *right away* with cases and other active learning.

Selecting the Right Cases

- The length and complexity of the cases should match the level and purpose of the course and the expectations of the students.
- Let the "Teaching Note" or "Instructor's Manual" (IM) be your guide. Most IMs describe the learning objectives of the case, and the courses for which the case is intended. The questions and analysis in the IM give a pretty good indication as to the issues and appropriate concepts to be applied.
- IMs don't know everything. Some of the best cases and learning experiences come from issues never touched upon by the IM.
- While Harvard Business School cases are perceived as the "gold standard," there are other sources to consider. NACRA and SCR cases are often a good bet. They are often of a "middle" length, they are well written, they have been reviewed, critiqued and edited, and they have IMs.
- Cases need to be interesting. Good cases tell a story . . . Good cases force the reader to take a stand and make decisions.
- Beware of the dreaded *"case wearout"*! After you have used a case a couple of times, and just when you are really becoming comfortable

in using it effectively, you will begin to hear your own words coming back to you. The fraternity files and the hand-me-downs will have struck. Put the case back on the shelf for a while, or find another case to use, or modify your expectations and objectives accordingly.

"Setting the Contract"

The single most important element of a successful case course is the establishment of a learning environment that is embraced by the community. It is critical that the students and the teacher are working with the same expectations and behavioral rules.

The case method scholar Professor C. Roland Christensen, in "Premises and Practices of Discussion Teaching" (1991, p. 16), notes:

1. A discussion class is a *partnership* in which students and instructor share the responsibilities and power of teaching, and the privilege of learning together.
2. A discussion group must evolve from a collection of individuals into a learning *community* with shared values and common goals.
3. By forging a primary (although not exclusive) *alliance with students* the discussion leader can help them gain command of the course material.
4. Discussion teaching requires *dual competency*: the ability to manage content and process.

At the beginning of a good focus group discussion, the moderator spends time encouraging all of the participants to talk, and then to expand their participation into the desired material. A good case teacher takes pains to set the appropriate tone and to encourage meaningful participation for all of the students in the early class periods of a course. My own goal for the first two weeks is to have every student take part in the discussion each day. Content is completely secondary until after the ground rules have been established.

Be careful! If you are directive in guiding the discussion early on, you have set the stage for the students to expect that from you in the future. You have kept control and the students will rightfully allow you to continue. After all, they are used to being observers rather than active learners. If you are less directive early on, the students will be encouraged to strike out on their own. It is the challenge of the case teacher to promote such adventurism while still guiding the overall direction.

Consistency is important. Students are suspicious when instructors offer them power and decision authority. At the first sign of an instructor trying to take power back, they will say, "I knew it." It will be very difficult to entice them back for a second try.

Some tools of the trade in setting (and maintaining) the contract are:

- opening ritual;
- closing ritual;
- syllabus and course outline;
- reaction to good and bad comments;
- indications of respect shown to students;
- flexibility in flow of discussion;
- knowing students' names;
- committing all to contribute;
- taking steps to eliminate stage fright;
- in early cases, involving subjects and issues to which the students can relate;
- in "process" courses, using broad cases early to set the tone.

Case Discussion Dynamics

Good case discussions are like stories or theatrical experiences. They should have a well-defined beginning, a middle and an end.

Class openings are part of the ritual and contract maintenance that define the learning environment. Announcements, questions, attendance, how one deals with tardiness, and so on all play a role at the beginning of class. The question "What did you learn from the last discussion?" can be a particularly useful tool in causing the students to rise to a higher level of abstraction or to take a step back and look at what they have been doing. Further, if done regularly, the students begin to see a pattern of learning and to connect elements of the class over the course.

Case openings differ from class openings. Class openings help to support "the contract," while case openings establish the direction of the particular case discussion to be held that day. There are several options:

- a. Faculty centered:
  - Decision oriented – "What should Sam do?"
  - Problem oriented – "What is the main problem Sam faces?"
  - Process oriented – "Where should Sam begin to analyze this situation?"
- b. Student centered:
  - Random selection – student presentation (creates pressure on students to be prepared).
  - Non-random selection – student presentation (sometimes there is a reason to have a particular student present: expertise, foreknowledge of exceptional preparation, etc.).

- Volunteer – student presentation (allows students to control the classroom and create an atmosphere of "going the extra mile").
- Group/team presentation (offers opportunity to teach team skills).

Case endings are critical to the learning outcomes.

Since cases are real histories of real situations, there is the opportunity to provide an epilogue. Students are fascinated to learn what the company really did. While this is often interesting, it gives the impression that this must be the right answer. Students crave "closure" and desperately want the teacher to validate one particular answer or outcome over all others. Students will go online to discover the "real" outcomes, usually before coming to class. Challenge the assumption that the company's actions were "correct" and ask how they could have been improved.

An alternative ending is to underline key learning issues. "Here are the things that you should have considered . . ." This is referred to in case teaching as "back-stopping." It gives the same "right answer" impression as an epilogue, but adds the additional insult that "the teacher knows best" and that the students cannot cover things on their own. It is a powerful message to the students that the teacher does not trust them. It will quickly cause discussion and risk taking to dry up as students wait for the teacher to provide "the answer."

Link to the next case by reviewing the main discoveries the students brought out and suggest that they might see some similarities or differences in the next case. Such an approach implies a structure in the material.

Similarly one might link to the last case. It is important to ask the students to explain what similarities or differences they saw rather than telling them. The question itself expressly shows that there is a structure to be seen, and underlines its importance.

Close by complimenting class performance as appropriate. Use sparingly to reinforce process and motivation.

Criticize class performance as needed. Again, use sparingly to reinforce responsibilities.

"Tricks of the Trade"

- Know each student's name as soon as possible. Take pictures. Use Facebook. Create a seating chart. Do whatever it takes. Work at it! There is an incredible transformation that takes place on the second day of class when you greet students by name. It says to them that you care about them as individuals. It tells them that you will hold them personally accountable. It shows that you are willing to work hard to hold up your half of the relationship.

- Don't be the "answer person." Students are used to having the teacher answer their questions, and they have become lazy in their expectation that this easy avenue is always open. Don't be afraid to say "I don't know." Don't be afraid to say "I think you should go look that up." Don't be afraid to say "I suggest that you look into the Myron Glurch theory on that subject and report back to the class on it."

- Use large name cards. Make sure that students have the names on both front and back and that they are readable by other students. Put them on desks or tables. You'd be surprised how many students don't know each other! When they get to know each other it creates a sense of community.

- When asked a question, turn it back to the class: "That's a good question! What do the rest of you think about that?" or "I hadn't thought about that. Not sure where to go with it. What do you think?"

- When a student makes a really good point, say so, go to your own notes and make a show of writing it down! If it is really a point that you hadn't thought of, say so . . . These are huge rewards for the student, and will motivate everyone!

- Live cases are a lot of fun for everyone. Bring a local or visiting business person to class with a short description or outline of a current issue. Give the students a few minutes to digest the information and then have them ask questions and discuss the matter as with a regular case. Such an experience reinforces the reality of the concepts and outcomes of the course.

- Board work is critical! *Plan* what your boards should look like before class. The instructor's board work does a great deal to set the structure of the discussion. When the instructor writes down what a student says, it is perceived as a reward. If it is not written down, it is perceived as a dismissal. The way the information is structured helps the students to organize their thinking and recognize relationships, and guides the discussion. Students learn quickly that a gap or space on the board signifies something that they have missed, and will begin searching.

- In "process" courses, use the same headings and topics in the same locations on the board to increase structure. For example, external or environmental analysis goes on one board, while internal, company information goes on a second, and proposals and action steps go on a third.

- A "scrap" board is always interesting and enlightening. Keep a corner or a separate board for unconnected or oddball thoughts, issues and comments. Sometimes the most creative and meaningful learning comes from the "twilight zone."

- If you want to continue the discussion on the same topic, call on the most recent hand that went up. If you want to change the discussion, call on the oldest. It doesn't always work, but it often does. The logic is that the newest hand came up as a result of the latest comment, while the oldest hand is there because of the fork way back in the road.

- Listen hard, and then restate if in doubt. Use the student's own words where possible.

- As case discussion classes mature, the discussions should become more "side to side." In other words, the students should begin to build off of each other's comments without interruption from the instructor. If the discussions continue to be "front to back," that is, student–instructor–student–instructor, there is probably too much direction going on. Stop it by simply calling on the next student without adding your two cents.

- When you like what students are saying and want them to continue, use your body language to support them by walking toward them and smiling and nodding. When you want a student to stop talking, look down and walk away. If it is really bad, shake your head.

- Map out the discussion ahead of time. Make certain that you have developed a good set of *transition questions*. In addition, there are probably some particular students on whom you can rely to understand the cases and make the transitions themselves. Keep them in mind as you wish to change the subject. Link your transition questions and plans to the board work design.

- Wait them out! When you ask a question and there is silence, it is more uncomfortable for them than it is for you! Take a cup of coffee with you and use the time to take a sip. Find something to erase at the side of the board. If they are really stumped, step back in the level of the question: "What was it that made it difficult to answer that last question?" Alternatively, restate the question and call for a "think–pair–share." Group the students in twos or threes, give them one minute to think about the topic and one minute to discuss it in their mini-groups, and then ask them to report out. It generates ideas through interaction and reduces the risk of sounding stupid by sharing the load.

- At least once in a term, don't read the case that you have assigned the class. Don't tell the students, and just carry on as usual. You will be amazed at what it does to your listening skills . . . and how you can cede power to the students! I did this each semester for 35 years. At the end of each term I told the students what I had done and asked them to predict which case it was. They *never* get it right, *and* it tells you something about how you performed on certain cases.

- At some point during the term, hand the chalk over to a student and sit down. Let the student run the show. Keep quiet. If the student appeals to you for guidance, just tell the student he or she is in charge. You'll be amazed at how well the student does *and* what it does for his or her confidence.
- A few weeks into the term some of your students will come to you, complaining that they just don't get it. They will ask you to show them a good analysis or to tell them the "right" answer, or some variation. Tell them to focus on the process or structure and to keep trying. Don't give in to them. What they are really asking for is a return to the good old days of passive learning.
- It is better to have 75 minutes or 90 minutes for a case discussion. Classes of 50–60 minutes make discussions awfully rushed.
- Tiered classrooms generate side-to-side discussions. Straight classrooms create front-to-back discussions. Try to schedule a room where the students can look each other in the eye.
- Assuming a 10- to 20-page case, a good student analysis should take three to four hours. A good instructor analysis will take twice that for a new case, plus a similar amount of time to consider what each student will gain.

Evaluation of Student Performance

Assuming a class size of 30 students the distribution of the discussion and participation will be, roughly:

- 6–8 non-participants: shyness or insecurity keeps them from talking;
- 4–6 frequent flyers: extroverts, sometimes intelligent, or just vocal;
- 16–20 midrange: will talk occasionally, when they have what they think is a good point.

Fear of looking stupid keeps some folks from participating. Gauge carefully before cracking their defensive shells with questions or comments. Students who are uncomfortable speaking in groups are often very well prepared and willing to talk one on one. An encouraging word during office hours can make all the difference in including them next time. Depending on the severity of the problem and your goals for the class, you might wish to make other options such as written outlines or one-on-one sessions available.

Because class participation is so important to case learning, there are two schools of thought about how to grade it:

a. High grade weight: As much as two-thirds of the class grade based upon the participation grade. Students are not commonly used to such a high proportion of their grade on participation, and it will put them under stress. Some will speak, just to get their points in for the day. The shy students will still not speak, and will have grade difficulties. You will receive complaints of "insufficient air time in class," "favoritism in calling on certain students," and the classic "attendance is the same as participation." High grade weight underlines the importance of preparation and participation.
b. Low grade weight: Creates less stressful discussion environment, but may also lead to lack of preparation, and a free ride for the non-talkers. Once the "contract has been set," grades often take a back seat.

If you are unsure of your ability to remember and account for the comments of the students, you can have a class member or an outsider take notes as an in-class recorder.

My own process has been to retreat to my office immediately after class and use the class list to record my impressions of the contributions of each student for that discussion. My grading rubric has always been: significant contribution advancing the understanding of the class – A; good comment or comments, on topic, keeping the discussion moving – B; marginal comment, perhaps a case fact without embellishment – C; weak comment, wrong content, wrong interpretation – D; no comment or disruptive behavior – F. I usually recreate the discussion and write a few notes on each student's comments or content.

CONCLUSION

We tend to believe that *our* content is the most important thing that the students will ever learn. The facts would seem to contradict this belief. Studies confirm that very little factual information is retained by students over time.

It is difficult to "switch" from a faculty-centered to a student-centered pedagogy. We are used to having control over the class, and it is hard to give up that power. And why should we? After all, we are the instructors! The answer is simple – active learning is more effective than passive learning.

There are many reasons it is difficult to "switch":

- There is less risk if you are in control – if the students control, you never know what will happen or when.
  A: That is what makes it both a challenge and a joy!
- It takes time and effort – we have our materials already set up.
  A: Being excellent at any endeavor requires work.
- My evaluations are okay now. "If it ain't broke, don't fix it!"
  A: Case instructors routinely receive teaching awards and accolades!
- I don't know how to do this!
  A: Of course you do! You can lead a discussion and have many times.
- I don't know where to find materials or how to select them.
  A: *Easy!* Go to the NACRA website: www.nacra.net. There are multiple links to online case publishers.
- If I don't produce and publish a certain number of articles, it won't matter how I teach – I won't be there!
  A: Start slowly – add a few cases at a time.

It really is simple – active learning is better than passive learning.

BIBLIOGRAPHY

Barnes, Louis B., Christensen, C. Roland and Hansen, Abby J. (1994), *Teaching and the Case Method*, 3rd edn., Boston, MA: Harvard Business School Press.
Christensen, C. Roland (1991), Premises and practices of discussion teaching, in C. Roland Christensen, David A. Garvin and Ann Sweet (eds.), *Education for Judgment: The Artistry of Discussion Leadership*, Boston, MA: Harvard Business School Press, pp. 15–34.
Christensen, C. Roland, Garvin, David A. and Sweet, Ann (eds.) (1991), *Education for Judgment: The Artistry of Discussion Leadership*, Boston, MA: Harvard Business School Press.
Leenders, Michiel R. and Erskine, James (1989), *Case Research: The Case Writing Process*, 3rd edn., London, Canada: Research and Publications Division, School of Business Administration, University of Western Ontario.
Mauffette-Leenders, Louise A., Erskine, James A. and Leenders, Michiel R. (1997), *Learning with Cases*, London, Canada: Richard Ivey School of Business, University of Western Ontario.
Mauffette-Leenders, Louise A., Erskine, James A. and Leenders, Michiel R. (1998), *Teaching with Cases*, London, Canada: Richard Ivey School of Business, University of Western Ontario.
Naumes, William and Naumes, Margaret J. (1999), *The Art and Craft of Case Writing*, Thousand Oaks, CA: Sage Publications.

8. The experiential learning portfolio and entrepreneurship education

Minet Schindehutte and Michael H. Morris

INTRODUCTION

Experiential learning is a pedagogical approach where students learn by doing or from observing the doings of others. When integrated with an entrepreneurship education program, it centers on the idea that students can learn entrepreneurship theories, principles and concepts by applying themselves to projects and activities rooted in real-world practice. Here, experiential learning allows a student to act and then learn a principle or concept, or to be introduced to the principle or concept and then reinforce that learning by applying it to some real-world situation. At their root, experiential approaches are about engagement and activity, where knowledge is created from interactions between students and the environment (Kolb, 1984).

A central concept in experiential learning is the importance of practice – the idea that students get to practice particular entrepreneurial behaviors and actions. Neck et al. (2014) use the term "deliberate practice" to describe meaningful performances by students that become habitual and help attain a state of mind. Hence, one is practicing so as to develop methods of thinking and acting – in short, to develop an entrepreneurial mindset. It is hard to imagine a successful pianist or gymnast who does not rigorously practice virtually every day. Extended to entrepreneurship education, the argument is that students must practice opportunity recognition, creative problem-solving, risk management, resource leveraging and other entrepreneurial competencies – not simply to get better at them, but to develop an entrepreneurial mindset.

Today, the discipline of entrepreneurship finds itself at the leading edge in terms of introducing new experiential learning methodologies and techniques in higher education. As the curriculum has expanded and degree programs have taken root in many schools, there has been an accelerated rate of experimentation with novel experiences. These are occurring both in the classroom and as co-curricular activities.

How to effectively manage experiential learning within an entrepreneurship program is a topic that has not received much attention. Rather, the focus has been on its value and importance, and ways to increase the amount of experiential learning. In this chapter, we introduce the concept of an experience portfolio as a key tool to aid both those managing entrepreneurship programs and the students enrolled in these programs. We argue that the portfolio should be tied to the learning objectives of programs and the learning styles of students. Key elements that might form an experience portfolio are reviewed.

WHAT IS AN EXPERIENCE?

Experiences are not merely practical applications. To experience something is to be engaged with it at some level, to process it cognitively and emotionally, to live through it. The student's imagination, problem-solving abilities, senses and feelings are being engaged in some sort of entrepreneurial scenario. Experiences have a structure and occur over some defined time period, such that there is a beginning, middle and end. With a well-managed experiential learning exercise or project, the educator attempts to structure the experience around the following questions:

- What should the student see?
- What should the student be thinking?
- What should the student be feeling?
- What should the student be doing?

Experiential learning approaches differ in their relative abilities to produce visual stimuli, cognitively challenge the student, elicit emotions, or require behaviors and actions. Hence trade-off decisions are being made by the faculty member in selecting an experiential learning vehicle. For instance, compared to a written case study that the student must read, analyze and discuss, a small business consulting project may generate more visual stimuli, produce a wider range of emotional reactions, and result in more tangible actions that students actually implement.

Levels of student engagement are especially critical in determining the learning impact of an experiential tool or approach. Engagement is the degree to which the student is attracted and his/her interest captured and held. High levels of engagement find the student more active than passive, and making connections that are more intimate than distant. A key factor impacting engagement levels is the gap or incongruity between the student's skills and the nature of the experiential challenges being faced (that is, context complexity) at any point in time (Nakatsu et al., 2005). Experiences produce incongruities that can be positive, where challenges exceed skills, or negative, where skills exceed challenges. Relative congruency between challenges and skills produces "flow" (Csikszentmihalyi, 1997). Flow is immersion based on high engagement and an energized focus, where emotions are positive and aligned with the task at hand. High amounts of negative incongruity can produce experiences of boredom or apathy, where the student is not especially engaged, is ultimately unsatisfied, and may withdraw. An example might be the use of a case study that is overly technical, uninteresting and hard to relate to course material. Of course, boredom could find the student looking for ways to increase the context complexity by trying new things, assuming the context lends itself to such experimentation. Alternatively, overly high positive incongruity can result in high levels of agitation and anxiety, which might also result in greater engagement, but also work against flow. A rigorous consulting project for a struggling small business in an industry where the student has little to no experience could produce such an outcome.

EXPERIENCES AND THE LEARNING STYLES OF STUDENTS

Seminal work on experiential learning can be found in Kolb's (1984) foundational book and the impressive body of literature that has been built on his foundation. He proposes a four-stage learning cycle that includes experiencing, reflecting, thinking/conceptualizing and acting. Knowledge is constructed as the result of a recursive process involving these four elements. Concrete experiences produce observations and reflections, which are assimilated and refined into abstract concepts from which action implications are then drawn, and these are actively tested and guide the creation of new experiences (Kolb, A. and Kolb, 2005).

Central to Kolb's work is the notion that students learn in different ways – they have differing learning styles. Arguing that knowledge is created by grasping and transforming experiences, the perspective centers on two opposed or conflicting modes of grasping experiences. One mode involves concrete experiencing (feeling) versus abstract conceptualization (thinking), and the other concerns active experimentation (acting) versus reflective observation (reflecting). Hence each of the four modes suggests a different kind of learning capability or skill. Taken a step further, four prevalent types of learning styles are identified. Convergers have stronger abilities with abstract conceptualization and active experimentation, and are good at the practical application of ideas. They prefer to deal with things rather than with people. Divergers are better at concrete experiencing and reflective observation. Able to view situations from multiple perspectives, they are more imaginative, emotional and people-oriented. Assimilators demonstrate more aptitude for abstract conceptualization and reflective observation, with abilities to create logical theoretical models. They can integrate disparate observations and are good at inductive reasoning, but prefer abstract concepts over practical applications, and are less people-oriented. Accommodators are superior at concrete experiencing and active experimentation. They like to take risks, engage in trial-and-error experiments, and get things implemented, and are good at moving away from the theory or plan and adapting to circumstances. Thus, accommodators have the opposite learning strengths to assimilators, and convergers have the opposite strengths to divergers. Note that these are not four discrete categories, but represent continuous positions on the two modes of grasping experiences.

Attempts have been made to link learning styles to academic fields of study (e.g., Kolb, 1981). Business students tend to be accommodators, engineers are often convergers, psychology students are typically divergers, and math and chemistry majors tend to be more assimilative. Such differences among disciplines are associated with differences in methods of inquiry and how knowledge is reported and in criteria for evaluating knowledge. In short, then, disciplines differ in terms of what constitutes valid knowledge. While management as a field of study, and by extension entrepreneurship, tends to emphasize pragmatism, it is inherently multidisciplinary and can require different learning styles.

A variation of Kolb's learning cycle is reproduced in Figure 8.1. Learning styles for which a student has a preference are reflected in the four regions within the cycle. Each region is also influenced by characteristics of the learning context. The fact that students learn in different ways is important when considering experiential learning. For example, teams of students working on a small business consulting project or putting together a business plan may be more productive if they have a sense of the different learning styles of teammates. Further, one should recognize that experiential learning projects and activities can differ in the relative importance of experiencing, reflecting, conceptualizing and acting for successful accomplishment of the task or assignment. In Figure 8.1, we provide examples of how different learning activities, including experiential tools, might place relatively more emphasis on skills related to a particular quadrant of the learning cycle. While this is influenced by instructors and how they design and manage experiential activities, we might find creating a business model is active experimentation, working in an incubator is concrete experience, interviewing an entrepreneur is

Experiential learning =
Hands on + Minds on

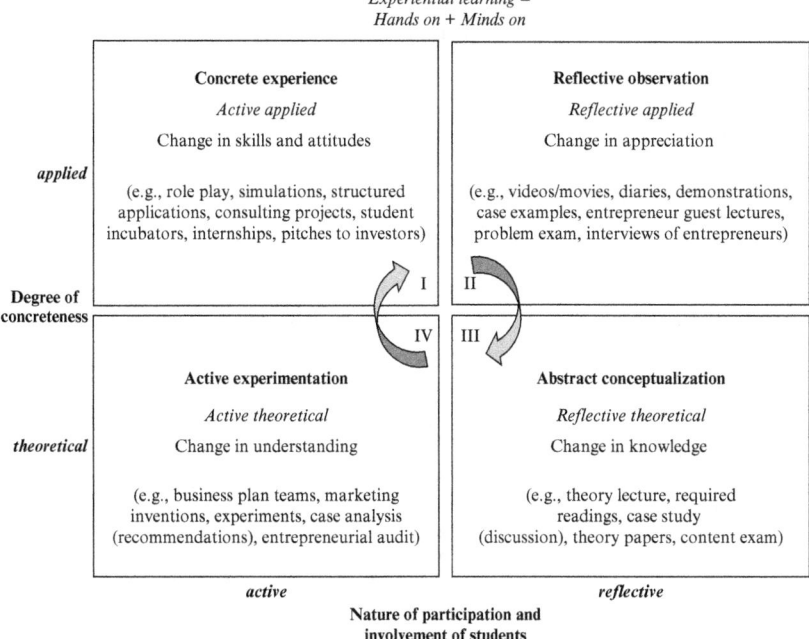

Source: Adapted from Schindehutte (2007), based on the original work by A. Kolb and Kolb (2005).

Figure 8.1   Learning styles and entrepreneurial experiences

reflective observation, and presenting a theory of venture life cycles is abstract conceptualization.

In the final analysis, experiential learning in entrepreneurship represents an attempt to move the educational focus away from a text-driven to an activity-driven approach, from telling to showing, from linear to recursive learning, and from theory to the integration of theory and practice (e.g., Kolb, A. and Kolb, 2005). The instructor is attempting to put the student in a situation where he/she interacts with elements or aspects of the entre-preneurial context, while introducing a more individualized and feeling-oriented education. Entrepreneurship especially lends itself to experiential techniques, as it involves the individual creating reality as he/she pursues an unclearly defined and uncontrollable path, with significant ambigu-ity and uncertainty, with a continual need for creative action, and where the entrepreneur must perform adequately in a number of different roles. While many possibilities exist in terms of such techniques, the ability to effectively build them into the learning process within an entrepreneurship program can be greatly enhanced through adoption of the experience portfolio concept, a subject to which we now turn.

THE EXPERIENCE PORTFOLIO CONCEPT

When students complete an entrepreneurship program, we believe they should graduate with a mix of experiences, and hence some basic level of experience. This mix can be captured in what we call an "experience portfolio." Analogous to that of a financial portfolio, the purpose is to build a mix of experiences that reflect different learning goals (for example, the abilities to analyze, apply, reflect, critique, conceptualize, create, solve and implement). And as with an artist's portfolio, the purpose is to demonstrate mastery of specific entrepreneurial competencies (for example, opportunity recognition, risk mitigation, resource leveraging, value innovation, and adaptation) (see Morris et al., 2013). Of note, the portfolio is not simply a valuable tool for the student, but a mechanism to help guide the design and management of the entrepreneurship program.

Students build their portfolio as they move through an entrepreneurship program, and present it for review upon program completion. Hence, proactive students may be able to produce two business models they developed for original concepts, a comprehensive business plan, a feasibility study, an idea diary, a consulting project for a small business, an entrepreneurial audit, an interview with an entrepreneur, four marketing inventions for existing firms, and a year's experience trying to run a business in a student incubator. The range of possibilities is limited only by the extent to which faculty approach the curriculum, campus and community as an experiential laboratory. Table 8.1 provides an illustration of the elements that could contribute to a student's entrepreneurial experience portfolio.

The cycle of observing, thinking, doing and feeling in A. Kolb and Kolb (2005) can be reflected in a student's experience portfolio. Those teaching entrepreneurship may want to ensure that the set of experiential activities available to students reflects some balance among reflective observation, abstract conceptualization, active experimentation and concrete experience. At the same time, it is likely that trade-offs are made in efforts to produce balanced portfolios. Thus, over-reliance on having students write business plans as a learning tool may find the student not doing enough reflective observation, or failing to gain the learning advantages produced by concrete experiencing. Having the student enter a competition using the same business plan might result in more reflection and experimentation. Similarly, the instructor can give a lecture or have students read about bootstrapping or guerrilla tactics, resulting in abstract conceptualization,

Table 8.1   Sample experiential learning portfolio

Course-based	Co-curricular
Idea diaries	Idea jams
Business models	Internships at local ventures and incubators
Business plans	Entrepreneurial mentors for students
Feasibility studies	Entrepreneurship study abroad programs
Written or video case studies	Elevator pitch competitions
Mini- and full case studies	Pitching to a banker
Live cases	Campus business plan competitions
Interviews of entrepreneurs	Students competing in regional or
YouTube videos of entrepreneurs	national competitions
Hollywood movies	Student venture hatcheries
Entrepreneurial audits	Campus-based businesses run by students
Marketing inventions	Prototype development/fab labs
Small business consulting projects	Website development
In-class games or exercises	Start-up weekends
Simulations	Shadowing entrepreneurs
Adopting a family firm	Student venture fairs
Role plays	Speaker series
Negotiations	Community outreach initiatives
Guest lectures by entrepreneurs	(e.g., bootcamps, women's symposia)
Lean start-up methodologies	Technology commercialization projects
Experiential exams	Students mentoring high school or
	disadvantaged students

but the ability to appreciate the need for balance between creative thinking and practical constraints in producing workable bootstrapping approaches might be enhanced with a live case study (active experimentation). Alternatively, the instructor who teaches the concept of entrepreneurial orientation (EO) requires that students read a case study of a company that has a track record of sustained entrepreneurial behavior, or asks students to find a company they believe is highly entrepreneurial and prepare a report on why, resulting in differing degrees of abstract conceptualization and reflective observation. The same instructor could require an entrepreneurial audit where students conduct an in-depth intervention with a company, actually measure its EO score, assess the work climate to identify facilitating and constraining elements affecting entrepreneurial behavior, and make recommendations. Further, as a consulting project, the students could work with the company to implement specific programs to increase levels of entrepreneurship, which from a learning perspective could produce degrees of active experimentation and concrete experiencing.

Student learning styles should also be considered. Assimilators may excel at learning activities that involve more abstract conceptualizing or thoughtful reflection. Accommodators may do very well at activities that center on experimentation and concrete experiencing. Yet Kolb and Kolb (2005, p. 201) describe experiential learning as "a process of locomotion through the learning regions that is influenced by a person's position in the learning space." Exposing the student to a diverse portfolio of experiential learning activities can facilitate their growth and development as they improve their capacities for different modes of learning.

BUILDING A BALANCED MIX OF ACTIVITIES WITHIN THE PORTFOLIO

Given the unlimited range of possibilities when it comes to experiential learning, one way to organize the portfolio is to distinguish: 1) activities that occur in the classroom or in conjunction with a course; 2) campus-based co-curricular activities that are not attached to a course; 3) outreach and community-based experiences; and 4) international experiences.

Experiences within or Tied to a Course

The beginning point in pursuing the portfolio approach concerns the embedding of experiences in the entrepreneurship curriculum. Again, there is a need to move beyond the business plan and consider the many creative possibilities. This can include activities done during class time, such as role plays, idea jams and case discussions. It may also involve activities discussed during class but with much of the work done in the student's own time, such as the development of business models, interviews of entrepreneurs, or developing a product prototype. Simulations represent an example of a mixed model involving heavy in-class and out-of-class time. The availability of entrepreneurship-specific simulations has increased significantly in recent years. Simulations are particularly effective in teaching entrepreneurship students about decision-making under time constraints (Cadotte, 2014), learning from failure (Shepherd, 2004), and contingency-based planning (Honig, 2004).

Table 8.2 presents an entrepreneurship curriculum from a university that offers an undergraduate major and minor in entrepreneurship. Each course in this curriculum has defined experiential components that reflect the purpose, nature and content of that course. Thus, the Entrepreneurial Marketing class requires students to create marketing inventions, where they must find existing small businesses and radically change one of the four elements of the marketing mix. Alternatively, the Corporate

Table 8.2   Linking experiential learning to the curriculum

Course title	Experiential learning requirements
Introduction to Entrepreneurship	Business model; interview of entrepreneur; short cases.
Women and Minority Entrepreneurship	Minority entrepreneur profile; research paper on practical challenges in women or minority entrepreneurship.
Entrepreneurial Marketing	Marketing inventions for existing companies; case studies.
Social Entrepreneurship	Business model for a new social venture.
Growing Small and Family Ventures	Adopting a family firm project.
Creativity and Entrepreneurship	Students create, present, modify ideas for five new products, services or ventures; imagination diary.
Business Plan Lab	Create original business plan; critique of an existing plan.
Special Topics in Entrepreneurship	Varies depending on topical focus.
Entrepreneurship and the Arts	Collaborative entrepreneurial project between art, theatre and music students.
Dilemmas and Debates in Entrepreneurship	Critique of notable entrepreneur; position paper on an entrepreneurial dilemma.
Green Entrepreneurship	Business model for for-profit green venture; environmental business case studies.
Corporate Entrepreneurship	Entrepreneurial audit of established firm; case studies.
Emerging Enterprise Consulting	Assessment model and full consulting report with deliverables for a small business client.
Entrepreneurship and New Technologies	Commercialization plan for a university technology project, technology case studies.
Strategic and Entrepreneurial Management	Full business plan; case studies.
Entrepreneurship Empowerment in South Africa	Consulting reports with four deliverables for each of two clients; student diary; case studies on former clients.
Entrepreneurship Practicum	Varies depending on topical focus.
Venture Capital	Five-year financing plan for start-up; case studies.
Economics of Entrepreneurship	Assessment of a country's GEM score and the underlying economic factors contributing to it.
Legal Aspects of Entrepreneurship	Legal plan for start-up venture, including enterprise form, intellectual property, employment and contractual issues.
New Product Development	Concept for new product including drawings or prototype.

Entrepreneurship class has students conducting an entrepreneurial audit in a mid-sized or large firm to determine how entrepreneurial the company currently is and how it might become more entrepreneurial.

A portfolio mindset is also supported when entrepreneurship programs create a logical flow among experiential learning projects and activities across the curriculum. One model would find an early course with activities that center on ideation and concept development (e.g., a Creativity course). This might be followed by a course where students develop a business model based on some original idea for a venture (e.g., an Introduction to Entrepreneurship course). Next might come courses with experiential projects linked to functional needs in a venture, such as marketing inventions, a legal plan or a financing model (e.g., Entrepreneurial Marketing, Business Law and Entrepreneurship, or New Venture Finance). The final, or capstone, course might then be the logical place to tie things together with a comprehensive, integrated business plan (e.g., Strategic and Entrepreneurial Management).

Campus-based Experiences

A growing number of universities are complementing what happens in the classroom with co-curricular activities that reinforce and extend the content delivered in courses. The most widespread of these has traditionally been a college-wide or campus-wide business plan competition. More recently, schools have instituted competitions that center on business models instead of plans, as well as elevator pitch competitions that focus on orally presenting concepts for new ventures. Beyond competitions, six types of campus-based initiatives that can contribute to experience portfolios include:

- *Student incubators*: Creating a dedicated space where students can launch and grow ventures while enrolled in school.
- *Technology commercialization projects*: Formal programs link entrepreneurship faculty, students and community resources to the process of moving a technology from the laboratory to the marketplace.
- *Entrepreneurship learning communities and dormitories*: Establishment of a creativity, innovation and entrepreneurship (CIE) residence hall allows programs to create a living environment dedicated to helping students recognize, act upon and celebrate their entrepreneurial potential.
- *Student venture funds*: A seed capital fund is created for investment in ventures launched by students. The university may take equity positions in these ventures. Students may also help run the

fund, making investment recommendations and performing due diligence.

- *Campus-based, student-run ventures*: The university allocates space and equipment to profit-generating businesses that are run by students and serve the faculty, staff and student body.
- *Mentoring programs*: Assigning entrepreneurial mentors to students for a semester or academic year represents a valuable way to expose them to the human side of the entrepreneurial process. Mentoring programs have also been extended from entrepreneur-to-student to peer-to-peer mentoring where upper-level or advanced students mentor those who are younger or face unique challenges in college or beyond.

The activities that make up a portfolio can also reinforce or impact one another. The student who resides in an entrepreneurship dormitory frequently ends up pursuing majors or minors in entrepreneurship, and competing in business plan competitions. Technology commercialization projects can end up inside student incubators. An interview of an entrepreneur might lead to an internship with the entrepreneur's company.

Community-based Experiences

The traditional role of the university as repository and conveyor of knowledge is complemented by its role as agent of economic and social development. As the latter receives more emphasis, community engagement becomes more prevalent. As entrepreneurship programs have launched a diverse mix of community engagement programs, new opportunities emerge for student experiences. Examples include start-up bootcamps that help local residents learn how to launch a venture, symposia focusing on unique challenges and opportunities confronting women or minority entrepreneurs, mentoring programs in inner-city schools, initiatives targeting disabled veterans attempting to start a business, and community-based breakfasts that feature entrepreneurial speakers. Students can volunteer to assist with such programs, in addition to playing leadership roles in managing them. A noteworthy example is the South Side Entrepreneurship Connect Program launched by the entrepreneurship center at Syracuse University. An incubator was created in the inner city to serve entrepreneurs attempting to build ventures in highly adverse circumstances. The incubator offers free consulting from students, a micro-credit fund that students help run, and training classes on topics such as QuickBooks taught by students, among other opportunities.

Some outreach programs represent attempts to invest in or give back to the community. Others represent revenue sources to support the entrepreneurship program. Regardless of the motives, the university positions itself in a leadership role in terms of entrepreneurial development within a city, state or region. It is also useful to approach community-based experiences as part of a three-way set of linkages where the classroom, experiential learning and community outreach are connected. Consider the example of a six-week bootcamp offered over six Saturdays to members of the community who own new and small businesses, or who are in the process of starting a business. Delegates attend class in the mornings, and then, in the afternoons, they receive consulting assistance from graduate students in entrepreneurship. The students, in turn, get credit within a course and build their experience portfolios.

International Experiences

In recent years, entrepreneurship programs have become more active in study abroad initiatives, providing another range of opportunities when building the experience portfolio. The simplest initiatives involve taking students to another country and having them receive some lectures and visit some entrepreneurial companies. Somewhat more involved might be programs where students work on a project with an entrepreneurial venture from abroad that is attempting to enter the US market, and as part of the project they visit the company in its home country. A higher level of engagement can be found in programs such as Entrepreneurship Empowerment in South Africa run by a consortium of universities led by the University of Florida. Here, 28 students and three faculty members go to South Africa for six weeks to work with historically disadvantaged entrepreneurs based in impoverished townships. The American students are paired with South African students and assigned to local entrepreneurs, resulting in a three-way transfer of knowledge, insight and learning experiences.

FORMAT OF AN EXPERIENTIAL PORTFOLIO

Ideally, the experiential portfolio should be treated as a purposeful part of the student's evolution as an entrepreneurial thinker and doer. The components of an experiential portfolio are creative deliverables. Not all entrepreneurship students want to (or can) create a new venture, but all of them can create a blog or a website, in addition to having several opportunities to "create" through their engagement in experiential learning activities. The portfolio of experiences (see Table 8.1) can also become an additional creative endeavor – in either a physical or a digital format.

A Physical Folder

The easiest approach is to require students to add printed copies of the items in their experiential portfolio to a folder (e.g., a three-ring binder) that must be kept up to date. Students create a table of contents for the folder, and may also be required to write a reflection of its contents to summarize the learning outcomes across the different experiences.

An e-Portfolio

Student entrepreneurs who participate in national competitions (e.g., for grants or business plans) are often asked to create a pitch video (typically two to five minutes long). It has also become customary for both graduate schools and employers to ask applicants to provide writing samples as well as a short video clip (e.g., about specific aspects related to the applicant's life, hobbies, skills, etc.). Transmission of these items is done electronically. In a similar vein, it makes sense to organize documentation related to experiential learning electronically. Furthermore, electronic portfolios (e-portfolios) are increasingly used to document learning – as a pedagogical tool (Wozniak, 2013), a measure of reflective practice (Parkes et al., 2013) and an assessment method (Cambridge, 2010).

The e-portfolio can take several forms, two of which are mentioned here as they might be used with an entrepreneurship course. First, it could be a course-specific blog in which students keep a journal of experiential activities they engaged in within the class or at home. Students take pictures of artifacts or the items created, post in the blog, and write an experience memo, thereby creating a log of all activities during the semester. This approach greatly facilitates grading, because the student updates the blog after each class, but the instructor only grades the blog intermittently. The blog can be kept private (shared only with the instructor) or it can be made public. The latter has the advantage that students are reminded that they have to be innovative; that is, they are encouraged to explore new ways to express themselves in a unique way and to blend their personal and academic lives. Additionally, plagiarism is discouraged because of public scrutiny. It also allows students to learn about themselves (becoming their own sounding boards for self-discovery) as well as from each other through feedback (and peer review).

Second, the e-portfolio can be in the form of a website that is created for the express purpose of documenting lifelong learning. Students can organize their past, present and future creative deliverables (e.g., project reports, business plans) into one experiential portfolio that documents their learning experiences in different courses, and even different life stages (e.g., pre-school, high school, university, work experience, etc.). The benefit of this approach is it presents a more holistic view of the student's competencies to future employers or other audiences, beyond the standard resume, which immediately gives the student an advantage during the interview process. An added advantage of this approach is that it significantly increases both the quality and the professionalism of project deliverables when students start to think of a career (long-term), rather than treat deliverables simply as an assignment for a grade (short-term). Importantly, the ease of transmission and portability of the e-portfolio enables students to permanently record their various achievements and their personal growth, in addition to creating a "legacy of learning" that transcends the classroom.

CONCLUSIONS

From a student vantage point, we believe learning can be much enhanced when the concept of an experience portfolio is adopted. More than just a compendium of experiential activities engaged in by a student, the portfolio concept is built around a mix of learning goals and outcomes. It is designed to reflect different learning styles. Students engage in experiences that develop their abilities at analysis, reflection, critique, creation and implementation, while also demonstrating mastery of particular entrepreneurial competencies such as opportunity recognition, risk mitigation and resource leveraging. Moreover, the portfolio can include a wide variety of learning activities that differ in the learning skills required, the time and rigor involved, the level of student engagement sought, and the possible outcomes. It typically includes a balanced mix of in-class and co-curricular (campus-, community- and internationally based) activities. Schools that capitalize on the potential of the portfolio do not see experiential activities as augmentations or add-ons, but as a pedagogical approach that is integral to the design of courses, curricula and overall entrepreneurship programs. They are a means of delivering content, not simply reinforcing or applying content.

REFERENCES

Cadotte, E.R. (2014), The use of simulations in entrepreneurship education: opportunities, challenges and outcomes, in M.H. Morris (ed.), *Annals of Entrepreneurship Education and Pedagogy – 2014*, Cheltenham, UK and Northampton, MA, USA: Edward Elgar, pp. 280–303.

Cambridge, D. (2010), *E-portfolios for Lifelong Learning and Assessment*, San Francisco: Jossey-Bass.

Csikszentmihalyi, M. (1997), *Finding Flow: The Psychology of Engagement with Everyday Life*, New York: Basic Books.

Honig, B. (2004), Entrepreneurship education: toward a model of contingency-based business planning, *Academy of Management Learning and Education*, **3**(3), 258–273.

Kolb, A. and Kolb, D.A. (2005), Learning styles and learning spaces: enhancing experiential learning in higher education, *Academy of Management Executive*, **4**(2), 193–212.

Kolb, D.A. (1981), Learning styles and disciplinary differences, in A.W. Chickering (ed.), *The Modern American College*, San Francisco: Jossey-Bass, pp. 232–255.

Kolb, D.A. (1984), *Experiential Learning: Experience as the Source of Learning and Development*, Englewood Cliffs, NJ: Prentice Hall.

Morris, M.H., Webb, J.W., Fu, J. and Singhal, S. (2013), A competency-based perspective on entrepreneurship education: conceptual and empirical insights, *Journal of Small Business Management*, **51**(3), 352–369.

Nakatsu, R., Rauterberg, M. and Vorderer, P. (2005), A new framework for entertainment computing: from passive to active experience, in F. Kishino, Y. Kitamura, H. Kato and N. Nagata (eds.), *Entertainment Computing – ICEC 2005*, Berlin: Springer, pp. 1–12.

Neck, H.M., Greene, P.G. and Brush, C.G. (eds.) (2014), *Teaching Entrepreneurship: A Practice-based Approach*, Cheltenham, UK and Northampton, MA, USA: Edward Elgar.

Parkes, K.A., Dredger, K.S. and Hicks, D. (2013), ePortfolio as a measure of reflective practice, *International Journal of ePortfolio*, **3**(2), 99–115.

Schindehutte, M. (2007), Play to learn and learn to play, Working paper, Syracuse University.

Shepherd, D.A. (2004), Educating entrepreneurship students about emotion and learning from failure, *Academy of Management Learning and Education*, **3**(3), 274–287.

Wozniak, N.M.C. (2013), Enhancing inquiry, evidence-based reflection, and integrative learning with the Lifelong ePortfolio Process: the implementation of integrative eportfolios at Stony Brook University, *Journal of Educational Technology Systems*, **41**(3), 209–230.

9. Deliberate Opportunity Design: a practical integrative product and business design framework to enable new frontiers in fostering innovation and entrepreneurship

Alex Bruton

INTRODUCTION

So What?

The work being reported here responds in large part to what I call the "many new approaches dilemma" in entrepreneurship education that has arisen in recent years – the problem that, in the face of so many approaches having become available for fostering entrepreneurship and innovation, curricular design decisions are not always made based on sound instructional design principles or with the right desired competencies in mind. It is not unusual to find entrepreneurship educators arguing – sometimes quietly, and sometimes vehemently with an approach founder's promotional materials in hand – that the approach he or she has selected has more merit than another. And, possibly worse than that, a good many of us are adopting approaches without having had the important debates that would help assure that our initiatives have an impact.

Tasked with developing a new course, for example, a junior faculty member might adopt tools such as the lean canvas of Ash Maurya, the business model canvas of Alex Osterwalder, or the idea modeling tools of Alex Bruton, because they are more readily available than others. A newly hired adjunct professor, on the other hand, might design the same course based entirely on the popular lean startup methodology developed by Eric Ries, guided by her exposure to it while running her last startup. A senior professor whose own businesses were able to raise funds based on the quality of their business plans might insist the course be based on the more formal and prediction-oriented approach of the business plan. The director of an incubator might adopt the design thinking approaches of David Kelley because he took one of the d.School's online courses while learning about social innovation. And a professor with experience in web-based product management might be inclined to structure things based on the customer development work of Steve Blank and Bob Dorf because of how well it served his experience.

This is not to say these approaches are not important, useful or valid; far from it, and this chapter aims to advance a framework that helps us work toward a common and actionable view of them, grounded in previously published work in various fields. Nor is it to say that the methodologies named here are alone on the menu of new and time-tested approaches from which we can choose today; they are not. Further, the supply side of this situation is likely not a problem; it is a good thing that so many options are available to educators, and it can be a great thing that new branded and packaged materials are so readily available to students and nascent entrepreneurs.

That said, the challenges of the "many new approaches dilemma" can arise, for example, when decisions are made without proper regard to the need for constructive alignment (see Biggs, 2011) between the desired learning outcomes, the choice of assessment methods, and the associated teaching and learning activities. They can arise when an approach is selected only because of a professor's history with it, an academic chair's personal preference for it, or the popularity of the associated brand with visiting entrepreneurs, or even just because an approach has more accessible packaging. Further, teaching innovations are limited when modules, programs, courses and co-curricular experiences are developed based on or become biased to only a subset of approaches.

In turn, these challenges can lead to significant detrimental outcomes for educators. To name a few examples: I have witnessed arguments between entrepreneurship professors because one felt very strongly about applying the business model canvas and the other felt just as strongly about using the traditional business plan; I have read Listserv emails, blog posts and even academic papers written to debunk or espouse various approaches over others; I have worked with untenured faculty seeking advice on how to explain their desire to implement "modern newfangled" approaches to their department chair who "just doesn't get it"; I have observed professors adopt an approach because students "gave better evaluations when I tried it" and not because it helped students meet the desired learning outcomes; I have advised academic program designers who had imported approaches not designed for their context, and others who were openly unclear about which methods to build into their courses; and I have worked with corporate leaders experiencing a dilemma about which approaches they should adopt for their staff and processes.

Calls for "New Frontiers" in Fostering Entrepreneurship

In addition to the significant opportunity that exists to serve program designers by addressing the "many new approaches dilemma," entrepreneurship education researchers have begun to recognize some of the same challenges while also calling for the use of some of the above-named approaches to help enable new paradigms in teaching and learning. The following provides limited but representative examples of that work.

Brinckmann and Grichnik (2010), Jones et al. (2013) and Lange et al. (2007) are among those to have recently tackled the "stubborn" and "intense" debate that still seems to persist about the role of business planning in enterprise and entrepreneurship education, for example. (Except in some circumstances, it seems to remain unclear whether writing a business plan actually helps as a tool for meeting some learning outcomes or whether it even leads to an increase in the eventual odds of one's success.) The business model continues to enjoy increasingly mainstream use in practice, but in recent research – such as that reported in George and Bock (2009) and Morris and Schindehutte (2015) – it is suggested that the literature on the topic remains "fragmented," "inconsistent" and "without consensus in regarding a definition." Additionally, publications can be found proposing and describing many of the other tools and approaches named here. Examples of the use of the business model for entrepreneurial learning include Morris et al. (2005) and Osterwalder et al. (2005), examples in design thinking for entrepreneurship include Bruton (2010) and Goldsby et al. (2014), and examples for lean startup in launching a new enterprise include Blank (2013) – just to name a few of many. However, one is challenged to find peer reviewed research that demonstrates the efficacy or superiority of these or the other earlier-mentioned approaches over each other, over other established approaches, or in helping meet the right learning outcomes.

Importantly though, some researchers have begun pointing to approaches such as those being highlighted here as being useful in enabling new paradigms, alternative models, and practice-based approaches to education. For example, Brush et al. (2015) make the case for practice-based entrepreneurship education in which educators "must create a classroom where 'being entrepreneurial' is a baseline behavior," and they name the business model canvas and the idea model as being useful in implementing what they call the Practice of Experimentation. Parts of the work of Blank and Dorf (2012) and Ries (2011), for example on hypothesis testing, also fall in this camp. In setting a vision for "new frontiers" in entrepreneurship education, Neck and Greene (2011) specifically outline the fit of "design-based learning" and "serious games and simulations" in approaching entrepreneurship as a value creation method (versus venture creation process). Lackéus (2014) specifically names design thinking, the business model, lean startup and customer development as "some of the more contemporary models and theories [that] have a more explicit focus on value creation rather than venture creation" in his work on how to make students more entrepreneurial by shifting practices from being dominated by outcomes focused on learning *about* entrepreneurship to outcomes *about, for and through* entrepreneurship. Along the lines of learning by taking action, Morris et al. (2013) outline specific competency-based learning outcomes our educational approaches need to teach if our students are going to take entrepreneurial action. So, while there is a lack of hard evidence that some of the approaches named here actually lead to better entrepreneurial outcomes, the argument is being made that, "in order to be entrepreneurial, students must do things . . . rather than just plan" and that traditional predictive and process-based approaches are not the most effective for the new paradigms (Brush et al., 2015).

This Chapter

On one hand, the above-mentioned research represents a call for entrepreneurship educators to shift their practices in order to help tomorrow's entrepreneur learn through more action and practice-based approaches, while, on the other hand, the earlier-described "many new approaches dilemma" speaks to the challenges to be faced when trying to do so.

This chapter responds to this situation by advancing a way of thinking and practice for educators. First, work in model-based learning in science education is built upon to establish a framework for a Deliberate Opportunity Design Learning Model that makes explicit the connection between key modeling tools available to educators today (such as the idea model, business model and business plan) and that can serve to guide the development of learning pathways and experiences in modern entrepreneurial contexts. Next, that framework is used to make the case for prototyping entire opportunities (not just products), and the four key ways of prototyping an opportunity are described. Examples are provided of how one can use the proposed framework to design different entrepreneurship curricula, and the framework is extended to the Deliberate Opportunity Design Learning Process, a generally applicable entrepreneurial learning process for designing opportunities. This is used to show the connection to other related processes (such as predictive planning, design thinking, lean startup and the minimum viable product). The case is made (and sample tools are shared) for the important task of enabling students and entrepreneurs to do their own (teacher-independent) critique and assessment of the potential of their work to create value. Finally, the imperative is made clear for providing learners with new enabling competencies if we are going to succeed in making the shifts being called for, and a model is advanced for structuring that work in a way that incorporates leading thinking on competencies and supports teachers and researchers moving into the new action-based paradigms.

MODEL-BASED LEARNING FOR ENTREPRENEURSHIP

Our First Fundamental Building Block: Model-based Learning

The goal of this section is to introduce thinking that will later allow us to connect the dots between entrepreneurial models such as the idea model, the business model and the business plan, and to recast those as "prototypes of opportunities" in the Deliberate Opportunity Design (DOD) framework.

A simple theory is shown in Figure 9.1 for thinking about modern approaches to pedagogical model construction in a classroom. This is modified only very slightly from the work of Clement (2000), which was published as part of a special issue of the *International Journal of Science Education* focused on the use of models in science education. It is intended to provide guidance to teachers by connecting concepts such as preconceptions, intermediate models (used in the classroom), target models (desired knowledge states to which we want the student to get), expert consensus models (currently accepted by scientists), and the learning processes that take the student from preconceptions to target models. It explains how models of increasing sophistication can be used to support the learning

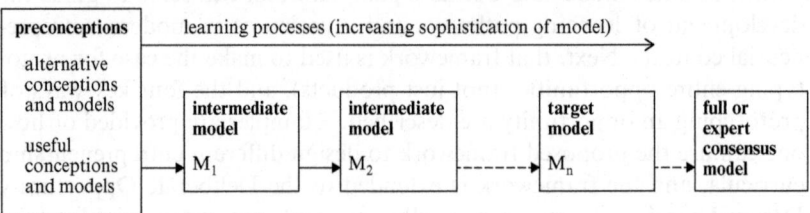

Figure 9.1   Framework for thinking about modern approaches to model construction for learning

processes found in science education. As Clement points out, this provides a framework for thinking about cognitive learning events in individuals and, at any point in time, instructional efforts are directed at moving the student from model M_n to model $M_n + 1$ along what he refers to as a learning pathway. Thus the horizontal axis reflects how learning pathways that connect models with increasing levels of sophistication can help learners gain a conceptual understanding at a level that goes beyond memorization of content or familiarization with process. He draws an analogy between the use of these models in a classroom and the ways in which they are used by expert scientists, and he argues that they are important because of "the suspicion that conceptual models help people attain 'conceptual understanding' in science at a level that goes beyond memorized facts, equations or procedures."

From Science Education to Entrepreneurship Education

In entrepreneurship, the learning models in Figure 9.1 are most closely related to entrepreneurial content and processes, that is, the declarative knowledge (or knowledge *about* a topic, knowing *that* it is, or *what* it is) and procedural knowledge (knowing *how* to do something, or the steps to achieve it) talked about by Biggs (2011), and a practice within the "process world" that was introduced by Neck and Greene (2011). These pieces of knowledge might be taught through activities such as lectures, textbooks, cases and sample concept models (idea models, business models and business plans), and assessed through quizzes, exams and case analyses.

By taking someone along learning pathways that connect the increasingly sophisticated models, you make room for learning outcomes that would be more associated with what Biggs (2011) refers to as conditional knowledge (knowing *when* and *why* to apply the earlier-mentioned categories of knowledge). You also deepen your practice in the "process world" and begin to develop a practice in the "cognition world" of Neck and Greene (2011). These pieces of knowledge might be taught through the development of concept models, by taking steps to incorporate a new venture, through analysis of deeper cases, via role-playing, and with serious games and simulations.

The Deliberate Opportunity Design Learning Model

The model-based thinking outlined above is extended in Figure 9.2 in ways that make possible a range of learning journeys that is more authentic to entrepreneurial contexts and, in turn, helps the student and the teacher develop more action and practice-based approaches. The top portion is no

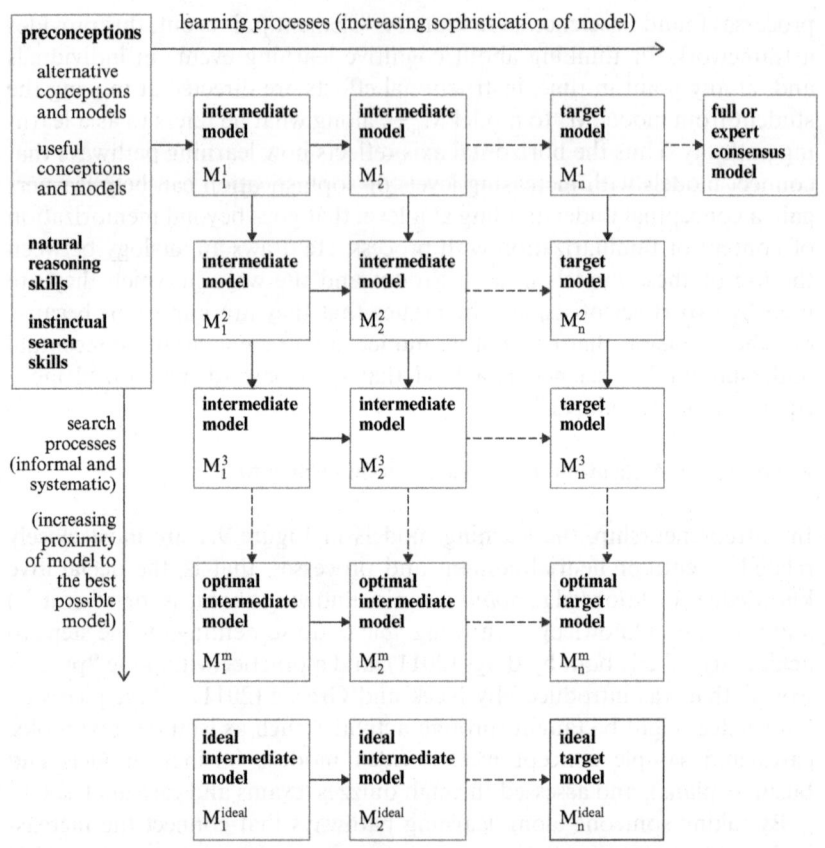

Figure 9.2   The Deliberate Opportunity Design Learning Model

different than the one shown in Figure 9.1; that is, it represents learning models of increasing sophistication connected by appropriately designed learning pathways. However, it now includes a second dimension along the vertical axis that represents instances of learning models that have increasing probability of creating value. In other words, the farther one goes down the page, the greater the potential becomes for creating and capturing value using the opportunity in question. I call the conceptual scheme in Figure 9.2 the Deliberate Opportunity Design Learning Model and propose that it is important both because it more authentically represents the learning that happens when entrepreneurs design high value opportunities (than does the one in Figure 9.1) and because it helps us design learning experiences through which nascent entrepreneurs can learn to do the same.

To further understand the important distinction between the two axes in Figure 9.2, first imagine that one's goal is to teach students *about* new businesses and the process of new business creation. One could design a learning process in which they are required to build increasingly sophisticated models of the underlying concepts; for example, one could task students with creating an idea model (M_1 in Figure 9.1), then a business model (M_2) and then a business plan (M_3) for a business. While this would help them gain an understanding of the underlying concepts represented by idea models, business models and business plans, it could still be quite disconnected from whether or not the underlying business is in fact "any good." You can learn about and understand concepts related to businesses without yours being a high impact business and without being any good at the process of turning your business into a high impact business, which is where the vertical axis in Figure 9.2 comes in. As well as increasing the level of sophistication of the models used in a learning context, one can also design the learning environment such that the underlying business concept being modeled is improved or made "better" as a result of doing the learning. Just as the expert scientist makes use of the kinds of models and learning pathways depicted in the horizontal axis in Figure 9.1, an entrepreneur who is good at coming up with successful business concepts will make use of the kinds of models and learning pathways depicted in the vertical axis in Figure 9.2. They will iteratively improve even a simple model (e.g., M_1^1) until it gets closer to the ideal version of itself (e.g., M_1^{ideal}).

While it is very unlikely that a serial entrepreneur who has become good at creating such businesses will think about his or her work in these terms, conceptualizing the underlying learning models and learning pathways in this way lends itself to helping others learn to do the same. By taking a student or nascent entrepreneur along learning pathways designed to cover combinations of the two dimensions in Figure 9.2, you open the doors to what Biggs (2011) refers to as functioning knowledge: a sophisticated level of ability that leads to value creation.

TREATING LEARNING MODELS AS PROTOTYPES OF OPPORTUNITIES

Our Second Fundamental Building Block: Prototypes of the Entire Opportunity

It is common for entrepreneurs to use the concept of a prototype when developing an offering (e.g., technologies, products and services), whether they use a 3D printer, a website mock-up, or role-playing for a service. It is less common however, and in my view even more important from a teaching and learning perspective, that they begin using the concept of prototyping the entire opportunity under development. I have been working with the framework in Figure 9.2 for years now to design classroom and corporate education experiences and, through doing that, have come to realize the power of helping the learner think about the learning model she is working with as a prototype of the opportunity she is after realizing. (Note that many conceptual definitions of the word "opportunity" are used in the entrepreneurship literature, which remains somewhat fragmented on the topic, for example Hansen et al. (2011). For the purposes of this work, I encourage thinking about an opportunity simply as *a set of circumstances with the potential to create value*, and the prototype of an opportunity as *a model of those circumstances that can be communicated to others*.)

I have also learned that tools such as the idea model, business model and business plan represent only one of four key ways in which entrepreneurs prototype opportunities. As shown in Table 9.1, the concept model is complemented by: a verbal model; a visual model; and a model of the offering. All of these forms of opportunity prototype can be created for any place in the Deliberate Opportunity Design Learning Model in Figure 9.2, and they will all evolve along with it as the underlying model becomes more sophisticated (moves to the right along the horizontal axis in Figure 9.2) and as one improves the likelihood that the opportunity will create value (moves down along the vertical axis). Further, all four of them are as important as each other because they play different roles in knowledge formation, knowledge evolution and knowledge communication. In other words, the notion of prototyping the whole opportunity in these ways is critical not just for sharing the opportunity with others; it also plays a critical role in designing and improving the opportunity itself.

The Idea Model and the Notion of Early-stage Opportunity Prototyping

As mentioned in Brush et al. (2015), I have developed and made available several tools that encourage very early-stage opportunity prototyping (e.g., Bruton, 2016a). One of these is included here in Figure 9.3 as an example because it may be less well known to the reader than others such as the lean canvas or business model canvas, and because it fills a gap for such models in the early stages of the opportunity design process (e.g., ideation and concept formation). Another even simpler prototyping tool includes only six of the same elements and shows them on the back of a napkin. Just as a business model does not aim to capture all the elements of business, models such as this are not intended to represent the full sophistication of the opportunity being prototyped. Rather, all of these tools serve us by

Table 9.1   The four ways of prototyping an opportunity

The concept model	This refers to the learning models shown in Figure 9.2 and might commonly take the form of an idea model, a business model or a business plan. At its simplest, this could take the form of an idea sketched on a Post-it Note or on one of the models outlined in the next section. Popular concept models include the lean canvas, the business model canvas, forms of the business model as described in Morris et al. (2005), and the traditional business plan. It can also take other forms.
The verbal model	This refers to a story or pitch told verbally by the entrepreneur or his or her team with the goal of communicating the nature and scope of the opportunity to others. It captures the range of possibilities from an informal pitch made to family or friends, to the more formal elevator pitch, to a full pitch to investors. Like the visual model and offering prototype to follow, such a model can be made for any position in the framework in Figure 9.2. And, like all the models, it plays a unique role not only in communicating knowledge but in its formation.
The visual model	This refers to some kind of visualization of the opportunity, also intended to communicate its nature and scope. It is treated as distinct from the verbal model because it appeals to different senses, requires different competencies to put together, and serves different and important roles in knowledge formation. It captures the range from a quick sketch, to the landing page of a website, to a teaser or animated whiteboard video explaining the opportunity, to a documentary or news report on your firm.
The model of the offering	Strictly speaking, this is a subset of the concept model (all instances of which require describing the offering in some way). However, it is important to consider on its own because of its power in communicating form and function of the opportunity being designed, and because of its importance to learning processes such as experimentation, hypothesis testing, empathy work, customer discovery and pre-order fulfillment. In the earliest stages, this could take the form of a sketch or simple cardboard prototype. As the opportunity evolves this will go through stages to fully functional versions of products and services.

reducing the number of variables that we are considering in our search, and by limiting the sophistication of the required cognitive or mental model at any point in the process. (A full business plan is no exception to this, itself also a pretty crude model or prototype of the actual opportunity in its real and complex landscape.) And, just as a business model does not stand on its own, even an early-stage idea model should be complemented by all of the other forms of prototype in Table 9.1.

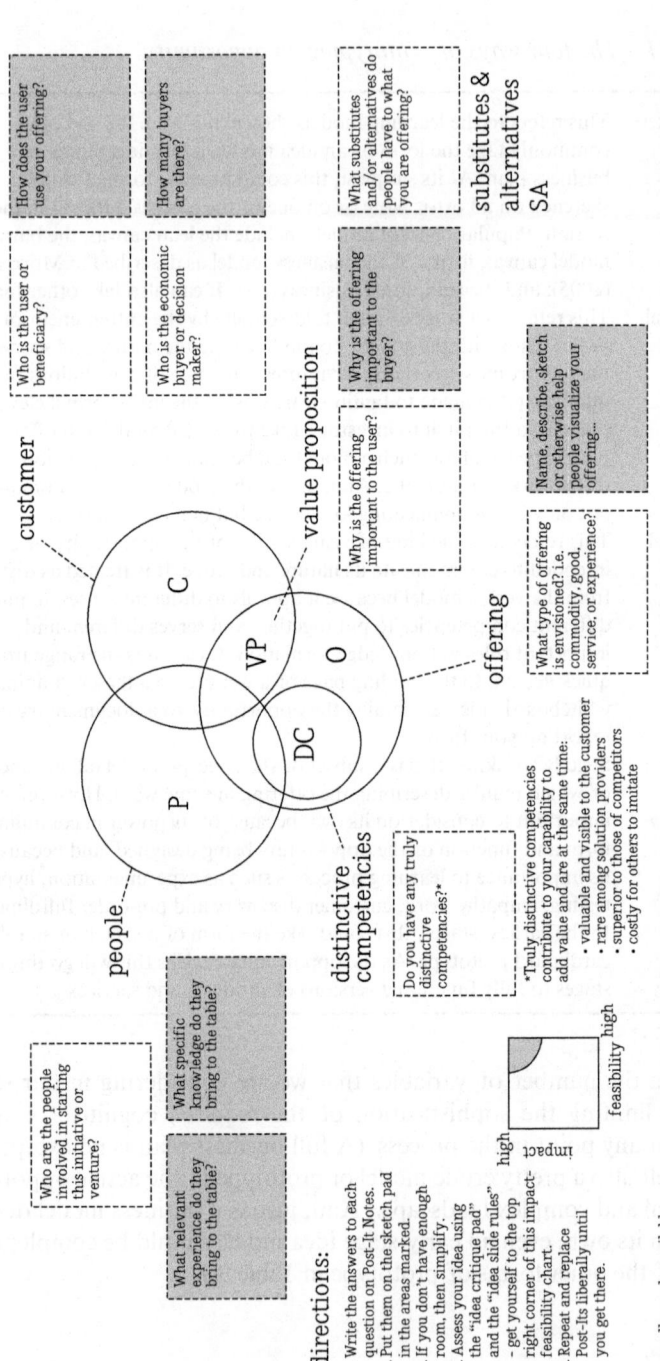

Idea Model for your Really Big Idea v.5.

These are the parameters to change when creating or refining a project or venture idea. Think of it as "sketching" the idea.

name of this idea: _____
designer's name(s): _____

customer

How does the user use your offering?

How many buyers are there?

Who is the user or beneficiary?

Who is the economic buyer or decision maker?

value proposition

Why is the offering important to the buyer?

Why is the offering important to the user?

substitutes & alternatives SA

What substitutes and/or alternatives do people have to what you are offering?

offering

What type of offering is envisioned? i.e. commodity, good, service, or experience?

Name, describe, sketch or otherwise help people visualize your offering...

people

Who are the people involved in starting this initiative or venture?

What relevant experience do they bring to the table?

What specific knowledge do they bring to the table?

distinctive competencies

Do you have any truly distinctive competencies?*

*Truly distinctive competencies contribute to your capability to add value and are at the same time:
· valuable and visible to the customer
· rare among solution providers
· superior to those of competitors
· costly for others to imitate

directions:

1. Write the answers to each question on Post-It Notes.
2. Put them on the sketch pad in the areas marked.
3. If you don't have enough room, then simplify.
4. Assess your idea using the "idea critique pad" and the "idea slide rules" - get yourself to the top right corner of this impact-feasibility chart.
5. Repeat and replace Post-Its liberally until you get there.

high | impact | high feasibility

proudly made available under creative commons: (t) ($) (=) **by the innographer**

print your own on Tabloid size paper (11x17 inch) at: theinnographer.com/toolkit/really-big-idea

get feedback on your idea using the Idea Critique Pad at http://theinnographer.com/toolkit/really-big-idea then take that feedback and chart it on the impact-feasibility chart using the idea slide rules at: http://theinnographer.com/idea-slide-rules

Figure 9.3   The idea model as opportunity prototype

Reducing Debate and Connecting the Dots between Key Prototypes

It might go without saying at this point, but I want to be explicit about how the Deliberate Opportunity Design Learning Model in Figure 9.2 can help reduce consternation and tension between people who might argue that one of the concept models is universally better than another. For example, the argument mentioned earlier between two entrepreneurship professors who felt equally strongly about the business model canvas and the traditional business plan could have been defused by explaining that both of those are just two of the possible prototypes in the broader entrepreneurial process; one is not better than another, and any priority given to one should only be a matter of the desired learning outcomes. Further, both are just examples of the many prototypes that can be engaged over a carefully designed learning pathway.

To this point, Figure 9.4 shows a specific route that learners might take through the opportunity design process in an introductory entrepreneurship course I designed at Mount Royal University in Calgary (e.g., Bruton, 2010): before embarking on the process, they are required to come up with ideas without using any formal modeling tool at all (we use a process called "ideastorming" to seed the ideation process); then as the course progresses they are required to prototype their selected opportunity in two early-stage iterations shown in Figure 9.4 as hunch[1] and hunch[2] (these are prototyped

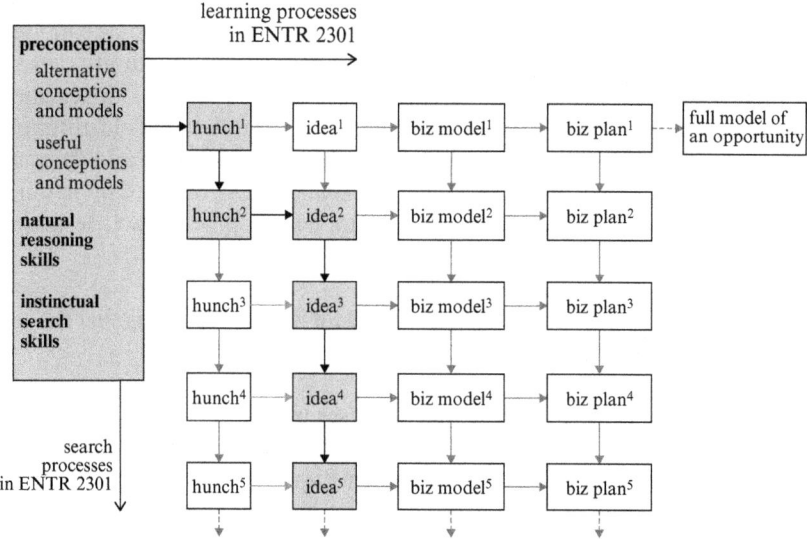

Figure 9.4   A sample Deliberate Opportunity Design learning pathway

using the back-of-the-napkin model described earlier); and then they do it again over several more iterations using an idea model like that in Figure 9.3, shown here as idea[2] through idea[5]. Another more senior course might be designed with different goals in mind to take the students through a learning pathway that moves more to the bottom right side of Figure 9.4, ending with a business plan for a relatively high potential new venture. And yet another course might only have desired learning outcomes related to the mechanics of writing a business planning document, not caring about how much value the venture could actually capture. The learning journey in that case might only have them occupy the upper rightmost cell in Figure 9.4 for the duration of a course.

It is hoped that this perspective on using the Deliberate Opportunity Design Learning Model to design modules and courses can help with the task of instructional and pedagogical design for action-based entrepreneurship education.

THE DELIBERATE OPPORTUNITY DESIGN LEARNING PROCESS

Even though they are relatively new to the scene, it turns out that the learning processes underpinning approaches like the lean startup and design thinking can be related to each other and to other traditional approaches, such as the more predictive business planning process, in a relatively straightforward manner. In this section we shift our focus from the models and *prototypes* of the opportunity to the *processes* of opportunity design, with the goals of: 1) making the relationship between some of the existing processes more explicit, in turn by building on the decades-old thinking of Argyris (1977, 1991) on single and double loop learning; and 2) using that thinking as a basis for defining what I call the Deliberate Opportunity Design Learning Process, a generally applicable process for designing opportunities.

Our Third Fundamental Building Block: Double Loop Learning and the Notion of Productive Reasoning

Two contrasting models of learning are described in Argyris (1977), a now-classic *Harvard Business Review* article. The first model of learning is called single loop learning, and it is depicted in Figure 9.5a. When a person or organization works in this way, plans and rules are operationalized within a set of governing variables, and those variables go unquestioned. Plans are written, for example, decisions are made based on those plans, actions

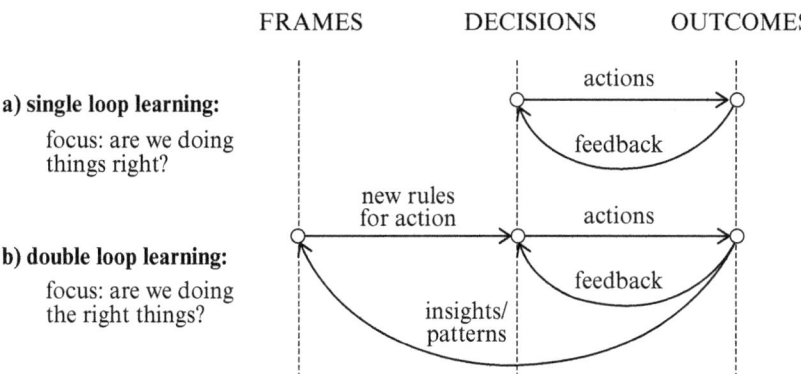

Figure 9.5   The concept of double loop learning

are taken, outcomes are achieved, and feedback received drives future actions – all within a single loop. The second model of learning, called double loop learning, is depicted in Figure 9.5b. It is different because the governing variables are deliberately questioned in ways that lead to shifts in the frames from which plans are written and decisions are made. Argyris (1991) goes on to tell us that single loop learning is dangerous because it is the result of "defensive reasoning" and "organizational defensive routines." This body of work has influenced thinking about organizational learning and encouraged the pursuit of double loop learning and the so-called "productive reasoning" that accompanies it.

Connecting the Dots between Key Processes such as Predictive Planning, Lean Startup and Design Thinking

If one redraws the single and double loop learning processes as has been done in Figures 9.6a and 9.6b, respectively, then one has a layout on the page that lends itself well to the mapping of some key entrepreneurial processes. For example, the traditional predictive project or business planning process can be mapped onto the single loop learning model, as shown in Figure 9.6c. This is not to say that all project and business planners work blindly, never testing their assumptions; there are clearly exceptions and ways to apply planning tools that rise beyond single loop learning. (That said, the reader is urged to read Argyris (1991) and more recent related publications for convincing arguments about how single loop learning, defensive reasoning and the resulting "doom loop" dominate our personal and organizational practices.)

On the other hand, the lean startup process (Ries, 2011) and the design

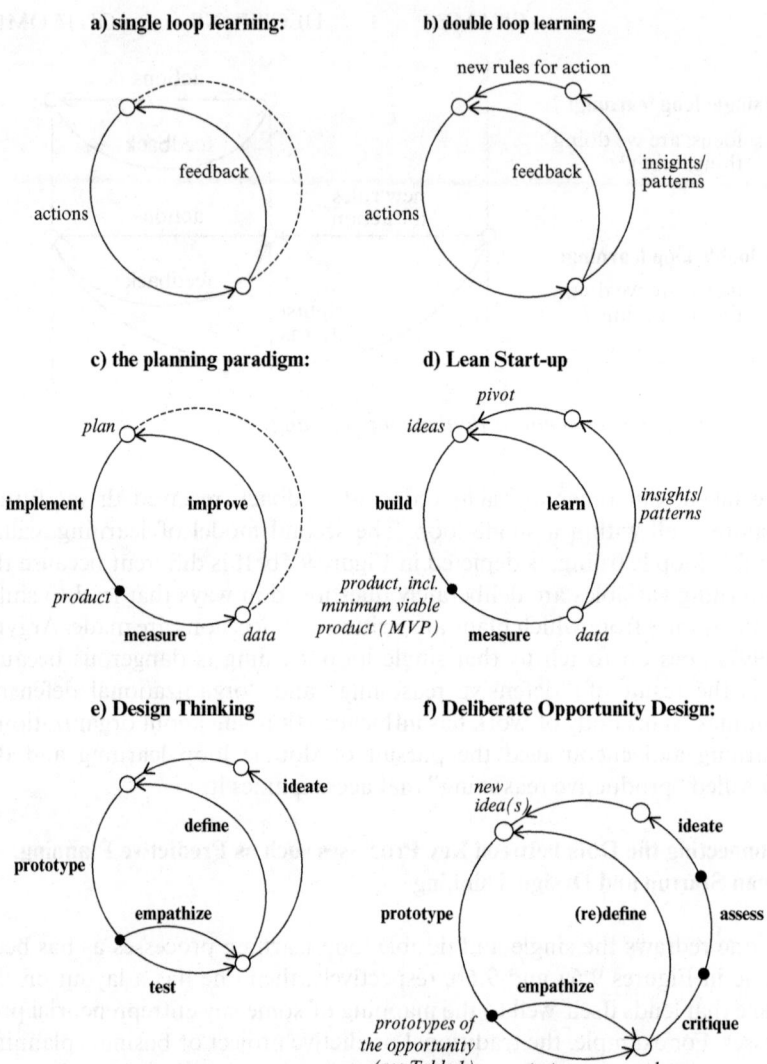

Figure 9.6   The Deliberate Opportunity Design Learning Process

thinking process (d.School, 2016) can both be mapped as double loop learning processes, as shown in Figures 9.6d and 9.6e, respectively. While this may explain their usefulness and appeal, it is not to say that those processes are the same as each other; anyone familiar with them will know that they differ greatly in detail. However, it is to say that these processes (and others that fall into this category but that have not been considered here) can be understood within a common conceptual scheme, and that by doing this we can break down some of the perceived differences between them that might have been cultivated as a result of their application in different domains and their own processes of commercialization.

The analysis summarized here culminates in the Deliberate Opportunity Design Learning Process shown in Figure 9.6f. This process is important for several reasons. First is that it is an action-based approach through which entrepreneurs can learn and develop their practices; it enables learning through authentic entrepreneurial action. Second, because it relates other processes popular today to existing bodies of work, such as the examples given above from the field of organizational learning, it can help researchers communicate and advance their calls for leaps in practice. For example, the practices of experimentation, play, empathy and creation outlined in Neck and Greene (2011) can all be situated in different parts of the process in Figure 9.6f and engaged through appropriate choice of the related tools and approaches.

Third, it serves as a more generally applicable extension of those other processes. By not being tied to any specific approach, it connects the other approaches in a sort of "framework of frameworks" (to borrow that concept from Morris et al., 2001). In turn, this helps put the focus of educational design on pulling from a portfolio of approaches, rather than depending on any one of them. In the same way, it also serves as a lens through which the instructional designer can look at her work. For example, the process itself enables the learning pathways an entrepreneur needs to experience in order to get between the learning models of Figure 9.2. Fourth, it helps put to rest debates about any one of the processes popular today being universally better than another; we propose that they can all be viewed as related processes in the educator's toolkit, each aimed at serving the general process in different ways. Finally, it places emphasis on the very important and often oversimplified and overlooked roles of critique and assessment within the cycle. It is this that helps entrepreneurs build competencies that allow them to reason productively, in the words of Argyris (1996), rather than just defensively. Doing this is the subject of the next section.

THE IMPORTANCE OF THE CRITIQUE AND ASSESSMENT PHASES OF THE OPPORTUNITY DESIGN PROCESS

The Deliberate Opportunity Design Learning Process in Figure 9.6f is explicit in emphasizing the importance of an entrepreneur (and her team) being able to carry out a critique and do a reliable assessment of the opportunity being designed. The goals of this section are to make more explicit the need for this, and to share an example of work being done to make it possible.

Our Fourth Fundamental Building Block: Enabling Learners to Assess the Value-creating Potential of Their Own Opportunities

If we are going to ask people to learn by actually trying to create value then it is required that we also give them tools with which they can assess their own progress in doing so. Although this is naturally an imperfect and imprecise process for any task as complex as those encountered in entrepreneurship, good work is being done to make it possible for students, entrepreneurs or managers to build a reliable critique of their work and, through that, be able to assess their success well enough to drive future iterations of the design process.

In Bruton (2010), for example, it was described that students could assess a new venture (or portfolio of new ventures) in such a way as to map its value creation potential to a chart like that shown in Figure 9.7a. In this example, the shaded dot represents the resulting measures of: 1) the venture's potential impact, in turn a function of its assessed situations in terms of customer (C), value proposition (VP) and substitutes and

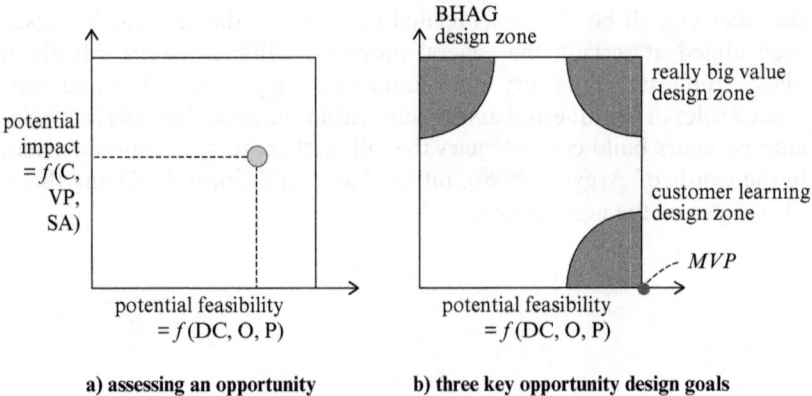

a) assessing an opportunity   b) three key opportunity design goals

Figure 9.7   On the importance of assessing one's own opportunity

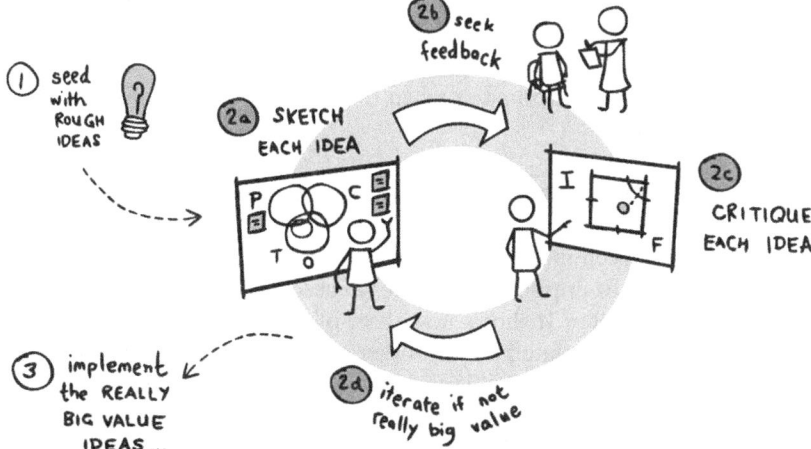

Figure 9.8   A simple critique and self-assessment process for opportunity design

alternatives (SA); and 2) the venture's potential feasibility, in turn a function of its assessed situations in terms of distinctive competency (DC), offering (O) and people on the team (P). These six variables are chosen to be the same as those modeled in the opportunity prototype in the first place (e.g., see Figure 9.3, which also uses C, VP, SA, DC, O and P), and the scores in each category come about through the critique phase of the process shown in Figure 9.6f. Translating between those scores and the potential impact and feasibility can be accomplished in one of several ways, including the use of a spreadsheet that implements the key relationship, and the use of the idea slide rules found at Bruton (2016b). In the ideation stage, this approach puts into students' hands a critique and self-assessment process like that summarized in Figure 9.8. In turn, this gives them the freedom to implement a version of the process in Figure 9.6f, and enables them to come up with a better opportunity by moving on their own down the vertical axis of the framework in Figure 9.2.

Generalizing, our task as educators is to enable the Deliberate Opportunity Design Learning Process of Figure 9.6f using appropriately selected tools and approaches that will help learners ideate, prototype, test, empathize, critique, and assess for greater value with only our guidance (i.e., it can no longer be our role to judge of the value-creating potential of their opportunity). It is clear that, although teachers need to support the student by assessing his or her learning, working in a truly authentic action-based educational paradigm will require that students can assess their own efforts to create value. If we do not teach methods that allow

them to do this, then they will not have the productive reasoning competencies required to navigate their way across Figure 9.2 toward really big
value in Figure 9.7a – either along the learning pathways we design for
them while in our classrooms or when they tackle the same tasks in their
own work.

Connecting the Dots between Key Opportunity Design Goals like the MVP

Figure 9.7b has been included to round out our work to connect the dots
between the various popular approaches in use today using the generalized
models in this chapter. It shows how three of the most common opportunity design goals are related to each other and to the assessment approach
shared in the last section. The first is the really big value (RBV) zone introduced by Bruton (2010) and refers to target opportunities that have the
highest potential impact and feasibility possible for the entrepreneur in the
conditions in which she finds herself. The second is the customer learning
(CL) zone, which refers to opportunity prototypes designed and implemented deliberately to help the entrepreneur learn as much as possible as
efficiently as possible about his or her context or customer. These put the
focus on what one can feasibly test as soon as possible, and the minimum
viable product (MVP) of Ries (2011) would fall into this zone. The third
is the big hairy audacious goal (BHAG) zone, which refers to opportunity
prototypes designed deliberately to put the focus on what would have the
most impact, without regard to whether or not it is feasible. The emphasis
in design thinking on solving wicked problems is an example of this last
design goal in action.

THE ENABLING COMPETENCY IMPERATIVE

Helping the Students Make the Leap Too

Before closing, it is important to consider how much more is being asked
of students or nascent entrepreneurs in learning contexts that require them
to succeed in the more action and practice-based approaches being enabled
here. For example, imagine a student who will only have to write an exam
on firm valuation techniques after working through the related problems
in a textbook. Think about how different the competencies are that he will
require to succeed (competencies both as a learner and as an entrepreneur)
from those that a student would require if challenged to create and capture
value in an authentic action-oriented entrepreneurial process (that might
in turn require her to master tools for valuing her own firm as one of many

such steps in the process). This is but one example of the importance of being realistic about and being able to articulate the competencies required for succeeding in such an educational paradigm. It is imperative that we design curricular and co-curricular experiences that will enable students to build the right competencies, a reality that points in turn to the research being carried out to provide frameworks for learning outcomes and competencies in modern entrepreneurship education (e.g., Duval-Couetil, 2013; Lackéus, 2014; Morris et al., 2013; Pittaway and Edwards, 2012; Siwan and Rowley, 2010).

Our Fifth Fundamental Building Block: The Enabling Competencies Model for Deliberate Opportunity Design

In Bruton (2015), the model of Biggs (2011) was extended to help pedagogical designers go about the task of framing and articulating their desired learning outcomes while also incorporating the leading edge work on competencies of the above-mentioned authors. The result is called the Enabling Competencies Model because it speaks to the competencies learners need to gain so that they will be able to learn and develop through action and practice-based approaches such as Deliberate Opportunity Design. Key ideas related to this model are shared here. The first is that these enabling competencies should be looked at as more than just "knowledge" or "skills" colloquially defined, and that considerable power can come from thinking about them in more of a structured way, as many of the above-mentioned authors have concluded. The second key idea is that, although competencies and learning outcomes are related concepts, they do not quite mean the same thing in the context of a Deliberate Opportunity Design approach. Rather, we suggest thinking of a competency as coming from the ability to apply a set of achieved learning outcomes in a certain context in order to create a benefit or achieve some real world results. This notion lends itself well to a practice-based perspective of entrepreneurship education where the goal is to learn by doing things that create value. The third key idea is that there are three fundamental levels of learning outcomes (or as Biggs (2011) might call them, levels of knowledge, or levels of knowing) that contribute to any competency. As shown on the left side of Figure 9.9, these are: 1) the necessary abilities; 2) the key behaviors that enable those abilities; and 3) the base knowledge, skills and attitudes that make the behaviors possible. The fourth key idea is that these levels lend themselves nicely as a framework upon which to hang six complementary categories of entrepreneurial learning outcomes. As shown in the boxes in Figure 9.9 and defined in detail in Table 9.2, these are: functioning knowledge; conditional

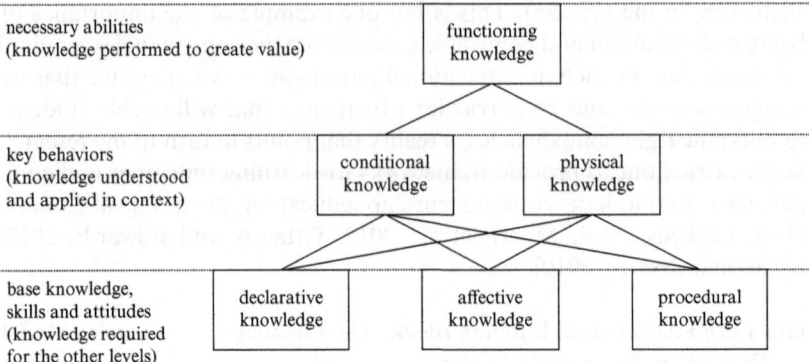

necessary abilities
(knowledge performed to create value)

functioning knowledge

key behaviors
(knowledge understood
and applied in context)

conditional knowledge

physical knowledge

base knowledge,
skills and attitudes
(knowledge required
for the other levels)

declarative knowledge

affective knowledge

procedural knowledge

Figure 9.9   The Enabling Competencies Model for Deliberate Opportunity Design

knowledge; physical knowledge; declarative knowledge; affective knowledge; and procedural knowledge. Finally, the fifth key idea is that the different types of knowledge (and associated learning outcomes) that make up a competency are related to and support each other as shown by the lines between the boxes in Figure 9.9; for example, truly functioning knowledge depends on the related conditional and physical knowledge, and those depend in turn on those that might apply at the base of the competency model.

SUMMARY

This chapter advanced a framework and way of thinking and practice referred to as Deliberate Opportunity Design and proposed that it has the potential to help shift entrepreneurial learning toward the more action and practice-based paradigms being called for in the field today. By building upon notions of model-based learning from the field of science education and foundational work in the area of organizational learning, it demonstrated how tools and approaches such as the idea model, the lean canvas, the business model (and business model canvas), the traditional business plan, lean startup and design thinking are actually all connected, complementary, and useful to the broader goal when used in appropriate forms and at appropriate times. Approaches to the often-overlooked areas of critique and self-assessment were provided, and an approach was shared for bringing into the instructional and pedagogical design processes leading thinking on the competencies students will require to make the leap to

Table 9.2   The enabling competencies

Level 1: The necessary ability	This level corresponds to one of several key abilities that need to be performed in order for the entrepreneurial learner to create value – it depends on achieving and being able to integrate the other related learning outcomes. It includes one kind of knowledge: *Functioning knowledge:* A sophisticated level of ability leading to value creation – knowing how to employ the other related types of knowledge and perform an understanding of them in order to solve complex problems and function as an effective entrepreneur; for example, learners will . . . be able to build and sell a new venture in order to solve a complex problem in society.
Level 2: The key behaviors	The learning outcomes at this level provide a bridge between the functioning knowledge (Level 1 above) and the related base knowledge (Level 3 below). They include: *Conditional knowledge:* Knowing *when* and *why* to apply the base knowledge, skills and attitudes, that is, when to apply or use certain approaches or access appropriate content or affective knowledge; for example, learners will . . . know when or why to use one form of business legal structure over another. *Physical knowledge:* Having knowledge to move things from concept to tangible reality; for example, learners will . . . build and test prototypes of their product and business concepts, or . . . establish one of the various forms of business.
Level 3: The base knowledge, skills and attitudes	These outcomes are the building blocks or foundation, and make the other levels and the overall competency possible. They are often easiest to articulate and assess, and they serve to enable the others. This level includes three kinds of outcome: *Declarative knowledge:* Knowing *about* something, knowing *that* it is, or *what* it is; for example, learners will . . . be able to recognize and name the different types of market segments, such as total addressable market (TAM). *Affective knowledge:* Knowing the *self* and *others*: values, attitudes, emotions, feelings; for example, learners will . . . be aware of the attitudes and desires of customers, or . . . know what deeply inspires them. *Procedural knowledge:* Knowing *how* to do something, or the steps to achieve it; for example, learners will . . . know how to do an empathy mapping session, or . . . value a firm.

these "new frontiers." It is hoped that this work provides guidance to educators both by connecting the dots between these traditional and popular approaches and by informing new principles for designing entrepreneurial learning experiences.

REFERENCES

Argyris, C. (1977), Double loop learning in organizations, *Harvard Business Review*, September–October, 115–125.

Argyris, C. (1991), Teaching smart people how to learn, *Harvard Business Review*, May–June, 4–15.

Argyris, C. (1996), Actionable knowledge: design causality in the service of consequential theory, *Journal of Applied Behavioral Science*, **32**(4), 390–406.

Biggs, J. (2011), *Teaching for Quality Learning at University*, Buckingham, UK: Open University Press/McGraw-Hill.

Blank, S. (2013), Why the lean start-up changes everything, *Harvard Business Review*, May.

Blank, S. and Dorf, B. (2012), *The Startup Owner's Manual: The Step-by-step Guide for Building a Great Company*, Pescadero, CA: K & S Ranch.

Brinckmann, J. and Grichnik, D. (2010), Should entrepreneurs plan or just storm the castle? A meta-analysis on contextual factors impacting the business planning–performance relationship in small firms, *Journal of Business Venturing*, **25**(1), 24–40.

Brush, C., Neck, H. and Greene, P. (2015), A practice-based approach to entrepreneurship education, in V.L. Crittenden, K. Esper, N. Karst and R. Slegers (eds.), *Evolving Entrepreneurial Education: Innovation in the Babson Classroom*, Bingley, UK: Emerald Group Publishing, pp. 35–54.

Bruton, A. (2010), The venture design studio: a design thinking approach to teaching and learning for the conception, communication and innovation of new venture concepts, Annual World Conference of the International Council for Small Business (ICSB), Cincinnati, OH.

Bruton, A. (2015), The enabling competencies model, Program materials of the Go Deep Entrepreneurship Teaching and Learning Scholars Program, July.

Bruton, A. (2016a), Tools for idea modeling, retrieved February 1, 2016 from https://theinnographer.com/toolkit/idea-modeling.

Bruton, A. (2016b), Idea slide rules, retrieved February 1, 2016 from https://the innographer.com/idea-slide-rules.

Clement, J. (2000), Model based learning as a key research area for science education, *International Journal of Science Education*, **22**(9), 1041–1053.

d.School (2016), Virtual crash course in design thinking, retrieved February 1, 2016 from http://dschool.stanford.edu/dgift.

Duval-Couetil, N. (2013), Assessing the impact of entrepreneurship education programs: challenges and approaches, *Journal of Small Business Management*, **51**(3), 394–409.

George, G. and Bock, A.J. (2009), The business model in practice and its implications for entrepreneurship research, *Entrepreneurship Theory and Practice*, **35**(1), 83–111.

Goldsby, M., Kuratko, D. and Nelson, T. (2014), Design-centered entrepreneurship: a process for designing opportunities, in M.H. Morris (ed.), *Annals of Entrepreneurship Education and Pedagogy – 2014*, Cheltenham, UK and Northampton, MA, USA: Edward Elgar, pp. 200–217.

Hansen, D., Shrader, R. and Monllor, J. (2011), Defragmenting definitions of entrepreneurial opportunity, *Journal of Small Business Management*, **49**(2), 283–304.

Jones, C., Penaluna, A., Matlay, H. and Penaluna, K. (2013), The student business plan: useful or not? *Industry and Higher Education*, **27**(6), 491–498.

Lackéus, M. (2014), *Entrepreneurship in Education: What, Why, When, How*, Entrepreneurship 360 Background Paper, Paris: OECD Publishing, retrieved February 27, 2016 from http://www.schooleducationgateway.eu/downloads/entrepreneurship/40.1%20OECD%20(2014)_BGP_Entrepreneurship%20in%20Education.pdf.

Lange, J.E., Mollov, A., Pearlmutter, M., Singh, S. and Bygrave, W. (2007), Pre-start-up formal business plans and post-start-up performance: a study of 116 new ventures, *Venture Capital: An International Journal of Entrepreneurial Finance*, **9**(4), 237–256.

Morris, M. and Schindehutte, M. (2015), Teaching entrepreneurship students how to design a business model, in M.H. Morris (ed.), *Annals of Entrepreneurship Education and Pedagogy – 2014*, Cheltenham, UK and Northampton, MA, USA: Edward Elgar, pp. 242–255.

Morris, M., Kuratko, D. and Schindehutte, M. (2001), Towards integration: understanding entrepreneurship through frameworks, *International Journal of Entrepreneurship and Innovation*, **2**(1), 35–49.

Morris, M., Schindehutte, M. and Allen, J. (2005), The entrepreneur's business model: toward a unified perspective, *Journal of Business Research*, **58**, 726–735.

Morris, M., Webb, J. and Singhal, S. (2013), A competency-based perspective on entrepreneurship education: conceptual and empirical insights, *Journal of Small Business Management*, **51**(3), 352–369.

Neck, H. and Greene, P.G. (2011), Entrepreneurship education: known worlds and new frontiers, *Journal of Small Business Management*, **49**(1), 55–70.

Osterwalder, A., Pigneur, Y. and Tucci, C. (2005), Clarifying business models: origins, present, and future of the concept, *Communications of the Association for Information Systems*, **16**(1).

Pittaway, L. and Edwards, C. (2012), Assessment: examining practice in entrepreneurship education, *Education + Training*, **54**(8), 778–800.

Ries, E. (2011), *The Lean Startup: How Today's Entrepreneurs Use Continuous Innovation to Create Radically Successful Businesses*, New York: Crown Books.

Siwan, S. and Rowley, J. (2010), Entrepreneurial competencies: a literature review and development agenda, *International Journal of Entrepreneurial Behaviour and Research*, **16**(2), 92–111.

10. New venture creation as a learning agenda: experiences, reflections and implications from running a venture creation programme

Leigh Morland and John Thompson

INTRODUCTION

This chapter explores the implications for various stakeholders – namely students, faculty and host institutions – of running venture creation degrees for undergraduates. It explores what is required to run (not just design) a successful venture creation degree. The chapter is conceptual but underpinned by longitudinal and reflective research (Morland and Thompson, 2015) focused in part on the authors' experiences with the BA in Enterprise Development (BAED), an undergraduate programme situated within a UK university business school. This innovative three year full time degree was launched in 2009, and is perhaps best defined as a *pracademic* programme, being both practical and academic at the same time. Participants pursue a degree award in tandem with conceptualising business opportunities and creating a business venture. There are, additionally, reflections on direct experiences with similar undergraduate programmes in other UK universities and emerging conceptual ideas on why there is likely to be continued tension between pracademic programmes of this nature and the strengthening research culture of the typical business school.

The purpose of this chapter is to inform the design and development of programmes for entrepreneurship, reconciling the learning experience, course philosophy and capabilities of the provider institution. The BAED reflections are based on three years of programme operation (between 2010 and 2013) and are informed by the experiences of a single cohort through the full degree programme. Our insights are specific to the provision of entrepreneurship education within a university context.

For our research we examined students' entrepreneur characteristics and their early expectations; we drew insights from reflective work; and we looked at students' academic and business achievements. Conceptual ideas reflect our emergent beliefs concerning entrepreneur development, specifically: the importance of learning from action and for action; the need for reflexive practice[1] from faculty and students; and finally, the critical role of the institution in resourcing and facilitating learning from and for entrepreneurship. This review of a single programme is seen as an instrumental case to those interested in the design and operation of entrepreneurship education and entrepreneurial learning experiences (Corbett, 2005).

Programme development must reconcile the interests of student participants and the capabilities of the provider institution. In this chapter we reflect primarily on our views, which were derived from active involvement in programme design and delivery. Our situation afforded understanding of participant needs as well as the interests and resources of the provider institution. There is no attempt to generate a general model of entrepreneurship education as participants, faculty and institution shape the manifestation of entrepreneurship learning programmes. This chapter is concerned with detailing and locating a programme with a view to informing the development and design of entrepreneurship education in relation to context.

Externally, there are considerations for market engagement and how providers attract, support and retain budding entrepreneurs in the university context. From a resource perspective, there are insights for acquiring and managing the contribution of faculty within the parameters and quality standards of the institution. In this respect we ground our work in selected views and concepts of both entrepreneurship and strategy.

ENTREPRENEURSHIP EDUCATION

Our discussion alludes to a programme that is both different and relatively rare, in both concept and practice, and this has implications for managing the interests of – and relationships between – participants and providers.

Drucker (1985) argued that effective entrepreneurship education should be practice based, and various approaches to 'practice' have been used in universities (Neck et al., 2014) for students on general business courses as well as those on enterprise related programmes. From a processual view, entrepreneurship must be enacted, facilitated and reflected upon if real learning is to occur (Pittaway and Cope, 2007). The implications are that practice must occur at different times for individual participants and may be placed and performed outside of the physical boundaries of the university. The relevant practice can be embedded within a degree programme or adjunct and parallel. We must equip participants and faculty to enable this.

The extent to which a provider integrates entrepreneurship with degree programmes or alternatively opts for enterprise skills depends upon the perceived participant need and nature of the resource base, specifically the ability of faculty to enable and support learning for practice (Rae and Woodier-Harris, 2012).

There is a growing awareness that graduates need employability and enterprise skills as soon as they transition into work roles (Gilbert, 2012). However there are significant differences between programmes for work based learning (WBL), where the context for practice may be known or predicted, and those for venture creation, where students will form an understanding of their context as the new venture is created. For would-be entrepreneurs, coping with uncertainty, and enjoying the challenge of undertaking a journey with a vaguely specified rather than clearly prescribed destination, is a significant learning priority. A 'true' venture creation programme (VCP)[2] provides this opportunity. A VCP is a distinct model and different from entrepreneurship education, which may fall short of the specific requirement to practice even though experiential opportunities are embedded. The BAED programme is a VCP and is concerned with 'knowing', 'doing' and 'being'. Understanding how individuals can use their skills, abilities and connections creates the capacity for effectual entrepreneurship (Read et al., 2010).

LOCATING THE BAED AS A LEARNING EXPERIENCE

The BAED is a three year, full time undergraduate venture creation degree created to enable entrepreneurship. Our assumption is that the ability to learn from and for action – aided by reflection – enables the practice of entrepreneurship. Participants are required to start up (and run) a small business alongside their formal studies in order to graduate with this award. Whilst venture creation degrees are becoming increasingly evident in the US (Neck et al., 2014) and parts of Europe (especially Scandinavia), they are relatively rare at undergraduate level as opposed to post-graduate level (Venture Creation Programs List, 2016). As mentioned earlier, they are different from degrees that feature aspects of experiential entrepreneurship more broadly, which are significantly more popular and, indeed, ubiquitous in the US. Skills-wise, many business courses integrate the concept and practice of entrepreneurship, but they are likely to differ in terms of the nature of experiences the participants are able to instigate and learn from. The BAED is one of a few stand-alone programmes, dedicated to theorising from and for new venture creation.

Whilst some students will have ambitions and aspirations for the business to have serious financial investment and growth potential, this is neither required nor important. What matters is the experience of actually creating a business from an idea and an opportunity, finding the necessary resources and customers, operationalising activities and at least covering the costs involved. The business can thus be modest in scope and scale. We believe this is an appropriate paradigm for undergraduates, who are usually (but not always) working alone; we recognise this distinguishes BAED from a typical post-graduate venture creation programme, where students are more likely, first, to work in small teams and, second, to engage with innovative technology. (The critical theme of the scope of the business is revisited later in this chapter.)

We do not propose either to enter into or to summarise the debates on an exact definition of those skills that should be developed – or present a definitive profile of entrepreneurial behaviours. Rather we declare a focus on entrepreneurship in terms of outcomes. We are concerned with the skills, knowledge and attitudes that enable the start of something that creates value and is recognised as a form of 'enterprise'. It might well be a conventional business (that involves employees); or it might be described as freelance self-employment; it could be a social enterprise. Importantly, the business enterprise functions as a learning vehicle. As highlighted above, the key issue is that there are real decisions to be taken about resources, customers and markets, and work organisation – these being the strategic and operational dilemmas that characterise the entrepreneurial context (Audretsch, 2012).

As the programme progresses, so participants direct learning towards personal development and the needs of the business. Fundamental to programme design is the requirement that participants can learn through cycles of action and reflection in order to effect new venture creation. The practice of experiential learning[3] is central to programme design. Experiential learning can encompass case studies, practitioner master-classes, writing a business plan, and problem based learning (PBL)[4] (Scott et al., 2016); all are relevant to the BAED. But the overriding purpose of creating a real business also requires that participants and faculty co-determine the learning agenda. Without attention to understanding the participants' learning aspirations, experiential learning could well manifest itself as a series of disparate exercises, each a learning opportunity but not necessarily a step on a development path that will enable new venture creation. Reflexivity and self-directed learning are required in order to give experiential learning direction. This need to inform and act in relation to venture creation creates an agenda for action learning.[5] Given that the individual learner's context for entrepreneurship cannot be known at the outset of the programme, the development of a curriculum with standardised learning milestones can be indicative but not a definitive model of learning. There is an action learning requirement for programme developers and participants alike.

As different learning approaches underpin the BAED, we acknowledge the programme is a different experience; the combination of experiential learning and action learning enable effectual entrepreneurship and the development of the participant as practitioner. Therefore the programme is best articulated by focusing on how participants learn, as opposed to what they need to know.

Breen (2000) argues that an enterprise is a creative response to opportunity, uncertainty and risk. Venture creation degrees do carry higher risks because there is a real chance that the business will not succeed over the duration of the programme or beyond the programme. In reality this is more a personal risk for the students than it is a business risk, as long as any financial exposure can be contained. Business risks[6] must be managed in conjunction with personal risks. Participants may encounter learning approaches that require more self-reflection and direction setting than in their previous experiences, contributing to a sense of the unknown. The heightened awareness of risk differentiates the overall learning experience, and therefore it is a factor that must be understood and embraced.

Individual academics will have skills and preferences that are influenced by institutional expectations and constraints, for example teaching departments and research groups formed around subject specialisms as opposed to learning approaches or a paradigm of venture creation. The concern is that 'know what' would take precedence over 'know how' and the need to engage in some form of entrepreneurship or entrepreneurial behaviour.

Figure 10.1 is an original conceptual framework developed for examining the thrust of any business programme, and BAED can be mapped against it.

The vertical axis depicts the subject related content that is likely to be taught within the remit of entrepreneurship. At the bottom of this axis we show practical enterprise skills – these may also be framed as transferable skills and are typically taught across a range of business programmes. They provide a foundation to entrepreneurship and include business skills such as opportunity spotting, opportunity screening, and conducting market research, those skills and knowledge that support the scoping of a business opportunity.

In the middle are the conceptual skills (underpinned by relevant knowledge) of envisaging or imagining a business enterprise, launching and running it, controlling it and dealing with related uncertainties and setbacks. Subjects and content are concerned with holistic thinking and

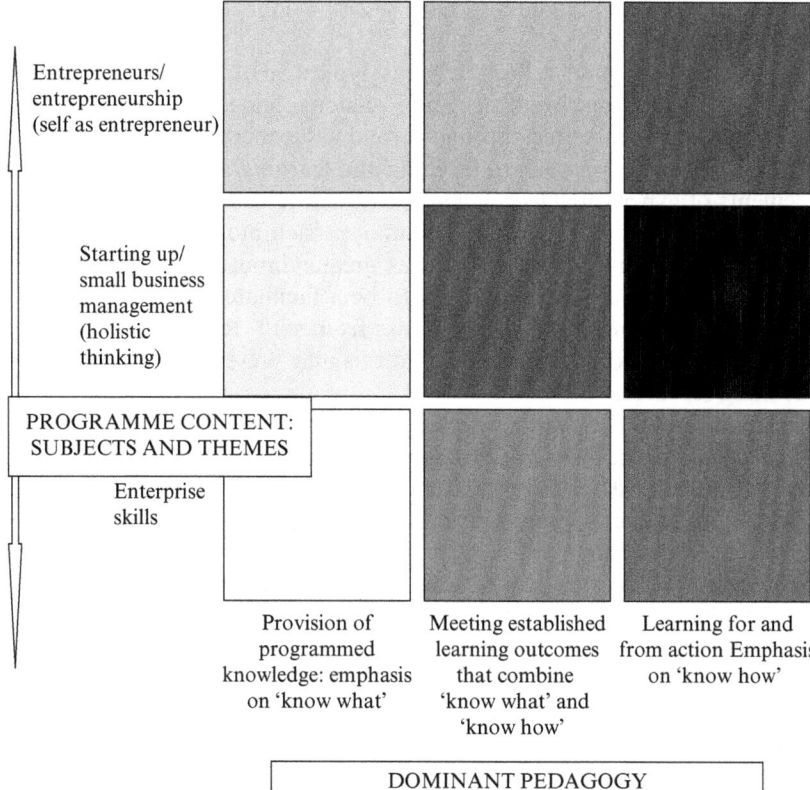

Figure 10.1   Locating the BAED as a learning experience (subjects, themes and pedagogy)

the ability to synthesise discrete enterprise related skills and knowledge in order to formulate and implement a business model and coherent business plans.

At the top of the vertical axis is the learning required for venture creation, specifically learning about the self in relation to the role and contribution of entrepreneurship. Learners reflect on their own actions in order to understand the practice of entrepreneurship and correspondingly raise awareness of their entrepreneurial and learning abilities.

The horizontal axis denotes the dominant pedagogy – choices in teaching and learning approaches – for entrepreneurship and new venture creation. On the left we identify a knowledge driven approach, supported by past and recent research. The learning agenda is concerned with the transfer of knowledge and expertise to willing practitioners; sources of knowledge include guest speaker sessions, independent research and conference sessions.

The middle ground reflects what is typical in teaching and learning provision that being formal teaching sessions guided by pre-established learning outcomes, tested through formal assessment. Here programmes reflect a planned approach to teaching and learning and may incorporate elements of experiential learning with assessed reflections.

Finally, on the right-hand side is an approach more closely associated with action learning. The learner has greater input in deciding what is learned, when and how. This needs to be a facilitated process, as 'learning to learn' requires different expertise from staff. Reflective capabilities must be developed and enhanced, and this may present challenges for the teaching resource.

The depth of the shading provides a view of the BAED in terms of what is taught and how. Programme design reflects a syllabus positioned on the right side of Figure 10.1, learning from and through action. Programme content spans practical skills, holistic thinking and importantly self-reflection – for the development of the self as entrepreneur. Other entrepreneurship programmes can be mapped and, in part depending on the nature and extent of the experiential element, the shading pattern may be quite different.

In short, then, the key themes of this particular degree are:

● assessment related to enterprise development in terms of concept and practice and development of the self as entrepreneur;
● on-going reflective practice for the purpose of action and an action learning orientation;
● a collaborative learning environment – in which students learn from each other as well as from (external) experts and 'conventional' tutors.

Given the differences between BAED and more 'conventional' business degrees, the expectations for the scale of the programme and the numbers that can be attracted are limited; this is a meaningful response to the perceived risks. We are asking faculty and participants to commit to a model of provision that is different and dependent on the ability of all to embrace action and reflection as the means to constructing the BAED experience. In this sense the BAED is aligned with an action learning philosophy and has an association with those programmes that are designed for professional development and practice.

LOCATING THE BAED IN TERMS OF GUIDING PHILOSOPHY AND CONTENT

We require undergraduate students to assume the role of practitioner at the outset of their studies, although their experiences to date and reflective skills may be limited. We embrace 'learning to learn' as an agenda that will extend over the programme. But the ability to undertake planned actions or concrete experiences is determined by the entrepreneurs' emerging sense of self in terms of understanding context and skills requirements.

Action learning is a mechanism for mediation between theory, practice and self and the means by which the participant makes sense of learning needs and takes action to address these. The emphasis may shift between personal development and task orientation, depending on how participants frame and engage with live issues born of venture creation.

Action learning sets are the typical means by which collective learning occurs (Clarke et al., 2006; Lee, 2006), but action learning continues to evade precise definition, and has the potential to grow into other forms. It is our assumption that action learning sets are not the only vehicle for action learning; acting and reflecting in relation to live issues can be achieved in different ways. In terms of ethos, action learning is a holistic approach, not subject bound, but rather driven by the participants' need to engage with and get movement on problem situations. Providing that sessions are not strictly subject bound, and there is space for rehearsal and talking through next steps, then action learning can take root. Classes with small numbers and dedicated modules for entrepreneurship can provide the right forum. It is the matter of reframing the role of teacher to that of facilitator. Participants surface and engage with live issues in order to direct their learning within a collective context of support and challenge. Simply put, action learning allows the learner as practitioner to drive and guide the learning agenda and contributions from others; it puts subject knowledge in its place. It is the means for directing learning experiences and in our view enables effectual entrepreneurship.

In summary, action learning and the development of learners as reflective practitioners requires space and time. On many programmes, knowledge (underpinned by research) is central, although it can be applied to support student sense-making. With BAED we encourage students to acquire knowledge when they need it; we also help them to appreciate what knowledge they need, and why.

Learning pathways and learning outcomes cannot be fully expressed as the sum of modular learning outcomes; there is more to aggregate. The programme must balance and address 'know what' with 'know how'. The institution's requirement for analytical skills and critical

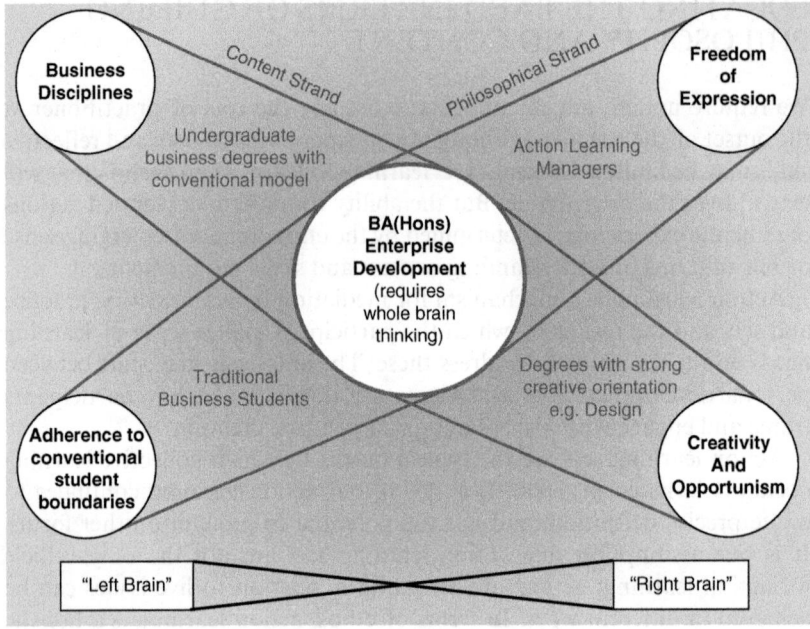

Figure 10.2   BAED: guiding philosophy, programme content and whole-brain thinking

evaluation must work alongside the participants' need to engage in new venture creation.

Figure 10.2 expresses the BAED programme design in terms of philosophy, content and thinking. It is not a typical business course, shaped around functional building blocks. The learning experience combines experiential learning with an action learning philosophy. BAED has some association with creativity and 'arts' programmes in which learners experiment and develop skills around self-expression and the creation of unique works.

We want to engender whole-brain thinking, providing learning opportunities that require creative and holistic thinking as well as analytical and critical reasoning (Hermann-Nehdi, 2010). Programme design is a matter of finding the balance between analytical left-brain thinking and providing the space and openness for imagination and creativity, right-brain thinking. 'Making the case' for new ventures benefits from both (Mercier, 2012).

We believe the provision of resources or content and guidance must be aligned with the autonomy for personal development, which is not only conversant with action learning but also seen as crucial in stimulating creativity and opportunity conceptualisation.

According to Figure 10.2, both right-brain and left-brain thinking matter for enterprise development to occur. Structuring this programme is about finding the balance between providing knowledge of business disciplines and creating the space for questioning insight and business conceptualisation.

The resource requirement for a VCP is less predictable for institutions than a typical business studies course, as learning needs are driven by participants' emerging interests and their individual ability to take action. It is inherently more uncertain.

MANAGING THE BAED

Managing the learning process was learned in action; our reflections were driven by our 'live issue' of proving the concept – that the BAED could work. Reflecting on the 2010–2013 cohort (our second cohort of students), we developed new insights on recruitment and selection, learning experiences and the attainment of learning outcomes.

The experiences of this cohort showed two things. Firstly, the performance data confirmed our belief and intention that students can obtain a good degree classification (demonstrated by the award of a high concentration of 2:1 and first classifications) and, at the same time, establish a business. Secondly, recruitment and selection must address the aspiration to 'be in business' as well as test for a propensity to learn from action and for action. In building an association with action learning, we require our participants to volunteer for action and practically engage with entrepreneurship from the outset. The Appendix to this chapter provides an (outline) analysis of the individuals in the cohort, in terms of key attributes and their achievements. It incorporates some of the themes we explore below.

Recruitment and Selection

In terms of recruitment and selection, our approach contrasts with the typical interview format that focuses on the academic competencies of applicants. We are looking for students who are 'right for the programme' but also students for whom this degree is an appropriate choice. Applicants must therefore be assessed in terms of their learning interests and practices; they need the capacity for both academic and practical learning.

We attempted to identify and test for entrepreneur attributes, by using the FACETS questionnaire and characteristics, but realistically this could only be initiated once participants had joined the programme. FACETS is an entrepreneur indicator designed by Bolton and Thompson (2003, 2013) which looks for evidence of six key characteristics: focus, advantage, creativity, ego, team and social. The indicator identifies the presence of key characteristics; it does not claim to predict the likelihood of entrepreneurial success. Applicants who are short-listed for interview are asked to account for any current or past entrepreneurial activity; they are being scrutinised for evidence of an 'entrepreneur in waiting'. There is a strong reliance on listening to how they make sense of their past experiences. For the staff involved, it is a matter of getting to aspiration, finding actions to validate student declarations and gauging reflective capabilities.

At interview and in the discussion of things tackled in the past we are looking for (although not actually opting to test) evidence of the candidate's 'advantage' attribute, which is primarily associated with opportunity spotting and taking. The advantage attribute also embraces the ability to envision a relevant future, to appreciate and secure the appropriate resources (but not necessarily at the outset) and to understand all the time how well the venture is progressing. This is seen as the defining characteristic of entrepreneurial talent.

We are also interested in, and probe for, what motivates the budding entrepreneur; the relevant FACETS attribute here is ego. Bolton and Thompson (2003, 2013) argue that motivation is a key component of the inner ego,[7] which also includes dedication and self-assurance. However, the inner ego must be matched and tempered with responsibility, accountability and courage (defined as the ability to deal with setbacks) and constituents of the outer ego.[8] Students complete the FACETS paired-question indicator during their first year at university (rather than at the interview stage), because at this point they are in a better position to appreciate the logic and the results they are given. Here, each attribute is scored out of 10, with a score of 10 being the highest. The BAED cohort studied for this research shows a strong link between high scores in ego (in particular, inner ego) and advantage and overall performance. In other words, the students who attained the highest degree awards also possessed key entrepreneur characteristics. This would, naturally, not necessarily be the case for other degrees. But it does suggest that (many – but not all) students attracted to a programme of this nature will be 'entrepreneurs in waiting'.

The interview is not – and it is not meant to be – a scientific approach to selecting candidates for the degree; rather we are looking for fit in terms of interest in entrepreneurship and willingness to engage in practice for the purpose of learning.

A number of our budding entrepreneurs were already active; examples ranged across school based microbusinesses, partnerships formed with employers, and engagement in family businesses.

Once the students had begun their degree, a number of self-perception tests were used, including learning styles inventories (Honey and Mumford, 2000) and a left-brain/right-brain questionnaire (as featured in Bragg and Bragg, 2005). Such tests are widely available to faculty and typically used for personal development agendas. Our purpose was to encourage participants to raise self-awareness and take ownership of personal development through finding the language to aid self-reflection and, importantly, understand the relationship between entrepreneurship motivations, behaviours and actions. In addition, and at two points, the very beginning and some weeks later during their first year, the students were asked to select from a number of possibilities which slogan they would be featuring on their metaphorical T-shirt at that point in time (based on the ideas of Mortiboys, 2010). Their choices are included in the Table 10A.1 in the Appendix. It can be seen that, of the eight students who ultimately graduated with BAED, three retained the same choice during their first eight weeks on the programme, whilst the other five had already started to see the world differently. Table 10A.1 also shows that the different students did not share a common view of the challenge and the opportunity; their journeys were different journeys.

Learning Processes and Learning Outcomes

Entrepreneurs must envision and shape the work context as their skills and insights for venture creation are formed; learning and skills transfer are vital to this.

According to *THE* (2015), undergraduates (from all disciplines) feel that certain 'soft skills' such as creativity, innovation and citizen awareness only marginally improve during their degree studies. Higher levels of development are instead perceived in terms of independent learning, analytical and critical thinking and the ability to work effectively with others. Not only are soft skills difficult to define (the learning requirement largely depends on the context for performance), but there is no best way to develop soft skills. There are times when skills can be developed through a planned approach and alternatively occasions when they result without clear intent; their enhancement might be a product of other planned actions (Ramsey, 2005).

Those students wishing to be entrepreneurial cannot realistically be committed to a clear and pre-determined business plan or self-development agenda. These emerge as the business context is conceptualised and created. Assessments are used to create learning milestones and opportunities for reflection. Students are not required to start with a clear idea; indeed our expectations are that they will pitch a sound business idea and opportunity at the end of the first year. A year later they will have a clear business plan and be ready to start trading, and they then run the business during their final year.

The underlying assumption, then, was that students would enter the degree with a clear commitment to the outcomes and experience but no firm business ideas – although some have started with clear intentions. During their first year they would be personally challenged in various ways; they would agree personal learning contracts; they would work individually and in teams on applied projects; they would evaluate opportunities for themselves. At the end of the year they would pitch a business idea. During their second year they would progress this idea, supported by relevant studies of key business functions. In their final year they would be running the business, albeit at a very modest level, and dealing with the challenges of satisfying orders and customers whilst remaining solvent and maybe seeking fresh opportunities.

For the tracked cohort (2010–2013) we were running the broad mix of programme content as illustrated in Figure 10.3.

The overarching aim of the programme is to engender the skills, knowledge and attitudes for participants to be enabled entrepreneurs. Course design must therefore balance the knowledge and analytical requirements (left-brain thinking) with practical skills development and the ability to create a business venture (right-brain thinking). The balance between these elements varied over the duration of the programme. There was a stronger

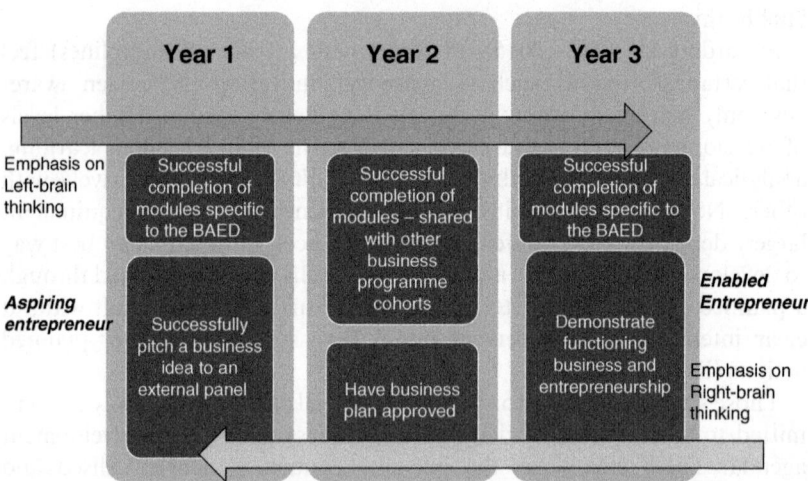

Figure 10.3　BAED: an alternative view of programme design, assessments and outcomes

association with right-brain thinking in Years 1 and 3 – the associated outputs being a business pitch and portfolio of learning based on the experiences of being in business. (Modules for Years 1 and 3 were specific to the BAED, affording the space and time for the cohort to develop as a learning community.) Year 2 concentrated more on the provision of programmed knowledge, specifically relating to law, finance and marketing, emphasising analytical reasoning (left-brain thinking), all contributing to the development of the assessed business plan. Year 2 modules were typically shared with other business related programmes.

The motivation to be an entrepreneur in order to establish a business must be significant, as the formative assessments of business pitches (Year 1) and business plans (Year 2) and the portfolio related to setting up the business (Year 3) earn credits towards the degree – although their overall contribution is limited. Furthermore, the assessments of pitch and business plan feed forward into business start-up. The business plan is not an isolated assessment (Gilbert, 2012); rather it provides the means to convert ideas expressed in the Year 1 pitch into the feasibility stage. The plan must be revisited in Year 3 as the learner moves into the action environment. These assessments function as practical gateways to enterprise development as well as providing key opportunities for reflection.

As would be the case in many universities, each module was required to have specific learning outcomes, but the overall desire to transform an aspiring entrepreneur into what one might describe as a 'competent practitioner' or an enabled entrepreneur provided the vision. This transformation embraces knowledge, experience and personal development. (It was always anticipated that students would learn more about themselves.) Correspondingly, of course, the faculty who enable this journey are also learning more about themselves and their beliefs in this approach to teaching and learning.

LOCATING THE BAED WITHIN THE INSTITUTIONAL CONTEXT

Having looked at one venture creation programme within the context of business education, it is now appropriate to consider the context of the host institution, relevant faculty and key stakeholder interests. The design and operation of programmes and courses must reconcile the outcomes required by the university and the contributing faculty with those pursued by individual participants.

The extent to which the learning environment is dynamic (Cope, 2003) depends on what can be freed up from planned progression and subject related modules. This will be determined by the ability to control and schedule resources. Institutions must contend with changes in learning processes and the measurement of learning outcomes. The aspirations of programme participants must be tempered with what is allowed in terms of tariffs of assessment, time, resources and the university view of performance measurement.

Scott et al. (2016) acknowledge the likelihood of 'constructive misalignment'. Their content analysis on master's-level reflective diaries linked to business planning assignments concluded that a number of arguably valuable enterprise skills and capabilities were reported that had not been specified as desired learning outcomes.

Any desire to engender enterprising behaviours and venture creation will need to contend with:

- the alignment between staff (teaching and programme management), institution and the learning needs or expectations of the participants;
- the need to capture, express and assess for learning outcomes, typically via assessments (which are in the spirit of doing, being and knowing);
- the allowance of risk and opportunity spotting to be realities, even within the confines of a taught programme.

Figure 10.4 provides a representation of entrepreneurship education in relation to stakeholder interests. In the centre is the learning agenda for those concerned with what is appropriate, feasible and desirable. Academics around the world are likely to see research outputs (in the UK, these will be linked to the periodic Research Excellence Frameworks or REFs) as being particularly significant in their career development. At the same time, where niche programmes (such as BAED) become associated with the individual staff who champion them, there will always be a danger that they are not scalable. Faculty face the live issue of 'resourcing' entrepreneurship education. The interactions between these three interested parties will affect the extent of opportunity spotting and taking and the accompanying willingness to take certain risks.

Students have their own motivations for being at university and choosing a particular degree; their choice will be influenced by their personal values and by what they see as being valuable to them in the future. Some universities are more committed than others to the 'entrepreneurship agenda', which can be manifested in various ways. Some are welcoming hosts, whilst others are constrained and challenged by a different way of

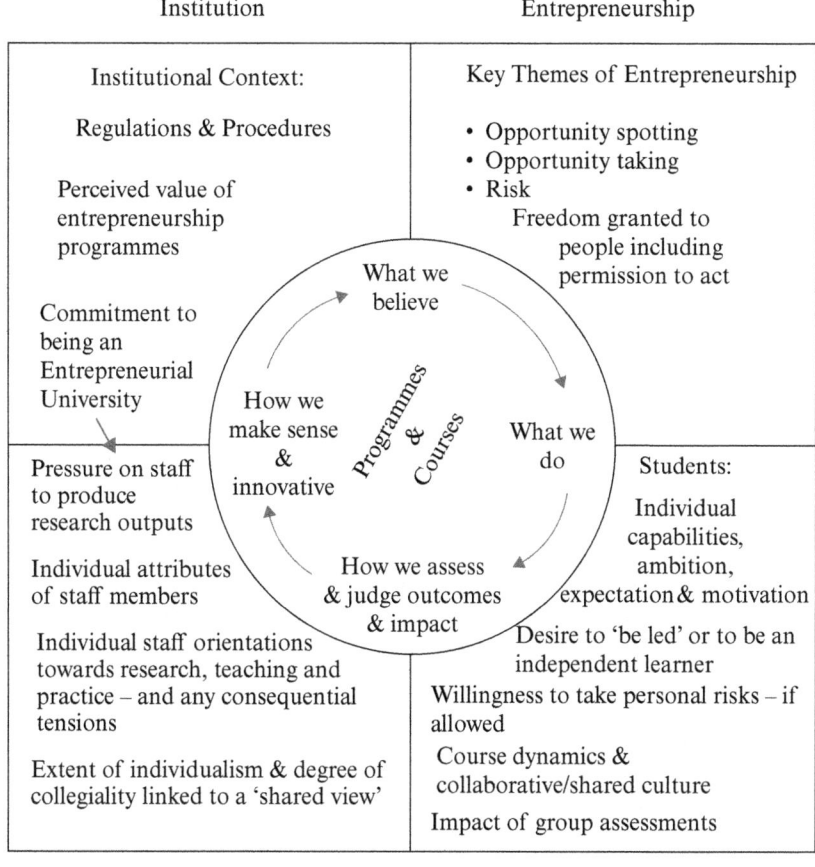

Figure 10.4 and surrounding labels:

Institution   Entrepreneurship

Institutional Context:

Regulations & Procedures

Perceived value of
entrepreneurship
programmes

Commitment to
being an
Entrepreneurial
University

Pressure on staff
to produce
research outputs

Individual attributes
of staff members

Individual staff orientations
towards research, teaching and
practice – and any consequential
tensions

Extent of individualism & degree of
collegiality linked to a 'shared view'

Key Themes of Entrepreneurship

• Opportunity spotting
• Opportunity taking
• Risk
  Freedom granted to
  people including
  permission to act

Students:

Individual
capabilities,
ambition,
expectation & motivation

Desire to 'be led' or to be an
independent learner

Willingness to take personal risks – if
allowed

Course dynamics &
collaborative/shared culture

Impact of group assessments

What we
believe

How we
make sense
&
innovative

Programmes & Courses

What we
do

How we assess
& judge outcomes
& impact

Staff   Students

*Figure 10.4   Locating programme design in relation to stakeholder
interests*

doing things; specifically a formal and planned approach to programme design can conflict with the relative freedom required for the practice of entrepreneurship.

Stevenson and Jarillo (1990), whilst focusing on opportunity, contend that entrepreneurship is a process by which individuals pursue opportunities without regard to the resources they currently control. Strategy texts (see, for example, Thompson et al., 2014) stress that to be effective any strategy needs to be implemented successfully; resources do matter. They also distinguish between strategies that are opportunity driven and those which are designed to exploit valuable organisational competencies, the so-termed resource based approach. Adopting a strategic perspective, BAED was driven by perceived opportunity and championed by a small group of committed staff. As any new course develops and matures, and more staff are required, given that the faculty available changes over time for a variety of reasons, resourcing issues can arise, making implementation that much more challenging. We believe that a core of programme champions is essential for a course such as BAED, but alone this is not enough. In addition, the values driven support and commitment of the institution will either ease or compound this issue. For these reasons, niche venture creation programmes will be 'more at home' in certain universities than others; the environment of the host institution will have a key impact on sustainability and resource development. Thompson et al. (2014) argue that strategic effectiveness is determined by the degree of congruency between the environment (E) (here, particularly, finding and retaining appropriate students), values (V) (the culture of the host institution) and resources (R) (where faculty are central). This model of E–V–R congruence can be used to judge the strategic strength of any venture creation programme, indeed of any entrepreneurship programme.

In summary, venture creation courses have a valuable contribution to make to entrepreneurship education; the challenge lies in running and developing them effectively, and this requires that we understand and embrace competing agendas, which in turn requires an approach to programme development and design that is underpinned by action learning, where reflexivity encouraged in students is mirrored within faculty and institution and fed through to programme design.

Figure 10.5 expresses the tension described above that might arise from competing agendas. The top element of the figure presents a notional reality – an even balance between taught theory and experience, with equal attention given to 'left-brain' and 'right-brain' learning. The implication is that staff view their personal and professional development in pracademic terms. A case can be made that the institutional pressure (and, indeed, external pressure from the paradigm of higher education in general) for academics to become renowned researchers has created a push to the left, to a greater emphasis on making sure teaching incorporates the most recent research thinking and publications. Some (many) students will thrive with this challenge and enjoy stretching their intellectual capabilities. We conclude that this is seen as more 'at home' in higher education than the notional normal distribution in the top element of the figure. Prioritising learning for practice and embracing enterprise (let alone entrepreneurship) require a countervailing push to the right. This will be particularly suitable for certain staff and students – but the stronger the push to the right (which is required for a venture creation degree) the greater the challenge

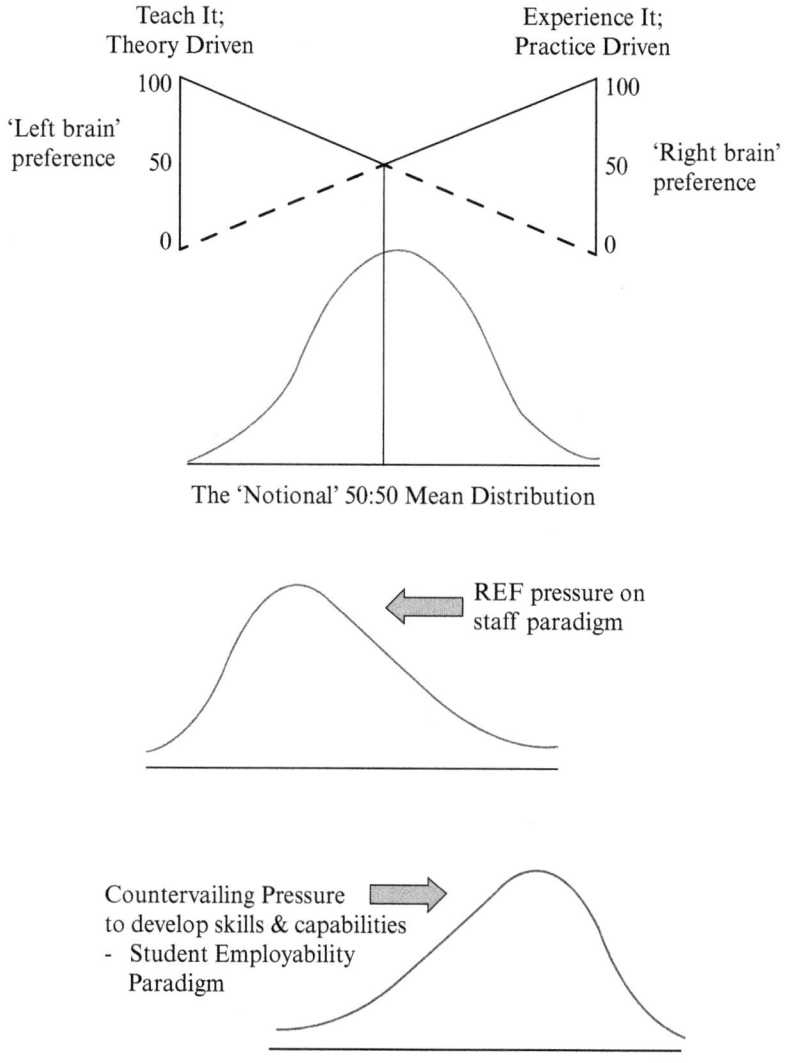

Figure 10.5   Conflicting pressures in programme design: the academic–pracademic tension

for the academics involved, because it is seen by some as challenging the conventional wisdom of the role of academia. In relation to this, it is worth highlighting the increasing trend in the UK for experiential entrepreneur-ship to be provided by university support services – outside of academic faculty – as providers of enterprise skills, assistance for start-ups and access to professional networks. While such services do support the practice of new venture creation, they may not assess for learning or contribute to the learning outcomes of the degree.

When faculty is considered as a resource, we need to ask questions about knowledge, skills and an orientation to learning. Is there a requirement for pracademics (as referred to by Posner, 2009; Susskind, 2013)? It is significant that for many academics their loyalty is to their discipline – or a specific sub-set of a discipline – whilst experiential and action learning paradigms switch the loyalty towards particular programmes and learner communities. This can cause internal issues if schools or departments are strongly based around disciplines and research themes, and staff are encouraged to focus on specific subjects. The challenge is to allow faculty to exercise loyalty to goals which are student centred and relevant for the university as a whole: to be interdisciplinary and to capture the contribution made to practice.

CONCLUSIONS AND REFLECTIONS

Our experience with venture creation degrees has cemented a view that experiential learning must be embedded within action learning (encapsulating live issues and personal goal setting) if there is to be effectual entrepreneurship with emergent practice and sense-making by those involved. This is illustrated in Figure 10.6.

The performance and achievements of a BAED cohort (2010–2013) suggested a 'proof of concept'. Students can achieve a solid degree

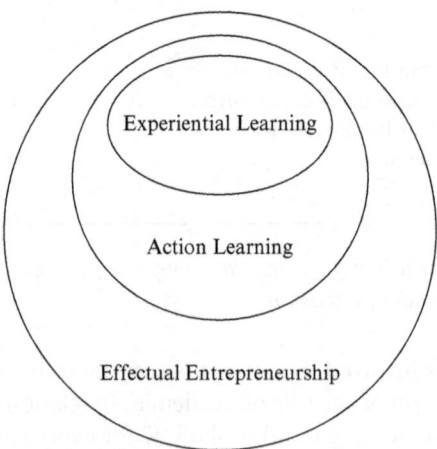

Figure 10.6   Effectual entrepreneurship

performance within traditional boundaries and start their own business venture. But, if it is to be effective and a valuable foundation for the future, the students involved must make sense of their achievements. 'Doing it' is essential but not enough in itself. Students must learn from doing as well as learn by doing. The education is certainly experiential, underpinned by a programme designed for extensive reflection and a commitment to the principles of action learning. A venture creation programme of this type can, then, work, assuming the appropriate students are recruited and retained and that committed faculty enable a suitable student experience and demand reflection on the part of students, all within an *accommodating* institutional environment.

That said, long-term sustainability is a different challenge and requires strength in depth amongst the faculty and a university that allows for such opportunities to be pursued. A programme that embraces action learning and experiential learning cannot be wholly planned; the pace of learning will vary between participants, as will the experiences they seek and undertake. Our experiences showed that dedicated modules and staff created a context for 'being entrepreneurial', and this provided sufficient structure and cohesion for a programme.

Entrepreneurship – for both entrepreneurs and students on entrepreneurship programmes – is a journey. There might or might not be clarity of the end point; there is likely to be much less clarity about the route and the uncertainties that have to be met. The journey involves opportunity and a belief that with appropriate actions the risks can be managed and the desired outcomes achieved. The reality of individuals' learning journeys is a sense of learning (with emergent themes from hindsight and knowing in the form of insight), as attested by what they do and are able to do. However, it may not be possible (permitted) for students to deconstruct learning in a way that a university would typically frame. Individual module assessments are important milestones – but a more holistic view of attainment is required.

The analysis and discussion of progress with the BAED cohort highlights the need for a different approach from faculty. Entrepreneurship and action learning requires facilitation (in collective sessions) as well as coaching and mentoring. Whilst institutions still need to provide modules that deliver the necessary programmed knowledge, one challenge for institutions is to think more creatively about how they support entrepreneurs to develop their businesses. The pressure on relevant staff to be researchers and focus on research outcomes is another challenge that has to be recognised.

Because of these various demands, and as highlighted earlier, these programmes are likely to be niche and attract only modest numbers. This route and approach is very different from the prior experiences that students will have and bring; it is understandable that it would be outside the comfort zone of many who have a more conforming perspective and welcome greater structure. For that reason it is likely to require some investment (as well as flexibility) on the part of the university; degrees like BAED will probably be less profitable financially than the more traditional (and more popular with students) programmes. That said, whilst venture creation programmes are different, their value is real. The number of graduates from across any university who will, at some point in their lives, be freelance or self-employed is significant – although this may not be uppermost in their minds before and during their studies. An experience which proves to people whether they can 'create their own job' and be self-sufficient, and which introduces them to the challenges and uncertainties of the entrepreneur's journey, is valuable for them and also for society as a whole. The real value of the contribution of a programme like BAED will ideally be assessed over a period of time that spans beyond the three years of the degree itself; and, therefore, tracking the on-going progress of the students from any cohort is important.

Entrepreneurship programmes enable students to undertake a very particular, special and important journey (involving starting and running a new venture) whilst studying for their degree. Their purpose is linked to the personal development of students who see this opportunity as welcoming, challenging, appropriate and desirable – which is not every student by any stretch of the imagination. These are the students for whom the programme is relevant; they can be characterised as being drawn to a different experience, but there will be no particular background that distinguishes who they are. Their compelling reason to opt for such a degree is based on their own desire to be different and a belief they can meet (and benefit from) the experience and the journey. In some cases, they will be students who would shun a more conventional approach, as they would see it as too structured and, for them, stifling. The key question for many faculties is: are they comfortable with the uncertainties involved, and do they believe they can cope with the challenge of moving away from conventional wisdom on the student experience? The key question for universities is: are they flexible enough and willing to champion small courses that are different and unconventional?

A final question is: for whom are undergraduate venture creation degrees attractive? We might embed an answer to this in the key themes of the business model – what, for whom and why (Thompson et al., 2014)? Venture creation degrees are programmes where students start and run a real business as an integral part of their studies. They are attractive to students who are excited by this opportunity – perhaps seeing it as less structured than other (business) programmes and more suited to their personal learning styles and needs. What, though, is their compelling reason for choosing it? To some extent confirmed by our research, we suspect many at least start out believing they want to run their own business after they graduate and this is an ideal route to achieve this. At the end, however, not all do this, or want to do this. Such an outcome is not a criticism of the programme. Rather learning to learn has allowed participants to realise what is involved in creating one's own job or business and whether they are suited to pursue this route, at the end of the programme. In their early 20s many other factors are involved in their immediate career decisions, and this degree might well be an experience that will be useful later in life.

NOTES

1. Reflexive practice refers to a continuum of reflections generated in pursuit of learning goals (Bruno et al., 2011). In the context of BAED, reflexive practice – from students and staff – underpins new venture creation and the on-going development of the programme.
2. VCP can be defined as 'entrepreneurship or business education on a higher education level with a pedagogy firmly based on the creation of a real-life venture as their primary learning vessel' (Venture Creation Programs List, 2016).
3. Experiential learning results from the undertaking of experiences (Kolb, 1984) and is enhanced by reflection with reference to feelings, conceptual ideas and future intent. Often learning experiences are of personal relevance and can be situated wherever the opportunity arises.
4. Problem based learning is concerned with real world problems to which experiential learning can be applied (Tan and Ng, 2006). PBL encourages holism and helps the learner to work with complexity and ambiguity. Attention is given to problem definition and draws on the reflective capabilities of the learner.
5. 'Action learning is the art of creating real results in real time . . . It is a process of accelerating people's learning about real work problems and on desired outcomes within the actual work context' (Bierema, 1998, p. 87). It is learning driven by the participant's desire to inform and get movement on 'live issues'.
6. Entrepreneurs may confront risks in terms of environmental variables that are beyond their control, as well as resource issues relating to skills and abilities (Macko and Tyszka, 2009).
7. The term 'inner ego' is used to reflect that these attributes are best understood by the person involved; they are not automatically visible to outsiders.
8. Attributes of the outer ego are more visible. The inner and outer attributes should be relatively balanced, as there are issues to deal with if they are not.

REFERENCES

Audretsch, D. (2012), Entrepreneurship research, *Management Decision*, **50**(5), 755–764.

Bierema, L.L. (1998), Fitting action learning to corporate programs, *Performance Improvement Quarterly*, **11**(1), 86–107.

Bolton, B. and Thompson, J. (2003), *The Entrepreneur in Focus: Achieve Your Potential*, London: Thomson Learning.

Bolton, B. and Thompson, J. (2013), *Entrepreneurs: Talent, Temperament and Opportunity*, 3rd edn., London: Routledge.

Bragg, A. and Bragg, M. (2005), *Developing New Business Ideas*, Harlow, UK: FT Prentice Hall.

Breen, J.P. (2000), Enterprise, entrepreneurship and small business, Paper presented at the ICSB Conference, Sydney.

Bruno, A., Galuppo, L. and Gilardi, S. (2011), Evaluating the reflexive practices in a learning experience, *European Journal of Psychology of Education*, **26**(4), 527–543.

Clarke, J., Thorpe, R., Anderson, L. and Gold, J. (2006), It's all action, it's all learning: action learning in SMEs, *Journal of European Industrial Training*, **30**(6), 441–455.

Cope, J. (2003), Entrepreneurial learning and critical reflection: discontinuous events as triggers for 'higher level' learning, *Management Learning*, **34**(4), 429–450.

Corbett, A.C. (2005), Experiential learning within the process of opportunity identification and exploitation, *Entrepreneurship Theory and Practice*, **29**(4), 473–491.

Drucker, P.F. (1985), *Innovation and Entrepreneurship*, Abingdon, UK: Routledge.

Gilbert, D. (2012), From chalk and talk to walking the walk: facilitating dynamic learning contexts for entrepreneurship students in fast-tracking innovations, *Education and Training*, **54**(2/3), 152–166.

Herrmann-Nehdi, A. (2010), Whole brain thinking (ignore it at your peril), *Training and Development*, **64**(5), 36–41.

Honey, P. and Mumford, A. (2000), *The Learning Styles Questionnaire*, Maidenhead, UK: Peter Honey.

Kolb, D.A. (1984), *Experiential Learning: Experience as a Source of Learning and Development*, Englewood Cliffs, NJ: Prentice Hall.

Lee, N.J. (2006), Action learning from a participant's perspective, *Action Learning: Research and Practice*, **3**(1), 89–96.

Macko, A. and Tyszka, T. (2009), Entrepreneurship and risk taking, *Applied Psychology: An International Review*, **58**(3), 469–487.

Mercier, H. (2012), Looking for arguments, *Argumentation*, **26**(3), 305–324.

Morland, L. and Thompson, J.L. (2015), How action learning can support under-graduate students on a venture creation degree, January, USASBE, Tampa, FL.

Mortiboys, A. (2010), *How to Be an Effective Teacher in Higher Education: Answers to Lecturers' Questions*, Maidenhead, UK: Open University Press.

Neck, H.M., Greene, P.G. and Brush, C.G. (2014), *Teaching Entrepreneurship: A Practice Based Approach*, Cheltenham, UK and Northampton, MA, USA: Edward Elgar.

Pittaway, L. and Cope, J. (2007), Simulated entrepreneurial learning: integrating experiential and collaborative approaches to learning, *Management Learning*, **38**(2), 211–233.

Posner, P.L. (2009), The pracademic: an agenda for re-engaging practitioners and academics, *Public Budgeting and Finance*, **29**(1), 12–26.

Rae, D. and Woodier-Harris, N. (2012), International entrepreneurship education: postgraduate business student experiences of entrepreneurship education, *Education and Training*, **54**(8/9), 639–656.

Ramsey, C. (2005), Narrating development: professional practice emerging within stories, *Action Research*, **3**(3), 279–295.

Read, S., Sarasvathy, S., Dew, N., Wiltbank, R. and Ohlsson, A. (2010), *Effectual Entrepreneurship*, London: Routledge.

Scott, J.M., Penaluna, A. and Thompson, J.L. (2016), A critical perspective on learning outcomes and the effectiveness of experiential approaches in entrepreneurship education, *Education and Training*, **58**(1), 82–93.

Stevenson, H. and Jarillo, C. (1990), A paradigm of entrepreneurship: entrepreneurial management, *Strategic Management Journal*, **11**, 17–27.

Susskind, L. (2013), Confessions of a pracademic: searching for a virtuous cycle of theory building, teaching and action research, *Negotiation Journal*, **29**(2), 225–237.

Tan, S.S. and Ng, C.K. Frank (2006), A problem based learning approach to entrepreneurship education, *Education and Training*, **48**(6), 416–428.

THE (2015), UK Engagement Survey, *Times Higher Education*, December 10.

Thompson, J.L., Scott, J.M. and Martin, F. (2014), *Strategic Management: Awareness and Change*, 7th edn., Andover, UK: Cengage.

Venture Creation Programs List (2016), Chalmers University of Technology, Sweden, retrieved April 2016 from http://vcplist.com.

APPENDIX

Table 10A.1   The BAED cohort (2010–2013): attributes, expectations and outcomes

Student	Advantage score (out of 10)	Ego score* (out of 10)	Honours level achieved at end of degree	Comment on business developed	T-shirt statement – freshers' week	T-shirt statement – two months later
1	9.5	10.0	First	Successful start-up in food business as a pop-up retail opportunity. Business closed after initial lease terminated.	There's so much to business I'm going to need help.	I'll like it if it's new and different.
2	9.0	10.0	Upper second	Successful start-up in food business – later sold the business on.	I'm here looking for the best ideas.	I want sound, practical advice.
3	7.0	9.5	Upper second	Number of small (micro) start-ups.	This is my chance to do something different.	This is my chance to do something different.
4	7.0	8.5	Upper second	Successful trading business – growing and employing staff. This represented the consolidation of activities that existed before starting the degree.	All that matters to me is being in business.	All that matters to me is being in business.
5	6.5	10.0	First	Working as an intrapreneur – new projects in existing high-growth SME.	All that matters to me is being in business.	This is my chance to do something different.
6	7.0	7.0	–	Inner ego exceeds outer – started a business but opted for academic route instead.	I want time to think my ideas through.	I want time to think my ideas through.
7	6.0	9.5	Upper second	Income from app businesses and pursuing trading opportunities.	I'm hoping I'll get ideas from others.	I'm hoping I'll get ideas from others.
8	6.0	5.5	Lower second	Comfortable self-employment with on-line trading business.	I want sound, practical advice.	I want time to think my ideas through.

Table 10A.1   (continued)

Student	Advantage score (out of 10)	Ego score* (out of 10)	Honours level achieved at end of degree	Comment on business developed	T-shirt statement – freshers' week	T-shirt statement – two months later
9	2.0	9.0	Upper second	Initially working with another on the cohort but now developing on-line trading opportunities, one from family business links. (Perceived to have overcome initial low advantage score.)	I want time to think my ideas through.	There's so much to business I'm going to need help.
10	2.0	7.5	–	Very low on focus although strong enabler profile. Left the programme.	I want to know the secret of success.	This is my chance to do something different.
11	7.0	8.5	–	Strong performer in first year of study. Left to join a business degree course linked to, and with sponsorship from, a leading retail chain.	There's so much to business I'm going to need help.	There's so much to business I'm going to need help.

Note: *The ego score is the mean average of inner and outer ego scores.

11. The principles and practices of delivering experiential entrepreneurship education to mega-classes

Christopher Pryor

If you were to visit my class – the introductory entrepreneurship course at the University of Florida – you'd feel right at home. The classroom would look about the same as yours: podium up front, tiered seating for about 50. The students would also sound and act the same: highly engaged, with either your lecture or whatever they're watching on their laptops. However, a few differences would stand out. Your classroom probably doesn't have five video cameras, run by a dedicated technical director from a hidden control room. Your classroom might not have rows of LED studio lights. You probably don't have to wear a microphone, and students probably don't have to speak into a padded, throw-able mic when they ask questions or pose comments. The biggest difference is one you would never notice: most of my students will never come to class at all. Each semester, about 500 students enroll in Principles of Entrepreneurship at the University of Florida, and in-class daily attendance averages about 10 students.

This is the world of the mega-class and of lecture capture, which is a technology that enables faculty to video-record their classroom presentations and easily share it, such as through a learning management system like Canvas, Blackboard or D2L (Owston et al., 2011). Mega-classes, or classes with 500 or more students, are a growing phenomenon at universities across the country (e.g., Pope, 2007). Lecture capture technology has enabled many more universities to offer mega-classes. The University of Central Florida, for instance, uses lecture capture technology in over 100 courses, some of which have enrollments of a thousand students (Rousson, 2015). At my university, lecture capture is used in the undergraduate business school to teach classes with 2000 or more students at once, which make my 500-student classes appear puny. Universities are rapidly adopting the mega-class model and lecture capture (Frenkel, 2012), and more entrepreneurship educators are likely to find themselves teaching to the digital masses.

When I entered the mega-class world, my intuition was to deploy what had worked so well for me in my previous small liberal arts university: interactive classroom sessions, fostering high student engagement, providing abundant personalized feedback, and having students produce written projects, such as business concepts and plans. (In the mega-class, students who sought feedback were more often than not students who attended the in-class sessions.) In short, I ignored the needs of the 99 percent of students watching online and taught to the students in the class. And no surprise: end-of-the-semester feedback was unpleasant. Something had to change.

This chapter is a summary of everything I learned and implemented while teaching in the mega-class environment. The outline of this chapter is as follows. First, I will describe the challenges – as well as resources – that are unique to the mega-class. Second, I will introduce an instructional framework that I have used to revise my own mega-class. Third, using the entrepreneurship course I have developed at the University of Florida as an example, I will describe several practices entrepreneurship instructors can use to provide a top-notch experiential journey to their own students. I hope that the lessons I have learned in the mega-classroom can also be applied by instructors of small classes and that you find something useful here to help you more fully deliver on the promise of entrepreneurship education.

MATTERS OF SIZE: THE PROBLEMS AND BENEFITS OF THE MEGA-CLASS

The Challenges of the Mega-class

Let's say you are one student enrolled in a 500- or 1500-person entrepreneurship class. You may be a freshman, and the sheer scale of the class shocks you, compared to the small classes at your high school (Mulryan-Kyne, 2010). You quickly determine that nobody knows you are in class or cares to know your name. You feel disengaged (Exeter et al., 2010): disengaged from the instructor, disengaged from your fellow students, and disengaged from the course content. This disengagement can lead you to believe that you are anonymous, that your presence in the class is not valued, and that you can simply "disappear" without any consequences (e.g., Gibbs, 1992). As you choose to skip class more frequently

– after all, who will notice? – your performance edges downward (e.g., Marburger, 2001). What's worse, your instructors, who are simply following well-meaning research (e.g., Terry et al., 2015) and advice from colleagues, dedicate themselves to delivering "engaging lectures," since that's what makes a "great" mega-class experience. Although you may think lectures are drudgery, the alternative, classroom engagement, is actually more painful for you to watch. Discussion sessions, in-class break-outs and group work don't lead to stimulating video and leave you feeling further alienated from the class.

You are now the entrepreneurship instructor. One of the first mega-class challenges that confronts you is logistical. For instance, administering and quickly grading exams, quizzes and other assignments pose serious challenges. To cope, you find yourself increasingly relying on multiple-choice exams and other non-written assignments (Bean, 2001), adversely affecting the learning potential in the course (Cuseo, 2007). Providing individualized, substantive student feedback is practically impossible. In fact, research suggests that large classes foster an environment inimical to interactions between instructors and students – instead, the culture imbues a message of "You leave me alone and I will leave you alone" (Kuh et al., 1991, p. 362). What's worse, you find that your large class size destroys the quality of the learning your students acquire. Class size appears to be inversely related to students' development of cognitive skills, as larger classes tend to focus on the rote memorization of facts rather than higher-order objectives, such as analysis or application or synthesis (e.g., Pascarella and Terenzini, 1991). Throughout the semester, as fewer and fewer students choose to attend the in-person session of your mega-class (Cuseo, 2007), you may become discouraged and burned out, which further reduces the potential for students' learning outcomes (e.g., Roeser et al., 2013).

In any classroom, these dynamics would be serious impediments to learning. In an entrepreneurship classroom, they are disastrous. The fundamental insight of research is that entrepreneurship is a process, which can be learned through practice (Corbett, 2005; Drucker, 1985; Kuratko, 2005). And, perhaps unlike the case for other disciplines found on the university campus, entrepreneurship students cannot practice their discipline by listening to lectures recorded on a video camera, taking multiple-choice tests, and offering a rote comment or two in an online discussion board with other students.

We Learn What We Do

As with the question Postman and Weingartner (1969) posed decades ago, we have to wonder what entrepreneurship students in mega-classes might actually be learning. They are not learning the content that we teach in lectures. Memorized definitions of "opportunity" or the steps of the entrepreneurship process are quickly forgotten after the final exam. However, our inability to engage students, our exclusive focus on lower-order memorization and comprehension skills, the absence of practice, our overreliance on the lecture, and the lack of any feedback *do* teach entrepreneurship students in mega-classes some important lessons:

- Entrepreneurship is easy. Entrepreneurship is acing two multiple-choice exams and a comprehensive final.
- Entrepreneurship is about me. I've written a one-page business concept or I've presented an elevator pitch. I wasn't required to interview customers or understand market conditions – my ideas came entirely from my own head. Entrepreneurship is a lot like the creative writing course I took as a freshman.
- Entrepreneurship ends when the class ends. I was "delivered" all of the content in the course through a series of lectures, and once I had listened to all of the lectures and completed all of the exams, I knew everything I needed to know.
- It is the instructor's job to make me an entrepreneur. I have no responsibility in leading my own learning experiences.
- Any feedback I receive will be rare and it will be positive. My fellow students were very supportive of my ideas, in online discussion boards, and I never received any individualized feedback from the instructor.

In short, the mega-class can hamstring any entrepreneur instructor's efforts and hamper our students' development of an entrepreneurial mindset.

Resources at Hand

Although the mega-class imposes a number of serious challenges, it is also accompanied by a number of resources, which the instructor can deploy. Ironically, many of the disadvantages of the mega-class can also be important resources for the entrepreneurship instructor, if recognized and used appropriately. The first resource is class size: although the individual instructor may be unable to directly connect with a large, diverse group of students, students can connect with each other. For instance, the use of peer assessment, which is the use of students to evaluate each other's work (e.g., Weaver and Cotrell, 1986), is increasingly seen as an important means of cultivating higher-order cognitive skills, such as critical thinking and analyzing information (Dochy et al., 1999). The mega-class, and its huge, diverse student population, has the potential to expose individual learners to perspectives and information that would be unavailable in a smaller class, with its relatively homogeneous population. The second resource is technology: the technological wave that made the modern mega-class possible also enables instructors to develop a vibrant, engaging learning experience for students (e.g., Grossman and Means, 2014). For instance, students' ability to create and customize their own blogs helps them create their own "seat" in the classroom, from which they may connect with other students and engage in their learning experiences (Kop, 2011). In addition, learning management systems, more often than not used by instructors to bludgeon students with more content, communication, testing or grades (Siemens, 2007), can instead be a powerful tool to stimulate student engagement, create interconnectivity, and curate students' work.

Other resources at the mega-class instructor's disposal, but which are not unique to their context, are the centers for teaching at our universities, faculty and administrative support, and the growing online communities dedicated to developing and spreading teaching techniques that are becoming increasingly necessary in our simultaneously digitalized and individualized world. One resource I deliberately do not mention is the instructor herself, specifically the pervasive notion that an engaging, passionate instructor is needed to carry the attention of the hundreds of students in a mega-class. Perhaps this advice is particularly common among entrepreneurship instructors because our field *is* inspirational and listening to successful entrepreneurs *can* be engaging. The suggestions I make in the following sections are based on our current understanding and research of how learning happens, which necessarily emphasizes "student-centered" learning.

DEFINING THE "FIRST PRINCIPLES" OF INSTRUCTIONAL DESIGN

In entrepreneurship, it is a truth universally acknowledged that experience is the foundation of learning (Corbett, 2005; Krueger, 2007; Kuratko, 2005). The experiences entrepreneurs have shape who they are (Morris et al., 2012). Therefore, if we want to foster an entrepreneurial mindset in our learners, our course design must place tremendous emphasis on shaping learners' experiences (Kickul and Fayolle, 2007). The experiential learning model (e.g., Kolb and Kolb, 2005) has been integral in guiding our shift from lecture-based, didactic methods of instruction to student-centered, action-oriented methods; nevertheless, this model, while effective at describing how learners learn, is less applicable when considering how teachers should teach. For that perspective, we draw on Merrill's "First Principles of Instruction" (2002), which provides explicit guidelines for instructional design that harness and enhance learners' experiences. Additionally, although generally applicable, Merrill's framework has been used to explore design issues related to teaching large classes (e.g., Margaryan et al., 2015; Tolley et al., 2012).

Merrill draws on a wide range of existing instructional design theories to coalesce five principles. The implementation of these principles in course design is positively related to the amount of learning in that course, he argues (2002). Before designing the entrepreneurship mega-class, instructional guidelines are important. As these principles are 1) applicable to any learning setting and 2) extrapolated from the commonalties among a broad array of existing instructional design models, I have used them to design my course. The principles, which are shown in the circle embedded in Figure 11.1, are as follows:

1. *Problem-centered.* Learning will increase when students are engaged in solving real-world problems. Problems are defined as "a wide range of activities, with the most critical characteristics being that the activity is some whole task rather than only components of a task and that the task is representative of those the learner will encounter in the world following instruction" (Merrill, 2002, p. 45). (This may appear obvious, but many of us are teaching courses based on the sequence of chapters in a book or based on a conceptual framework, such as the entrepreneurship process. The real-world applicability of entrepreneurship can be lost in the jumble of frameworks and concepts, which are often presented *before* students have had a chance to experience them.) Problem-centered instruction emphasizes the relevance of the course to students' lives (e.g., Postman and Weingartner, 1969), as well as recognizes that, unless students are able to anchor frameworks and concepts with real-life problems and situations, they quickly forget (Brown et al., 2014). In addition, students should be presented with a progression of problems, each of which adds complexity and each of which is explicitly built on the experiences of the preceding problems.

2. *Activation of experience.* The acquisition of new knowledge is aided when learners are able to connect it to previous experiences (Merrill, 2002). This principle contrasts against the practice of introducing abstract concepts to students, who may not have the experience basis with which to interpret and make sense of abstract information. Importantly, if learners do not have adequate experience it is incumbent upon the instructor to provide that experience. This is particularly important for the undergraduate entrepreneurship instructor. While

Activation practices

- **Micro-exercises**: Provide students experience with common entrepreneurial tasks
- **Peer feedback**: Students' exposure to multiple viewpoints helps them more rapidly develop mental schemas to understand the exercises
- **Short, practical lectures**: Provide concepts and frameworks that enable students to place their own experiences within the broader context of entrepreneurship

Demonstration practices

- **Student blogs**: Each student provides a report on their experience with a given entrepreneurial skill or task; these reports demonstrate to other students how to complete these skills or tasks
- **Short, practical lectures**: Instructors produce "How To" videos, demonstrating the skill or task being learned and providing comparisons of good and bad examples

Integration practices

- **Student blogs**: Incorporate "reflection;" at the end of the semester, blog posts form a cohesive story of student's path to the entrepreneurial mindset
- **Micro-exercises**: Regular practice of skills requires students to reflect and adapt
- **Peer feedback**: Blogs enable students to comment on each other's posts; in providing feedback in these comments, students rely and reflect on their own experiences to evaluate others' performance

Application practices

- **Micro-exercises**: Provide students with opportunities to apply the skills and tasks they learn in class; micro-exercises also facilitate regular practice

Problem-centered

- **Micro-exercises**: Clearly and explicitly link exercises to the solution of real-world problems

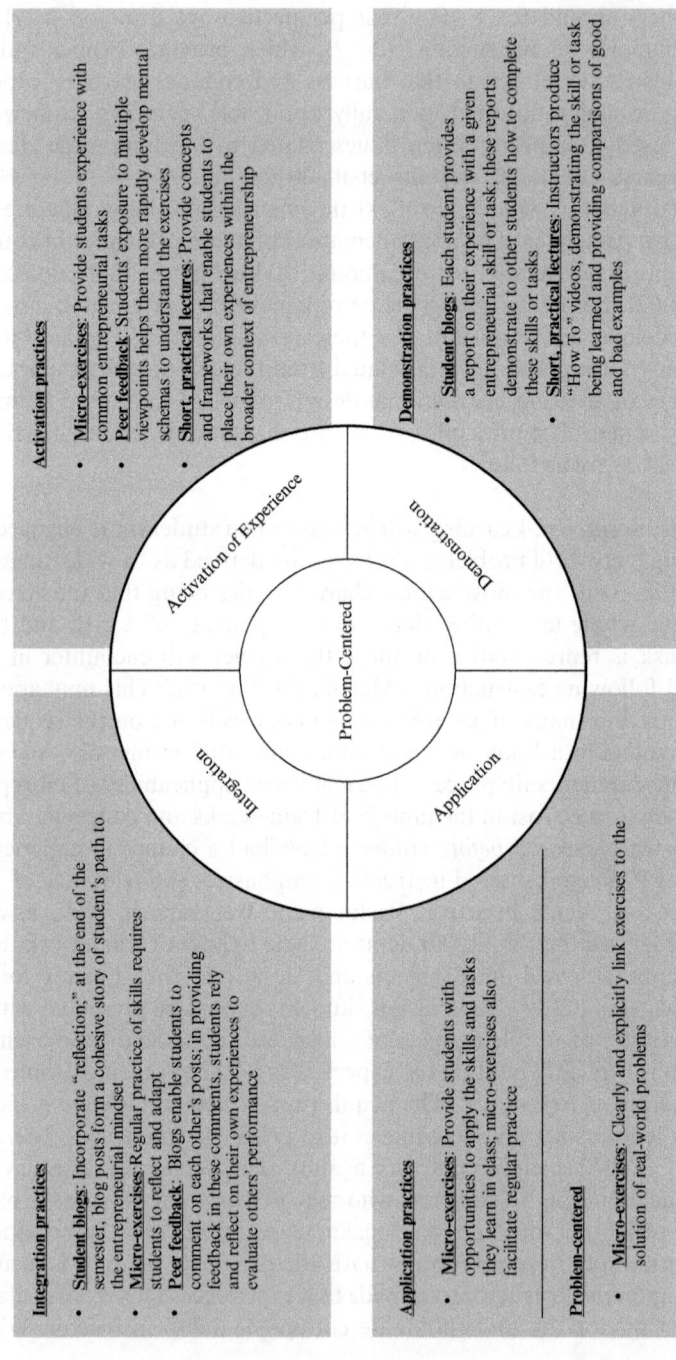

Figure 11.1   The principles and practices of an experiential entrepreneurship course

we may be able to discuss, abstractly, notions of an entrepreneurship process or describe the competencies most important to entrepreneurs, our students are not likely to have experience with skills, such as risk mitigation or guerilla thinking (e.g., Morris et al., 2013), which can hamper our ability to inculcate this knowledge. Activation also involves the stimulation of mental models or abstract frameworks to assimilate students' experiences as knowledge. For entrepreneurship, these mental models might include the entrepreneurship process or the business model canvas.

3. *Demonstration.* Show, don't tell. When instructors demonstrate the skills they want their students to acquire – as opposed to telling them information – learning is enhanced (Merrill, 2002). The underlying notion is that, if students are shown how the information they are being taught can apply to specific problems, they are more likely to find relevance in the information and retain it (Margaryan et al., 2015). Effective demonstration will show both bad examples and good examples of the practice. For instance, if teaching students how to talk to customers, it is important to show them the *incorrect* ways of interviewing customers alongside the correct ways. Effective use of the demonstration principle also involves task progression. For instance, students are presented with a real-world objective that must be completed. Then, in a progression, students are presented with a sequence of tasks that lead to the completion of the objective. Effective progressions run through simple tasks to complex tasks, to reduce students' cognitive load (Merrill, 2007). Finally, pare down your demonstrations – simple and precise is more effective than effulgent and mellifluous. Over-complex media can compete with students' attention and distract them from the demonstration.

4. *Application.* Students who practice using the information and skills they have acquired learn more than students who do not (Merrill, 2002). The positive effect of practice, especially regular, distributed practice (as opposed to practice lumped all together at the same time – such as cramming), has been firmly linked to learning (Cepeda et al., 2006). To promote learning, courses should be designed in a way that affords students many opportunities to practice the skills they have been told about; these opportunities should be frequent and consistent with learning objectives. When preparing a series of practice opportunities, instructors should plan to focus more time coaching earlier and reduce their support as students acquire more practice (Merrill, 2002). At the same time, instructors should not stifle their students with coaching and support: students who are granted room to make errors tend to learn more effectively, especially when they are provided

feedback on their practice efforts (e.g., Huelser and Metcalfe, 2012). Finally, to follow this principle means providing students with varied practice, rather than simply repeating the same task. Students who have varied practice develop fuller understanding of the conceptual dimensions of a skill and are better able to apply the skill in different situations (Kerr and Booth, 1978).

5. *Integration.* This principle could also be internalization, reflection or personalization. Merrill's (2002) fifth principle suggests that, when students adopt a skill as their own, they augment their learning. To facilitate the integration of new skills, students may demonstrate their newly acquired skills to friends and peers, they may reflect, either to themselves or by sharing with others, and they may recombine their new skills with other skills in their repertoire to "create" new skills and enlarge their knowledge and abilities. For instance, reflection, which occurs as we mull over past experiences, discuss those experiences with others, or meditate on those experiences, is an important but frequently overlooked element of course design (e.g., Boud, Keogh, and Walker, 2013). Importantly, reflection strengthens students' acquisition of knowledge through retrieving or recalling past learning, which reinforces the information in students' memory (Brown et al., 2014), and students' reflection transforms new information by attaching personal meaning to it and incorporating it into their existing mental frameworks.

FROM PRINCIPLES TO PRACTICE IN THE ENTREPRENEURSHIP MEGA-CLASS

The instructor's close adherence to these principles and a clear vision of the course objectives – together with appropriate practices and a deft use of resources at hand – can result in an amazingly engaging course and a fruitful learning experience. Below, I describe a number of the practices I use to implement the first principles. These practices are pragmatic approaches I have adopted to provide a serious entrepreneurship experience for my students toward fostering an entrepreneurial mindset. I describe how each practice helps me overcome the challenges related to teaching the mega-class, as well as how they enable me to fulfill the principles. The field in Figure 11.1 displays how each practice aligns with the principles and provides descriptions of how each practice aligns with each principle.

Micro-exercises: We Learn What We Do, One Step at a Time

Glance through the syllabi of many entrepreneurship courses, and a particular trend emerges: assignments tend to be few in number and require significant effort. For instance, students may be teamed to write a business plan through the course of a single semester. Elsewhere, a class may require students, in teams again, to produce a case analysis and presentation, take three exams, and write a comprehensive business model. Repetition of any of these exercises in a single course is rare, to students' detriment. Empirical evidence on how we learn points to the usefulness of repeated and varied practice (e.g., Brown et al., 2014), the power of leaving time between exercises to stimulate forgetting (e.g., Carey, B., 2014), and reflection (Boud et al., 2013). In other words, rather than major, one-time exercises, it could be better to break exercises into smaller pieces and incorporate repetition.

In my course, I have doubled down on the notion of regular practice. Students make not one elevator pitch but four (and they are also asked to provide feedback on others' pitches as well as reflect on how they improved their own pitch over time); students produce four descriptions of a business concept over a semester, not one (again, with feedback and reflection in between); and students interview five potential customers a week over three weeks (with feedback and reflection). While implementing our best current understanding of how students learn, this practice is also practically necessary in a mega-class. Exercises that are complex and multi-faceted tend to require careful instructor attention and feedback along the way, or else the exercise loses its effectiveness and students become frustrated. In the mega-class, one instructor simply does not have the capacity to monitor the progression of hundreds of business plans, business model canvases, or market analyses. However, many of these complex entrepreneurial behaviors may be broken into pieces (e.g., Pryor et al., 2016), which can be made into simple micro-exercises and practiced. The exercises are simple enough for students to be able to achieve them and also to be able to provide feedback and suggestions to their peers.[1] Students write reports on their experiences for each exercise and post them to personal blogs they create for the course.

Using micro-exercises enables me to achieve several of the first principles: problem-centering, activation, application and integration:

- *Problem-centering*. Entrepreneurship educators are lucky that, compared to the case in other academic fields, their students are clearly and actively engaged in solving real-world problems. In outlining instructions for each exercise, care should be given to explicitly describing how the exercise applies to the student's journey toward the entrepreneurial mindset.

- *Activation.* Students coming into an introductory entrepreneurship course do not often have the requisite experiences to activate, so these experiences must be provided to them, which I do through the micro-exercises. Aristotle said that we learn what we do, and the exercises I include are those that entrepreneurs might reasonably do. That includes, for instance, looking for and conceptualizing opportunities, developing networks, speaking with customers and potential investors, and even failing. That does not tend to include case analyses, exams and quizzes.

- *Application.* This fundamental understanding of experiential learning – that the content, concepts and frameworks of entrepreneurship are better understood when they are experienced than when they are discussed in a lecture – requires the application of knowledge to address real-world problems. Additionally, incorporating repeated and varied micro-exercises provides students a chance to practice what they have learned, which is central to application.

- *Integration.* Students' blog posts reporting on their completion of exercises always include a component that asks them to reflect on what they learned, what part of the exercise was surprising to them, and what they will change the next time they undertake the exercise.

Student Blogs: Recreating and Turbo-charging the "Seat"

Students in my course are required to create personal blogs during the first week of class. They submit the web addresses of their blogs to me, and I input them into a class blog directory, which I post to our LMS. Students use the blogs to "hand in" all of their assignments, which I call experience reports. Each experience report is published to the student's blog as an individual post. Many (or all) of these posts are shared with other students in the class, who are asked to read and provide evaluative feedback via comments on the blog post.

In any small class, or even larger classes that do not use lecture capture technology, students take their seats in the room or auditorium. They actually have presence in the classroom, and may, from their seat, engage in the lessons presented each day. In the mega-class, where lectures are often recorded to be watched later, students have no classroom presence. As I describe above, the lack of students' presence in mega-classes harms engagement and negatively affects learning outcomes. Students' use of blogs, in lieu of a seat in an actual classroom, can give them a sense of presence in the classroom. Their blog is their seat, and, because they have much more personal control and ownership of their blog than they do of a seat in a classroom, blogs can actually increase students' sense of engagement and belonging in the class (e.g., Kerawalla et al., 2009). The sense of engagement can be further enhanced through the network-creating potential of using student blogs. For instance, in my course, which has an average enrollment of 500 a semester, students are located all over the country and the world. Providing a blog directory and asking students to read each other's posts and comment on them exposes them to a huge array of student experiences (Kop, 2011), which is not possible in a smaller class. Finally, the students are undertaking the same journey together and describing their experiences in completing the same exercises through their blogs. Sharing each other's experience can recreate, on a smaller scale, the actions and interactions that are essential to the entrepreneurship experience (e.g., Venkataraman et al., 2012).

Blogs enable instructors to meet several of the first principles, especially demonstration and integration:

- *Demonstration.* In an entrepreneurship course, students may be required to interview customers or present an elevator pitch or even present a case. The instructor may demonstrate these activities in lectures or by showing recordings online of others' demonstrations. However, blogs harness the amazing creative output of the mega-class. Suddenly, a student can record an interview with a potential customer, post it on YouTube, and share it in a blog post. Next, hundreds of other students are able to see the interview and, using a rubric that I have provided in the lecture or in the LMS, they assess for themselves the good aspects and poorer aspects of the interview. Not only is the instructor responsible for demonstrating the entrepreneurship-relevant tasks, but students also demonstrate their performance of the tasks.
- *Integration.* Blogs create a space for students to discuss their experiences in the course, describe and defend the actions they took to achieve a task, and reflect on what they learned. I require students to keep their blogs public and encourage them to comment on each other's posts. Moreover, blogs tell a story over time, and each new post is located alongside the subsequent posts. A student's individual experiences come together to form a cohesive whole, and each exercise is described by the student and read by other students in the context of each student's journey through the entire course.

Peer Feedback: Leveraging the Mega-class's Most Abundant Resource

The primary challenge in a mega-class is the student–faculty ratio: there are hundreds of students for only one instructor. The odds are against any instructor providing substantive one-on-one student feedback. However, the practice of using blogs and micro-exercises 1) enables students to comment on each other's exercise experiences and 2) keeps the exercises simple enough that students can provide valuable feedback to each other. Peer feedback is not only a practical solution to a mega-class problem – it works, too. For instance, research has shown that students' performance after receiving a variety of peer feedback from multiple students increases more than when they receive feedback from a single instructor (Cho, K. and MacArthur, 2011). Moreover, students' provision of feedback has also been found to have learning benefits (Nicol et al., 2014). Providing and receiving feedback is also a critical task in entrepreneurship (e.g., Haynie et al., 2012). Taken together, the learning benefits alone warrant the use of peer feedback in the entrepreneurship mega-class, aside from practical considerations.

Peer feedback also delivers on the first principles of activation and integration:

- *Activation.* Compelling students to provide feedback on several students' experience reports presents them with alternative perspectives on an experience they all share, which can help students develop abstract understandings or schemas, which is a facet of activation (Margaryan et al., 2015). Feedback also takes place within the context of practice: students report on an experience exercise, receive feedback from students, and are able to put that feedback to use in subsequent exercises.
- *Integration.* The learning benefits of peer feedback occur as students evaluate others' work and provide support and suggestions for improvement, which can reinforce their own understanding of the exercise (Cho, Y. and Cho, 2011). In addition, students reflect on their own experiences to provide feedback to their peers, which further supports integration.

Drop the Mic, Really: Keeping the Lecture Short and Practical

The ratings are in, and they aren't great: if you are the instructor in a mega-class using lecture capture, you have about 6 minutes before your students stop watching (Guo et al., 2014). If you are instead lecturing to a room of hundreds, the numbers are not much better in terms of attention and knowledge retention. When I began teaching a mega-class, I treated the course like an in-person class with an out-of-sight, out-of-mind online component. Out came our usual bag of tricks: short lectures, break-out groups, lots of student interaction and participation, all captured in one 1-hour, 50-minute video. The in-class experience was wonderful (at least, I perceived it to be wonderful), but it was miserable to watch online. And eventually very few students were.

Evidence suggests that effective recorded lectures are short, practical and demonstrative (e.g., Bates, 2005; Guo et al., 2014). Merrill's first principles also suggest an instructional role for demonstration, which such lectures can fulfill. In my mega-class, I now record "how to" videos for each exercise students are asked to complete. These videos' explicit purpose is to demonstrate the skill students should learn, and I try to include good and bad examples of the skill applied. For instance, for a "how to" video on elevator pitches, I asked a student entrepreneur who had obtained national attention for his elevator pitch to make an in-class demonstration; I also asked a student who was involved in a start-up, but still a novice, to make a demonstration of his pitch. The video concluded with my extemporaneous discussion of the differences between the two pitches as well as a short run-down of elevator pitch "best practices." I also record short segments that present abstract concepts and frameworks in entrepreneurship. This content is presented as a "road-map" for students, and its intent is to provide students with interpretive frameworks, which they can use to meaningfully understand their experiences and place them within the broader entrepreneurship context (i.e., the principle of activation).

Hack the LMS: A Practicality of the Experience-driven Mega-class

One consequence of 1) breaking larger exercises into micro-exercises and 2) giving students a chance to repeat exercises several times in order to practice is that there are a lot of opportunities for students to earn points. In my course, there are 77 columns in my gradebook. If you visit the blog (ent3003backstage.blogspot.com), which I have created for entrepreneurship instructors and which is based on my class, you can see the variety of exercises students perform. The second, more important consideration of providing students ample opportunity to practice is that they will improve as they perform each task. Lots of theoretical and empirical research has been conducted on what is known as the growth mindset – or one's belief that one's intelligence and skills can improve over time (as opposed to remaining more or less fixed) (Dweck, 2006). This means that student performance on early tasks will tend to be weaker than on later tasks. Together with the consideration that entrepreneurs learn from failure (e.g.,

Kuratko, 2014), it seems inappropriate to grade students harshly for poor performance early in a series of tasks. Therefore, I mostly designate 1 point for all exercises in the class, with a few more onerous tasks worth 2 points: in other words, if students complete the task, they earn the point. The purpose is to reward students for their practice and accumulation of experience rather than reward them for achieving a task the way I think they ought to or by measuring them against some moving, arbitrary classroom distribution.

On Grading

Simplifying grading in a class with 500 students who must complete 77 tasks still means making 38 500 entries in a gradebook. Even if I had the time to do this, logging students' points is a much less effective use of my time than generating feedback, curating content and providing enthusiastic support. This is where your LMS can come in handy. Simply have the students log their own points.[2] In my course, for instance, I have created 77 quizzes in our LMS, each with one question (or "declaration"). I simply ask the students whether they have completed each exercise, met all of the requirements detailed in the instructions, and published their report to their blog. If a student marks "true" in the quiz, the LMS automatically logs the point. If students have not completed the exercise, they simply do not take the quiz, and the LMS assigns a zero once the deadline expires. For two exercises a week, I also require students to upload (or "share") the URL to a particular blog post they have written in the LMS. Using the peer evaluation function, our LMS will randomly assign that URL to students in the class, who are then asked to write comments and feedback on the posts they are assigned. D2L and Blackboard provide similar peer evaluation functions.

The initial concern any instructor might have before implementing such a system is that students might claim points for exercises they did not complete. That has not been my experience. Three things keep students honest: 1) there is the promise of peer evaluation, when other students will be able to read and comment on posts; 2) the blogs they create are public, and I upload a class blog directory at the beginning of the semester; and 3) many exercises require students to upload a video of themselves (e.g., doing an elevator pitch). Indeed, the case could be made that students are much *less* likely to cheat in this system than they would during a high-stakes exam, when they might be one of 500 or more anonymous faces in an auditorium and you're the only proctor. The second concern an instructor might have is simply the lack of any evaluative grading and assessment. That is, how can we *know* students are learning if we aren't actually critiquing their work and adjusting points on each assignment? Abundant research suggests that traditional grading is actually harmful to the learning process (please see Carey, T. and Carifio, 2012; Kohn, 1999, 2011; McMorran et al., 2015). Research and empirical evidence suggest that grades reduce students' interest in learning, reduce students' risk propensity in approaching assignments, and reduce the quality of their thinking. However, the alternative system used in my course is informed by current assessment and learning theory, and it is a powerful means for achieving the following:

- Instructors are freed to provide *true* experience and *true* practice to their students. In the mega-class, freedom from the gradebook can also afford the instructor time to enhance more important aspects of the class, such as the nature and progression of the micro-exercises and the content of the short lectures.
- Students are afforded room to fail. And, if they miss one exercise, there are other opportunities for them to practice the task.
- Students are treated like adults. They are responsible for their own grades and their progression through the class – truly a student- and action-centered classroom.
- Students are actually exposed to entrepreneurship experiences. Although the question of "How many experiences does it take to foster an entrepreneurial mindset?" has not been answered in research, the answer is much more likely to be 77 (or beyond) than 4 (e.g., case analysis, two exams, and the production of a business model canvas).

FROM BIG TO SMALL TO SMALLER

Each week I put on the microphone and step in front of the cameras and the bright lights to talk to hundreds of students at once. Rather than channeling Charles Kingsfield, the anxiety-producing professor in *The Paper Chase*, I'm aiming for Jim Nantz, the CBS sports broadcaster and play-by-play analyst. If I have done my job right and followed the principles and practices that I have described above, my students are *already* on the path toward an entrepreneurship mindset before I ever speak a word. My job is mostly that of the sports analyst when the game, or journey, is in progress: to describe how each student's experiences fit within the broader context of entrepreneurs and the entrepreneurship process and to give them a few of the tools they need to succeed on their journey.

With a compass of instructional principles firmly in hand, the instructor's next course of action is to start thinking small and get out of the way: micro-exercises, mini-lectures, earn one point here and another there. Outline the students' path toward an entrepreneurial mindset – and always be there to help – but always remember that it's the *students'* journey and not yours. Going forward, I anticipate the possibility of introducing some of these techniques in smaller classes. My initial challenge was to scale *up*, but on reflection I suspect that these principles and practices can scale *down*, too. I'm excited about the small-class possibilities of micro-exercises, of providing students ample opportunity to practice tasks, and of setting them down new paths to develop their own entrepreneurial mindset.

NOTES

1. You may access and use all of the exercises I have used in the Principles of Entrepreneurship course at ent3003backstage.blogspot.com. I have also provided other information, such as a course outline, syllabus and reading list, which you may use. Many of the exercises were developed with the help of materials provided by Dr. Alex Bruton and Diana Kander.
2. I learned of this practice from Professor Laura Gibbs, who teaches literature at the University of Oklahoma. Her blog, which provides much more detail about this technique and others, can be found at anatomy.lauragibbs.net.

REFERENCES

Bates, A. (2005), *Technology, E-learning and Distance Education*, London: Routledge.

Bean, J. (2001), *Engaging Ideas: The Professor's Guide to Integrating Writing, Critical Thinking, and Active Learning in the Classroom*, San Francisco: Jossey-Bass.

Boud, D., Keogh, R. and Walker, D. (2013), *Reflection: Turning Experience into Learning*, London: Routledge.

Brown, P., Roediger, H. and McDaniel, M. (2014), *Make It Stick: The Science of Successful Learning*, Cambridge, MA: Belknap Press.

Carey, B. (2014), *How We Learn: The Surprising Truth about When, Where, and Why It Happens*, New York: Random House.

Carey, T. and Carifio, J. (2012), The minimum grading controversy: results of a quantitative study of seven years of grading data from an urban high school, *Educational Researcher*, **41**(6), 201–208.

Cepeda, N., Pashler, H., Vul, E., Wixted, J. and Rohrer, D. (2006), Distributed practice in verbal recall tasks: a review and quantitative synthesis, *Psychological Bulletin*, **132**, 354–380.

Cho, K. and MacArthur, C. (2011), Learning by reviewing, *Journal of Educational Psychology*, **103**, 73–84.

Cho, Y.H. and Cho, K. (2011), Peer reviewers learn from giving comments, *Instructional Science*, **39**, 629–643.

Corbett, A.C. (2005), Experiential learning within the process of opportunity identification and exploitation, *Entrepreneurship Theory and Practice*, **29**(4), 473–491.

Cuseo, J. (2007), The empirical case against large class size: adverse effects on the teaching, learning, and retention of first-year students, *Journal of Faculty Development*, **21**, 5–21.

Dochy, F., Segers, M. and Sluijsmans, D. (1999), The use of self-, peer and co-assessment in higher education: a review, *Studies in Higher Education*, **24**, 331–350.

Drucker, P. (1985), *Innovation and Entrepreneurship: Practice and Principles*, New York: Harper & Row.

Dweck, C. (2006), *Mindset: The New Psychology of Success*, New York: Random House.

Exeter, D., Ameratunga, S., Ratima, M., Morton, S., Dickson, M., Hsu, D. and Jackson, R. (2010), Student engagement in very large classes: the teachers' perspective, *Studies in Higher Education*, **35**, 761–775.

Frenkel, K.A. (2012, January 5), Echo 360 pushes "lecture capture" tech into classrooms from Qatar to the US, *Bloomberg*, retrieved from http://www.bloomberg.com/news/articles/2012-01-05/echo360-pushes-lecture-capture-tech-into-classrooms-from-qatar-to-the-u-s-.

Gibbs, G. (1992), Control and independence, in G. Gibbs and A. Jenkins (eds.), *Teaching Large Classes in Higher Education: How to Maintain Quality with Reduced Resources*, London: Kogan Page, pp. 37–59.

Grossman, E. and Means, T. (2014), From tablet and stylus to tablet and stylus: an almost 6000 year revolution in technology for teaching and learning, in M.H. Morris (ed.), *Annals of Entrepreneurship Education and Pedagogy – 2014*, Cheltenham, UK and Northampton, MA, USA: Edward Elgar, pp. 44–59.

Guo, P., Kim, J. and Rubin, R. (2014), How video production affects student engagement: an empirical study of MOOC videos, in *Proceedings of the First ACM Conference on Learning @ Scale Conference*, New York: ACM, pp. 41–50.

Haynie, J., Shepherd, D. and Patzelt, H. (2012), Cognitive ability and an entrepreneurial task: the role of metacognitive ability and feedback, *Entrepreneurship Theory and Practice*, **36**, 237–265.

Huelser, B. and Metcalfe, J. (2012), Making related errors facilitates learning, but learners do not know it, *Memory and Cognition*, **40**, 514–527.

Kerawalla, L., Minocha, S., Kirkup, G. and Conole, G. (2009), An empirically grounded framework to guide blogging in higher education, *Journal of Computer Assisted Learning*, **25**, 31–42.

Kerr, R. and Booth, B. (1978), Specific and varied practice of motor skill, *Perceptual and Motor Skills*, **46**, 395–401.

Kickul, J. and Fayolle, A. (2007), Cornerstones of change: revisiting and challenging new perspectives on research in entrepreneurship education, in A. Fayolle (ed.), *Handbook of Research in Entrepreneurship Education*, Vol. 1: *A General Perspective*, Cheltenham, UK and Northampton, MA, USA: Edward Elgar, pp. 1–18.

Kohn, A. (1999), De-grading to degrading, *High School Magazine*, **6**(5), 38–43.

Kohn, A. (2011), The case against grades, *Educational Leadership*, **69**(3), 28–33.

Kolb, A. and Kolb, D. (2005), Learning styles and learning spaces: enhancing experiential learning in higher education, *Academy of Management Learning and Education*, **4**(2), 193–212.

Kop, R. (2011), The challenges to connectivist learning on open online networks:

learning experiences during a massive open online course, *International Review of Research in Open and Distance Learning*, **12**, 19–37.

Krueger, N. (2007), What lies beneath? The experiential essence of entrepreneurial thinking, *Entrepreneurship Theory and Practice*, **31**, 123–138.

Kuh, G., Schuh, J., Whitt, E., Andreas, R., Lyons, J., Strange, C., Krehbiel, L. and MacKay, K. (1991), *Involving Colleges*, San Francisco: Jossey-Bass.

Kuratko, D. (2005), The emergence of entrepreneurship education: development, trends, and challenges, *Entrepreneurship Theory and Practice*, **29**, 577–598.

Kuratko, D. (2014), *Entrepreneurship: Theory, Process, Practice*, Mason, OH: Cengage.

Marburger, D. (2001), Absenteeism and undergraduate exam performance, *Journal of Economic Education*, **32**, 99–109.

Margaryan, A., Bianco, M. and Littlejohn, A. (2015), Instructional quality of massive open online courses (MOOCs), *Computers and Education*, **80**, 77–83.

McMorran, C., Ragupathi, K. and Luo, S. (2015), Assessment and learning without grades? Motivations and concerns with implementing gradeless learning in higher education, *Assessment and Evaluation in Higher Education* [online], 1–17.

Merrill, M. (2002), First principles of instruction, *Educational Technology, Research and Development*, **50**, 43–59.

Merrill, M. (2007), A task-centered instructional strategy, *Journal of Research and Technology in Education*, **40**, 5–22.

Morris, M., Pryor, C. and Schindehutte, M. (2012), *Entrepreneurship as Experience: How Events Create Ventures and Ventures Create Entrepreneurs*, Cheltenham, UK and Northampton, MA, USA: Edward Elgar.

Morris, M., Webb, J., Fu, J. and Singhal, S. (2013), A competency-based perspective on entrepreneurship education: conceptual and empirical insights, *Journal of Small Business Management*, **51**, 352–369.

Mulryan-Kyne, C. (2010), Teaching large classes at college and university level: challenges and opportunities, *Teaching in Higher Education*, **15**, 175–185.

Nicol, D., Thomson, A. and Breslin, C. (2014), Rethinking feedback practices in higher education: a peer review perspective, *Assessment and Evaluation in Higher Education*, **39**, 102–122.

Owston, R., Lupshenyuk, D. and Wideman, H. (2011), Lecture capture in large undergraduate classes: student perceptions and academic performance, *Internet and Higher Education*, **14**, 262–268.

Pascarella, E. and Terenzini, P. (1991), *How College Affects Students: Findings and Insights from Twenty Years of Research*, San Francisco: Jossey-Bass.

Pope, J. (2007), Colleges cope with bigger classes, *Washington Post*, retrieved January 31, 2016 from http://www.washingtonpost.com/wp-dyn/content/article/2007/11/24/AR2007112400679.html.

Postman, N. and Weingartner, C. (1969), *Teaching as a Subversive Activity*, New York: Delacorte Press.

Pryor, C., Webb, J., Ireland, R. and Ketchen, D. (2016), Toward an integration of the behavioral and cognitive influences on the entrepreneurship process, *Strategic Entrepreneurship Journal*, **10**(1), 21–42.

Roeser, R., Schonert-Reichl, K., Jha, A., Cullen, M., Wallace, L., Wilensky, R., Oberle, E., Thomson, K., Taylor, C. and Harrison, J. (2013), Mindfulness training and reductions in teacher stress and burnout: results from two randomized, waitlist-control field trials, *Journal of Educational Psychology*, **105**, 787–804.

Rousson, G. (2015), Mega-classes at UCF prompt students to scramble for seats, *Orlando Sentinel*, retrieved January 18, 2015 from http://www.orlandosentinel.com/features/education/os-ucf-first-week-crowded-20150828-story.html.

Siemens, G. (2007), Learning management systems: the wrong place to start elearning, *elearnspace*.

Terry, N., Macy, A., Clark, R. and Sanders, G. (2015), The impact of lecture capture on student performance in business courses, *Journal of College Teaching and Learning*, **12**, 65–73.

Tolley, L., Johnson, L. and Koszalka, T. (2012), An intervention study of instructional methods and student engagement in large classes in Thailand, *International Journal of Educational Research*, **53**, 381–393.

Venkataraman, S., Sarasvathy, S., Dew, N. and Forster, W. (2012), Reflections on the 2010 *AMR* decade award: whither the promise? Moving forward with entrepreneurship as a science of the artificial, *Academy of Management Review*, **37**, 21–33.

Weaver, R. and Cotrell, H. (1986), Peer evaluation: a case study, *Innovative Higher Education*, **11**, 25–39.

12. Entrepreneurs in Action! An authentic learning experience

R. Wilburn Clouse, Terry Goodin and Joseph Aniello

INTRODUCTION

In 1996, Vanderbilt University professor Wil Clouse and two graduate students, Terry Goodin and Joe Aniello, began the development of a problem-based learning (PBL) approach to teaching entrepreneurship. All three members of the team not only were skilled in academics but also had extensive experience in business and industry. Themselves the products of public school education and state and private universities, they saw a need to develop new learning strategies that would lead to the development of the next generation of entrepreneurs.

The team, utilizing both academic and practical skills, conceptualized and developed a multidisciplinary approach to teaching entrepreneurship, one that began in elementary school and carried through to the university level. Being organized around the theme of entrepreneurship, the new approach was targeted at students who would like to create their own business. Students were given the opportunity to develop a business plan from one of their own ideas, which itself was generated in response to a problem posed by the instructor. While elementary school is naturally multidisciplinary in nature, the division of subject matter that begins in middle school meant that this organizing theme was necessary in order to unite disparate areas of learning. Beginning at the K–12 level, students were given the opportunity to interact with real-world problem solvers. The curriculum was designed to progress in complexity from early grades, and to progress in terms of interactions. At the collegiate level, for example, students from many different disciplines were encouraged to collaborate. It was not uncommon for students from the Human and Organizational Development program at Vanderbilt to team with students from business, engineering, the arts and natural sciences in a cross-disciplinary model. The approach was designed to teach students how to dream about new ideas and how to take a new business venture to the marketplace.

In part our workable definition of entrepreneurship was represented as "a state of mind – an artful, insightful and innovative mentality rather than a business management or administrative concept." It is a way of perceiving and exporting opportunity wherever it is found. Through open-ended, problem-based authentic cases, students at every educational level were given the opportunity to explore markets for their own ideas and to conceptualize a business enterprise for such markets. In this approach a wide variety of teaching strategies are introduced in the problem-based scenario – including vignettes to set the stage, so-called "lecturettes," guiding questions, peer group learning strategies, telephone/video conferencing, outside speakers and online searches, with heavy emphasis on developing a learning environment that contains "just-in-time learning strategies," emphasizes "whole–part–whole" techniques, and develops "beginning with the end in mind" (Clouse and Goodin, 2008).

Thus, the concept of Entrepreneurs in Action! (EIA) was born at Vanderbilt University. Since the inception of the model it has been expanded to include other "action"-oriented programs, including Creativity in Action, Humor in Action, and Ideas in Action. In later years this process became known as Learning in Action (LIA), an innovative, creative process for developing the next generation of entrepreneurs (Clouse, 1997, 2010; Clouse and Miller, 1996).

PURPOSE

Reflecting on our work experiences and university experiences, we sought to develop a series of experiences that would teach students to expand their thinking to be outside of "right or wrong answers" and linear thinking. We wanted students to learn to deal with chaos and uncertainty and to see new opportunities that come from a changing world. But yet we realized that most formal educational systems teach students how to work and live in a stable and structured organizational world. Most curricula teach structure, order, linear thinking and certainty, while the world is filled with chaos, ambiguity and uncertainty. This understanding led us to develop a learning environment to include new idea development, creativity, humor and entrepreneurship as a way of thinking about life in the twenty-first century. However, we realized we were going against the norm. Where the current schooling process teaches students how to work inside a structured and oftentimes bureaucratic organization, it teaches certainty.

OPERATIONAL PREMISE

We surmised that the work environment will change drastically in this millennium. Twenty-first-century entrepreneurs, if they are to succeed, must think differently and more creatively. We envisioned learning environments that teach about uncertainty, helping students learn how to deal with ambiguity and how to manage chaos. Instead of reinforcing uniformity and conformity, we saw the need to develop citizens who will be creative and original thinkers, who will "make jobs instead of take jobs." We want Americans to be prepared to compete effectively in tomorrow's diverse global economic environment. Entrepreneurs in Action!, with its emphasis on a problem-based learning experience, was ideal for cross-disciplinary, case- and web-based learning environments. Our first efforts centered on the development of the Entrepreneurs in Action! model, which was later developed into Learning in Action.

RATIONALE

Much of our learning, from kindergarten through to doctorate, seems to be unrelated. For example, we learn to memorize dates and facts, the multiplication tables, the periodic table, algebraic equations, quadratic equations, principles of chemistry and physics, the laws of nature, and situational problem solving. We learn the bits and pieces but frequently do not see the total application of knowledge. Our curricular-based learning, throughout our formal learning process, is usually oriented around a single discipline, and thus may be characterized as being myopic. Seldom do we have the opportunity to apply our knowledge in such a way as to accelerate our learning and to connect to our current knowledge base. Thus, students frequently say, "Why do I have to know this? I will never use this idea or concept. Will this be on the test?" Where do students learn to think creatively and entrepreneurially if most of our teaching is disciplinary, myopic and highly structured? The student learns a concept or idea within the framework of a particular course, and not in the framework of the world environment.

Generally speaking, public schools and universities are established around a disciplinary approach to education. Young children starting the schooling process are usually very eager to learn and eager to try new and interesting ventures. In many cases, students who are ready for the first grade are intrinsically motivated by the many different stimuli that they encounter in the learning environment. Usually by the third grade students have learned that creativity is not rewarded, and in most cases is not tolerated in the classroom. Therefore, the student conforms to school-related norms and proceeds with his/her life. This single-focused learning strategy is generally infused throughout the formal training of the student. When the student finally graduates from the university, he/she is faced with living in a complex, chaotic, uncertain world. The difficulty of applying knowledge acquired over the years is sometimes frustrating and overwhelming to the young person entering the work world.

These assumptions have led us to spend the past 20-plus years of our research developing an approach that encourages creativity and entrepreneurial venture development. Using problem-based learning as our anchor, we have established a program that teaches and encourages entrepreneurial venture development within a real-world framework. The Entrepreneurs in Action! model was developed on the following principles.

LEARNING THEORIES

Every person has the potential for entrepreneurial thinking. From preschool age, children show entrepreneurial tendencies. Too often, the formal schooling process moves them away from entrepreneurial thought, shutting them into intellectual "boxes." It is our job as educators to help break these walls down, and to assist in the growth of entrepreneurial thinking. Entrepreneurs in Action! was designed with that goal in mind.

Using the "whole–part–whole" teaching model (see Figure 12.1), teachers can link learning with real-life applications (Clouse and Goodin, 2001a, 2001b; Clouse et al., 1999, 2000; Goodin, 2003).

Student projects progress from the local to a global scope and from simple to complex topics and ideas. One unique feature is the use of "online experts" to relate local real-world situations to traditional curricular goals. Relating subject matter to the real needs of students has never been easy to do, and it seems that it is getting more difficult all the time. Changes such as the shift in demographics, the growth of populations with special needs, and overcrowding are just a few of the factors that prevent

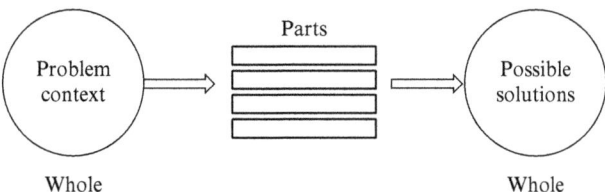

Figure 12.1   Whole–part–whole instruction

good teachers from connecting the needs of the individual child with the curriculum. On top of that, it seems that, just when they think they have a handle on it, teachers are given a new program to implement. Increasingly, school systems are adopting more demanding curricula and expecting teachers to deliver the content in meaningful ways. Often, overwhelmed educators resort to a lecture and memorization model of teaching and learning in an effort to satisfy the requirements of the new programs (Donsky, 1999). Rather than solving the problem, such methods seem to make matters worse. In many cases, students are able to master the material for a test but show little ability to transfer that learning into other domains. How can we overcome this obstacle?

There is a body of research that suggests that one way to involve students in the kind of learning which transfers to other tasks is to employ teaching methods built around the concept of situated cognition. Brown et al. (1989) hold that students learn more effectively if they are presented with materials in realistic contexts. In such scenarios, students can attack problems from a "global" perspective, actually using the tools of their cognitive "trade." Thus, students who learn to "think like a mathematician" are more likely to solve problems mathematically. How does it work?

The Cognition and Technology Group at Vanderbilt University (CTGV, 1990) argues that situated cognition goes hand in hand with a concept called "anchored instruction," in which problems are anchored (situated) in a videodisc-based problem-solving scenario, which is naturally interdisciplinary. One of the fundamental principles is the use of problem presentations that contain all the data necessary for a solution. By focusing on the holistic nature of the task, learners are able to employ a variety of problem-solving techniques that may be grounded in altogether different disciplines.

There are numerous examples of situated cognition in action. One such is the Jasper Woodbury Series, which was produced by Vanderbilt University (CTGV, 1997). The Jasper series is a set of problem-based learning scenarios that are for use in middle school. Students are presented with real-life problem scenarios that require them to apply critical thinking skills along with content knowledge. One such is entitled "The Big Splash" and focuses upon a middle school student's efforts to raise money at school using a dunking pool. The students have to calculate not only the amount of water needed to fill the pool but also the most cost-effective method for them to fill it. The goal of this work is to "help people understand the kinds of problems and opportunities that experts in various areas encounter, and to see how experts use knowledge as tools to identify, represent, and solve problems" (CTGV, 1997, p. 24). As a second goal, the authors state the desire to encourage viewing problems from "multiple points of view" in an effort to have students integrate knowledge from different domains.

The Entrepreneurs in Action! program is built along the same lines as the Jasper series. It is targeted at students at many levels. Its goal is to help them to integrate multiple disciplines, such as math, science and social studies skills, through a contextual teaching method. Our intention is to present a problem scenario and to have our students react by solving the problem using the skills teachers are already teaching them and the clues provided in the story. Put simply, this is an opportunity for them to put their knowledge to a "real-life" test, or at least to that of a close simulation of the real world.

RESEARCH EFFORT

Curriculum Design

A major portion of our research work is designed to investigate ways in which entrepreneurship can be taught in various learning environments. Our work is based on the following assumptions and learning theories.

Over the years our work has been based on a set of assumptions about how people learn and how schools prepare students to live in the real world. Our assumption is that most of traditional schooling in America is built around a system of compliance and control. This approach tends to stifle students' creative and entrepreneurial instincts. Our research has been exploring a different approach to education, one that involves capturing the interest of the student through the use of problem-based learning and project-based instruction delivered via the Internet – Entrepreneurs in Action! This program seeks to involve students in an entrepreneurial problem at the outset and to promote learning of traditional subject areas as a part of the problem-solving activities that are undertaken. This strategy is designed to teach students to think entrepreneurially by the use of local cases and/or scenarios. Unlike many curriculum strategies that teach conformity, structured learning and unrelated learning, our strategies support creative and entrepreneurial thinking across the curriculum.

As previously stated, the process emphasizes the whole–part–whole instructional strategy that we have developed. This approach involves seeing the big picture first, breaking it into parts (instructional units) and then putting it back together again into a new whole (see Figure 12.2).

This instructional design supports the teaching strategy where the concept being taught is connected (hooked) to the framework of the learner. Students learn and then apply new knowledge in situations that will reinforce their learning. Termed "recursive design," this strategy

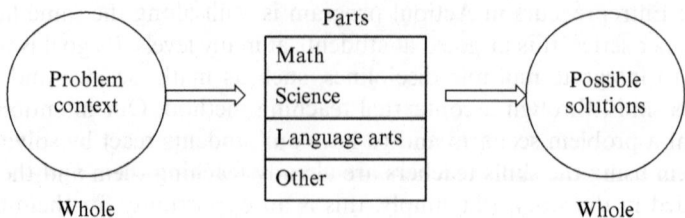

Figure 12.2   The whole–part–whole instructional process

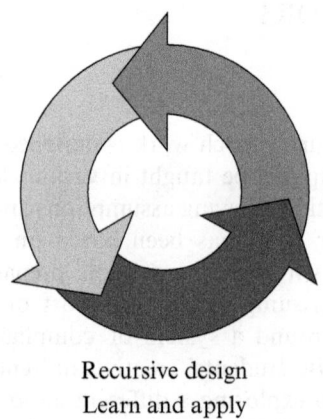

Recursive design
Learn and apply

Figure 12.3   The recursive design strategy

supports long-term learning of important concepts versus short-term memorization learning (see Figure 12.3).

In addition to using the whole–part–whole concept and a recursive design, we also use just-in-time learning techniques, which involve the local community and entrepreneurs. By presenting curricular content just at the moment when the need for it arises, this feature addresses the issue of maintaining the relevance of the content being learned. In general, this means that the students are given an opportunity to respond to a case developed for a local community. Students are given the opportunity to think creatively about the entrepreneurial application of the case. When students want more information about an issue, they are able to e-mail their questions to local online experts. Experts and entrepreneurs are selected from the local environment to provide relevant information just at the time the students need to learn it. This is what we call "learning the parts." Once the students have the information they need, they put together a new entrepreneurial "whole" for the case. Students are required to develop an entrepreneurial approach to the case and find ways to implement the entrepreneurial activity.

The fourth teaching method in the Entrepreneurs in Action! project is this use of online experts. Experts from the community are identified to serve each case as online experts. These professionals provide the students with a reality check as well as valuable information for developing solutions to the cases. Online experts must agree to respond to questions from students via e-mail, telephone discussion and at times personal interviews.

As indicated by the Entrepreneurs in Action! model, problem-based learning is an attempt to develop a real-world learning environment where students are faced with complex issues, the need to develop innovative and creative approaches to business ventures, and the need to learn despite ambiguity and deadlines. PBL offers a realistic approach to the inexact world of creativity and entrepreneurship. PBL cases show cross-sections of the real world. In developing creative solutions to the problem-based cases, students learn how to deal with incomplete information, from which they must extrapolate, generalize and find meaningful business ventures. Our PBL exercises are always based on true local situations. The scenarios are written to leave one "hanging" and wondering what to do next. There are no preconceived solutions to our PBL activities. Every activity is unique and designed to be hooked to the interests and framework of the learner. Once the problem-based activity has been identified, a scenario is then written to connect to the framework of the learner.

Identifying Resources

The next step in the PBL exercise development is to identify a number of online resources that students can use to help develop possible business ventures from the scenario presented. This is usually the first place that the student goes to gather information about the scenario. In some cases, students may access trade journals that can provide the newest innovative technologies relating to the PBL exercise. It is always necessary to connect the learning with the latest established research literature. Therefore, a number of research articles are also recommended.

Online Experts

The online experts play an important part in this PBL model, because they connect the learner with an experienced person in the field related to the case. Selecting these individuals is critical to the success of the program, in that they must be willing to respond to students' e-mails and telephone calls and/or have meetings with students.

In this model, the case presents the students with an unresolved issue, provides some resources and permits the students to take charge of their own learning and to develop a new business venture out of the given situation.

FEATURED CASES

Entrepreneurs in Action!

Our work first began with these cases related to entrepreneurship and involved working with 14 universities and at least five different public school systems.

Elementary Level

The case of the neighborhood renaissance

This case was written for the fifth grade level and was implemented in a public school system in Schenectady, New York. Here, students learn the effects of the closing of a neighborhood mini-market. The mini-market had been a neighborhood business for almost 50 years. The closing of the market is seen through the eyes of fifth grade students who have passed by and bought items from this store for their entire lives. The store has become a symbol of the local community, somewhat like the Cheers restaurant in Boston. The students are very saddened to see this icon being closed. Therefore, their task is to develop a new business venture around the concept of the mini-market in a local community facility. They want somehow to re-establish the old-fashioned soda-pop cooler filled with delicious ice cream, soda and banana splits. The students learn a multitude of concepts related to community decay and revitalization, changing value systems, changing demographics, the risk involved in running a small business and other social and political issues. However, the students see this as an opportunity to rebuild a neighborhood icon; thus, they learn of the rewards and opportunities of establishing their own business enterprise.

So, what are you going to do this summer?

This fifth grade level case was implemented at the Mitchell Nelson Middle School with 20 gifted children from across the city of Murfreesboro, Tennessee. This case is about two middle school students in Murfreesboro who face the disturbing prospect of having nothing to do during the upcoming summer, so they decide to involve their colleagues in the development of a series of activities for teenagers. Having learned of the closing of a theme park, Opryland USA, in the nearby city of Nashville, Tennessee, they decided to investigate the possibility of developing plans for a theme park. In so doing, they learn about land acquisition, zoning ordinances, loans, equipment costs, operational costs, public acceptance and, and a special interest of theirs, the science of the roller-coaster. They interact with bank presidents, university professors, real estate agents and local citizens to collect the information they need to develop their business venture.

When summer sun is no fun
This same approach was used in the Wilson County School District in Tennessee, and the students developed the concepts of a local park, which later became the Charlie Daniels Park – named and supported by this famous country and western musician.

The great rollerblade challenge
This case focuses on the transition time between elementary and middle school. In order to make this case more generally applicable, it is based on the fictional community of Elkmont, where just about everything and everyone is within walking distance. The main characters are three classmates in Elkmont Middle School, where they are finishing the fifth grade. It is May, and school is about over for the year. The kids want to have a great summer, and they have a plan! They love to rollerblade, and they want to practice all summer for the community's big team contest to be held at the end of July. The only problem is that they each have old equipment. To really compete, they need new gear! How will they go about earning the money to purchase what they need? This case requires students to think through the basic elements of a summer business, with an eye toward earning enough money to compete in the big challenge.

Middle School Level

The case of the disappearing school
This case has been developed for and implemented in two middle schools in Sumner County, Tennessee. The case involved the closing of a public school in a community neighborhood. Students were given the opportunity to investigate new, creative and entrepreneurial uses of the school building. The students were charged with the responsibility to develop a business plan whereby they could use the facilities in an entrepreneurial venture. In doing so they were forced to learn about zoning laws, political

issues, taxation, venture capital, risks, income projection, architectural issues and a host of other multidisciplinary concepts. The students put together plans for a range of potential entrepreneurial uses of the building.

Signs of a storm

This case was written for students at the eighth grade level and was implemented in the Manzano Vista Middle School in Los Lunas, New Mexico. The narrative deals with the problems of children growing up in a small and somewhat isolated neighborhood. The case is grounded in learning related to family issues and those of teenage children in a small community where there is not much productive activity available for students. In the story, one student becomes involved in gang activities and is eventually arrested for vandalism. The case challenges students to develop a new business venture around activities that would encourage their peers to dis-associate from gangs and become productive citizens. Social, political and economic issues of New Mexico are addressed as well.

Class of '11, a mosaic of America: developing the new norms

(This case can also be used at the high school level.)

Every year in the United States during the months of May and June, millions of high school students graduate. This is the first time in their lives that they have had an opportunity to spread their wings out of the nest of their parents. In the spring of 2011, more than 3 million American teenagers graduated from high school – one of the largest, most diverse and most challenged classes in US history. Morley Winograd referred to the class of 2011 as the mosaic of a new America. Thus this case introduces the millennial student to the new world of "real life." The class of 2011 is the midpoint of a millennial generation – born 1982 to 2003 – that is bigger than the baby boomer generation. These students are the first to live half their lives after 9/11, and their views of security and authority have been heavily shaped by the 9/11 event. They have also lived at least 10 years of their lives during two wars. They have been slower to grow up than their parent's generation and faster to integrate their lives with the Internet than even their brothers and sisters. This group is entering adulthood in the worst economy since the 1930s, and social scientists say they are forming attitudes similar to the generation that grew up in the great depression. Morley Winograd and Michael D. Hais, co-authors of the book *Millennial Momentum: How a New Generation is Re-making America*, state the economic challenges facing the millennial generation (Clouse, 2013b). This case investigates how millennials begin to integrate their ideas for new ventures into a changing world.

Demographic changes: USA
(This case can also be used at the high school level.)

The United States is a land of immigrants. In the early development of the United States many immigrants from various European countries sailed the seas to enjoy the freedom and the blessings that the United States could offer. During the early 1900s through the 1920s huge numbers of immigrants came through Ellis Island into a land of freedom and opportunity. Throughout some of the larger cities in the United States, special ethnic groups began to cluster and build a community. For the most part these immigrants held onto some of their old customs and fashions but also melted into the newly developing freedom and entrepreneurship environment of the United States. These immigrants were primarily from European descent and were Caucasian. This group of immigrants began to marry and to bear children. Their children maintained some of the old customs and culture, but also picked up a new custom and culture from their colleagues at school and at work. Over the years the European immigrants have declined, and Hispanic and Asian immigrants have replaced the European immigrants. Up until the 1960s the United States was primarily a white working middle class country. Beginning in the 1960s with the passage of the Civil Rights Act, the composition of the United States began to change. The population of the African-American community began to rise with the increasing birthrate among this group of people. In the 1970s, 1980s, 1990s and 2000s the United States experienced a large increase in immigrants from Asia and Central and South America. These two population groups were both legal and illegal.

In 2011 the non-white birthrate exceeded the white birthrate. It is predicted that by 2040 the white population in the United States will be the minority and the black, Asian and Hispanic population will exceed the white population. Now, if this prediction comes true, how will the environment, the economy and culture change in the United States?

This case provides the backdrop for a changing world environment that will greatly influence the next generation of entrepreneurial students.

High School Level

(Some middle school and university cases can also be used at the high school level.)

The case of the slippery slope: black gold in paradise
This case was developed for and implemented in a high school in Mandeville, Louisiana. This case is about entrepreneurship, risk, social issues, political issues, environmental concerns and other issues related to

offshore drilling for oil in the United States. Students at the high school level in a biology class were required to study this situation and to develop a new business venture around these issues and concerns. The results of this case led to new sources of energy and their impact on the world supply of oil.

University Cases

Blackout in America
This case is about the great electrical energy blackout that began in the west and continued through the eastern part of the United States a few years ago. The case encourages students to look at multiple solutions to the electrical power energy business. The case deals with social, political and economic issues related to electricity. Students are encouraged to find new business ventures related to power cells, windmills, solar energy and nuclear power. We have been able to connect this case with the Tennessee Valley Authority (TVA), which is the major supplier of electricity in the south. We have been able to secure video interviews with the director of the power transmission system for TVA. This greatly enhances and makes this project real and alive to students. This case can be used by several different disciplines or in a technical course.

A question of power
This case is associated with the oil industry. At the present time, this is a very timely and meaningful case, since it deals with the rising or falling cost of oil and the implications that this has on the world supply of oil. This case provides students the opportunity to look at the history of the oil business, the rise of power in the Middle East, and the shortage of crude oil or over-supply of oil. It encourages students to develop new sources of energy.

Chasing the dragon
This is an illegal drug-related case. In recent years, we have seen an increase in methamphetamine labs developed in the country. The problems caused by this illegal activity are very troublesome. The impact of the drug industry on our society and the cleanup of harmful drug residues left in the path of the labs is a tremendous problem facing our country. Students from a wide range of disciplines can tackle this problem.

Not in my backyard!
This is a recycling case. Our society in the United States is a throwaway society. Frequently, we buy items where the cost of packaging is worth

more than the item itself. We discard our beer cans on the side of the road, and we leave our McDonald's Styrofoam cups on the table to be disposed of. This case cuts across many different disciplines and offers many new opportunities for business ventures.

Music city blues
This is a case about the music business. How does one write lyrics and find a means through which to support oneself? This case deals with the opportunities associated with creating your own music career. In addition to teaching creativity and entrepreneurship, this case also investigates copyright issues and other related legal matters.

Talking to the air
This is a wireless technology case. This case was written specifically for the small college environment and proposes the opportunity for students to develop a business that would bring wireless technology to a college campus. It also includes assisting the downtown area in rejuvenating itself by proposing to develop a wireless downtown community.

The Santa Fe effect
This case is designed to help rejuvenate a small downtown area where businesses have moved out as the result of the interstate highways. It is designed to permit students to investigate new and innovative ways to bring business life back to small downtown areas. The concepts of this case could be related to any Small Town, USA.

The phoenix
This case was written to encourage students to develop a cyber-café where cross-disciplinary learning can take place in an informal environment that is not part of the university or college structure.

Long lines, short tempers
This case was written for engineering design classes interested in small device designs for homeland security and terrorism prevention. One of the most pressing problems facing the United States at this time is the threat of terrorist attacks, on both homeland and foreign soil. This case provides a scenario for students to develop micro-electro-mechanical systems (MEMS) to help protect the security of the homeland (Clouse et al., 2003).

Fashion, fashion everywhere and nothing to wear
This case is designed to investigate the impact of fashion on creativity, ethics, culture and international development. Students enjoy working on this case.

EIA Research

All of our EIA cases are designed to follow a specified format that provides the student with an introduction, a learning vignette, text, online resources, online experts, and in some cases video clips that further explain the issues. The cases can be used as an entire course, with sources from outside, readings related to entrepreneurship, new venture opportunities, product pricing and future projections. However, the cases are best used as an activity for an existing course. Usually, faculty members use the case as an activity to stimulate thinking about the entrepreneurship spirit and how to take an idea to the marketplace. As the cases currently stand, they are not designed to be all encompassing and should have additional support from the instructor to make the learning localized. The entire process is designed to stimulate interest among students and to connect learning with everyday life.

Creativity in Action (CIA)

The cases developed in this section are designed to create a learning environment that will encourage creative thinking and thus lead to entrepreneurship. Our world is driven by the desire to maximize life by developing self-sufficiency, self-determination, and individuals who have a passion for new venture creation (Aniello and Clouse, 2005; Clouse et al., 2013). These cases are designed to set the stage for future ventures.

Night of celebration
This is an introductory case to engage students in thinking creatively and entrepreneurially about a new business venture. It also involves the transfer of wealth from generation to generation. This case is usually used as a teaching strategy to introduce the major concepts of entrepreneurship.

The call
This is a case about a senior university football player who is faced with the issue of being rejected by the NFL draft and then using his accumulated skills, knowledge and experience to establish a business. Of course, all of the issues related to being a senior faced with this kind of situation are

frightening to many potential pro football players, and it happens more often than not. This case is based on the life of a college senior football player who was involved in our entrepreneurship class at Vanderbilt University.

The big question

University students are presented with the problem of a K–12 private school located in a suburban area. This case is concerned with the risk of a private school startup that does not offer conference athletics. In the case, students are interested in enrolling in the highly qualified academic institution, but find it disconcerting that it does not have organized conference-based sports. The university students, in solving the case, are required to develop a new business plan venture for this K–12 private school. Issues related to state and federal requirements for school startups, venture capital, student recruiting and marketing, school accreditation, and other related issues are faced by students as they develop a business plan for this K–12 learning environment.

Changing generations

This case presents university students with the problem of a young college graduate who wants to pursue a career but who feels obligated to take over the family business that helped to send him through school. When young Michael receives a purchase offer from a local real estate development firm it places him in a dilemma. Should he sell out and pursue his dream of being a professional musician, should he refuse and continue to run the business, or is there an alternative that will allow him to do both? University students must wrestle with social issues such as responsibility to family and community, along with career development concerns common to graduating seniors. Along the way, they must develop a business plan that will resolve all of the issues identified in the problem.

Dark clouds rising

This graduate level case is targeted at school administrators as they struggle to address the problem of increasing violence in schools, and is meant to encourage the growth of entrepreneurial problem solving in an audience that is not often presented with the opportunity to experience such thinking. Administrators are asked to identify with the troubles of a first-year principal who is attempting to deal with the complex issues underlying the growth of conflict in a middle school setting. Different solutions are proposed in the narrative, each with its own research support and each with its own adherents. Graduate students who participate in this problem-based learning activity must reach an understanding of the multitude of social and systemic causes of conflict, and are given the task of crafting their own effective and marketable solution to the problem.

From the vine to the wine

The world is changing drastically; if you don't believe the world is changing just ask a small family farmer. Agribusiness has undergone perhaps more innovation and changes than any other industry within the last 100 years. In the late 1800s and the early 1900s farming was the way of life. The organizational unit was the farm family. Every member of the family had a unique job and responsibility to fulfill. Family farming went from handheld tools to horse-drawn tools to gasoline and diesel combustion engines. Seldom did the members of the family farm find it necessary to take Sominex or Ambien to sleep at night. After working a 10- to 12-hour day in the fields their bodies and minds were ready to rest and sleep. There were no labor unions; if you wanted to eat it was necessary to work. Perhaps the original family farmers were the greatest of all entrepreneurs. They risked everything, but at the end of the day they were their own boss – self-employment to its fullest. This case is filled with entrepreneurial challenges.

Humor in Action

Humor in Action (HIA) is part of a process designed to teach students to think creatively and entrepreneurially. We believe that life should be fun and that humor should play a part in our personal and organizational lives. Thus, these HIA cases are designed to introduce the students to the field of humor and to help start creative thinking. These cases are designed to stimulate the thinking process and to make learning fun and exciting. Furthermore, HIA is a process that will help make work fun and will help us deal with everyday personal and organization stress. We seek to develop learning environments that will encourage creativity and entrepreneurial thinking. The cases included are developed in part from colleagues who have been a part of the Learning in Action research. The cases are to be considered a work in progress and are undergoing changes and updating. For privacy reasons, pseudonyms or fictitious names have been given to all individuals and organizations mentioned in these cases. The storylines come from real-life experiences, and credit is given to those persons who have contributed, while the editor of a case assumes all responsibility for its content. These exercises are mini-cases and are used to begin the creativity thinking process. In most cases they are used as an "eye opener" and as a "stimulator" to break away from traditional learning environments.

Humor mini-cases

The following is a listing of case titles that have emerged from the Humor in Action segment:

- Case 1: Power and paradox in humor: imitation isn't always flattery;
- Case 2: Humor rings true: a humor case;
- Case 3: Case of the empty vase;
- Case 4: Case of indigestion;
- Case 5: Waitressing woes;
- Case 6: Letting your boss know how you feel: an example of benign humor;
- Case 7: Did you say what I thought you said?
- Case 8: The red, red rose or just the thorn in its side? The story of a flower girl flare-up;
- Case 9: Carnival capers;
- Case 10: Corny situations;
- Case 11: Learning to laugh;
- Case 12: The case of the up-tight teacher;
- Case 13: Sarah's sore ankles;
- Case 14: Attempt at humor fails miserably and lands me in hot water;
- Case 15: Elvis as a social lubricant;
- Case 16: Cardinal rule no. 1: never embarrass the boss;
- Case 17: Ricky, no relation to Edgar;
- Case 18: Hunter found himself hunted: Ivory Coast case.

All of our work is designed to develop a series of experiences that teach students to expand their thinking to be outside of "right or wrong answers" and linear thinking. We want students to learn to deal with chaos and uncertainty and to see new opportunities that come from a changing world. Our cases are designed to help create the next generation of entrepreneurs.

Implementation – The Santa Fe Effect Case

(See the Appendix.)

In this case, students develop a comprehensive plan to redevelop the small town with emphasis on creating the *entrepreneurial spirit* as the vehicle to rejuvenate the small town. A formal document is developed and presented to the local chamber of commerce or city council. Students learn cross-disciplinary concepts related to social, political, economic, legal and demographic matters, as well as see opportunities to start new business ventures in areas of great need.

A complete copy of the case is shown in the Appendix, showing the contents and process for developing a possible solution to one of the favorite EIA cases.

SUMMARY

As indicated by the Entrepreneurs in Action! model, problem-based learning is an attempt to develop a real-world learning environment where students are faced with complex issues, the need to develop innovative and creative approaches to business ventures, and the need to learn despite ambiguity and deadlines. PBL offers a realistic approach to the inexact science of creativity and entrepreneurship. PBL cases are authentic cross-sections of the real world. In developing creative solutions to the problem-based learning cases, students learn how to deal with incomplete information, from which they must extrapolate, generalize and find meaningful business ventures. Our PBL exercises are always true local situations. The scenarios are written to leave one "hanging" and wondering what to do next. There are no preconceived solutions to our PBL activities. Every activity is unique and designed to be hooked to the interests and framework of the learner. Once the problem-based learning activity has been identified, a scenario is written to connect to the framework of the learner.

Learning in Action expands the EIA concept and is a process related to connecting learning with the framework of the learner. LIA is a holistic approach to the learning process involving the whole–part–whole teaching strategies that connects the learning to live cases written across several different disciplines to develop an authentic learning experience. Through a problem-based case experience, the student learns multiple concepts and different disciplines simultaneously. LIA is developed through problem-based learning cases that are multidisciplinary in nature. The overriding theme is to produce students who can be creative thinkers in the twenty-first century. Our world is filled with uncertainty in our social, economic and political systems. Certainty and stability are no longer a given. In recent years, political systems have failed, terrorists' activities have increased to be worldwide, world energy systems are changing, world markets are changing, products and process development systems are being modified, and natural disasters have occurred with worldwide impact. So our cases are designed in part to help students deal with an unstable and changing world.

IMPACT

Since we first developed this concept and began to implement the LIA–EIA cases we have reached over 5000 students in at least 14 universities and several public schools in Tennessee, New York, Louisiana, New Mexico, Kentucky, Georgia and South Carolina, thus connecting with thousands of students and infusing entrepreneurial ideas into the minds of the next generation of citizens. At least 10 doctoral dissertations have been completed using the concepts of this effort. Also, a new venture called Commercialization in Action began in 2013 at Western Kentucky University (WKU) and led to the development of a new Center for Engineering Commercialization at WKU as a part of this effort (Clouse, 2013a).

We began this effort in entrepreneurship when entrepreneurship was not "cool" in most universities. In fact it was necessary for us to refer to our work as "faculty initiated," thus placing distance between our efforts and the university administration. We were only permitted to pursue this line of research because we could generate our own funding and never required direct university funding.

SO WHAT?

When we began our efforts in entrepreneurship 20-plus years ago, entrepreneurship was not considered to be an academic field of study by most academics. Academics usually thought of the field as vocational and business-orientated and frequently stated that there was not a sufficient body of knowledge to justify the field. The three of us were at a major private research university, Vanderbilt, and thus felt the pressure of working in a field of study not always appreciated by the tier one universities. Working with the Coleman Foundation and joining the United States Association for Small Business and Entrepreneurship gave us encouragement to continue our efforts.

At the time we began our work only the more aggressive colleges and universities across the country were engaging in some form of coursework and/or experiences related to entrepreneurship education. Most of these efforts were found in either the school of business or the school of engineering. Some schools offered one course in entrepreneurship in order to acquaint students with the general field of entrepreneurship. Other schools might offer one or two more courses to further enhance the student's understanding of entrepreneurship. Still only selected other colleges and universities offered a complete four-year degree program and/or master's degree or doctorate. The vast majority of schools offered little or nothing to teach students about self-employment, creative thinking, and the process of generating new and creative ideas for opportunity development. They taught the content courses with minimal connections to new idea development and creativity and minimal application to real-world problems.

There were at least two general underlying assumptions about entrepreneurship education at that time. Some schools, especially some schools of business, assume that entrepreneurship cannot be taught. To them, it is an inborn skill that is derived from your gene base. In these types of schools, students appear already either to be starting a company or to have entrepreneurial tendencies. These schools emphasize more about how to develop a business venture and seek venture capitalists for funding. Corporate buyouts are also an important feature of this approach. Generally speaking, some of these programs taught more about how to manage and develop a corporate environment than they did to seek new and different opportunities. Usually, these programs were single-discipline focused.

In programs associated with schools of engineering, students are more frequently involved in innovation than they are in true entrepreneurship. The schools of engineering are usually great at teaching the technical concepts related to disciplines but frequently do not have courses that cut across technical subject areas, thus combining multiple subjects simultaneously. While there was a trend among schools of engineering to introduce selective courses that introduce entrepreneurship into the curriculum, it is usually taught as an entity within itself and does not involve cross-discipline activities.

The second approach is centered on the general concept that all students can learn, to some extent, to be creative and entrepreneurial. The focus of this approach is to be broad-based, to take a cross-discipline approach, to be focused on seeing opportunities that others do not see and to stress self-fulfillment and sustainability. The general theme is to create a job and not take a job. Building on this idea, our assumption was that all students can be encouraged to think creatively and entrepreneurially in a cross-discipline, problem-based learning environment if the learning can be connected to the framework of the learner and made authentic (Clouse and Goodin, 2001b).

As of 2016, universities all over the world are developing entrepreneurship programs, from cross-disciplinary programs to doctoral programs. Centers for innovation and entrepreneurship as well as endowed chairs in entrepreneurship are in most universities. Incubators and accelerators exist in universities, community colleges, local governments and private venture organizations. Much of this credit is given to USASBE, ASEE, and programs like the Experiential Classroom founded by Michael Morris in 1999.

Universities have at last begun to infuse experiential learning into many classes and opened up entrepreneurship to non-business and engineering majors.

As developers of the Entrepreneurs in Action! and Learning in Action programs, we are proud to have had a very small part in this paradigm shift in universities. The following paragraphs provide the reader with tangible outcomes from this research and the impact it has had on the original three developers.

IMPACT ON DEVELOPERS

While it is impossible for us to know the total impact of the Entrepreneurs in Action! project, we do have evidence of its impact on the three primary developers of the project. For example:

- The Entrepreneurs in Action! project was developed at Vanderbilt University in its College of Education and Human Development, which was a major breakthrough in entrepreneurship education 20 years ago. This became the home for the project in the first 14 years of development and implementation.
- As the project developers moved on in their careers, the impact of the project continued to be forceful. After receiving emeritus status at Vanderbilt University, Dr. Clouse moved his work to Western Kentucky University in Bowling Green, Kentucky, to serve as the first Executive Director of the Center for Innovation and Entrepreneurship and to serve as the Mattie Newman Ford Endowed Chair in Entrepreneurship – part of a $10.6 million endowment. In this role, utilizing the concepts of the EIA, Clouse expanded the minor in entrepreneurship to a four-year major in entrepreneurship, and developed a statewide business plan competition – where his students won first or second place for four consecutive years, and where his students earned the Governor's Innovation award for two consecutive years. Utilizing the concepts of EIA, Clouse secured the largest grant ever to be received by the Gordon Ford College of Business to develop a regional entrepreneurial plan in a 10-county area around Elizabethtown, Kentucky. As part of the Coleman Foundation's cross-disciplinary program, 10 faculty members from various disciplines participated in the EIA project at WKU. A close collaboration was developed with the vice president for research, with the dean of the school of engineering, and as a result a new center was developed for engineering commercialization and a student accelerator was developed. After 4.5 years at WKU, Clouse

moved his work to Middle Tennessee State University (MTSU) and established the Clouse Elrod Foundation, Incorporated – designed to support the concepts of the LIA project. To date the following projects have been developed:

- Learning in Action: saving the American farm – think tank sessions ending in new entrepreneurial projects for small farms, and a project between MTSU and WKU agricultural programs;
- Learning in Action: learning by doing, innovation in agri-business, rebuilding old farm equipment as a venture, MTSU agribusiness;
- Learning in Action: teacher education training program – problem-based with
- College of Education, MTSU;
- Learning in Action: Creativity–Innovation–Entrepreneurship Culture award, College of Education, MTSU;
- Learning in Action: problem-based teacher education program: Residency 1 ASPIRE, College of Education, MTSU;
- Learning in Action: Womack Educational Leadership Department graduate improvement process, College of Education, MTSU;
- Learning in Action program: Second-Tier Business Idea awards, Jones College of Business, MTSU;
- Scholarship Grant: The Ralph and Mary Lou Gentry Innovation and Creativity Scholarship, College of Business, University of Tennessee (UTC), Chattanooga, Tennessee;
- Learning in Action – agribusiness: connecting the Clouse Farm with the Tennessee Technological University (TTU) Oakley Sustainability Farm;
- Learning In Action: South Carolina entrepreneurship incubation center – collaborative effort between Francis Marion University (FMU) and Florence South Carolina business community;
- Learning In Action: Creativity–Innovation Scholars award, MTSU.

After completing his requirements for the doctorate at Vanderbilt University, Terry Goodin joined the faculty at Middle Tennessee State University, where he implemented the core concepts related to Entrepreneurs in Action! and developed an award-winning problem-based learning teacher education program, modeled after the MD residency program. Dr. Goodin has become internationally known for his work in problem-based learning with applications especially in creativity and innovation in the field of teacher education.

Likewise, after completing his requirements for the doctorate at Vanderbilt University, Dr. Joe Aniello joined the faculty at Francis Marion University in Florence, South Carolina, where he established the Small Business Development Center, played a major role in entrepreneurship development and is currently involved in developing a collaborative regional incubation center with the local business community and with students at Francis Marion University.

REFERENCES

Aniello, J.A. and Clouse, R.W. (2005), Improving adult creativity using therapeutic models, *Journal of Entrepreneurship Education*, **8**, 85–112.

Brown, J.S., Collins, A. and Duguid, P. (1989), Situated cognition and the culture of learning, *Educational Researcher*, **18**(1), 32–41.

Clouse, R.W. (1997), Entrepreneurship education for the 21st century, in J. Canjemi (ed.), *Psychology: A Journal of Human Behavior*, **34**(1), 36–40.

Clouse, R.W. (2010), Learning in Action: a problem based experience for developing the entrepreneurship spirit, Progress report, Center for Innovation and Entrepreneurship, Western Kentucky University.

Clouse, R.W. (2013a), Learning in Action: a commercialization process model, Atlantic Marketing Association Conference proposal, Atlantic Marketing Association.

Clouse, R.W. (2013b), Living the American Dream: but what is it? *American Journal of Management*, **13**(1).

Clouse, R.W. and Goodin, T.L. (2001a), Entrepreneurs in Action: a case-based model, *Proceedings of the Academy of Free Enterprise Education*, **5**(1).

Clouse, R.W. and Goodin, T.L. (2001b), Creating an entrepreneurial culture: breaking the disciplinary boundaries, *Proceedings of the 2001 American Society for Engineering Education Annual Conference and Exposition*, American Society for Engineering Education.

Clouse, R.W. and Goodin, T.L. (2008), Entrepreneurs in Action: case manual and entrepreneurship cases, Forum for Entrepreneurship Education, Vanderbilt University.

Clouse, R.W. and Miller, R. (1996), Entrepreneurship: views from educators and business executives, in J. Canjemi (ed.), *Psychology: A Journal of Human Behavior*, **33**(1).

Clouse, R.W., Goodin, T.L. and Helbig, J. (1999), Cyberspace entrepreneurship program, in J. Richards (ed.), *United States Association for Small Business and Entrepreneurship: Sailing the Entrepreneurial Wave into the 21st Century*, San Diego, CA: University of San Diego Press, p. 788.

Clouse, R.W., Goodin, T.L. and Aniello, J. (2000), Entrepreneurship education for the third millennium: taking over the world with the "E" spirit, in A. Nadim (ed.), *United States Association for Small Business and Entrepreneurship: The Entrepreneurial Millennium*, San Antonio, TX: United States Association for Small Business and Entrepreneurship, p. 248.

Clouse, R.W., Aniello, J. and Biernacki, J. (2003), Entrepreneurs in Action! A problem-based learning environment for engineering entrepreneurship, *Proceedings of the American Engineering Society*.

Clouse, R.W., Goodin, T.L. and Aniello, J. (2013), Leadership metaphors: developing innovative teaching strategies, *American Journal of Management*, **13**(3).

CTGV (Cognition and Technology Group at Vanderbilt) (1990), Anchored instruction and its relationship to situated cognition, *Educational Researcher*, **19**(6), 2–10.

CTGV (Cognition and Technology Group at Vanderbilt) (1997), *The Jasper Project: Lessons in Curriculum, Instruction, Assessment, and Professional Development*, Mahwah, NJ: Lawrence Erlbaum.

Donsky, P. (1999, April 5), Math teachers trade old drills for group skills, *Tennessean*, pp. 1A, 11A.

Goodin, T.L. (2003), *Evaluating the Entrepreneurship Education Initiative: Entrepreneurs in Action*, Doctoral dissertation, 2003. 3117516, Nashville, TN: George Peabody College of Vanderbilt University, ProQuest Dissertations Publishing.

APPENDIX: THE SANTA FE EFFECT CASE

At this point we are listing one of the favorite cases to show the reader the format and content of a case. This case has been used at several different universities and has been applied to regenerate the following small cities: Old Hickory, TN; Florence, SC; Athens, TN; Madison, TN; Bowling Green, KY; Paducah, KY and Maryville, TN. The Santa Fe Effect Case was named after the entrepreneurial spirit that permeates the small town of Santa Fe, New Mexico.

Introduction

All across America, small towns are facing a similar plight – the gradual decline of their downtown area. Shopping centers, industrial parks, interstate highways and changing demographics have changed the way people live in America, thus leaving the small town or in some cases the suburban area to drift from the mainstream of American life. Today, businesses are moving out of central areas as more and more people elect to go "where the shoppers are," generally to the larger highways that bypass the small towns. In addition, large stores, the so-called "big box" (e.g., Home Depot, Wal-Mart, etc.) retail operations, tend to locate in these outlying areas to take advantage of the increased flow of customers. This traffic encourages the growth of specialty retail stores, as well as hospitality and industrial development all outside of the "old town square concept." Where do these trends leave the small town? Once the cycle has begun, it seems difficult to arrest. Usually, older buildings are left to crumble and decay, with the only holdouts often being the city offices, a few professional buildings, and a few "mom and pop" stores.

Learning Vignette – The Santa Fe Effect

This is a case about Small Town, USA and has been used to study several small towns, such as Athens, TN, Madison, TN, Florence, SC, Paducah, KY, Maryville, TN and selected other small cities or suburbs of larger cities. The opportunities are all the same. The following is a brief introduction to the case. (Space in this chapter does not permit listing the entire case, thus this is just a beginning for the case.)

Assignment

Dr. Tim Smith, Professor of Business, has made an assignment in his Business Communications class to investigate the downtown area of Small

Town, USA, and to develop a strategy to revitalize the downtown area. Five students, including Mark Davenport, Jeff Goodwill, Robert Jackson, Sue Williamson and Jackie Robinson, obtained a digital camera from the resource center and set out to film the downtown area. Through the eyes of the camera, the students saw a visual description of Small Town, USA. The camera first was used to videotape some of the famous streets that run through the city and to film some of the unique buildings and other places of historical interest. Using the camera, the students videotaped the remaining part of the city of interest to the case and then analyzed the situation and developed a plan for new business startups and redevelopment of the "old city."

The Challenge

1. What do you think?
2. What solutions would you recommend if you were a member of this student team?
3. What business ventures could be developed from this case?

After raising these questions, the students are free to begin deliberations on possible solutions to the case.

Guiding Questions

1. What types of political problems do you expect?
2. What groups contribute toward community development? How?
3. What other communities have similar issues and how have they addressed them?
4. What makes this town unique?
5. What external issues can arise from development?
6. What new startups are best suited for this area?

Core Concepts

1. Demographics of small towns.
2. Social factors affecting small town exodus.
3. Arts and cultural cohesiveness.
4. Laws and regulations.

Learning Objectives

1. Role of government and law in establishing new business.
2. Business organizations.

3. Social resistance to change.
4. Appreciation of town history.

Resources

Resources related to the case are listed here, such as:

- city planning;
- urban design;
- community and environmental development;
- consensus planning;
- architectural design;
- performing arts;
- historic preservation;
- infrastructure, such as traffic, roads, water (how sustainable?);
- other resources for small business development and startups.

13. Using the SEE model in entrepreneurship consulting courses and programs

Michael H. Morris

INTRODUCTION

The Supporting Emerging Enterprise (SEE) model provides a simple and logical framework to guide the consulting efforts of student teams. It has been developed and refined based on experience in managing interventions with small businesses over 20 years. The model is specifically designed for consulting engagements involving emerging businesses owned and managed by local entrepreneurs. It has proven highly successful with early stage ventures operating under conditions of adversity.

The ability of student teams to help entrepreneurs is tied to their understanding of the business in its entirety. Developing a marketing plan or an improved bookkeeping approach requires that the student understand operations, the basic cost structure of the business, and internal resources, among other issues. The SEE model is a tool that enables students to effectively "wrap their head around the business," determine consulting needs, and set priorities for what can realistically be accomplished over the term of the consulting engagement.

The model structures the front end of the consulting engagement as an evolving process that moves through three inter-connected layers or levels of analysis (see Figure 13.1). In essence the consultant moves from 1) an examination of the fundamental core of the business to 2) an assessment of internal operations and issues to 3) an analysis of how the entrepreneur interacts with external publics and resource providers. Each layer also consists of a number of sub-areas. For instance, internal issues include the basic operations of the business (how the product is produced or the service is delivered) as well as the infrastructure in the business (skill levels of staff, adequacy of facilities and equipment, use of technology).

It is expected that teams will comprehensively explore all three layers within the first weeks of the consulting engagement, so that the majority

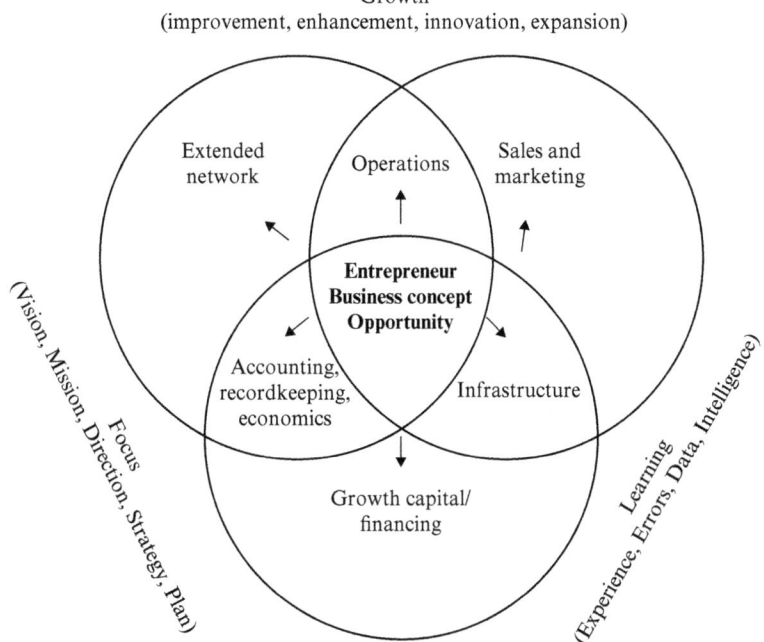

Figure 13.1   Supporting Emerging Enterprise (SEE) consulting model

of the semester can then be spent on problem solving and value creation. The expression "comprehensively explore" indicates that the current situation must be described or characterized, analyzed, and then critiqued. It is also expected that, while contributions will be made in multiple areas, the key outcomes or deliverables from the team's consulting engagement will be concentrated in particular sub-areas within one of the layers. Thus, a given engagement may be especially concerned with solving a marketing need, which lies at the third or outer layer of the model. It might be concerned with designing a bookkeeping and accounting system or an inventory management system at the second or internal layer of the model.

The model is further designed to produce three types of outputs. The first of these is *learning* by those in the organization, and it is concerned with ensuring that there is some documentation of experiences, lessons learned, information and records available, and the intelligence gathered in support of the firm's operations. The second output is *focus*, or the specification of vision, setting of priorities, ensuring of consistent strategic direction and the existence of a plan of operation. The third output is *growth*. Growth is concerned with untapped opportunities, the expansion of the business, acquiring new equipment or facilities, increasing the customer base or entering a new market, and so forth. While the consulting team is likely to make contributions in all of these areas, any given consulting engagement should concentrate principally on one major type of output. Further, while these outputs overlap, the team should prioritize the relative importance, at the present time, of learning versus focus versus growth in terms of the entrepreneur's attention and allocation of resources. Thus, it would make little sense to emphasize growth opportunities if there is insufficient focus.

A BRIEF NOTE ON THE MAPS

During the process of putting together the SEE model, seven "maps" are developed that capture key areas of the business in a diagram or flow model. These are:

1. *Map of "how the entrepreneur spends his/her time in a given week."* This is a map of the percentage of time the owner spends on major activities in the business (administration, selling, producing, supervising, solving client problems, purchasing, etc.). It is used to assess the efficiency of the entrepreneur's time allocation while also evaluating delegation and leadership skills.
2. *Map of "customer buying process."* This map illustrates the identifiable decision making process or set of steps that a customer goes through when making a purchase of the product or service.
3. *Map of the "economics of the business."* This diagram looks at the relationship between the margins, volumes, cost structure, and revenue drivers in the business. The consultant should have a sense of where the firm is making its money in terms of different revenue drivers or product categories.
4. *Map of "bookkeeping process."* This map lays out the proper steps in recording expenses and revenues and transforming these inputs into financial statements and useful managerial reports or forms, and notes where flaws exist in the client's current approach.
5. *Map of the "operations process."* This map captures the production or service delivery process of the business as a flow of inputs, throughputs and outputs. In some cases, the consultant may need to develop two maps, one for "front stage" operations and the other for "back stage" operations.
6. *Map of "points of customer contact" or "moments of truth."* This is a map of all the moments where a customer makes a judgment about a

company based on a point of contact that is either direct or indirect. These points will be numerous and range from interacting with a sales person to simply walking or driving past the storefront, receiving an invoice, or even using the bathroom on the premises.

7. *Map of the "marketing and sales process."* This is a map of the way in which the organization moves a potential client from awareness creation through a closed sale and a growing relationship.

While these seven maps capture critical elements affecting the business, the instructor may want to have students map other activities or processes taking place within the company.

LAYER ONE OF THE MODEL: THE ENTREPRENEURIAL CORE

Layer one is concerned with the entrepreneurial core of the business. The challenge is to get acquainted with what is being produced and sold, to whom it is sold, and the people who drive the business. It has three sub-components: 1) the entrepreneur himself or herself; 2) the business concept; and 3) the opportunity (or market).

The business is a projection of the personality of the founder or owner. In conducting analysis and ultimately making recommendations, it is vital that you take into account the personal characteristics and background of the people running the business. Student recommendations can be technically sound but useless if they do not fit with the personality and capabilities of the client. This is a critique, so it must include a *table of both strengths and weaknesses* (financial skills, selling skills, production skills, IT skills, etc.). Key issues to be assessed and documented with regard to *the entrepreneur* include:

- age;
- family circumstances;
- work history and experience;
- educational background;
- training;
- skills (bookkeeping, marketing, production, supervisory, etc.);
- motivation for starting the business;
- financial circumstances and commitments;
- maturity;
- future outlook;
- growth orientation.

This is where the consulting team should map "how the entrepreneur spends his/her time in a given week."

Survival and growth of a venture are dependent upon a clearly defined and somewhat unique business concept. The concept is concerned with the essence of the business, the value it creates, and the benefits it delivers to a customer. The *business concept* should be examined with regard to:

- the basic product or service being offered;
- the complete product or service mix;
- sources of differentiation;
- sources of value being created for customers;
- packaging;
- how the business makes its money (e.g., low margin/high volume);
- core attributes or benefits;
- location if retail or consumer service;
- brand identity if any exists;
- unique aspects of pricing, sales or distribution that in effect define the business.

One can have a great business concept and high quality products, but still fail in the marketplace (or generate anemic returns) simply because there is no opportunity. The opportunity is in the marketplace, and so is concerned with market needs that have profit potential. In looking at *the opportunity (market)*, the major concerns include:

- forces creating the opportunity;
- market definition;
- market size and growth potential;
- profit opportunity in this market;
- how well segmented the market is;
- buyer descriptors;
- customer buying behavior;
- customer switching costs and loyalties to competitors;
- how low barriers to entry are;
- competitor shortcomings and strengths;
- competitive intensity;
- fit between opportunity and concept.

Here is where the team should map the "customer buying process."

LAYER TWO OF THE MODEL: INTERNAL OPERATIONS AND RESOURCES

Based on the foundation established in terms of the entrepreneurial core, the team must explore the basic workings of the business. Three sub-components are involved here: 1) business numbers (accounting, bookkeeping, and the economics of the business); 2) operations; and 3) infrastructure.

The first of these can be quite a sensitive issue with the entrepreneur, but is vital to the completion of any consulting engagement. Early on, the teams must thoroughly review (and, in some cases, construct) the financial records of the business. Further, the entrepreneur must be an integral part of this process. In many instances, the team must help educate the entrepreneur both in terms of the benefits of systematic recordkeeping and in terms of fundamental accounting issues. Systems should be kept simple, as it serves no purpose to develop either a system or a set of procedures that the entrepreneur will simply ignore. The team should stress that:

- adequately tracking costs in proper categories allows the owner to see what expenses are more significant and where increases or changes are occurring;
- by properly recording revenue and expenses in a systematic manner, profit can be regularly determined (some clients do not really know how profitable they are);
- comparisons of financial information can be made on a period to period basis only if consistent recordkeeping is used;
- many of the businesses will rely on cash-based accounting as opposed to an accrual basis, and the team should be aware of the implications (especially in terms of distorting the true financial picture, since revenues and expenses are not properly matched) and share these with the entrepreneur;
- there is a need for basic internal controls, such as distinguishing whether the person keeping the books has access to the cash.

In looking at the firm's numbers, the concern is the *financial records* and what they say about the viability and needs of the business. Critical issues include:

- existence of records;
- existence of a bookkeeping system;
- level of sophistication;
- completeness of the system;

- ease of system use;
- accuracy of records;
- system for collection and payment of sales tax (or VAT) and other taxes;
- costing structure (key fixed and variable costs);
- breakeven point;
- cash flow;
- receivables (timeliness and amount);
- payables (timeliness and amount);
- financial controls;
- budgeting and financial planning;
- performance benchmarking ratios;
- revenue drivers and profitability of each.

The team also wants to note the linkages between accounting information and the marketing, production and financing needs of the business. For instance, in the marketing area, are sales expenses tracked properly and are all marketing costs built into the price of the product? In production, is inventory turnover properly tracked and is the cost of goods sold broken down into direct material, direct labor, and other costs related to sales? In the financing area, what is the interest expense and how much is it as a percentage of total expense?

Here is where you should map the firm's "bookkeeping process."

A key issue is to determine what the breakeven point is for the business on an annual basis, and how much that means the entrepreneur must be selling each day. This requires a clear delineation of fixed and variable expenses.

Here is where you should map the "economics of the business."

Moving to operations, key operational considerations address: how the product is made or produced; if a service business, how the service is actually delivered; and, if a retail business, how the store is run and the customer experience managed. It is a day in the life of the business. The team will want to develop a step-by-step diagram of the production or service delivery system. The critique of *operational considerations* includes issues such as:

- modeling of the production or service delivery process;
- key bottleneck points;
- process and information flows;
- capacity versus demand patterns;
- purchasing policies;
- inventory management;

- inventory storage costs;
- value of inventory;
- obsolete inventory;
- internal controls;
- health and safety;
- administrative procedures;
- handling complaints and returns;
- hours of operation;
- resource productivity;
- customer service;
- delivery or shipping;
- outsourcing (of what particular activities?);
- quality controls;
- theft and pilferage.

Here is where you should map the firm's "operations process."

Turning to the internal infrastructure, the team's concern becomes assets and resources that the entrepreneur has accumulated to support operations. Thus, assessing *the internal infrastructure* of the business involves an evaluation of the adequacy of:

- operating facilities;
- production equipment;
- the staff (other than the entrepreneur);
- information systems;
- the employee compensation package;
- cars and trucks;
- computers, cash registers, accounting machines and administrative equipment;
- customer parking;
- security;
- formal registration of business (CC, partnership, etc.);
- databases and records (other than financial);
- location.

LAYER THREE OF THE MODEL: EXTERNAL RELATIONSHIPS AND ACTIVITIES

In moving to layer three, the team's focus now shifts to external publics, the principal ones of which can include customers, financiers, suppliers, tax, regulatory and municipal authorities, community authorities or bodies, and distributors or middlemen. These have been organized into three major sub-components: 1) marketing and selling; 2) financing; and 3) the external network.

The first of these, marketing, is a common problem in many client enterprises. While marketing is an internal function, its purpose is to interface with external publics. It is vitally important that the team obtain a first-hand feel for the customer interface. Further, team members should be made to study the ways in which the entrepreneur approaches and interacts with current and prospective customers. Teams should strive to interview some customers, and to observe the entrepreneur when he/she is involved in selling, customer relations and customer service. A key issue concerns the steps or process for making a sale happen.

The marketing efforts of client firms typically involve doing more with less. Teams should assess the use of "guerrilla techniques," or creative mechanisms for communicating with the market, bartering for services, co-marketing or sharing resources with other businesses, tapping into under-utilized vehicles for promotion, and so forth. In examining *marketing efforts*, the team should specifically explore the following:

- positioning;
- targeting of segments;
- selling efforts and approach;
- distribution channels;
- signage;
- the marketing plan;
- market research;
- customer relationship building;
- marketing media;
- branding and the brand identity;
- advertising;
- sales promotion;
- pricing;
- collection of receivables from customers;
- tracking of market performance;
- capturing customer data;
- customer screening (for high risk customers who cannot make payments).

Here is where you should map the firm's "marketing and sales process."
Here is where you should map "points of customer contact."

Many clients need money, but they do not really know how much. They are heavily reliant on their own resources, those of friends and family, and banks for financing, and many would not attract equity sources of funding. Analysis of their *financing needs*, resources and relationships should include:

- ownership structure;
- financial structure and debt position;
- ability to service debt;
- access to capital;
- business and personal credit;
- cost of capital;
- short term versus long term assets and liabilities;
- availability of alternative financing;
- current and future capital needs;
- financing preferences of the entrepreneur (e.g., self versus debt versus equity, control versus risk);
- number of people the entrepreneur is attempting to support through the business.

Entrepreneurial success is frequently associated with a well-established network of people, agencies and organizations outside the firm. The network will be extensive, with stronger and weaker components. The entrepreneur will cultivate this network, ensuring regular communication with key members. It is helpful to try to diagram a summary picture of this network. Thus, when looking at and characterizing the *extended network*, primary issues are:

- relationships with suppliers;
- relationships with legal experts;
- relationships with bankers;
- relationships with distributors;
- other financial contacts;
- government contacts;
- contacts with community agencies;
- access to sources of labor;
- sources of free or cheap advertising and promotional assistance;
- sources of publicity or low cost visibility;
- other advisors.

CONCLUSIONS

This discussion is not intended as a comprehensive listing of all the facets of the enterprise that teams must investigate. Rather, it represents a logical and systematic process for taking the business apart and putting it back together again. It is expected that other issues are likely to come up along the way, but these issues will still fit within the general SEE model.

Importantly, teams must follow the logic of the model, starting with the core, and only then examining internal issues, after which external relationships and activities are reviewed. The team should adhere to the discipline of this approach in spite of potential resistance from the entrepreneur, who is likely to want to focus only on a particular interest at a point in time. Obviously, some of the areas will be investigated simultaneously. The important thing is that the team does not "put the cart before the horse" or, mixing metaphors, try to "jump the gun."

It is also critical to recognize that the three layers and the various sub-components of the model are not independent. Instead, they work together. For instance, an examination of the bookkeeping and accounting issues can help clarify problems in production, operations and marketing. Similarly, the assessment of marketing and customer issues may serve to identify a problem with the infrastructure of the company. These inter-dependencies must be reflected in the team's review of the business. It is critical that, once they have moved through the three layers of the model, the team conduct a detailed review of the internal consistency among the nine sub-components of the model. Those areas least consistent with the others must be identified.

Approached in this manner, the SEE model will enable consulting teams to clearly distinguish problems from symptoms from causes. Further, it will enable teams to establish clear-cut priorities in terms of where they and the entrepreneur should focus. Figure 13.2 provides a logical step-by-step process for prioritizing client deliverables once the SEE model is completed. Finally, our experience suggests the model itself can be instrumental in helping the entrepreneur to better understand his/her own business from an outsider's perspective, and to manage it more effectively and efficiently.

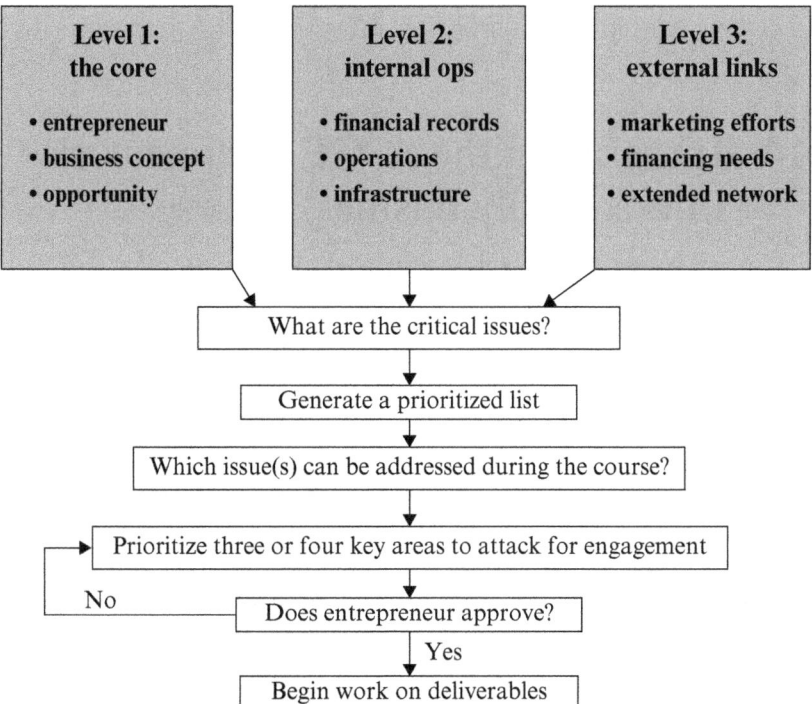

Figure 13.2   Setting priorities based on the SEE mode

14. Integrating the A-GES framework into a family business course

Erik Markin, Clay Dibrell and Richard J. Gentry

INTRODUCTION

Family businesses might constitute as much as 80–90 percent of all the businesses in the free world (Astrachan and Shanker, 2003), contributing nearly 75 percent of all jobs and roughly 70–90 percent of global GDP each year (Craig and Moores, 2015). Given their centrality to the global economy, it is strange that there is no predominant canon for teaching courses on managing family businesses in colleges and universities.

Part of that gap comes from the difficulty the field has had in developing a solid consensus on the definition of family business management (Astrachan et al., 2002). Perhaps the most widely employed definition of family business is offered by Chua et al. (1999) as "a business governed and/or managed with the intent to shape and pursue the vision of the business held by a dominant coalition controlled by members of the same family or a small number of families in a manner that is potentially sustainable across generations of the family or families."

Through increased theoretical and empirical research, we have a greater understanding and appreciation for the unique attributes of family businesses and those who are stakeholders of family businesses. The global number of family businesses and interest in the academic world suggest that more family business courses are needed in higher education institutions. To develop the talent family businesses need, many entrepreneurship programs in the country now offer courses in managing family firms (Morris et al., 2013). Unresolved, and relatively unexplored since these programs began to appear, is a proper concept of what and how family business should be taught and to what extent it differs from the traditional business canon. The most common treatments of family business stem from agency theory and a resource-based view (Chrisman et al., 2010; Pieper, 2010). Folding these perspectives together, Craig and Moores

(2015) introduced the A-GES framework as a foundation for exploring the definition of family business. We introduce that framework here as an organizing framework for coursework in teaching family business.

Additionally, given that family business courses are typically not a part of the business school's curriculum, traditional instructional techniques are less effective at developing students to participate in these businesses. Although family businesses and traditional businesses share commonalities that can be taught, it is as important that students learn how to identify the differences between family businesses as it is crucial that they learn the nuance in those differences through experiential learning. Krueger (2007) offers a framework that helps move the focus of teaching from a purely behavioral approach (i.e., acquire information and recite) to a more constructive approach (i.e., trial and error in a social setting) which leads to a focus on knowledge structure versus just knowledge content. The latter approach places the locus of learning on the student and thus encourages students to be self-directed learners as well as assessors of their own work. Combining appropriate instructional techniques with a coherent organizing framework for family business coursework can create an exciting and differentiated business course in any entrepreneurship program, and we will explore some techniques that instructors can use to effectively teach family business.

Further, the teaching of a family business course is a different type of course teaching compared to most other offerings in a business school, as both traditional and non-traditional students have had personal interaction with family businesses through family ownership of a venture, through employment, or as a customer. In effect, these students often already have a basic understanding of how family businesses operate. For a student whose family does own a family business and has been involved in the business, this course is very personal and intimate, as the course topics are directly related to the dynamics of not only their business but also their family. Similarly, for students who are not from a family business, many of them still have a family and can personally relate to the family dynamic. Instructors should be cognizant of these points as they approach the course. From our experiences, student interactions in this class are vastly different than those in other classes.

We first present and explain a framework for teaching family business as a unique content domain and what students should appreciate at the conclusion of a course in family business. We present the framework as a structure to arrange a course and develop its four primary components individually. We then integrate the aforementioned components with contemporary pedagogical methodologies that emphasize teaching-centered, learner-centered and learning-centered approaches (Krueger,

2007). Finally, we summarize our concepts and conclude with a general discussion of how universities might implement or adapt the approaches presented in this chapter to the development and improvement of family business courses.

FOUNDATIONS AND APPLICATIONS

To begin, we examine the underpinnings of the A-GES framework and how it can be utilized in teaching family business. Craig and Moores (2015) sought to differentiate family business from the traditional entrepreneurship domain by focusing on four inter-related platforms: architecture, governance, entrepreneurship and stewardship (Figure 14.1). These platforms serve as key points of differentiation between a traditional business that is serving the interests of investors and a family enterprise that is much more focused on continuity and transitioning the business across generations. Architecture refers to the various systems and structures to support the planned strategy of the organization – how the management executes an intended strategy. Governance is representative of the framework of rules,

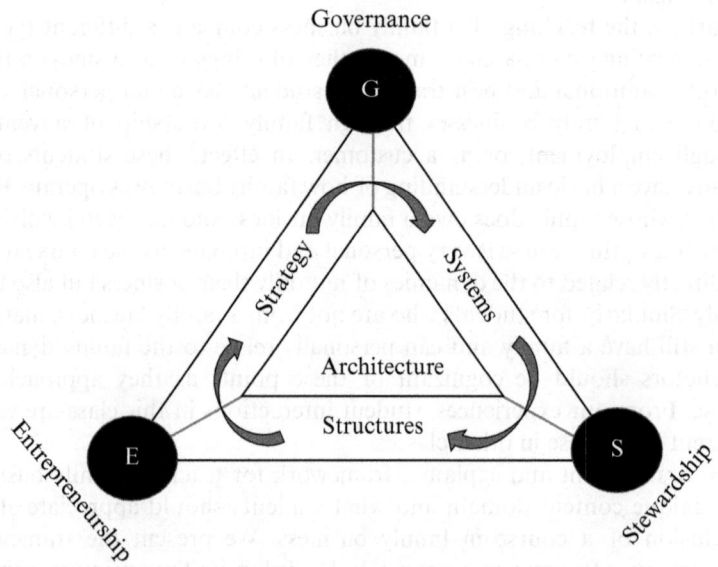

Source: From Craig and Moores (2015).

Figure 14.1   The A-GES framework

practices, structures and systems by which organizations are governed and the unique governance mechanisms in family firms. Entrepreneurship within the A-GES framework refers to the leadership and formulated strategies. Stewardship, a key differentiator between family businesses and other businesses (Zahra et al., 2008), suggests that leaders are motivated to act in ways that are more favorable to the firm's collective good over self-interest.

We will first describe each of the four components of the A-GES framework and highlight the unique components of each that present, for family business education, unique content areas that form the corpus of a family business management course.

Architecture

Architecture denotes the organization's formal structures and systems, the mechanisms organizations use to execute strategy. The organization's structures pertain to the choices concerning the breadth of management's authority and activity. In particular, family business management structures are often relatively flat for organizations of their size and with predominantly centralized authority. Systems are the processes and incentive programs that support the firms' formulated strategy. Such systems include management control, performance management, and systems at various functional levels (e.g., human resources, marketing, finance and accounting).

Structures
Organizational design and its management structures are the formal policies and reporting lines through which the firm's operations are managed. According to Galbraith (2014), there are three basic organizational structure forms: 1) functional; 2) multidimensional; and 3) matrix. Small and medium-sized firms are typically organized by functional form, which can be best described as the division of functional areas by their relative job responsibilities (i.e., human resources, production, accounting, etc.). As firms grow more complex and develop corporate settings, we tend to observe these as operating within the multidimensional structure. This structure consists of multiple departments or business units overseen by unit leaders (e.g., division manager). Finally, matrix type structures, or cut-through reporting lines, are multidimensional structures that typically exist in large, more complex organizations that consist of multiple business units and perhaps broad geographic operations.

Family firms face a particular conundrum in formal organizational structure because members of the family might be placed throughout the organization as part of a family manager development plan. It is no simple task to assign managers to oversee the activities of family members, who might have a direct line of communication to the family CEO. This open communication between the organizational levels facilitated by family relationship ties can be a strength for the upper managers, but it might unsettle some managers and it could destroy the ability for non-family members to influence top managers when they disagree with a family member subordinate. Classes could spend time talking about how non-formal communication channels will influence and change the management relationship as well as how best to mentor non-family managers. However, the systems that are in place to help manage employees will also need to incorporate a process to encourage non-family managers to maximize their performance in the absence of the traditional motivation to achieve organizational promotion, since that space is probably reserved for a family member.

Systems
Systems are the firm's processes, policies and procedures to set strategy and dictate how strategy is to be conducted and managed. Strategic planning systems for instance aid in understanding a firm's current position, short- and long-term goals, and plan for achieving those goals. Control systems are those that enable management and other constituents to influence personnel behavior and activity toward achieving strategic goals. These controls can include formal or informal areas such as business culture, socializing programs and workshops, or external demands from government, charities or customers. Performance management systems are utilized to measure effectiveness at multiple levels (i.e., individual, team and organizational), which enables an organization to assess the efficacy of its current strategy. The A-GES framework proposes that family firms differ in both their formal control systems and the extent to which culture is used to influence employee behavior.

The balanced scorecard (Kaplan and Norton, 1992), a measurement technique that provides financial measures of past actions and operational measures considered to be the drivers of future financial performance (i.e., customer satisfaction), is particularly relevant in family organizations. However, the scorecard will need to focus more heavily on preserving the socioemotional wealth of the managers, and it will need to formalize the risk attitude of family firms (Gentry, R. et al., 2014). Classes might focus on determining how much industry, ownership, and individual job roles interact to shape employment contracts in family firms.

Additionally, family firms tend to employ more clan- and culture-focused management techniques (Ouchi, 1980). The special emphasis placed on founders and family values lends another level of implied strategic direction over and above the firm's mission statement. While these types of culture can be very difficult to change, a major concern of the family firm is to maintain balance between the preservation of that culture and monitoring the external environment. Classes might devote time to how the hiring relationship and process need to adjust for the need to protect a culture and to what extent a firm can protect its culture without becoming insulated from the market and its environment.

Lastly, for both structures and systems, this is an excellent opportunity for the instructor to reinforce the lessons learned from other entry-level business classes, such as principles of management, finance, or accounting courses, which may serve as pre-requisites to this course. A family business management course builds off these preliminary courses, and this section of A-GES is a wonderful opportunity to apply these principles and to see different forms of structures and systems in practice through cases or through interactions with existing family businesses.

Governance

Chua et al. (1999) note that collective definitions for family business suggest that an entity should include any of three qualifiers to be considered a family business: 1) family owned and managed; 2) family owned but not family managed; or 3) family managed but not family owned. As the firm grows and becomes more complex and concerned with professionalism, family businesses will consist of more non-family members. Governance in a family firm is the balance between family, managers, employees, customers and, potentially, other investors. Unique to family business is the prevailing control and governance of family members. In contrast to a firm with a board of independent members, family-controlled organizations often rely on family assemblies, family councils, and constitutions to coordinate the family's attitude and influence within the firm (Poza, 2013). These structures and forums play a role in communication, strategy, and maintenance of sustainable competitive advantage.

Classes could focus on how to establish a family council, which might function independently of or in conjunction with the firm's formal board of directors. For larger families, entire assemblies exist to communicate the firm's direction and performance to a vast family group. These assemblies serve as a further conduit for family members to secure employment and development training inside the family firm. Classes might propose and debate the bylaws for such an assembly, the merits and problems with this open communication approach and whether a family firm should be interested in hiring *all* family members as opposed to the immediate family of the current CEO or chairman. If every family member will have an opportunity to participate in the firm, how should the careers of non-family talent be protected?

Entrepreneurship

Entrepreneurship, as it relates to the A-GES framework, concerns the leadership and strategies adopted by the governing body of the organization. Gupta et al. (2004), drawing from a variety of others (DuBrin, 2015; Kuratko and Hornsby, 1999; Slevin and Covin, 1990), define entrepreneurial leadership as "leadership that creates visionary scenarios that are used to assemble and mobilize a 'supporting cast' of participants who become committed by the vision to the discovery and exploitation of strategic value creation" (p. 242). This definition emphasizes the task of assembling resources and gathering competent and committed members to carry out the vision. These two concepts are interdependent since a bundle of resources alone cannot become a strategy without people to execute it. However, as discussed earlier, the participants in a family firm can range from family to non-family members. These more complicated relationships between employees can create unique challenges and opportunities for family firms that may not exist in other non-family organizations (Dyer and Handler, 1994, p. 75).

Entrepreneurial strategy concerns "the what" of the organization or more specifically the core ideology and envisioned future of the firm. Strategy then is an organizational-level process consisting of activities that firms engage in to establish and activate their mission and goals (Dess et al., 1997). Hart (1992) notes that these activities include analysis, planning, decision-making, strategic management, and other cultural aspects of the organization. There have been numerous definitions for entrepreneurial strategy offered by scholars (Hart, 1992; Lumpkin and Dess, 1996; Miles and Snow, 1978; Miller, 1988; Mintzberg, 1973). In general, entrepreneurial strategy involves an organization's posture toward opportunity-seeking, risk-taking, and experimentation with regard to processes or products (Dess et al., 1997). Family firm strategies incorporate the internal workings of the business and the external environment as well as the interests of the family in regard to goals, culture, values and succession issues (Goel et al., 2012). Evidence shows that long-running family businesses typically do not engage in grand strategizing but instead are driven by more substantive missions (Goel et al., 2012; Pieper, 2010).

To frame this component of the course, the instructor might first introduce the concept of entrepreneurial orientation (EO), and how it can be used to characterize differences between firms (Lumpkin and Dess, 1996). EO is a wonderful foundation for understanding "entrepreneurial" organizations, and it serves as a useful starting point for a discussion of long-term orientation (LTO) in family firms (Lumpkin and Brigham, 2011). Here, though, rather than focusing on the governance or structure aspects of the LTO, students need to think about the premise of a manager pursuing an opportunity with an unusual focus on preserving the family business. In much the same way that managers are often quoted as thinking of risk as the potential to lose money (Shapira, 1995) rather than the risk/return trade-off popularized in the capital asset pricing model tradition, family businesses often undertake projects with a first look at the money that can be lost rather than the growth that can be achieved. Professors might take the opportunity in this module, because it is essentially about decision-making, to examine more deeply the endowment effect – a reluctance to part with assets that belong to an endowment (Kahneman and Tversky, 1984; Thaler, 1980) – and other biases in decision-making. Students might also take the opportunity to look for ways to advance past the conservative decision-making inherent in family firms while learning to appreciate that this decision-making is what makes family businesses what they are. This module can be an extensive component of the course, as it can become a starting point to distinguish the value of decision-making contingent on the family's requirements, as opposed to an exclusive focus on positive NPV projects.

Stewardship

Stewardship is "the why" of the organization and can best be described as an interactive term consisting of individual, psychological characteristics and that of the situational, organizational nature. Individual stewardship depicts the actions of governing members that are more collectivistic, pro-organizational and trustworthy (Davis et al., 1997). Psychological or individual stewarding is based on the assumptions of the self-actualizing person. The self-actualizing agent gains the greatest utility from pro-organizational, collectivistic behaviors. When faced with a choice between an individualistic, self-serving option and a collectivistic, pro-organization option, the steward will choose the latter for the attainment of organizational objectives. Situational or cultural context refers to the family-controlled business's involvement orientation, as well as the extent to which the organization values individualism versus collectivism and the level of power distance accepted within the ranks of employees. Thus stewardship theory accommodates the family business milieu and aids in separating the field from entrepreneurship. Stewardship theory's use of more psychological and sociological systems of behavior holds that there is no conflict of interest between managers and owners (Donaldson and

Davis, 1989). According to Davis et al. (1997) there are three psychological dimensions that define and differentiate stewardship from agency theory: 1) intrinsic motivation; 2) identification with the organization; and 3) the use of power. This portrays managers as team players in place of opportunistic agents and thus suggests that managers act in the best interest of owners. It has been posited that family business leaders and their long-run orientation will behave as stewards and act accordingly to preserve the greater good of the firm (Craig and Moores, 2015; Lumpkin and Brigham, 2011). The addition of stewardship to the field of family business has aided in our understanding of family business (Craig and Moores, 2015) and the relationships among key members within family firms where agency theory was somewhat limited in scope.

Classes might spend time looking at the stewardship components in two related veins. The first is how to build and maintain a steward orientation in the firm. How can intrinsic motivation be encouraged and selected into the firm? Students might find and report on the hiring materials they are exposed to and debate the kind of approach most likely to attract people interested in working for a family business. Students can also debate the limits to which this stewardship and long-term orientation should extend. Do family firms owe a special obligation to their employees? Do family businesses have an unusually strong need to protect the environment? Research suggests that they frequently behave as though they do (Gomez-Mejia et al., 2011). Stewardship theory often suggests that firms with a high stewardship orientation have lower power distance than other organizations. Students could be invited to explore how much formal power family members should exercise.

Additionally, courses investigating stewardship need to spend time exploring the negative side of work/life balance. Family firms and their managers run the risk of assuming an unhealthy level of responsibility for their employees and the business. A third-generation family manager might feel an enormous amount of pressure to maintain and protect the firm. This pressure can lead to conservative decision-making, potentially leading to fatal outcomes, but also might cause negative health consequences such as anxiety and depression (Entrepreneurs Anonymous, 2014; Staw et al., 1981). To properly equip students to manage or work for family businesses, and for entrepreneurship generally, it is important that we equip students with the tools to deal with the negative aspects of any kind of entrepreneurship. Students and employees in family businesses must confront these pressures more forcefully, as the success of the business is now not only connected with relationships to employees but also with the often more intimate relationships with family.

LEARNING AND PEDAGOGY

Traditional approaches to teaching involve more of a transfer of information to a passive audience. Many of the methods used in the entrepreneurial and family business milieu take on more of an active learning approach. Current cognitive psychology views suggest that people learn through trial and error in their daily lives (Krueger, 2007). Experiential learning has been of interest to educators for decades (Hoover, 1974; Wolfe and Byrne, 1975), and the notion of "learning by doing" dates back to the days of Sophocles and Confucius (Gentry, J., 1990). Teaching family business requires a mixed approach that focuses on the transfer of useful information alongside practical hands-on experience. We offer the distinction between a teaching-centered approach and a learning-centered approach to frame a mindset we suggest in teaching family business.

Teaching-centered Approach

The teaching-centered approach recognizes learning as a process and has been dubbed a "pedagogy of answers" (Astolfi et al., 1997, as quoted by Potvin et al., 2010, p. 4), which often provides students with tools that will become useful at some point in the future (Astolfi et al., 1997, p. 143). This model is somewhat traditional in the sense that teachers develop lesson plans, deliver instruction concurrently to a classroom of students, make the majority of decisions in regard to learning methods and resources, conduct the class as a central entity, and make assessments (Branson, 1998). In this approach, students learn the skills and exercises necessary for carrying out routine operations. In a family business course, such skills and exercises would be delivered via lecture, interactive digital content, readings, problem sets (e.g., financial metrics for analysis, succession and estate planning), and large group projects which entail students visiting and interviewing family businesses to apply the concepts learned in class. The large group project often differs from a more traditional course group project, which normally relies heavily on the textbook and secondary data sources. Given that family businesses are ubiquitous in the economy, we ask students to select, interact with and analyze existing family businesses through a dialogue with the family running the business and receive the family's support to participate in the family business project. In effect, the project forces students to apply the principles learned in class through analyses of the family firm. The student project is directly related to the A-GES framework.

Learning-centered Approach

Learner-centered approaches suggest that students take ownership in the learning process. The traditional role of the teacher changes from that of information provider and evaluator to more of a coach, mentor, facilitator and participant, by providing educational recommendations and suggestions to students (Huba and Freed, 2000). Allen (2004) suggests that teachers ought to engage students in their learning and assist them in mastering their learning goals. Many suggest that it is the engagement of students, accompanied with thoughtful guidance, sound feedback and educational recommendations, that leads to learning and not simply the delivery of information (Dascalu et al., 2015; Hattie and Timperley, 2007; Shute, 2007). Learner-centered approaches instill a deeper level of learning (Marton and Sääljö, 1976), which is connected to transformative learning and the development of knowledge, skills, attitudes and abilities (Baartman and de Bruijn, 2011). It is in this notion of ownership and reflection that students discover the significance of self-motivation and self-awareness that potentially lead to intellectual and personal growth (Slavich and Zimbardo, 2012). Case studies, guided interviews, guest speakers and in-class group projects are good examples of teaching tools that allow students to take ownership of learning objectives.

TEACHING FAMILY BUSINESS USING A-GES

In Table 14.1, we propose a sample 15-week course structure built around the A-GES framework and a short description of each week's topic. This course setup is useful for MBA programs and undergraduate entrepreneurship majors or minors, as well as focused undergraduate programs. The course can be adapted to a shorter term by removing cases or specific topics that might be covered in other courses in the curriculum.

A course on family business should seek to emphasize the special problems and skills involved in the creation and management of family business. Such a course would integrate skills and concepts developed in other functional areas, while also addressing specific family business issues such as succession planning, innovation in the family business, and transgenerational wealth creation. Perhaps describing the elements of a business model and explaining how these can be drivers of specific family business concerns would complement the A-GES framework quite well. A primary objective would be to encourage students to have a greater understanding of the unique form of business venture which is family. Students should

Table 14.1   Sample course outline

Week	Topic	Description
1	What is a family business?	Overview of the definitional problem, A-GES framework
2	Heterogeneity	Differences in family firms and other organizations, key resources and key activities
3	Architecture: structure	How much formalization is necessary?
4	Architecture: systems	Evaluating performance contracts, examples from industry
5	Governance: family structures	Assembly bylaws, merits of employing family members, problems, case: Ambani clan in India
6	Family communication	Managing priorities
7	Entrepreneurship: building EO	Description of EO and its measurement, managing firms to be more EO and maintaining strategic direction
8	Entrepreneurship: balancing EO and capital protection	How to frame uncertainty, real options learning, lean strategy
9	Biases in decision making and balancing LTO	Setting a discount rate, endowment effect game
10	Stewardship: building a culture	Power distance, responsibility to employees and the environment
11	Stewardship: protecting yourself	Stress, failure, dealing with anxiety and work/ life balance.
12	Change and adaptation	Management for the long term, change management, and problems with restructuring a family enterprise
13	Family business modeling	Elements and importance of a business model in family business
14	Succession	Power transfer: passing the reins to future generations
15	Field project report-outs	

also understand the basic concepts and language of family business. Measurable outcomes include the following:

1. the ability to describe what constitutes a family business;
2. identifying and describing distinctions between family and non-family businesses;
3. identifying and describing the components of the A-GES framework;
4. the ability to apply the A-GES framework in order to structure solutions to business problems in family firms.

Within a teaching-centric approach, lectures and digital content are typical means of critical information conveyance. These methods are good for introducing concepts such as the nature, importance and unique-ness of family business, as well as discussing the usefulness of theoretical frameworks such as the A-GES framework, along with agency theory. Guest speakers, such as family business owners, award students a real-time interaction and an opportunity to ask questions regarding the key ele-ments of the A-GES framework. Outside readings and problem sets aid in solidifying learning objectives through application and create knowl-edge and skills inventories for students to draw upon. Such exercises are fundamental for understanding and insight, leading to implementation of routine operations in professional settings.

For students to take ownership in the learning process, instructors should adopt more of a mentoring role where possible and appropri-ate. Activities such as case studies and in-class group projects encourage students to take ownership of learning objectives. Individual or group assignments of this nature inspire students to gather insights from their peers and/or instructor in order to devise strategic approaches to problem solving and investigation. By extending recommendations and suggestions instructors guide students and engage in their learning rather than simply providing material and evaluating based on erudite information (Dascalu et al., 2015). Engaging students in these ways encourages the mastering of learning goals, instilling a deeper level of learning and self-regulation, while leading students to discover the significance of self-motivation and self-awareness that potentially fosters a lifetime of learning (Allen, 2004; Marton and Säaljö, 1976).

The learning-centered approach places students at the center of the learning process, meaning they play an active role in directing their own learning and are thus able to evaluate their own progress (Branson, 1998). Being learner-centric evokes creativity, improvisation, student action, and empowerment, proposing that students decide more than just whether they will learn (Palmgren-Neuvonen and Korkeamäki, 2015). Referencing research by Zappe et al. (2009), Teegan Green (2015) notes that "the implementation of interactive student-centered activities and learning experiences enriches the learning process much more than . . . traditional education modes. When the learning environment is enriched with differ-ent types of educational experiences for students to encounter . . . students are likely to become more engaged with the course content" (Green, 2015, p. 180). The more engaged students are with course content the more likely they are to learn, achieve, and investigate things on their own (Green, 2015).

According to Wenger (1998), student engagement includes participating in activities with others, talking, and producing outcomes. Shadowing, a unique student opportunity that many alumni are willing to provide, offers students the opportunity to engage in, and witness, real-time events and decision-making processes that family business owners and/or managers face. Sorenson and Milbrandt (2015) found that, when people learn new concepts collaboratively, they are more likely to share an affinity for those concepts and apply them in practice. Collaborative learning also encourages open communication, which promotes intergenerational learning and acquisition of tacit knowledge regarding both family and business (Sorenson and Milbrandt, 2015). Learning for a second-generation manager differs significantly from the founder's education (Salvato et al., 2015). Learning from family members and formalizing mentoring can enhance talent development, both personally and professionally, in next-generation members, especially regarding cognitive, emotional and social skills (Barbera et al., 2015).

Structured interviews built to a targeted set of questions related to a specific area of the A-GES framework are another opportunity for students to actively participate in the learning process by obtaining feedback on specific topical areas pertaining to the A-GES framework. Additionally, self-directed learning, where students are given an unstructured assignment and asked to complete the assignment in the best way they see fit, provides social learning opportunities in that students can interact with one another and discuss related issues. Such an approach to problem solving encourages students to construct their own understanding and educational meaning from experiential interactions (Green, 2015). Problem-based learning opportunities are those that may be lacking in information for clear resolving, or perhaps have multiple solutions with varying degrees of success (Gallagher, 1997). Often such problems are ambiguous and change as new information is gained. Shin and McGee (2003) refer to such problems as ill-structured problems and suggest that, working through such problems, students are more apt to: 1) develop a significant body of content knowledge and make use of it in the future; 2) regulate their own thinking and evaluate their progress toward goal completion; and 3) defend their arguments with evidence gained throughout the investigation.

Lastly, preparing the next generation to take the reins of leadership is essential for family business continuity (Barbera et al., 2015). Thus a wonderful option for a final project is self-managed field projects and live case studies. A family business analysis group project encourages students to interact with the members of a family firm. The objective of this task is to assess and carefully analyze the current situation and compare with best practices. This is essentially a living case study of the family business where students apply evidence-based concepts proven to be successful at sustaining businesses across generations. Students should first develop an in-depth understanding of the family business by generating a genogram, a representation of the family's structure and relationships. This can be developed by interviewing family members and developing a history of the family, its origins, and the narrative for the family from founder to present. Such a diagram is useful in identifying conflicts or deficiencies in the family's succession planning and offers an opportunity to discuss the potential for contingency planning alternatives aside from the traditional succession sequence. Students should include each member's role and responsibilities, including those who are not working full-time.

The second step in the analysis builds on the four inter-related platforms of the A-GES framework: architecture, governance, entrepreneurship and stewardship. Regarding architecture, students will highlight the importance of various systems pertaining to the formulated strategy of the firm, focusing on strategy implementation and the systems that support it. Also, students should discuss the managerial structures (e.g., authority and activity) of the family business, paying particular attention to the organizational structure and degree of centralization of authority. The purpose of the governance section is for students to highlight the unique family governance structures, forums and processes, and the role that these structures and forums play in firm strategy, communication and competitive advantage. Students should also take note of differences in the family governance structures compared to other business governance structures. If none are present, students should note whether objective, independent members improve the governance of the family business and then reflect on best practices. Also, students should explain how firms could avoid agency costs associated with entrenchment while reaping the benefits of long-tenure family and non-family management.

In the entrepreneurship section, students should identify the match between the entrepreneurial leaders in the family and the firm's strategies. They should reference how leaders develop insights into the business, family, and self through their understanding of appropriate leadership behavior. The strategy portion of this section should focus on the importance of formulating a values-driven vision and mission. How has the family developed its core ideology, and what is the envisioned future of the business? What values are most prevalent in the firm, and does the family participate in grand strategizing or is it driven by more substantive missions? For the stewardship section, students should present three psychological factors which differentiate the assumption of stewardship from agency theory, namely intrinsic motivation, identification with the organization, and use of power, when considering this complex, noneconomic model of human behavior. In addition to the three psychological factors, students should further differentiate the family-controlled business from its counterparts by discussing how each differs in terms of its situational or cultural context. This includes the involvement orientation of the family, as well as the levels of individualism versus collectivism and power distance among the ranks of employees.

DISCUSSION AND CONCLUSION

As business schools search for sources of differentiation, instructors may wish to consider adding a family business course to the business curriculum, given the role that family businesses play in the local, state, national and global economies. We have offered a clear, concise framework that can serve as a distinct organizing framework for a course in family business that is firmly rooted in extant research. Teaching the A-GES framework encourages students to take ownership of their learning goals by actively experiencing real-life cases in a collaborative manner. Classroom lectures and exercises construct an inventory of knowledge and skill for students to draw upon after they graduate and enter the workforce. While many other excellent frameworks are available, we believe that the A-GES framework offers students a comprehensive but simple and intuitive structure for understanding the many degrees of formalization within family firms. Using a broader framework, students can grapple with the benefits and concerns associated with working with family members, the value of maintaining strategic direction and entrepreneurship, and the advantages and disadvantages of a collectivist culture. It is our hope that instructors find this framework useful in their classrooms in the forging of future family business scholars and practitioners.

REFERENCES

Allen, M.J. (2004), *Assessing Academic Programs*, Boston, MA: Anker Publishing.

Astolfi, J.P., Darot, É., Ginsburger-Vogel, Y. and Toussaint, J. (1997), *Mots-clés de la didactique des sciences: repères, définitions, bibliographies*, Paris: De Boeck Université.

Astrachan, J.H. and Shanker, M.C. (2003), Family businesses' contribution to the US economy: a closer look, *Family Business Review*, **16**(3), 211–219.

Astrachan, J.H., Klein, S.B. and Smyrnios, K.X. (2002), The F-PEC scale of family influence: a proposal for solving the family business definition problem, *Family Business Review*, **15**(1), 45–58.

Baartman, L.K. and Bruijn, E. de (2011), Integrating knowledge, skills and attitudes: conceptualising learning processes towards vocational competence, *Educational Research Review*, **6**(2), 125–134.

Barbera, F., Bernhard, F., Nacht, J. and McCann, G. (2015), The relevance of a whole-person learning approach to family business education: concepts, evidence and implications, *Academy of Management Learning and Education*, **14**(3), 322–346.

Branson, R.K. (1998), Teaching-centered schooling has reached its upper limit: it doesn't get any better than this, *Current Directions in Psychological Science*, **7**(4), 126–135.

Chrisman, J.J., Kellermanns, F.W., Chan, K.C. and Liano, K. (2010), Intellectual foundations of current research in family business: an identification and review of 25 influential articles, *Family Business Review*, **23**(1), 9–26.

Chua, J.H., Chrisman, J.J. and Sharma, P. (1999), Defining the family business by behavior, *Entrepreneurship Theory and Practice*, **23**, 19–40.

Craig, J.B. and Moores, K. (2015), Appreciating the nature of the family business difference: the A-GES framework, in Scott L. Newbert (ed.), *Small Business in a Global Economy: Creating and Managing Successful Organizations*, 2 vols, Santa Barbara, CA: Praeger.

Dascalu, M.I., Bodea, C.N., Moldoveanu, A., Mohora, A., Lytras, M. and Pablos, P.O. de (2015), A recommender agent based on learning styles for better virtual collaborative learning experiences, *Computers in Human Behavior*, **45**, 243–253.

Davis, J.H., Schoorman, F.D. and Donaldson, L. (1997), Toward a stewardship theory of management, *Academy of Management Review*, **22**(1), 20–47.

Dess, G.G., Lumpkin, G.T. and Covin, J.G. (1997), Entrepreneurial strategy making and firm performance: tests of contingency and configurational models, *Strategic Management Journal*, **18**(9), 677–695.

Donaldson, L. and Davis, H.J. (1989), CEO governance and shareholder returns: agency theory or stewardship theory, Paper presented at annual meeting of the Academy of Management, Washington, DC.

DuBrin, A. (2015), *Leadership: Research Findings, Practice, and Skills*, Mason, OH: Cengage Learning.

Dyer, W.G. and Handler, W. (1994), Entrepreneurship and family business: exploring the connections, *Entrepreneurship Theory and Practice*, **19**, 71–83.

Entrepreneurs Anonymous (2014, September 20), *The Economist*, **412**(8905), 64.

Galbraith, J.R. (2014), *Designing Organizations: Strategy, Structure, and Process at the Business Unit and Enterprise Levels*, San Francisco: John Wiley & Sons.

Gallagher, S.A. (1997), Problem-based learning, *Journal for the Education of the Gifted*, **20**(4), 332–362.

Gentry, J.W. (1990), What is experiential learning? in J.W. Gentry (ed.), *Guide to Business Gaming and Experiential Learning*, East Brunswick, NJ: Nichols, pp. 9–20.

Gentry, R., Dibrell, C. and Kim, J. (2014), Long-term orientation in publicly traded family businesses: evidence of a dominant logic, *Entrepreneurship Theory and Practice*, **40**(4), 733–757.

Goel, S., Mazzola, P., Phan, P.H., Pieper, T.M. and Zachary, R.K. (2012), Strategy, ownership, governance, and socio-psychological perspectives on family businesses from around the world, *Journal of Family Business Strategy*, **3**(2), 54–65.

Gomez-Mejia, L.R., Cruz, C., Berrone, P. and De Castro, J. (2011), The bind that ties: socioemotional wealth preservation in family firms, *Academy of Management Annals*, **5**(1), 653–707.

Green, T. (2015), Flipped classrooms: an agenda for innovative marketing education in the digital era, *Marketing Education Review*, **25**(3), 179–191.

Gupta, V., MacMillan, I.C. and Surie, G. (2004), Entrepreneurial leadership: developing and measuring a cross-cultural construct, *Journal of Business Venturing*, **19**(2), 241–260.

Hart, S. (1992), An integrative framework for strategy-making processes, *Academy of Management Review*, **17**, 327–351.

Hattie, J. and Timperley, H. (2007), The power of feedback, *Review of Educational Research*, **77**(1), 81–112.

Hoover, J.D. (1974), Experiential learning: conceptualization and definition, *Developments in Business Simulation and Experiential Learning*, **1**.

Huba, M.E. and Freed, J.E. (2000), Learner centered assessment on college campuses: shifting the focus from teaching to learning, *Community College Journal of Research and Practice*, **24**(9), 759–766.

Kahneman, D. and Tversky, A. (1984), Choices, values, and frames, *American Psychologist*, **39**(4), 341–350.

Kaplan, R.S. and Norton, D.P. (1992), The balanced scorecard of measures that drive performance, *Harvard Business Review*, January–February.

Krueger, N.F. (2007), What lies beneath? The experiential essence of entrepreneurial thinking, *Entrepreneurship Theory and Practice*, **31**(1), 123–138.

Kuratko, D.F. and Hornsby, J.S. (1999), Corporate entrepreneurial leadership for the 21st Century, *Journal of Leadership and Organizational Studies*, **5**(2), 27–39.

Lumpkin, G.T. and Brigham, K.H. (2011), Long-term orientation and intertemporal choice in family firms, *Entrepreneurship Theory and Practice*, **35**(6), 1149–1169.

Lumpkin, G.T. and Dess, G.G. (1996), Clarifying the entrepreneurial orientation construct and linking it to performance, *Academy of Management Review*, **21**(1), 135–172.

Marton, F. and Säaljö, R. (1976), On qualitative differences in learning, II: outcome as a function of the learner's conception of the task, *British Journal of Educational Psychology*, **46**(2), 115–127.

Miles, R. and Snow, C.C. (1978), *Organizational Structure, Strategy and Process*, New York: McGraw-Hill.

Miller, D. (1988), Relating Porter's business strategies to environment and structure: analysis and performance implications, *Academy of Management Journal*, **31**(2), 280–308.

Mintzberg, H. (1973), Strategy-making in three modes, *California Management Review* (pre-1986), **16**(2), 44–53.

Morris, M.H., Cornwall, J.R. and Kuratko, D.F. (2013), *Entrepreneurship Programs and the Modern University*, Cheltenham, UK and Northampton, MA, USA: Edward Elgar.

Ouchi, W.G. (1980), Markets, bureaucracies, and clans, *Administrative Science Quarterly*, **25**(1), 129–141.

Palmgren-Neuvonen, L. and Korkeamäki, R.L. (2015), Teacher as an orchestrator of collaborative planning in learner-generated video production, *Learning, Culture and Social Interaction*, **7**, 1–11.

Pieper, T.M. (2010), Non solus: toward a psychology of family business, *Journal of Family Business Strategy*, **1**(1), 26–39.

Potvin, P., Riopel, M., Masson, S. and Fournier, F. (2010), Problem-centered learning vs. teaching-centered learning in science at the secondary level: an analysis of the dynamics of doubt, *Journal of Applied Research on Learning*, **3**(5), 1–24.

Poza, E. (2013), *Family Business*, Mason, OH: Cengage Learning.

Salvato, C., Sharma, P. and Wright, M. (2015), From the guest editors: learning patterns and approaches to family business education around the world – issues, insights, and research agenda, *Academy of Management Learning and Education*, **14**(3), 307–320.

Shapira, Z. (1995), *Risk Taking: A Managerial Perspective*, New York: Russell Sage Foundation.

Shin, N. and McGee, S. (2003), *Designers Should Enhance Learners' Ill-structured Problem-solving Skills*, Wheeling, WV: Virtual Design Center.

Shute, V.J. (2007), Focus on formative feedback, *ETS Research Report Series*, **2007**(1), i–47.

Slavich, G.M. and Zimbardo, P.G. (2012), Transformational teaching: theoretical underpinnings, basic principles, and core methods, *Educational Psychology Review*, **24**(4), 569–608.

Slevin, D.P. and Covin, J.G. (1990), Juggling entrepreneurial style and organizational structure, *MIT Sloan Management Review*, **31**(2), 43–53.

Sorenson, R. and Milbrandt, J. (2015), A family affair – teaching families versus individuals: insights gained from 24 years of family business education, *Academy of Management Learning and Education*, **14**(3), 366–384.

Staw, B.M., Sandelands, L.E. and Dutton, J.E. (1981), Threat rigidity effects in organizational behavior: a multilevel analysis, *Administrative Science Quarterly*, **26**(4), 501–524.

Thaler, R. (1980), Toward a positive theory of consumer choice, *Journal of Economic Behavior and Organization*, **1**(1), 39–60.

Wenger, Etienne (1998), *Communities of Practice: Learning, Meaning, and Identity*, Cambridge, UK: Cambridge University Press.

Wolfe, D.E. and Byrne, E.T. (1975), Research on experiential learning: enhancing the process, *Developments in Business Simulation and Experiential Learning*, **2**.

Zahra, S.A., Hayton, J.C., Neubaum, D.O., Dibrell, C. and Craig, J. (2008), Culture of family commitment and strategic flexibility: the moderating effect of stewardship, *Entrepreneurship Theory and Practice*, **32**(6), 1035–1054.

Zappe, S., Leicht, R., Messner, J., Litzinger, T. and Lee, H.W. (2009), *"Flipping" the Classroom to Explore Active Learning in a Large Undergraduate Course*, Washington, DC: American Society for Engineering Education.

15. Entrepreneurial ecosystems and entrepreneurship education: the role of universities in fostering ecosystem development

Diana M. Hechavarria, Amy Ingram and Justin Heacock

INTRODUCTION

Entrepreneurship is a crucial element for any country that aims to be competitive in today's global knowledge-based economy. The pivotal role of entrepreneurship in fueling economic growth can be facilitated with well-developed and coordinated entrepreneurial ecosystems (Isenberg, 2010), which can be defined as a set of

> interconnected entrepreneurial actors (both potential and existing), entrepreneurial organizations (e.g., firms, venture capitalists, business angels, banks), institutions (e.g., universities, public sector agencies, financial bodies) and entrepreneurial processes (e.g., the business birth rate, numbers of high growth firms, levels of "blockbuster entrepreneurship," number of serial entrepreneurs, degree of sell-out mentality within firms and levels of entrepreneurial ambition) which formally and informally coalesce to connect, mediate and govern the performance within the local entrepreneurial environment. (Mason and Brown, 2013, p. 214)

An entrepreneurial ecosystems approach highlights the complex inter-linkages among a variety of participants in an entrepreneurial society (e.g., entrepreneurs, educators, corporations, the media and a diverse set of government agencies), and the importance of the incentives the various actors encounter as they push towards an entrepreneurship-friendly environment (Bloom and Dees, 2008; Wessner, 2005). As a result, practitioners and educators note the importance of entrepreneurial ecosystems in linking multiple stakeholders to foster and sustain venturing (Isenberg, 2013).

Entrepreneurial ecosystem proponents argue that the formation of new businesses is driven by two dynamic elements: the entrepreneur (or, more accurately, the would-be entrepreneur) and the entrepreneurial environment. In addition to stressing the dynamic interaction between the entrepreneur and the environment, this perspective also suggests that the ecosystem is not fixed but evolutionary, growing and evolving according to new needs and new circumstances and that the system can change as a result of initiatives enacted by local agents to support and develop the ecosystem.

The ecosystems concept is arguably important because it highlights the dynamic nature of entrepreneurial activity by calling attention to the changes that take place in an ecosystem while also focusing on the need for local actors to address the complex challenges faced by entrepreneurs. Within the ecosystem, myriad factors support the development of an entrepreneurial society, including human capital and workforce supply, funding and finance, support systems and mentors, government and regulatory frameworks, education and training, cultural supports, leadership and intermediaries, among others (e.g., Feld, 2012; Isenberg, 2010; World Economic Forum, 2013). However, there is no "one size fits all" approach to ecosystems throughout the world, as every ecosystem is unique. Components and interactions within the ecosystem will differ from one context to another.

Among the many factors embedded in a flourishing entrepreneurial ecosystem is the role of education (Isenberg, 2010; World Economic Forum, 2013). Here, we focus on educational programming which stimulates entrepreneurship, because it is targeted at the pre-start, start-up and post-start-up phases of the entrepreneurial process, and is designed and delivered to address the areas of motivation, opportunity and skills, aimed encouraging more people to start their own businesses (Peterman and Kennedy, 2003). Entrepreneurship education creates and uses educational initiatives to establish entrepreneur-friendly legal and regulatory frameworks to increase entrepreneurial activity in an economy. Moreover, as scholars note, educational institutions are an essential factor of the ecosystem because education helps develop entrepreneurial intentions among members of the community (Honig, 2004; Liñán et al., 2011). Research work employing both institutional theory and population ecology perspectives provides additional evidence to support the fundamental role of educational organizations in the evolution of entrepreneurial ecosystems (Neck et al., 1999; Spilling, 1996).

ENTREPRENEURIAL ECOSYSTEMS

An ecosystem refers to the complex juxtaposition of organisms and their environment. The systematic study of ecosystems is rooted in the biological sciences, where the term "ecology" is most commonly applied to the natural habitats of animals. "Human ecology" is a more recent term extending to the domain of geographers and sociologists who are interested in the distributions of human populations. The term "social ecology" has evolved mainly from the efforts of behavioral scientists to direct their inquiries toward a more complete view of humans interacting with their physical and social environment (Insel and Moos, 1974). An ecosystem approach to the study of human behavior is a framework for viewing the interactions that occur between individuals and their environment. As the ecosystem approach is dynamic, accounting for complex interactions between the individual (entrepreneur) and the dynamic environment, this study adopts an ecosystem framework to gain insights into one dimension of entrepreneurship, new business start-ups. Specifically, this chapter describes the relationship between the would-be entrepreneur and the economic environment utilizing an ecosystem framework.

Work on entrepreneurial ecosystems goes back to Alfred Marshall (1920), who stressed certain benefits from co-location such as the availability of skilled labor and knowledge when studying industrial clusters. Contributions that emerged from industrial clusters include work by Arikan (2009), Breschi and Malerba (2001), Enright (1996), Gordon and McCann (2000), Markusen (1996), Martin and Sunley (2003), Maskell (2001), Matthews (2010), Mesquita (2007), Miller et al. (2009), Sabel (1989) and Saxenian (1994). Porter (1998) views clusters as geographical concentrations of interconnected companies, specialized suppliers, service providers, firms in related industries, and associated institutions (e.g., universities, standard agencies, trade associations) in a particular economic field, which compete but also cooperate (e.g., Porter, 1998, 2000). Furthermore, Moore (1997) argues that businesses don't evolve in a vacuum; thus the relationally embedded nature of how firms interact with suppliers, customers and financiers is also an important attribute of industrial clusters. The work on industrial clusters identified that there are spillover effects that are beneficial to the growth of other firms in the same locality (Mason et al., 2009). In all, this research stream argues the advantages of clusters in terms of co-location, social embeddedness and value creation (Pitelis and Pitsa, 2012). As work in this area advanced, it evolved towards an understanding that industrial clusters are really dynamic ecosystems in which new firms have better opportunities to grow and create employment, especially when compared to firms in other locations (Rosted, 2012).

Although there are several conceptualizations of the entrepreneurial ecosystem, we adopt Mason and Brown's (2013, p. 5) definition of an entrepreneurial ecosystem as a set of

> interconnected entrepreneurial actors (both potential and existing), entrepreneurial organizations (e.g., firms, venture capitalists, business angels, banks), institutions (e.g., universities, public sector agencies, financial bodies) and entrepreneurial processes (e.g., the business birth rate, numbers of high growth firms, levels of "blockbuster entrepreneurship," number of serial entrepreneurs, degree of sell-out mentality within firms and levels of entrepreneurial ambition) which formally and informally coalesce to connect, mediate and govern the performance within the local entrepreneurial environment.

Thus, the entrepreneurial ecosystem emphasizes the interaction of people, roles, infrastructure, organizations and events. The multiple stakeholders in an entrepreneurial ecosystem need to be inclusive and embrace other members of the start-up community who want to be involved (Mason and Brown, 2013). A regional ecosystem requires a culture of openness and information exchange, which fuels regions like Boulder, Austin and Silicon Valley's success. As technology evolves, people are better positioned to share information, adopt new trends, leverage innovation and respond to new conditions. Closed systems don't work. Creative people want to be around other creative people, because they know they need each other to create meaningful new ideas and solutions.

Entrepreneurial ecosystems therefore concentrate on bridging assets that serve to connect people, ideas and resources. These bridging assets are often embodied as individuals whose mission is to connect the dots and have a considerable role in further facilitating the knowledge spillovers needed to create an entrepreneurial society. The entrepreneurial society perspective contends that venturing is a key driver of economic growth (Audretsch, 2009). The entrepreneurial ecosystem serves as a catalyst in potentially speeding up the economic progress of stable economies, but it also can act as the prime mover when it comes to rescuing economies that have faced a sharp decline. Accordingly, the entrepreneurial ecosystem approach tends to focus on high potential start-ups, arguing that this type of entrepreneurship is an important source of innovation, productivity growth and employment needed to foster an entrepreneurial society (Mason and Brown, 2014).

Entrepreneurial ecosystems have a positive effect on high potential venture creation because of their unique character, and the co-existence of competition and cooperation (Romero-Martínez and Montoro-Sánchez, 2008). For instance, studies find that the entrepreneurial ecosystems fuel venturing as well as having a significant impact upon macroeconomic development (Ács et al., 2014). Bernardez and Mead (2009) showcase how entrepreneurial ecosystems played a key role in economic recovery in Argentina, the United States, Israel, India, China and Mexico despite adverse economic and social conditions. Bernardez and Mead (2009) demonstrate how each entrepreneurial ecosystem grew around a specific competency, such as tourism, gastronomy and hospitality for Palermo, Argentina, software and high-tech for Silicon Valley, finances for Wall Street and London, manufacturing for China, and engineering and business processes outsourcing for India.

Hence, research in entrepreneurial ecosystems demonstrates that the environment the entrepreneur is embedded in promotes productive venturing activity. Indeed, Levie and Autio (2008) empirically demonstrate that the entrepreneurial ecosystem can have a direct effect on overall regional entrepreneurial activity. Further, Hechavarria and Ingram (2014) extend this finding, providing evidence that declining ecosystem factors from 2001 to 2010 in the United States were considerably related to the declining prevalence of overall national entrepreneurial engagement.

Overall the entrepreneurial ecosystem is composed of factors or framework conditions that are said to either foster or hinder venturing activity. Conceptually, different informal and formal intuitions (North, 1990) or framework conditions have been identified as the core components of the entrepreneurial ecosystem. For instance, GEM research conceptualizes the conditions in which entrepreneurship is productive (Baumol, 1996): access to entrepreneurial finance, government support and policies, the presence of government-based entrepreneurship programs, entrepreneurship education, policies conducive to R&D transfer, legal and commercial infrastructure, market dynamics associated with change and openness, ease of entry regulations to start a business, and protection of intellectual property. Isenberg (2010) highlights six areas of the ecosystem: finance, culture, policy, human capital, support and markets. Arguably, all of these factors are important in promoting entrepreneurial activity. For instance, scholars have noted and empirically demonstrated that access to finance influences the entry into entrepreneurship (Levie and Autio, 2008). Others call attention to the importance of government programs nurturing entrepreneurial activities. Governments can support start-ups through programs that provide subsidies, material and informational support for new ventures (Dahles, 2005; Keuschnigg and Nielsen, 2001, 2002, 2004). However, education, and its influence upon entrepreneurial activity, is a burgeoning topic (Levie and Autio, 2008), and undoubtedly a pivotal aspect of the entrepreneurial ecosystem. Education increases the supply of entrepreneurs (Liebenstein, 1968) by providing skills that are necessary to create a start-up (Honig, 2004). Thus, promoting education through the entrepreneurial ecosystems is an essential part in providing the human capital necessary to create the foundation of agents needed to sustain and develop an entrepreneurial ecosystem. Next, we discuss the impact of entrepreneurial education programs as part of the broader entrepreneurial ecosystem.

ENTREPRENEURIAL EDUCATION

Historically, education is one of the most studied and discussed factors influencing entrepreneurial activity (Levie and Autio, 2008); however, the empirical findings are mixed. Some studies identify a positive relationship between entrepreneurial education and/or entrepreneurial programs at universities and the perceived attractiveness and feasibility of actual start-up activity (Delmar and Davidsson, 2000; Fayolle et al., 2006). Contrastingly, others discover that the effects of entrepreneurial education are negative on the perceived attractiveness and feasibility of actual start-up activity (Oosterbeek et al., 2010). Furthermore, research highlights gender differences in entrepreneurial education, where women are more strongly affected by entrepreneurship educational programs than men (Oosterbeek et al., 2010). Scholars suggest this occurs because female entrepreneurs have less self-confidence than male entrepreneurs in their entrepreneurial abilities (Wilson et al., 2007). Thus, participating in entrepreneurial educational programs can affect a person's self-efficacy, or a person's confidence in performing a particular task, which fosters entrepreneurial intentions and actions (Peterman and Kennedy, 2003).

Although the majority of the research about entrepreneurship education mainly focuses on the university level (e.g., Raposo et al., 2008; Sánchez, 2009) or the secondary school level (e.g., Paço et al., 2010; Raposo et al., 2008), scholars highlight that the educational process linked to developing venturing skills can begin earlier (Landstrom and Sexton, 2000). Landstrom and Sexton (2000) suggest that children are seen as entrepreneurial by birth, and thus entrepreneurship education should begin at the youngest age possible. It is imperative to have in mind that entrepreneurship and entrepreneurship education, from an early age in one's life, are not just about start-ups and new ventures, but predominantly surround the ability that an individual has to turn his/her inspirations into actions, and are about fostering values and skills that could be useful to develop entrepreneurial intentions. With more education and encouragement, youth should be able to realize their entrepreneurial aspirations, and this ultimately will increase economic growth in communities and open new job and career opportunities, regardless of economic circumstances.

Although not all youth will become entrepreneurs, all students and society benefit when individuals have a solid education that gives them entrepreneurial knowledge and skills to use over their lifetime and facilitate the development of an entrepreneurial society.

Overall evidence on entrepreneurship education tends to lean slightly in favor of its efficacy, although general research findings are not as convincing as one would expect (Fairlie et al., 2012; Martin, et al., 2013; Rideout and Gray, 2013). These mixed findings likely occur because of variance in pedagogical approaches, program goals, educational environments and student categories. Davidsson (2015) highlights that it is quite surprising that the extant literature is limited about this variance and influence of different educational frameworks upon entrepreneurship, where some findings suggest pros and cons of more academic-theoretical versus more practical approaches (Martin, et al., 2013; Piperopoulos and Dimov, 2015).

As a result, we follow Maritz and Brown's (2013) focus on entrepreneurial education as *any* course, program or process of education for the development of entrepreneurial attitudes and skills which involves developing personal qualities. Content is usually a combination of theory and practice (Rae, 2010), and generally a debated issue among entrepreneurship educators (Maritz et al., 2013). This is grounded on the differences in ideologies and beliefs on outcomes, approaches in content, and deliverables. For instance, business plan content is taught significantly differently to newer content including the Lean Startup (Ries, 2011) and Business Model Canvas (Osterwalder and Pigneur, 2010). Regardless of approach, the underlying goal of entrepreneurial education is to empower both entrepreneurs and nascent entrepreneurs with the tools necessary to undertake a new business. Entrepreneurial education programs are burgeoning internationally among students, with the primary goal being to increase the quantity and quality of entrepreneurs (Matlay, 2009) and influence behavior (Davidsson, 2015; Fayolle, 2010), entrepreneurial tendency (Neck and Greene, 2011; van Gelderen et al., 2015) and entrepreneurial outcomes (Matlay, 2008).

Scholars argue that entrepreneurship education currently can be best described as heutagogical (Hase and Kenyon, 2000, 2013; Maritz et al., 2015). Heutagogy refers to self-determined learning, where students are primarily guided by their passions and genuine interests, and educators subsequently respond by providing mentoring and facilitation, instead of instruction in a prescribed pedagogical manner. For instance, the educator can pedagogically plan to introduce topics such as business planning and entry strategies to students. Conversely, the students can introduce their personal contexts into the learning environment, and be supported by the educator (Maritz et al., 2015). The interaction between pedagogy and heutagogy is dependent on a process of academagogy (McAuliffe and Winter, 2013), or scholarly leading. In essence, academagogy is a process of negotiation between educator and student whereby the nature of content and resource identification and acquisition are negotiated, along with other processes, for example assessment processes (Maritz et al., 2015). Consequently, entrepreneurial education that uses an academagogical approach, arguably, should be the most successful in fostering an entrepreneurial ecosystem. Education is an important aspect of an entrepreneurial ecosystem because it affects the readiness of individuals to pursue business creation (Reynolds, 2015). And the supply of potential entrepreneurs is a national characteristic that has a major impact on the vibrancy of entrepreneurial ecosystems. We subsequently review the role of universities in nurturing the environment conducive to venturing.

ENTREPRENEURSHIP EDUCATION AND ENTREPRENEURIAL ECOSYSTEMS: FOSTERING AN ENTREPRENEURIAL SOCIETY

Indeed, as Isenberg (2013) argues, you cannot have a flourishing entrepreneurship ecosystem without large companies and educational institutions to cultivate it, intentionally or otherwise. Universities as institutions can drive changes in other local institutions and cultures. The actions of universities can contribute to the creation of an environment that encourages yet more entrepreneurship and can even form a positive feedback loop. Therefore, universities can have an impact on the direction and quality of organizations valued by entrepreneurial ecosystems by shaping the direction and potential rewards of alternative courses of technological development and even the types of organizational forms that will be accepted as legitimate. In sum, universities can play a pivotal part in the entrepreneurial ecosystem because they can be very influential in encouraging values for entrepreneurial intentions and for an entrepreneurial society (Honig, 2004; Liñán et al., 2011; Peterman and Kennedy, 2003).

There are three main explanations relating to the impact of universities on the formation and functioning of ecosystems. The first explanation, based in economic theory, is agglomeration economies (Marshall, 1920). This line of analysis argues that companies located in an area benefit from external economies of scale. Emerging companies need some common inputs, and by sharing a common geography companies can share the fixed costs of these resources external to the company. As the pool of start-ups in the area share the cost of specialized inputs, the average cost per start-up drops for the specialized inputs, which provides direct economic benefit to companies located within the start-up community. Research universities can have a significant impact on the evolution of an ecosystem through primary research and the education of skilled workers (Bruno and Tyebjee, 1982; Neck et al., 2004). Therefore, universities that specialize in certain fields of study (e.g., engineering) can impact the source of supply for ecosystems by increasing the amount of skilled labor in a region. Accordingly, entrepreneurial education and training, arguably, enhance the supply of potential entrepreneurs (Liebenstein, 1968). Education increases this supply through several mechanisms. First, education increases the supply of entrepreneurs through the provision of the instrumental skills required to start up and grow a new firm (Honig, 2004). Second, education increases the supply of entrepreneurs through the improved cognitive capability of people to manage the dynamic and complex process of opportunity recognition, assessment and exploitation (DeTienne and Chandler, 2004). Finally, education increases the supply of entrepreneurs through behavioral dispositions that encourage venturing as a viable career option (Peterman and Kennedy, 2003). Therefore, universities play an integral role in developing entrepreneurial human capital.

The second explanation is derived from sociology, and is based on horizontal network effects. Horizontal network effects purport that a culture of openness and information exchange among members in a system will enhance value for existing network members (Saxenian, 1994). Such attributes allow members in a network high flexibility to adapt quickly to change. The development of these values and attitudes calls individuals to consider entrepreneurship as an attractive and valid alternative to paid employment or unemployment (Holmgren et al., 2004; Sanchez, 2010). Accordingly, a university can facilitate openness by encouraging knowledge sharing and knowledge spillovers through value change. Indeed, research by Hellerstedt et al. (2014) concludes that knowledge spillovers from universities in terms of R&D played a particularly important role in positively influencing the number of firms' births in 286 Swedish municipalities. This highlights that university research is an important ingredient for promoting the level of entrepreneurship and the potential of new industries.

Finally, the third explanation for entrepreneurial ecosystems is based on the work of Florida (2002) in the field of economic geography. According to Florida (2002), the creative class (e.g., entrepreneurs, engineers, professors and artists) creates meaningful new forms. The existence of a critical mass of creative class members in an area will create a competitive geographic advantage over other geographies because creative class members have a vested interest in creating an environment that is pleasant and culturally diverse, and tolerates novel and contrarian ideas. Entrepreneurship education within universities not only teaches the skills and abilities needed to start a business, but also develops and fosters the attitudes and motives of creative problem solving. Again, the university plays a fundamental role in connecting creative individuals to facilitate entrepreneurial ecosystem development.

However, one of the most important prerequisites for successfully starting a new business is the desire or the ability to do so. Therefore, entrepreneurial education often focuses on developing attitudes that value entrepreneurial careers by fostering entrepreneurial self-efficacy and intentions (Mason and Brown, 2014). Entrepreneurship education seeks to engage people, regardless of age, to be responsible, enterprising individuals who are creative thinkers and can contribute to economic development through the exploitation of opportunities. Accordingly, entrepreneurship education is not just about teaching someone to run a business; it is also about fostering creative thinking and promoting a strong sense of self-worth and empowerment. Entrepreneurship education not only teaches students to create business, but also fosters other essential abilities. For instance, entrepreneurial education develops the ability to recognize opportunities, the ability to pursue opportunities by generating new ideas and gathering the necessary resources, the ability to create and operate a new firm and the ability to think in a creative and critical manner (Fetters et al., 2010). Entrepreneurs are central players (leaders) in the creation of an entrepreneurial ecosystem and in keeping the system healthy, and entrepreneurial education is an important predecessor to instill the values and attitudes needed to increase the supply of potential entrepreneurs.

Higher education institutions not only directly influence entrepreneurial education and venturing in the university setting through educational programming for students, but also play a pivotal role in developing the regional entrepreneurial ecosystem by working with business and government to promote the entrepreneurial society. Fetters et al. (2010) argue that, for universities to successfully develop the broader regional ecosystem, there must be an entrepreneurial champion within the university community (usually a member of the administration or faculty). These entrepreneurial leaders will often create pilot programs in order to gain visibility in the community, attract additional talent, acquire resources from donors, and acquire sponsors in the business community and from government agencies. As pilot programs develop, additional initiatives grow, and often the entrepreneurial ecosystem grows organically until it reaches critical mass. For example, a university incubator or accelerator helps facilitate and develop the broader regional entrepreneurial ecosystem by connecting several of the inter-organizational institutions and agents needed to successfully launch a new organization. This is because a university has the capacity to understand, develop and promote innovation and opportunity driven organizations (Rice and Habbershon, 2007).

It is important to stress that local conditions do drive differentiation among entrepreneurial ecosystems. Different universities have different resource bundles, which create specific kinds of competencies. These competencies are generally leveraged by universities in their role as entrepreneurial ecosystem facilitators. For instance, some universities may focus on enhancing technology transfer, which leads them to be more involved in science and engineering colleges. This ultimately will facilitate knowledge spillovers related to technology and science from colleges linked to STEM fields. On the other hand, universities with a strong history of philanthropy might be more likely to have engagement with disciplines that advance sustainability or solve social problems. Ultimately, this could lead universities to be more involved in disciplines associated with the liberal arts, and facilitate knowledge spillovers related to ecological or socially oriented opportunities.

In sum, we present seven key insights identified by Fetters et al. (2010) that were gleaned by a case analysis examining six universities and their role in developing their local entrepreneurial ecosystems (Table 15.1).

First, universities must leverage senior local entrepreneurial leadership to engage senior university administration to develop an entrepreneurial vision for the community and university. Strategic intent from university leadership and local entrepreneurial leaders will enhance commitment from individuals, governments, media and other academic institutions.

Second, universities need to focus on strong programmatic emphasis on entrepreneurship, and faculty leadership. It takes a team of skilled people in program development and program management to execute the strategic intent and vision of entrepreneurial leaders and university administration.

Third, there must be sustained commitment over a long period of time from key stakeholders within the university and local community. Building

Table 15.1   Universities' role in developing the entrepreneurial ecosystem

---

1. University–local entrepreneurship leaders craft the entrepreneurial vision for the university and the community.
2. University pragmatic focus on entrepreneurship and faculty leadership.
3. Long-term commitment from key university stakeholders.
4. University long-term financial commitment to the local entrepreneurial ecosystem.
5. University commitment to continuing education.
6. Proper university infrastructure.
7. University commitment to build and extend the entrepreneurial ecosystem.

---

a successful entrepreneurial ecosystem requires intensity and commitment, often over decades. In their review of universities such as Babson College, EM Lyon Business School, the University of Southern California, the University of Texas (Austin), Tecnológico de Monterrey, and National University of Singapore, the authors highlighted the continuity of leadership in champion sponsors as a key success factor in creating a thriving entrepreneurial ecosystem.

Fourth, long-term financial commitment from the university to the development of a local entrepreneurial ecosystem will likely increase its probability of success. This is because such an investment reduces the time and energy expended by local sponsors and champions who are in a constant scramble to secure ongoing funding to execute the strategic intent of the university administration. In addition, it insulates the university's entrepreneurial ecosystem development process from the resistance or obstruction that could arise from other university units.

Fifth, commitment to continuing innovation in curriculum and programs is vital. The contexts in which universities operate are constantly changing, and in turn universities must lead the charge to respond to change. Therefore, it is necessary that there is continuing innovation in how programming is delivered and developed to meet the environmental changes that are instrumental to a thriving and effective entrepreneurial ecosystem.

Sixth, universities must ensure they have proper organizational infrastructure. The structural organization of universities into profit centers can make the cross-disciplinary collaboration needed for effective ecosystem development difficult. Concerns about sharing tuition revenues, faulty salaries, and general expenses often create barriers that are difficult to overcome (Allen and Lieberman, 2010). Therefore, it is important to start with a small number of initiatives that are aligned with the rest of the organization, and that clearly advance institutional priorities before broadly network-building the ecosystem.

Finally, there must be a commitment to build and extend the entrepreneurial ecosystem and achieve critical mass. A strong entrepreneurial ecosystem has not only a strong regional impact, but the potential to achieve global reach and impact as well. This can be achieved through a global network of partner institutions. Achieving a sufficient scope and impact for the ecosystem to sustain itself requires that the university have a broad vision and commitment to achieving considerable outcomes locally, regionally, nationally and globally.

CONCLUSION

Over the last 60 years there has been an evolution in the manner in which governments in advanced countries have undertaken industrial and enterprise policies (Warwick, 2013). Indeed, the evolution of how we have conceptualized the entrepreneurial phenomenon has given rise to different enactments of entrepreneurial education. We contend that globally, for the United States economy to remain competitive, stakeholders involved in the entrepreneurial ecosystem must employ an entrepreneurial society position toward entrepreneurial education and entrepreneurial ecosystems. Furthermore, a long-term, integrated regional action plan for bringing about cultural value change is instrumental to promoting an entrepreneurial society. In order to coordinate or expand educational activities into an effective entrepreneurial ecosystem that promotes an entrepreneurial society, educators and university administrators need to advocate a more strategic and integrative framework for building the curricular and co-curricular programming, cross-disciplinary research, community engagement, and infrastructure components across university programs, specifically outreach programs into the local community, thereby extending the "ecosystem" view beyond the campus and the students into the broader regional context (Morris et al., 2013).

Universities and colleges encourage and stimulate the creation of new ventures through developing human capital, which subsequently leads to local economic development within their respective communities (Shane, 2004; Vincett, 2010). According to Siegel (2013), universities are a key part of the ecosystem because education enhances knowledge useful to entrepreneurship, increases the use of techniques to examine business situations and create actions plans, identifies and stimulates entrepreneurial skills, develops empathy and support for entrepreneurship, encourages positive attitudes towards change and promotes new start-ups and other ventures. Thus, the goal of entrepreneurial education should be to develop enterprising individuals and encourage an attitude of autonomy using suitable learning processes.

In its essence, entrepreneurship is about a proactive mindset that takes ownership of surrounding problems in society, sees them as opportunities, and embraces the risks and failures involved in finding a solution. Moving forward, universities and others working on creating an entrepreneurial ecosystem should leverage this change to empower citizens to become entrepreneurs. Therefore, the multiple stakeholders in an entrepreneurial ecosystem need to be inclusive and embrace other members of the start-up community who want to be involved (Mason and Brown, 2013). Entrepreneurial ecosystems should concentrate on bridging assets that serve to connect people, ideas and resources. These bridging assets are often embodied as individuals whose mission is to connect the dots and have a considerable role in facilitating the knowledge spillovers needed to create an entrepreneurial society. The entrepreneurial society perspective is a key driver of economic growth (Audretsch, 2009). Consequently, the entrepreneurial ecosystem not only can act as a catalyst in speeding up the economic progress of stable economies, but also can act as the prime mover when it comes to rescuing economies that have faced a sharp decline.

REFERENCES

Ács, Z.J., Autio, E. and Szerb, L. (2014), National systems of entrepreneurship: measurement issues and policy implications, *Research Policy*, **43**(3), 476–494.

Allen, K. and Lieberman, M. (2010), University of Southern California, in M.L. Fetters, P.G. Greene, M.P. Rice and J. Sibly Butler (eds.), *The Development of University-based Entrepreneurship Ecosystems*, Cheltenham, UK and Northampton, MA, USA: Edward Elgar, pp. 76–95.

Arikan, A.T. (2009), Interfirm knowledge exchanges and the knowledge creation capability of clusters, *Academy of Management Review*, **34**(4), 658–676.

Audretsch, D.B. (2009), The entrepreneurial society, in D.B. Audretsch, G.B. Dagnino, R. Faraci and R.E. Hoskisson (eds.), *New Frontiers in Entrepreneurship*, New York: Springer, pp. 95–105.

Baumol, W.J. (1996), Entrepreneurship: productive, unproductive, and destructive, *Journal of Business Venturing*, **11**(1), 3–22.

Bernardez, M. and Mead, M. (2009), The power of entrepreneurial ecosystems: extracting boom from bust, *PII Review*, **2**(2), 12–45.

Bloom, P.N. and Dees, G. (2008), Cultivate your ecosystem, *Stanford Social Innovation Review*, **6**(1), 47–53.

Breschi, S. and Malerba, F. (2001), The geography of innovation and economic clustering: some introductory notes, *Industrial and Corporate Change*, **10**(4), 817–833.

Bruno, A.V. and Tyebjee, T.T. (1982), The environment for entrepreneurship, *Encyclopedia of Entrepreneurship*, **2**(4), 288–315.

Dahles, Heidi (2005), Culture, capitalism and political entrepreneurship: transnational business ventures of the Singapore-Chinese in China, *Culture and Organization*, **11**(1), 45–58.

Davidsson, P. (2015), Entrepreneurial opportunities and the entrepreneurship nexus: a re-conceptualization, *Journal of Business Venturing*, **30**(5), 674–695.

Delmar, F. and Davidsson, P. (2000), Where do they come from? Prevalence and characteristics of nascent entrepreneurs, *Entrepreneurship and Regional Development*, **12**(1), 1–23.

DeTienne, D.R. and Chandler, G.N. (2004), Opportunity identification and its role in the entrepreneurial classroom: a pedagogical approach and empirical test, *Academy of Management Learning and Education*, **3**(3), 242–257.

Enright, M. (1996), Regional clusters and firm strategy, in U. Staber, N. Schaefer and B. Sharma (eds.), *Business Networks: Prospects for Regional Development*, Berlin: de Gruyter, pp. 190–213.

Fairlie, R.W., Karlan, D. and Zinman, J. (2012), *Behind the GATE Experiment: Evidence on Effects of and Rationales for Subsidized Entrepreneurship Training*, No. w17804, Cambridge, MA: National Bureau of Economic Research.

Fayolle, A. (2010), *Handbook of Research in Entrepreneurship Education*, Vol. 3, Cheltenham, UK and Northampton, MA, USA: Edward Elgar.

Fayolle, A., Gailly, B. and Lassas-Clerc, N. (2006), Assessing the impact of entrepreneurship education programmes: a new methodology, *Journal of European Industrial Training*, **30**(9), 701–720.

Feld, B. (2012), *Startup Communities: Building an Entrepreneurial Ecosystem in Your City*, Hoboken, NJ: John Wiley & Sons.

Fetters, M., Greene, P.G. and Rice, M.P. (eds.) (2010), *The Development of University-based Entrepreneurship Ecosystems: Global Practices*, Cheltenham, UK and Northampton, MA, USA: Edward Elgar.

Florida, R. (2002), The economic geography of talent, *Annals of the Association of American Geographers*, **92**(4), 743–755.

Gelderen, M. van, Kautonen, T. and Fink, M. (2015), From entrepreneurial intentions to actions: self-control and action-related doubt, fear, and aversion, *Journal of Business Venturing*, **30**(5), 655–673.

Gordon, I.R. and McCann, P. (2000), Industrial clusters: complexes, agglomeration and/or social networks? *Urban Studies*, **37**(3), 513–532.

Hase, S. and Kenyon, C. (2000), *From Andragogy to Heutagogy*, Melbourne: Ultibase.

Hase, S. and Kenyon, C. (2013), *Self-determined Learning*, London: Bloomsbury.

Hechavarria, D.M. and Ingram, A. (2014), A review of the entrepreneurial ecosystem and the entrepreneurial society in the United States: an exploration with the Global Entrepreneurship Monitor dataset, *Journal of Business and Entrepreneurship*, **26**(1), 1–35.

Hellerstedt, K., Wennberg, K. and Frederiksen, L. (2014), University knowledge spillovers and regional start-up rates: supply and demand-side factors, *Advances in Entrepreneurship, Firm Emergence, and Growth*, **16**, 137–168.

Holmgren, C., From, J., Olofsson, A., Karlsson, H., Snyder, K. and Sundtröm, U. (2004), Entrepreneurship education: salvation or damnation? *International Journal of Entrepreneurship*, **8**, 55–71.

Honig, B. (2004), Entrepreneurship education: toward a model of contingency-based business planning, *Academy of Management Learning and Education*, **3**(3), 258–273.

Insel, P.M. and Moos, R.H. (1974), Psychological environments: expanding the scope of human ecology, *American Psychologist*, **29**(3), 179–188.

Isenberg, D.J. (2010), How to start an entrepreneurial revolution, *Harvard Business Review*, **88**(6), 40–50.

Isenberg, D. (2013), Babson Entrepreneurship Ecosystem Project.

Keuschnigg, C. and Nielsen, S.B. (2001), Public policy for venture capital, *International Tax and Public Finance*, **8**(4), 557–572.

Keuschnigg, C. and Nielsen, S.B. (2002), Start-ups, venture capitalists, and the capital gains tax, Research document, University of St. Gallen and Copenhagen Business School, June.

Keuschnigg, C. and Nielsen, S.B. (2004), Start-ups, venture capitalists, and the capital gains tax, *Journal of Public Economics*, **88**(5), 1011–1042.

Landstrom, H. and Sexton, D.L. (eds.) (2000), *The Blackwell Handbook of Entrepreneurship*, Oxford, UK: Blackwell Business.

Levie, J. and Autio, E. (2008), A theoretical grounding and test of the GEM model, *Small Business Economics*, **31**(3), 235–263.

Liebenstein, H. (1968), Entrepreneurship and development, *American Economic Review*, **58**(2), 392–415.

Liñán, F., Urbano, D. and Guerrero, M. (2011), Regional variations in entrepreneurial cognitions: start-up intentions of university students in Spain, *Entrepreneurship and Regional Development*, **23**(3–4), 187–215.

Maritz, A. and Brown, C.R. (2013), Illuminating the black box of entrepreneurship education programs, *Education + Training*, **55**(3), 234–252.

Maritz, A., Waal, G.A. de, Buse, S., Herstatt, C., Maclachlan, R. and Heidemann, A. (2013), Innovation education programs: towards a conceptual framework, *European Journal of Innovation Management*, **17**(2), 166–182.

Maritz, A., Jones, C. and Shwetzer, C. (2015), The status of entrepreneurship education in Australian universities, *Education + Training*, 57(8/9), 1020–1035.

Markusen, A. (1996), Sticky places in slippery space: a typology of industrial districts, *Economic Geography*, **72**(3), 293–313.

Marshall, A. (1920), *Principles of Economics: An Introductory Volume*.

Martin, B.C., McNally, J.J. and Kay, M.J. (2013), Examining the formation of human capital in entrepreneurship: a meta-analysis of entrepreneurship education outcomes, *Journal of Business Venturing*, **28**(2), 211–224.

Martin, R. and Sunley, P. (2003), Deconstructing clusters: chaotic concept or policy panacea? *Journal of Economic Geography*, **3**(1), 5–35.

Maskell, P. (2001), Towards a knowledge-based theory of the geographical cluster, *Industrial and Corporate Change*, **10**(4), 921–943.

Mason, C. and Brown, R. (2013), Creating good public policy to support high-growth firms, *Small Business Economics*, **40**(2), 211–225.

Mason, C. and Brown, R. (2014), Entrepreneurial ecosystems and growth oriented entrepreneurship, Final report to OECD, Paris.

Mason, G., Bishop, K. and Robinson, C. (2009), *Business Growth and Innovation: The Wider Impact of Rapidly-growing Firms in UK City-regions*, London: NESTA.

Matlay, H. (2008), The impact of entrepreneurship education on entrepreneurial outcomes, *Journal of Small Business and Enterprise Development*, **15**(2), 382–396.

Matlay, H. (2009), Entrepreneurship education in the UK: a critical analysis of stakeholder involvement and expectations, *Journal of Small Business and Enterprise Development*, **16**, 355–368.

Matthews, J. (2010), Renewing healthy competition: compulsory licenses and why abuses of the TRIPS Article 31 standards are most damaging to the United States healthcare industry, *Journal of Business, Entrepreneurship and the Law*, **4**, 119–150.

McAuliffe, M. and Winter, A. (2013), Distance education and the application of academagogy: a case study, *International Journal of Innovation, Creativity and Change*, **1**(2), 1–15.

Mesquita, L.F. (2007), Starting over when the bickering never ends: rebuilding aggregate trust among clustered firms through trust facilitators, *Academy of Management Review*, **32**(1), 72–91.

Miller, B.K., Bell, J.D., Palmer, M. and Gonzalez, A. (2009), Predictors of entrepreneurial intentions: a quasi-experiment comparing students enrolled in introductory management and entrepreneurship classes, *Journal of Business and Entrepreneurship*, **21**(2), 39–62.

Moore, J.F. (1997), *The Death of Competition: Leadership and Strategy in the Age of Business Ecosystems*, Chichester, UK: Wiley & Sons.

Morris, M.H., Kuratko, D.F. and Cornwall, J.R. (2013), *Entrepreneurship Programs and the Modern University*, Cheltenham, UK and Northampton, MA, USA: Edward Elgar.

Neck, C.P., Neck, H.M., Manz, C.C. and Godwin, J. (1999), "I think I can; I think I can": a self-leadership perspective toward enhancing entrepreneur thought patterns, self-efficacy, and performance, *Journal of Managerial Psychology*, **14**(6), 477–501.

Neck, H.M. and Greene, P.G. (2011), Entrepreneurship education: known worlds and new frontiers, *Journal of Small Business Management*, **49**(1), 55–70.

Neck, H.M., Meyer, G.D., Cohen, B. and Corbett, A.C. (2004), An entrepreneurial system view of new venture creation, *Journal of Small Business Management*, **42**(2), 190–208.

North, D.C. (1990), *Institutions, Institutional Change and Economic Performance*, Cambridge, UK: Cambridge University Press.

Oosterbeek, H., Van Praag, M. and Ijsselstein, A. (2010), The impact of entrepreneurship education on entrepreneurship skills and motivation, *European Economic Review*, **54**(3), 442–454.

Osterwalder, A. and Pigneur, Y. (2010), *Business Model Generation: A Handbook for Visionaries, Game Changers, and Challengers*, Hoboken, NJ: John Wiley & Sons.

Paço, A., Ferreira, J., Raposo, M., Rodrigues, R.G. and Dinis, A. (2010), Universities' entrepreneurship education and regional development: a stakeholder approach, University of Beira Interior, Portugal.

Peterman, N.E. and Kennedy, J. (2003), Enterprise education: influencing students' perceptions of entrepreneurship, *Entrepreneurship Theory and Practice*, **28**(2), 129–144.

Piperopoulos, P. and Dimov, D. (2015), Burst bubbles or build steam? Entrepreneurship education, entrepreneurial self-efficacy, and entrepreneurial intentions, *Journal of Small Business Management*, **53**(4), 970–985.

Pitelis, C.N. and Pitsa, E.M. (2012), Entrepreneurship, appropriability and the co-creation of markets and ecosystems, available at SSRN 1963726.

Porter, M.E. (1998), Clusters and competition: new agendas for companies, governments, and institutions, in M.E. Porter, *On Competition*, Boston, MA: Harvard Business School Publishing, pp. 197–287.

Porter, M.E. (2000), Location, competition, and economic development: local clusters in a global economy, *Economic Development Quarterly*, **14**(1), 15–34.

Rae, D. (2010), Universities and enterprise education: responding to the challenge of the new era, *Journal of Small Business and Enterprise Development*, **17**(4), 591–606.

Raposo, M.L.B., Ferreira, J.J.M., Paço, A.M.F. do and Rodrigues, R.J.G. (2008), Propensity to firm creation: empirical research using structural equations, *International Entrepreneurship and Management Journal*, **4**(4), 485–504.

Reynolds, P.D. (2015), Business creation stability: why is it so hard to increase entrepreneurship? *Foundations and Trends in Entrepreneurship*, **10**(5/6), 321–475.

Rice, M. and Habbershon, T.G. (2007), The place of entrepreneurship, in M. Rice and T.G. Habbershon (eds.), *Entrepreneurship: The Engine of Growth*, Vol. 3, Westport, CT: Praeger Publishers.

Rideout, E.C. and Gray, D.O. (2013), Does entrepreneurship education really work? A review and methodological critique of the empirical literature on the effects of university-based entrepreneurship education, *Journal of Small Business Management*, **51**(3), 329–351.

Ries, E. (2011), *The Lean Startup: How Today's Entrepreneurs Use Continuous Innovation to Create Radically Successful Businesses*, New York: Random House.

Romero-Martínez, A.M. and Montoro-Sánchez, Á. (2008), How clusters can encourage entrepreneurship and venture creation: reasons and advantages, *International Entrepreneurship and Management Journal*, **4**(3), 315–329.

Rosted, J. (2012), *Understanding Business Ecosystems*, Istanbul: FORA Group.

Sabel, C.F. (1989), *The Reemergence of Regional Economies*, Berlin: WZB.

Sanchez, A. (2010), Capitalism, violence and the state: crime, corruption and entrepreneurship in an Indian company town, *Journal of Legal Anthropology*, **2**(1), 165–188.

Sánchez, J.C. (2009), Social learning and entrepreneurial intentions: a comparative study between Mexico, Spain and Portugal, *Revista Latinoamericana de Psicología*, **41**(1), 109–119.

Saxenian, A. (1994), *Regional Networks: Industrial Adaptation in Silicon Valley and Route 128*, Cambridge, MA: Harvard University Press.

Shane, S.A. (2004), *Academic Entrepreneurship: University Spinoffs and Wealth Creation*, Cheltenham, UK and Northampton, MA, USA: Edward Elgar.

Siegel, D. (2013), Academic entrepreneurship: lessons learned for university administrators and policymakers, in D. Audretsch and M. Lindenstein Walshok (eds.), *Creating Competitiveness*, Cheltenham, UK and Northampton, MA, USA: Edward Elgar, pp. 116–135.

Spilling, O.R. (1996), The entrepreneurial system: on entrepreneurship in the context of a mega-event, *Journal of Business Research*, **36**(1), 91–103.

Vincett, P.S. (2010), The economic impacts of academic spin-off companies, and their implications for public policy, *Research Policy*, **39**(6), 736–747.

Warwick, K. (2013), *Beyond Industrial Policy: Emerging Issues and New Trends*, OECD Science, Technology and Industry Policy Papers No. 2, Paris: OECD Publishing.

Wessner, C.W. (2005), Entrepreneurship and the innovation ecosystem: policy lessons from the United States, in D.B. Audretsch, H. Grimm and C.W. Wessner (eds.), *Local Heroes in the Global Village: Globalization and New Entrepreneurship Policies*, New York: Springer Science + Business Media, pp. 67–89.

Wilson, F., Kickul, J. and Marlino, D. (2007), Gender, entrepreneurial self-efficacy, and entrepreneurial career intentions: implications for entrepreneurship education, *Entrepreneurship Theory and Practice*, **31**(3), 387–406.

World Economic Forum (2013), *Entrepreneurship Ecosystems around the Globe and Company Dynamics: Report Summary from the Annual Meeting of the New Champions, 2013*, Davos, Switzerland: World Economic Forum, Stanford University, Ernst & Young, and Endevor.

PART II

Model university entrepreneurship programs

16. Entrepreneurship at the University of Southern California

Kathleen R. Allen

Located in one of the most active regions in the United States for entrepreneurship, the University of Southern California (USC) provides a vibrant environment and opportunity for students and faculty to become entrepreneurs. With a University Park Campus and a Health Sciences Campus, in addition to various clinics and laboratories around Los Angeles, USC is home to 19,000 undergraduates, 24,000 graduate and professional students, and more than 4000 faculty. Recognized as one of the most ethnically diverse student bodies in the United States, its enrollment includes 24 percent international students. The university's alumni, widely known as the "Trojan Family," span 44 countries and are an enormous source of job opportunities and new venture support for our students.

A BRIEF HISTORY OF ENTREPRENEURSHIP AT USC

Entrepreneurship has been a part of the USC academic environment since the 1960s, when the first graduate courses dedicated to helping students understand the entrepreneurial mindset and how to start businesses were offered. To appreciate why the study of entrepreneurship developed so early at USC, it is important to understand the regional environment in which the university resides. The Southern California region (Santa Barbara to San Diego) is home to a number of important technology clusters that include aerospace, media and entertainment, port technologies, biotechnology, engineering, and medical devices. For decades these industries have produced significant companies to fuel the regional economy. Over the past two decades, Southern California has been rivaling New England and the New York metropolitan area to claim the number 2 spot behind Silicon Valley as an innovation and entrepreneurship hub. With more than 200 colleges and universities that offer opportunities in entrepreneurship, Los Angeles county universities produce more engineering graduates than any other county in California. Home to only five Fortune 500 companies, the Los Angeles area tends to attract people who want to start businesses or work for mid-sized entrepreneurial companies. Investors in new ventures increasingly target Southern California. In 2015 alone, venture capital investment in Southern California-based new ventures reached more than $6 billion.[1]

In 1971, the USC Marshall School of Business's entrepreneur program offered a concentration in entrepreneurship at the MBA level as well as the first undergraduate course in entrepreneurship. The popularity of the undergraduate course led to the offering of an undergraduate concentration in entrepreneurship in 1980. In 1997, USC became the first U.S. university to have its entrepreneurship center endowed by an alumnus of an entrepreneur program; it was named the Lloyd Greif Center for Entrepreneurial Studies (the Greif Center).

The Greif Center, which is housed in the Marshall School of Business, reached out to the Engineering School and the School of Medicine to support their growing interest in entrepreneurship. In 1998, under the leadership of Professor Kathleen Allen, the Technology Commercialization Alliance was formed, the first such collaboration at a university in the United States. An NSF Partners for Innovation grant eventually led to the establishment of a formal USC Marshall Center for Technology Commercialization in 2004. The Center's purpose is to work with scientists and engineers to commercialize their research through a variety of programs, including matching MBAs with scientific or engineering teams to bring business expertise to the commercialization effort. Students from across campus can also earn a Certificate in Technology Commercialization by completing four designated courses.

In 2007, under the leadership of Professor Adlai Wertman, a social entrepreneurship program was started to provide opportunities for students, faculty and others to use business principles to solve world problems. So successful was the program that, in 2014, it was endowed as the Brittingham Social Enterprise Lab (BSEL). It now offers education, programs, events and career development focused on social entrepreneurship. USC was the first U.S. university to offer a Master of Science in Social Entrepreneurship degree.

THE USC ENTREPRENEURIAL CULTURE AND ECOSYSTEM

The entrepreneurial culture at USC and its associated ecosystem have grown organically from efforts dating back to the 1960s. Whereas for many decades entrepreneurship emanated largely from the Marshall School of Business and, more specifically, from the Greif Center, today the university offers 22 organizational units that touch entrepreneurship. Most recently, a university-wide effort has produced Incubate USC (incubate.usc.edu), a portal that serves as a resource to the USC entrepreneur ecosystem. The resources found at Incubate USC are designed to support students, faculty, and those who wish to become involved in mentoring, advising, guest-lecturing, investing and sponsoring as well as providing jobs and intern-ships. The resources include course offerings, research, financial resources, incubators and accelerators, legal and intellectual property assistance, pitch competitions, and student organizations focused on entrepreneurship.

A few examples of specific programs in the USC ecosystem outside of the Marshall School of Business include:

- USC Annenberg's Media, Economics and Entrepreneurship Program;
- USC Games Program;
- Jimmy Iovine and Andre Young Academy for Arts, Technology and the Business of Innovation;
- mHealth Collaboratory;
- Viterbi School of Engineering Student Innovation Institute;
- Center for Body Computing;
- USC Coulter Translational Research Partnership Program;
- USC Institute for Creative Technologies (artificial intelligence, graphics, virtual reality).

In addition, USC is home to 10 incubators and accelerators, some of which focus in specialized areas such as healthcare, devices, gaming, and prototype fabrication. The Stevens Center for Innovation serves as the technology transfer office to manage the flow of intellectual property at the university.

LLOYD GREIF CENTER FOR ENTREPRENEURIAL STUDIES

As the oldest U.S. entrepreneurship center, the Greif Center functions as both a department and a center. Its Academic Director, Professor Helena Yli-Renko, is responsible for faculty, entrepreneurship curriculum, and research. She holds the Orfalea Director's Chair in Entrepreneurship, endowed by alumnus Paul Orfalea, the founder of Kinko's. Executive Director David Belasco leads the Center's venture incubation and outreach efforts and the Advisory Council. The Center works to advance the core tenets of the USC Marshall School of Business Strategic Plan: infusing an entrepreneurial mindset within the Marshall community, emphasizing the international scope of curriculum and research, and engaging the Southern California community.

The Greif Center has enjoyed consistently high rankings since the Center was founded. Its current rankings are: Number 3 Undergraduate Program in *US News and World Report* 2016; Number 9 Graduate Program in *US News and World Report* 2016; and Number 4 Graduate Program in *Financial Times* 2015. The Center has an active Advisory Council of 47 alumni entrepreneurs, non-alumni entrepreneurs, and professionals who support the Center by speaking in classes, judging and mentoring, and sponsoring events.

Three pillars of excellence guide the work of the Center: curriculum, thought leadership, and venture incubation.

Curriculum

The Greif Center curriculum emphasizes rigor, relevance and currency in its academic programs, which had a total enrollment of over 3300 in the academic year 2015–2016. Building skills that can be applied immediately to a student's chosen career is an important emphasis. The Center reaches out to students from most of the schools on campus to take courses and secure certificates and degrees in entrepreneurship. The following programs are currently serving students from all parts of the campus and from outside the university, and they also serve as "concentrations" to help students differentiate themselves.

Undergraduate minors and concentrations

- Marshall Business Major with an Entrepreneurship Concentration;
- Minor in Entrepreneurship;
- Minor in Social Entrepreneurship;
- Minor in Media Economics and Entrepreneurship, with the Annenberg School for Communication and Journalism;
- Minor in Technology Commercialization, with the Viterbi School of Engineering;
- Minor in Innovation: The Digital Entrepreneur, with the Viterbi School of Engineering;
- Minor in Game Entrepreneurism, with the School of Cinematic Arts.

Graduate degrees and concentrations

- Master of Science in Entrepreneurship and Innovation;
- Master of Science in Social Entrepreneurship;
- USC Marshall Certificate in Technology Commercialization.

The Center currently offers 49 different courses in entrepreneurship at the graduate and undergraduate levels, taught by 12 full-time professors and 19 adjunct faculty. The Greif Center is unique among entrepreneurship programs in that all of its faculty are assigned exclusively to entrepreneurship instead of being borrowed from other departments. Many of the Center's faculty have specialized expertise in areas such as technology commercialization, venture capital, business acquisitions, social impact investing, social entrepreneurship, and Internet ventures. In addition to academic credentials, most of the faculty are experienced in starting and growing businesses.

Thought Leadership

Over the past decade, the Greif Center has been focused on fostering entrepreneurship as a research field and supporting high-quality entrepreneurship research conducted by USC Marshall faculty and doctoral students. These efforts have been led by the Greif Center's Research Director, Professor Nandini Rajagopalan, who holds the Simonsen Chair in Strategic Entrepreneurship. Research initiatives include the Greif Research Impact Award, a national prize of $5000 given at the annual Academy of Management Meeting to the researcher(s) who published the most impactful entrepreneurship article six years earlier in the top management and entrepreneurship journals. Impact is measured as the number of Social Sciences Citation Index citations in the five years following publication. In addition, the Center offers the Greif Faculty and Doctoral Student Research Awards, which recognize USC Marshall faculty and doctoral students for their outstanding research in entrepreneurship, and the Greif Entrepreneurship Research Seminars, which bring leading researchers to USC to discuss their most recent work. The Center also serves as one of the sponsors and organizers of the West Coast Entrepreneurship Research Symposium, which invites researchers from around the world to come together to improve their research, stimulate new ideas and form new collaborations.

Beyond academic research, the Greif Center contributes to pedagogical thought leadership in entrepreneurship through the newly launched Entrepreneurship and Innovation Case Series. The teaching cases focus on Southern California and/or USC alumni ventures. Featuring entrepreneurial stories around space, video games, cleantech, fashion, healthcare and fantasy sports – to name just a few – this case series showcases the extended Southern California region and the global entrepreneurial companies that are started in the region. The cases are currently distributed through the Case Centre and are available through Harvard Business School Publishing as of summer 2016. All of the cases are accompanied by comprehensive and tested teaching notes.

Venture Incubation and Support

The Greif Center offers a myriad of opportunities for students and alumni to seek funding and guidance for their startups and to connect with other entrepreneurs and community professionals.

USC Incubator

Run by the Greif Center, the USC Incubator is designed to take founders from feasibility and early customer discovery to testing a business model, building a team and preparing for investment. It also provides work space for early-stage ventures. To date participating companies have run successful Kickstarter campaigns, raised venture capital and shipped product to customers. They have also been successful in various venture competitions, including Silicon Beach, the Stevens Student Innovator Showcase, and the New Venture Seed Competition.

Blackstone Launchpad Accelerator

Funded by the Blackstone Charitable Foundation to provide aspiring entrepreneurs with the tools and mentors they need to transform ideas into opportunities and new ventures, the Accelerator is housed in the Marshall School of Business and supported by the Greif Center. It provides guidance and mentoring to ventures in the earliest stages.

Venture competitions

The Greif Center organizes and supports a wide range of venture competitions at USC:

- *New Venture Seed Competition*: a university-wide competition open to students, faculty, staff and recent alumni, who compete for $50,000 in prize money.
- *Silicon Beach Awards*: a university-wide competition for new ventures focused on technology, media and/or entertainment. Prizes total more than $50,000.

- *Maseeh Prize Competition* (with Viterbi School of Engineering): open to all USC students and faculty, but must have a Viterbi student on the team. A $50,000 grand prize provides seed funding to translate ideas into products.
- *Min Family Engineering Social Entrepreneurship Prize* (with Viterbi School of Engineering): focuses on using innovations in engineering and technology to develop sustainable and effective solutions to global problems. Offers multiple prizes from customer discovery to project implementation.
- *MBA Women's Venture Competition*: teams of Marshall MBA women compete for $40,000 in prize money.
- *Stevens Student Innovator Showcase*: open to USC students from all disciplines who present their innovations in a variety of media, competing for prize money.
- *University Venturing and Angel Summit*: the top ventures from Southern California universities present to more than a dozen angel investment groups. The event is the largest gathering of angel investors in California.
- *Mayor's Cup Civic Challenge*: open to all two- and four-year colleges and universities in Los Angeles County. Students compete for $25,000 in prize money for solving problems of civic engagement.

COMMUNITY OUTREACH

In addition to the entrepreneurial activities on campus, the Greif Center is engaged in a number of outreach efforts in the broader Southern California community.

NFTE (Network for Teaching Entrepreneurship)

The Greif Center has a long-standing partnership with NFTE, a non-profit organization that supports entrepreneurship education in inner-city middle and high schools. Many of the Greif faculty have their classes conduct "E-Challenges" – experiential learning exercises in which students run pop-up ventures with the profits donated to NFTE. In the academic year 2014–2015, these E-Challenges generated more than $32,000 in funding for NFTE. Greif faculty also mentor NFTE students and serve as judges in NFTE's venture competitions. In addition, the Greif Center hosts NFTE's annual Transform LA Youth Entrepreneurship Conference. At this event, NFTE students from several inner-city schools have the opportunity to hear from and speak with entrepreneurs as well as participate in workshops. Since 2007, NFTE has also received two scholarships annually for program graduates to attend USC's summer Exploring Entrepreneurship program.

NSF I-Corps Regional Node Grant

USC serves as the headquarters for the NSF Innovation Corps (I-Corps) national program in Southern California, which provides to engineering and science-based startup teams education, Launchpad training, and links to the investment community. The Greif Center participates in the research and teaching activity of the regional node, collaborating with the Viterbi School of Engineering.

Angel and Venture Capital Communities

Southern California is home to the Tech Coast Angels (TCA), one of the largest angel investment groups in the United States, and Pasadena Angels, a highly respected group of local accredited investors. TCA, Pasadena Angels and various other angel groups are active at USC as mentors to startups and early-stage investors. The angel groups have internship programs that give USC students an opportunity to better understand how the investment community works.

Venture capitalists are active in many networking events: as judges in pitch competitions, teaching workshops on fund raising and effective pitching, and serving as adjunct faculty and on the Greif Center's Advisory Council. Graduate students are often recruited as associates and interns in VC firms in the area.

CONCLUSION

USC did not have to engineer an entrepreneurial environment; it grew organically out of a student body, alumni network and faculty who embraced the idea of starting new ventures as a viable alternative to finding a job or engaging in a more traditional profession. Some of the prominent businesses started by USC alumni include Qualcomm, Colony Capital, California Pizza Kitchen, PMI Mortgage Insurance, Vizio, and Public Storage. Since the 1960s, the Greif Center has served as the focal point and impetus for entrepreneurship at the university; and the success of its efforts is reflected in the number of name-brand companies its students have created – Salesforce, Kinko's, Tinder, Telesign, and Box, to name a few – and in the number of entrepreneurial initiatives that now blanket both campuses of the university. Over the years, as the environment for startups has changed in response to economic conditions and the emergence of new technologies, USC has met the challenge with the faculty and resources required to ensure that our students are prepared to be successful entrepreneurs and to lead rapidly growing companies.

NOTE

1. PricewaterhouseCoopers 2015 MoneyTree Report, https://www.pwcmoneytree.com/.

17. Entrepreneurship at Lancaster University

Eleanor Hamilton, Helen Fogg, Sarah L. Jack and Fionnuala Schultz

HISTORY OF OUR ENTREPRENEURSHIP PROVISION

In the 1980s, Lancaster University Management School (LUMS) started teaching entrepreneurship; the first dedicated unit teaching and research-ing entrepreneurship was established in 1999. This became the Institute for Entrepreneurship and Enterprise Development (IEED), which was founded in 2003 and gained departmental status in 2008. In 2014, the department re-launched the Centre for Family Business with the involvement of inter-nationally distinguished scholars and practitioners. The latest development has been the re-naming of IEED as the Department of Entrepreneurship, Strategy and Innovation (DESI), founded in August 2015. The Sir Roland Smith Centre for Strategic Management was re-positioned within IEED to form DESI.

DESI is well known for producing high quality and engaged research which has been primarily funded through a range of external funding bodies. It is also a department which has achieved high visibility in the global entrepreneurship, strategy and innovation research communities. DESI is increasingly recognized as an international leader for research and education in entrepreneurship and innovation, in partnership with business and the community.

Today DESI consists of 22 full-time academics, three distinguished scholars, 23 honorary scholars, 10 members of staff working in business engagement and 21 Ph.D. students.

CURRICULUM

At every level of learning and teaching, from undergraduate to Ph.D. research, the Department strives to improve the student learning experience and provide transferable skills. It encourages direct involvement with businesses and the acquisition of work-based experience. This shapes the programs we run within DESI and the service teaching we do on the LUMS consortial programs.

Undergraduate Studies

The Department runs a three-year Bachelor degree in Management and Entrepreneurship as well as a four-year Bachelor degree in Management and Entrepreneurship which includes a one-year industry placement.

Employers want graduates who are able to act entrepreneurially, evaluate new ideas and understand the challenges of taking ideas to market. In our degree programs, we do this by immersing students in a network of world class academics and entrepreneurs-in-residence.

What does it mean to be an entrepreneur? Throughout the degree students will be challenged to explore this question in different contexts and from different world views to develop their skills and extend their knowledge.

Small- and medium-sized enterprises (SMEs) are often the most innovative and entrepreneurial. We use this context as an important foundation for understanding how entrepreneurship comes about. It also provides an important foundation for exploring entrepreneurship within other contexts, such as large global organizations, family businesses, social enterprises and franchises. These different contexts for entrepreneurship challenge students to develop new skills and knowledge, in a way which is underpinned by an evolving entrepreneurial and innovative mindset.

With over 50 entrepreneurs-in-residence, alongside our world-class researchers, we ensure that the integration of theory and practice is embedded in the program. Learning throughout our degree programs comes from more than lectures. Enacted, observational and situated learning styles are used to help build a deeper understanding of theory and how theory works (or does not work) in practice. Throughout the degree, students engage with the business community, visit practitioners and learn from their experiences. The four-year degree provides an opportunity for students to spend a year on industrial placement. During this year the emphasis is on the practical application and evaluation of theories and concepts learned on the program. This gives our students unique insights that will underpin the final year of their studies, provide students with skills and knowledge that are valued by potential employers, and provide experience for future business ventures.

In addition to our degrees, the Department is at the cutting edge of engagement with the business community on a national and international stage. In many ways, this is crucial to supporting what we are able to offer students during their studies. These business engagement activities provide invaluable opportunities. Students also have the option to study abroad in the second year in top universities around the world.

A new Bioscience with Entrepreneurship Bachelor program will be running from autumn 2016. This degree is aimed at students with an interest in a range of bioscience topics but who are also looking to understand the challenges of entrepreneurship and innovation. The degree is situated in the Faculty of Health and Medicine within Lancaster University.

Postgraduate Studies

There are two Master's programs dedicated to entrepreneurship: the MSc in Entrepreneurship, Innovation and Practice and the MSc in International Innovation (Entrepreneurship). DESI also runs two further Master's programs which have a focus on strategy.

The MSc in Entrepreneurship, Innovation and Practice is a yearlong Master's program. Along the way, students study entrepreneurship and how it works in practice, corporate entrepreneurship, family enterprise, innovation in practice, new venture creation and strategic management. This exciting Master's program, through its strong focus on the practical application of theory, equips able business and non-business graduates with the knowledge and skills they will need to be more innovative and enterprising in their future careers.

The program emphasizes theoretical rigor and practical learning. It benefits from the academic excellence and broad business networks provided by DESI. Several modules draw on our entrepreneurs-in-residence program.

The program is designed for students who want to start their own business, work as an "intrapreneur" and be an innovator in an existing company, take over a family business, or work in entrepreneurship and innovation-related fields (e.g., consulting, public support programmers). The program is designed for both business graduates and graduates from other disciplines with some work experience or a family business background.

The MSc in International Innovation (Entrepreneurship) is a unique program which offers a ground-breaking curriculum, blending academic studies and company projects with UK and Chinese business and cultural experiences. Students receive a tax-free bursary (tuition fees still apply), and students can join one of six specialist pathways including entrepreneurship. Through this program, students gain in-depth studies in entrepreneurship and also foundation-level studies in design and technology. Students will also be able to study Chinese language and culture (or equivalent for Chinese speakers) and undertake two substantial collaborative projects, one with a UK business and one with a business based in China. Throughout their studies, students study corporate entrepreneurship, design-driven innovation, family enterprise management, innovation in practice and new venture creation.

The European Master in Management is delivered in partnership with EMLYON Business School and Ludwig Maximilian University of Munich (LMU). It is co-designed around the MSc in Management and the MSc in Entrepreneurship Innovation and Practice (EIP). The program is a two-year general management master based in France, Germany and the United Kingdom.

The International Business and Strategy MSc combines the global perspective of international business with the up-to-date strategic thinking required to develop and defend competitive advantage and implement effective organizational designs. Students examine contemporary issues and developments in many different areas of international business and strategy, from market entry, mergers and acquisitions, global trade and exchange rates to leadership in cross-cultural settings. A feature of the program is its recognition of the influence of political, historical and cultural factors on international business issues. Overall, the program gives a strong interdisciplinary grounding in all aspects of international business and strategy.

Ph.D. program
Within the Department there is also a vibrant and thriving Ph.D. community, which is an integral part of the departmental research environment. Ph.D. students are invited to engage across the breadth of departmental activities and are given the space and support to develop their interests. They not only have access to experienced staff and resources in the University but also are often invited to contribute to programs of research within the Department. Currently DESI hosts 21 Ph.D. students.

RESEARCH

Research activities within the Department of Entrepreneurship, Strategy and Innovation focus around three main themes:

- entrepreneurship, with specialisms in entrepreneurial learning, family business, enterprise policy and regional development, networks, and small- and medium-sized businesses;
- strategy, with specialisms in a strategy-as-practice perspective that foregrounds the work of strategy actors, strategy process and micro-level aspects of strategy in various contexts;
- innovation, with a focus on innovation as social process and social practice.

DESI is one of the leading centers for research in entrepreneurship, ranked number seven in the world by a recent Elsevier publications and citations analysis, and ranked second in the UK after London Business School. The Department houses a very strong business engagement group that offers a distinctive link to practice, and it is also the home of two leading research centers, the Sir Roland Smith Centre for Strategic Management and the Centre for Family Business. In September 2015 *Family Capital*, an influential practice-oriented journal, listed LUMS among the top 25 in the world for family business. Strategy-as-practice forms a unifying theme for the Sir Roland Smith Centre for Strategic Management. It encompasses both the formulation of strategy and how strategies are put into action to deliver strategic renewal and change.

The co-location of the different research interests and the business engagement activities offers opportunities for high quality research which supports, and is supported by, research-led business engagement, ensuring an impactful and distinctive research profile strongly linked to practice.

AWARDS AND RECOGNITION

- In February 2016 the Wave 2 Growth Hub (W2GH) program was one of 30 innovations picked out at the Deans Conference of the AACSB International (the global accrediting body and member-ship association for business schools) following the Association's "Innovations That Inspire" initiative.
- The Academy of Management Practice Theme Committee Research Centre has further awarded the Wave 2 Growth Hub program with the 2015 Impact Runner-up Award.
- Small Business Charter Gold Award: DESI played a leading role in LUMS achieving Gold Status in the Small Business Charter initiative in 2014.
- LUMS in conjunction with the Greater Manchester Chamber of Commerce was recognized in 2013 by the judging panel in a special

Network Partnership category for the LEAD (see below) program's impact on SMEs.

- DESI won an inaugural national award from the Economic and Social Research Council (ESRC) for its Outstanding Impact in Business in 2014.
- In November 2012 LUMS was named as Business School of the Year at the Times Higher Education awards, and was commended for its "demonstrable, consistent and considerable impact locally, regionally, nationally and internationally." A particular focus of the submission was the work undertaken by LUMS with SMEs.
- North and Western Lancashire Chamber of Commerce invited DESI to provide research to underpin the categories in their annual business awards – the BIBAs. In 2014 Professor Ellie Hamilton was the head judge, and LUMS was also a headline sponsor. This initiative received substantial PR.

ENGAGEMENT ACTIVITY AND PROGRAMS FOR SME

DESI's business engagement strategy is integral to its research and teaching strategies. It is informed by and informs research, maximizes opportunities to expand and diversify income including research income, delivers impact, enhances student recruitment, experience and employability, and contributes to policy.

Entrepreneurs-in-residence (EiR)

In 2008 Ian Gordon became IEED's founding "EiR," funded by the ESRC. His remit was to act as a "cultural irritant," challenging assumptions and informing SME program delivery. Lancaster University's experience is summarized in "What Is (the Point of) an Entrepreneur-in-residence?" (George et al., 2010). Spring 2012 saw the induction of 29 EIRs who are active across our teaching and business engagement, making diverse contributions as ambassadors and advocates. This suite of activity demonstrates our sustained effort to engage practitioners in the co-design and delivery of business support. In 2016 we increased the number of EIRs to 54, and aim to continue to grow this number and also invite key international stakeholders to join.

Lancashire and Cumbria Growth

The program involves the establishment of a "forum" – a facilitated network for a select group of successful and aspirational SMEs to come together and cross-fertilize ideas and opportunities and further be directed towards wider Lancaster University business engagement programs across the faculties.

The Lancashire Forum is part of Boost Business Lancashire, the Lancashire Business Growth Hub. This program is a peer network and business masterclass program designed for SME owner-managers. The Forum, designed to inspire and foster a culture which supports and brings together ambitious growth businesses, supports 80 SMEs. This model has been extremely successful, and we plan to roll out this program across other counties throughout the Northwest of England.

Aspiring Business in Cumbria (ABC) was an innovative six-month program that drew upon the integrated learning model developed through the LEAD program. The ABC program gives owner-managers the opportunity to engage with likeminded businesses, Lancaster University and its associates. This provides support to 50 SMEs.

Berkeley Innovation Forum (BIF)

In 2012 LUMS was invited to join the Berkeley Innovation Forum. BIF is an exclusive membership group consisting of carefully selected corporate directors who are deeply involved in managing innovation within their company. We remain the only university in a unique global network of Fortune 100 companies, led by Henry Chesbrough. This has informed the development of programs that link small and large organizations, both public and private.

Regional Growth Fund – Wave 2 Growth Hub Program

The W2GH program, led by Lancaster University in conjunction with Business, Innovation and Skills and Cities Policy Unit, Cabinet Office and funded by £32 million from the Regional Growth Fund, supported the launch of 15 growth hubs across the UK to promote economic growth. LUMS managed funds disbursed across 16 English city regions. The program started in 2013 and was finished in 2015. Research is still being produced on the W2GH program.

The program created a national network of local networks. Through dedicated events and digital networking tools the hubs regularly came together to share experiences, ideas and challenges. There were 17 Local Enterprise

Partnerships, 19 chambers of commerce and 42 universities throughout England directly involved in the delivery of the program and a wider network of public and private partners delivering a range of business support from face-to-face advice through to investments and grant schemes – making this a hugely complex set of local partnerships. The W2GH program linked up the local and national levels of business support by creating a constructive dialogue and partnership between the various levels, reducing duplication and confusion in the landscape. By bringing all the partners at different levels around the table with a neutral broker – the university – national and local support gained a better understanding of what each had to offer, and how to link up their provisions to ensure the best service for businesses. The Lancaster W2GH program accelerated the availability of responsive and accessible business support across the country and created powerful networks of locally based organizations that had the opportunity to learn about what worked best for business growth and job creation.

- The program was worth approximately £100 million in allocated funding and regional private sector match.
- The number of jobs created was over 2500 by the end of the program.
- Over 18 000 SMEs have been engaged through the growth hubs.
- Over 1400 SMEs have received over five hours' business support or grants in excess of £1000.
- There were 361 contracts with SMEs to the value of £16.5 million:
    - £11.3 million private sector match;
    - £5.2 million Regional Growth Fund.

LEAD

LEAD is a 10-month leadership and management development intervention for SME owner-managers, which was developed in 2003. Participants cover all business sectors and demonstrate strong growth. The LEAD program has grown from provision within one English region to a model increasingly and widely promoted by other providers nationally, thereby demonstrating the transferability of the integrated learning model it deploys. In 2014, DESI launched LEAD 2 Innovate. This program leverages LEAD principles towards innovation outcomes and recognizes the particular challenges facing SME owner-managers attempting to innovate successfully while maintaining sustainable core businesses. Participants make a significant contribution to the cost of this program, via fees.

REFERENCE

George, M., Gordon, I. and Hamilton, E., (2010), What is (the point of) an entrepreneur-in-residence? *Industry and Higher Education*, 24(6) (December), 495–503.

18. Baylor University: entrepreneurship for everyone through innovative programming

Kendall Artz

EDUCATIONAL OBJECTIVES

Baylor University began offering a major in entrepreneurship in 1977 and was one of the first schools to provide its students a formal entrepreneurship education. In the years since, the breadth and depth of our entrepreneurship research and teaching capabilities have expanded dramatically. Today, multiple degrees exist at the undergraduate, graduate and doctoral levels, and virtually all students on campus have the ability to obtain an entrepreneurship degree. This ability to provide an entrepreneurship education to everyone is a result of a long term commitment to innovative programming that has resulted in a wide range of unique and impactful programs that are applicable to a large and diverse group of students.

We also believe it very important to our success that, despite the vast changes that have occurred since the program was created, our two core objectives have remained constant, that is, to foster the entrepreneurial spirit in all students by providing them the skills needed to create profitable entrepreneurial companies while simultaneously encouraging them to reflect on the core values and ethics that are necessary for building a meaningful life.

We achieve the first objective by immersing our students in a comprehensive and demanding education that begins when students first arrive on campus and continues after their graduation. Based on the belief that the best way to learn entrepreneurship is by actually being an entrepreneur, all courses offered have a large experiential component. We are committed to providing our students the resources needed to support their ventures immediately upon their arrival at Baylor. As they continue through the program, the extent and sophistication of resources available to the students increase.

Our second primary objective is fundamental to our mission as a

Christian university. We believe that entrepreneurial pursuits are a reflection of an individual's purpose. Therefore, offering an education that simply provides students with the tools needed to be a successful entrepreneur is not enough. We believe that our student-entrepreneurs are most inspired by serving a higher purpose – not simply making more money. To that end, we provide our students guidance and encouragement to consider their core values and beliefs, to examine their life and work in relation to the larger society in which we live, and to reflect on their responsibilities to that world. This focus on helping develop the whole student has proven to be an attractive component of our education.

HISTORY

Building a comprehensive entrepreneurship program takes time: time to build momentum, acquire administrative support, create a curriculum and staff organizational units, acquire funding, develop partnerships, and build a culture attractive to faculty, staff and students. At Baylor, this process has taken nearly four decades, with each decade marked by some particularly notable milestones. In the 1980s, the entrepreneurship area was raised to department status, with the creation of the Management and Entrepreneurship Department. The Center for Entrepreneurship, one of the first of its kind, was created in 1983, and later endowed by the John F. Baugh Family, and in 1985 the Institute for Family Business was launched to promote research and teaching in family business. Importantly, six endowed entrepreneurship chair positions were funded during the 1980s, which allowed Baylor to attract numerous high-profile faculty members.

In the 1990s, Baylor began to expand globally, with programs and partnerships developed in Europe and Central America. The curriculum at the undergraduate and graduate level was greatly expanded so that students could specialize in one of six areas: family business, technology entrepreneurship, social entrepreneurship, franchising, corporate entrepreneurship or international entrepreneurship.

From 2000 to 2010, Baylor added global programs in Africa and China, created multiple joint graduate and undergraduate programs with other schools across campus, launched the Technology Entrepreneurship Initiative and the Baylor Angel Network in 2007, and opened the Entrepreneurship Living and Learning Center in 2008. Since 2010, the 21-acre research complex, the Baylor Research and Innovation Collaborative, was opened, the Center for Entrepreneurship and Free Enterprise was created in 2012, Entrepreneurship became a stand-alone department in 2013, and in 2015 the Ph.D. program in Entrepreneurship was launched. Currently, the Department of Entrepreneurship employs over 25 full-time faculty and staff and offers a wide range of courses to its students at all levels. Baylor is consistently ranked among the top entrepreneurship education programs in the world.

CURRICULUM – OPPORTUNITY TO ACTION

Innovativeness in curriculum and teaching methods has long been an emphasis at Baylor. Our faculty has developed a unique curriculum where students are challenged to learn effective techniques for 1) developing ideas for new products or services, 2) evaluating whether those ideas represent an actual business opportunity, and 3) assimilating the actions required to turn the opportunity into a successful business. We base our teaching philosophy on the fundamental idea that entrepreneurship is a vision-driven process whereby students form mental images of "what could be" and then act to make those dreams a reality.

We name our curriculum "Opportunity to Action" because students' visions are centered on identifying or creating circumstances where new products, services or business models can be profitably introduced to one or more markets. Recognizing that this is an inherently uncertain endeavor, we use the latest advances in entrepreneurship research to develop a set of best practices regarding ways to think creatively, evaluate the attractiveness of an opportunity and effectively pursue the opportunity via the launch of a new venture.

At the heart of the curriculum is learning from experience. Baylor professors share their combined years of experience starting and running businesses with their students. Mentoring from practicing entrepreneurs is an integral part of the program as successful entrepreneurs share their journey and wisdom with students. Perhaps more critically, students engage in a variety of curricular and co-curricular experiential activities designed to stimulate ideas, scrutinize them with colleagues, and research their feasibility by getting out in the field and talking to potential customers and suppliers. Through these experiences students learn that entrepreneurship is a set of interdependent decisions, and by engaging in research, experimentation and iteration the decision path becomes much clearer.

The Opportunity to Action framework is at the core of all of our undergraduate and graduate experiences. As students' progress through the curriculum these experiences focus attention on various aspects of opportunities and actions that are critical for success.

Undergraduate Entrepreneurship

Students in the Hankamer School of Business can declare a major in entrepreneurship, while students in other areas of study across campus can pursue an 18-hour entrepreneurship minor or participate in one of our entrepreneurship certificate programs. All entrepreneurship majors are required to take three courses, Entrepreneurial Process, Entrepreneurial Finance and Entrepreneurial Leadership. These three courses build upon each other and are organized to be consistent with the Opportunity to Action framework. The skills the students first learn, such as the theory and practice of opportunity identification, feasibility analysis, concept validation and IP protection, prepare them to proceed into building revenue, expense and cash flow projections, acquiring outside capital and valuing their firms. This knowledge then leads into how to manage growing firms, promoting ethical business practices and leading with integrity.

Graduate Entrepreneurship

The graduate level entrepreneurship program consists primarily of an entrepreneurship track for master's level students, and our most recent curriculum addition, a Ph.D. program in entrepreneurship. The master's program allows students to follow the Opportunity to Action framework through a number of innovative courses that lead them through the new venture creation process. This includes a sequence of team-taught courses with engineering students that focus on technology and corporate entrepreneurship.

Our new Ph.D. program makes Baylor one of only a handful of schools in the United States to offer a doctoral degree in entrepreneurship. It builds on Baylor's long-standing tradition as a leader in entrepreneurship and equips students with the skills to conduct rigorous research that advances the discipline, eventually launching high-impact careers as faculty members at leading research-oriented universities. Faculty members in this area work with the students to help them develop deep knowledge of the field of entrepreneurship and appreciation for theory, research methodology and the publication process. The program also emphasizes excellence in teaching and does so in a way that is consistent with Christian principles of stewardship as students take part in a phased mentorship plan that builds teaching skills.

INNOVATIVE CURRICULAR AND CO-CURRICULAR PROGRAMS

While a strong core curriculum is at the heart of the Baylor education, great emphasis is also placed on developing innovative curricular and co-curricular programs to meet the needs of our diverse students. This includes four global programs that are led by entrepreneurship faculty.

Curricular Programs

- *Accelerated Ventures*. Open to all majors across campus, Accelerated Ventures is an innovative and real-world two-semester course that combines startup education and execution. Led by two practicing entrepreneurs, students learn the foundational principles needed to spot an opportunity, assemble a functional team, and execute on a high-potential venture. As a complement to traditional education, the program allows student teams to execute and test the ideas they learn in the classroom while surrounded by a team of mentors. Each student venture has $5000 in seed capital as well as a semester-long pairing with a seasoned entrepreneur to mentor the firm on the path to success.
- *Baylor Angel Network Analyst Program*. The Baylor Angel Network (BAN) offers undergraduate students a two-semester internship program with extensive involvement in the operations and management of the Baylor Angel Network. Student interns – BAN analysts – are responsible for most aspects of BAN, including analyzing potential deals, presenting analyses to the BAN screening committee, sourcing deals through online portals, and organizing and conducting company presentation meetings. To date, dozens of BAN student analysts have completed the program and launched their careers in a variety of fields such as entrepreneurship, investment banking and private equity.
- *Quantum Leap*. Developed and taught by Gary Keller, co-founder and chairman of the board for Keller Williams Realty International, the Quantum Leap program focuses on helping entrepreneurship students from across campus pursue personal achievement through intentional development of ethics-based goal planning and discipline habits. Believing and teaching that the foundation of a life of purpose comes from clear missions, visions, values, beliefs and perspective (MVVBP), Keller explains the six key disciplines that help a person achieve a purposeful life.

- *McLane Teammates Scholar Program.* Led by entrepreneurship faculty members, McLane Scholars is a highly selective one-semester group that reads and discusses classic and contemporary works in political economy related to entrepreneurship, economic freedom and social progress. McLane Scholars draws some of the brightest students at Baylor with diverse political and academic backgrounds to discuss key topics in society today.
- *Venture Fellows.* Open to graduate entrepreneurship students only, Venture Fellows is a unique two-semester program that provides hands-on experience working in a venture capital firm. Students evaluate business plans for potential investment, conduct market research and provide feedback to entrepreneurs.
- *Technology Entrepreneurship Initiative (TEI).* Led by a cross-functional faculty team and board of advisors from the Schools of Business, Engineering and Law, TEI cultivates cross-campus collaborations and global partnerships. All courses in the sequence are team taught, and designed to develop science and technology insight, business expertise and global cultural competency in both graduate and undergraduate participants.

Global Curricular Entrepreneurship Programs

The Department of Entrepreneurship is home to four for-credit international programs. While all have a common goal of helping students understand the unique cultures and entrepreneurial environments in the particular region, each has a significantly different structure and emphasis.

- *Social Entrepreneurship in Africa.* In a two-week program open to all majors, students spend 15 days in Rwanda with a focus on developmental entrepreneurship and business as a mission. Students experience the challenges faced by entrepreneurs in developing countries. They use their entrepreneurial skills to formulate innovative responses to economic and social problems in Rwanda in particular and Africa in general by conducting research to help local microfinance operations and providing entrepreneurship training to Rwandan students.
- *Technology Entrepreneurship in Asia.* In a six-week program, Baylor students team with Chinese students with a technical and business background to work on the innovation development process of actual ventures in China. Working on a team technology project for a partnering inventor or corporation, students help them validate and communicate their technology-based ventures.

- *Entrepreneurship in Latin America.* In a two-week program open to all majors, students learn from local entrepreneurs and other experts who cover local and global problems, including details of recent trade agreements, the role of environmental entrepreneurship and other important economic, political and cultural issues. Recent host countries include Cuba, the Dominican Republic and Costa Rica.
- *Baylor Entrepreneurship in Europe.* In a five-week program for business majors, traveling to 10 cities and seven countries, students work with local entrepreneurs and executives, visit dynamic organizations and are briefed at leading international organizations, while building a business plan focused on starting a global new venture.

Co-curricular Programs

- *Baylor Angel Network.* The BAN has been part of the Baylor Entrepreneurship Department since 2008. It facilitates the engagement of angel investors and early stage companies while providing real-world, hands-on educational opportunities for students. Today's nearly 60 BAN members recognize the benefits of supporting our students and the entrepreneurial community and have invested over $10 million in new ventures. Baylor Entrepreneurship receives an investor-designated portion of the profits from the angel members' investments upon exit. Since its inception, BAN has grown into a platform that engages and impacts multiple stakeholders both inside and outside Baylor, including alumni, industry, students, multiple schools across campus, and the entrepreneurial community at large.
- *Entrepreneurship Living–Learning Center.* Available to all majors and age groups, the Entrepreneurship Living–Learning Center was established in 2008 as a state-of-the-art residential facility to provide an apartment-style living environment for entrepreneurially minded students from all majors and age groups. Students may enter this facility as freshmen and continue to call it home until graduation. Students engage in a wide range of activities to prepare them to be successful entrepreneurs and to live a service-oriented life, including creating businesses, hosting speakers, and leading service activities that benefit the University and the local community.
- *Baugh Center for Entrepreneurship and Free Enterprise.* The Baugh Center's original intent was to support entrepreneurial research and education and to build ties with the larger entrepreneur community. In 2013, its role was expanded to include a focus on conducting and disseminating free enterprise research with the objective of becoming a national leader in research, teaching and outreach at the

intersection of entrepreneurship and public policy. Today, Baugh Center faculty and staff lead a wide range of activities that support entrepreneurship education and research

- *Institute for Family Business.* The Institute for Family Business promotes the tenets of Firm–Family–Faith on a global scale through transformational education, rigorous scholarship, and Christian engagement between family-owned businesses and Baylor. Its contributions have resulted in Baylor being nationally recognized in the family business field for nearly 30 years. Its flagship program, the Texas Family Business of the Year Awards, is in its 26th consecutive year of honoring the best family-owned businesses in the state of Texas.

- *New Venture Competition.* The Baylor New Venture Competition is our flagship business plan competition. In 2016, over $150 000 in cash was awarded to student entrepreneurs to support the pursuit of their entrepreneurial dreams. The competition process involves several rounds of elimination, and the finalists are evaluated by a panel of expert judges during a two-day event hosted on the Baylor University campus. A large roster of judges and other volunteers provides competitors with feedback, mentorship and coaching during each stage of the competition process.

- *LAUNCH* is housed at the Baylor Research and Innovation Collaborative (BRIC). It serves Baylor researchers and students who need help commercializing their inventions, and members of the Waco and surrounding community who need the same assistance. LAUNCH provides coaching and training for innovators, hosts networking opportunities, and makes available the commercialization tools and processes inside BRIC to startups. Baylor students join LAUNCH as interns and play a vital role by conducting market research and social media strategy development, and creating product videos for incubating firms.

- *Trep Expo* Trep Expo is a partnership between Baylor Entrepreneurship, the Town of Addison, Texas Economic Development group and the Dallas Entrepreneur Center. Trep Expo is a two-day entrepreneurship education conference held annually at the Treehouse in Addison. Startups and early stage companies are provided informational seminars on topical issues such as intellectual property, crowdfunding, marketing for startups, online market optimization and raising capital. Companies are also provided opportunities for quick pitches to potential investors and networking time with successful serial entrepreneurs and funding strategists.

CONCLUSION

The entrepreneurial culture is deeply ingrained throughout Baylor University. Much has been accomplished in terms of developing impactful educational programs, and hundreds of successful businesses have been launched by our students. The rapidly evolving climate in entrepreneurial education means that many more innovative programs will need to be developed to keep pace with the changing needs of all students who seek to pursue an entrepreneurial life. While these challenges are very real, we are confident the educational philosophy of Baylor faculty and staff, which emphasizes innovative programming and attention to helping our students find their place in the larger world, will allow Baylor to remain a leader in entrepreneurship education.

19. Entrepreneurship education at the University of Maryland

Elana Fine

The Dingman Center for Entrepreneurship at the University of Maryland ranks among the nation's preeminent institutions of higher education in which research, education, and the practice of entrepreneurship are pursued vigorously. The Center develops and executes curricular and co-curricular programs that uniquely leverage the Smith Business School's thought leadership, experiential learning, and broad network of practitioners to provide maximum resources to our startup community. Every Dingman initiative is designed to support the Center's mission: to build within the Smith School of Business a community that discovers, equips, connects and celebrates entrepreneurs.

The Dingman Center is a vital organization at the Robert H. Smith School of Business, an internationally recognized leader in management education and research. One of 12 colleges and schools at the University of Maryland, College Park, the Smith School offers undergraduate programs, full-time, part-time, online and executive MBAs, specialty master's programs, Ph.D.s, and executive education programs, as well as outreach services to the corporate community. The Smith School of Business has been recently ranked:

- No. 7 executive MBA program, U.S. (*Financial Times*, 2015);
- No. 11 Ph.D. program, world (*Financial Times*, 2014);
- No. 22 undergraduate program, U.S. (*U.S. News and Report*, 2015);
- No. 22 part-time MBA program, U.S. (*U.S. News and Report*, 2014);
- No. 24 full-time MBA program, U.S. (*Financial Times*, 2015);
- No. 24 research, world (*Financial Times*, 2014).

BACKGROUND AND HISTORY

"It takes entrepreneurs to instill an entrepreneurial culture," says academic and business entrepreneur and the founder of the Dingman Center,

Dr. Rudy Lamone. In 1986, when Lamone set out to establish an entrepreneurial support center for the Smith Business School, he found a willing partner in Michael D. Dingman, founder of the Signal Corporation, now part of Honeywell International. With a generous grant from Mr. Dingman, the Dingman Center emerged as a top-ranked entrepreneurship center owing to the efforts of Dr. Lamone and future directors Charles Heller (1990–1999) and Don Spero (2000–2004).

In the 1980s, Dr. Lamone lamented the criticism that business schools "did little to fan the spark of entrepreneurship." As Dean of Maryland's business school, Dr. Lamone was concerned that entrepreneurship, new venture management, and issues related to emerging growth companies were absent from the school's courses and programs. Business and political leaders also urged the university to provide an environment to stimulate entrepreneurial spirit and activities.

Demonstrating his own commitment to creativity and innovation in business, Michael Dingman responded with significant seed funding for the development of new courses and programs in entrepreneurship for both undergraduate and graduate students at Maryland. Furthermore, Dingman funding supported a team of experts in management, finance, marketing and accounting to prepare and assist entrepreneurs in the Baltimore–Washington corridor and beyond in starting up and expanding companies with high growth potential.

University of Maryland, College Park is located within the Baltimore–Washington corridor, a major international hub of business activity, representing the fourth-largest market area in the nation. Just eight miles from the White House and downtown Washington, D.C., the Smith School is wired to the circuitry of government, corporate and international power. The region is rich in unparalleled professional opportunity, smart people, jobs, and diverse cultural and recreational resources. The campus is easily accessible to agencies of the federal government and information, biotech and defense technology, and highly ranked Fortune 500 companies such as Fannie Mae, Lockheed Martin Corporation, General Dynamics, SAIC, Freddie Mac, Northrop Grumman, Capital One Financial, and Marriott International. The Washington metropolitan area is the most educated and, by some measures, the most affluent metropolitan area in the United States. As of the 2014 U.S. Census Bureau estimate, the population of the Washington metropolitan area was estimated to be 6 033 737, making it the seventh-largest metropolitan area in the country.

Not surprisingly, the Baltimore–Washington corridor has generated a vibrant startup community with business incubators such as ETC, Bethesda Green, Betamore, and the Technology Development Corporation (TEDCO). Betamore, for example, is a co-working space, incubator, and campus for technology and entrepreneurship that aligns businesses, government, not-for-profit entities, and centers of education with entrepreneurs who drive creative commercialization. TEDCO was created by the Maryland State Legislature in 1998 to facilitate the transfer and commercialization of technology from Maryland's research universities and federal labs into the marketplace, and also to assist in the creation and growth of technology-based businesses in all regions of the State.

The District of Columbia startup scene offers major networking events and meetups, access to venture capital, companies, competitions, blogs, programs, and organizations that strengthen and promote entrepreneurism. One example, 1776, an international business incubator, connects startups in regulated fields, such as education, energy, healthcare and government, with resources in the Washington metropolitan area. Membership is granted through an application process that selects startups with high growth potential; as of February 2014, 1776 had over 200 member companies.

LEVERAGING THE REGION

The Dingman Center capitalizes on and maximizes the many assets and resources of the Baltimore–Washington corridor to enrich entrepreneurism for Maryland students, alumni, community members and the economy. Two key offerings, the Dingman Center Angels and Student Fellowships, are prime examples of regional programming.

Dingman Center Angels (DCA)

Dingman Center Angels, a Maryland-based angel investment group, provides funding to early-stage companies located within the Mid-Atlantic region. The Dingman Center Angels includes more than 40 entrepreneurs, CXOs, venture capitalists and business leaders who have founded, funded and built world-class companies. Dingman angel investors represent a wide array of industry expertise and, in association with the Dingman Center of Entrepreneurship, create an extensive entrepreneurial community. Angels look for innovative, technology-driven startup companies which address a significant market opportunity where their investment and expertise can make a difference. They introduce entrepreneurs to potential investors through presentations at monthly meetings held between September and June.

The group looks to invest $100 000 to $1 000 000 in seed/early-stage companies, and will often syndicate with other angel groups and venture capitalists for deals up to $2 million. The Dingman Center Angels is not a fund and does not invest as a group. Members collaborate on due diligence but make individual investment decisions. Members make their own thorough review of all information, including speaking with representatives of the company. In FY 2015, the group invested $1.4 million in regional companies. The current portfolio of over 50 companies includes several startups, such as Social Tables, Distil Networks, and Zero Fox, that have generated significant traction and venture funding.

Student Fellowship Programs

Hisaoka Fellowship program
The Hisaoka Fellowship is designed for first-year Smith MBA students who are highly interested in entrepreneurial innovation and/or start-ups. The program is a partnership between the Dingman Center for Entrepreneurship and the Office of Career Services. To be selected as a Hisaoka Fellow, students must secure summer internships with venture capital or angel-funded startups and early-stage companies. The Dingman Center provides each Hisaoka Fellow a $5000 stipend to supplement students' summer salaries.

Kathryn Stewart Fellowship program
The Kathryn Stewart Fellowship is designed for undergraduate students who are interested in entrepreneurship and want to intern at a startup. To be selected as a Stewart Fellow, students must secure a summer internship with venture capital or angel-funded startups and early-stage companies. Through this program, startups benefit from increased access to the Smith School's most talented and vibrant students. Meanwhile, students benefit from experience with the challenges of forming and growing new ventures. The Dingman Center provides a stipend of up to $5000 to supplement the salary offered by the startup.

CAMPUS LANDSCAPE AND PROGRAMMING

After 29 years, the entrepreneurial spirit at the University of Maryland is as bright as ever. In its 2014–2015 annual report, *A Connected Community of Remarkable Entrepreneurs*, Dingman Center Managing Director Elana Fine notes that the Center had been recognized for regional, national and international leadership in the field:

- 2006: Dingman Center received the GCEC Enterprise Creation award.

- 2010: Dingman Center received the GCEC Entrepreneurship Teaching and Pedagogical Innovation award.
- 2012: Dingman Center Founder Rudolph P. Lamone was given the Inaugural Legacy award.
- 2013: Dingman Center Managing Director, Elana Fine, was named a "Tech Titan" by *Washingtonian Magazine*, and named in "Power Women in Tech" by *Tech Bisnow* and "50 on Fire" by *InTheCapital*. Fine is also an Academy of Innovation and Entrepreneurship Distinguished Fellow.
- 2014: Nearly 210 students pitched their ideas to entrepreneurs-in-residence, while more than 60 startups were launched by University of Maryland students.
- 2014: The Dingman Center received the NASDAQ Award for Entrepreneurial Excellence at the Global Consortium of Entrepreneurship Centers, in London.
- 2015: The Center's accelerator program, Fearless Founders, was awarded "Outstanding Contribution in Venture Creation" by the Global Consortium of Entrepreneurship Centers.

HIGHLIGHTING TWO OUTSTANDING PROGRAMS FOR STUDENTS

Fearless Founders Accelerator

In October 2013, the Dingman Center launched its signature venture creation program, Fearless Founders, an evidence-based accelerator. Fearless Founders provides student teams with the tools necessary to develop business ideas using Lean Launchpad methodologies. Fearless Founders demystifies the venture creation process by breaking it into three stages: Idea Shell, Hatch, and Terp Startup.

Idea Shell (not-for-credit) and Hatch (for-credit) are both structured courses offered over a semester, while Terp Startup, a summer student incubator, is offered to select student teams which have completed the first two stages of the Accelerator. The Idea Shell and Hatch courses include weekly class meetings plus advising sessions. Terp Startup participants use co-working space at the Dingman Center over the summer and participate in mandatory workshops and optional advising sessions three days per week.

Throughout these stages, teams leverage the customer discovery process to assess and mitigate product, customer and market risk. Successful teams are able to distill key insights from customer interviews, validate or invalidate hypotheses, and refine their business model. Upon completion of each stage, student entrepreneurs present their progress to Dingman Center staff and entrepreneurs-in-residence. During the 2014–2015 school year, Fearless Founders provided student startups at various stages with a total of $65 500 in awards and sponsored grants.

AdVENTURE Challenge: China

This four-credit study abroad course for MBA students includes eight weeks of preparation, during which teams develop business ideas for the Chinese market. The pre-travel study is about developing and presenting new venture business models relevant to the Chinese market. Using the NovoEd platform, cross-national teams are formed to develop a business idea using the business model canvas.

During the in-country portion of the course, Smith students travel to Shanghai, Bengbu and Beijing exploring venture creation and global operations in China's rapidly evolving economy. Throughout the eight-day experience, students earn points as they visit Chinese startups, multinational corporations, venture capital firms, and cultural sites like the Great Wall and the Forbidden City. The trip culminates with a final competition at Peking University's Guanghua School of Management. Students compete for cash prizes alongside peers from Smith, Guanghua and other Chinese business schools, as well as the Technion-Israel Institute of Technology.

Most recently, at the ninth annual China Business Model Competition, 17 Smith MBAs and three Technion MBAs participated in the course, while the final competition featured 49 students on 13 teams. The winning team, StyleStar, developed a personal stylist mobile app.

STUDENT COMPETITIONS AND SEED FUNDING

Seeding student ventures is a hallmark of the Dingman Center. Through generous donor gifts, grants and corporate partnerships, the Center offers students many opportunities to receive seed funding. Competitions are just one of the avenues through which students can secure funding.

Pitch Dingman Competition

The Center's Pitch Dingman Competition is the University of Maryland's only business competition exclusively for University of Maryland students. Held annually, the Pitch Dingman Competition gives students an opportunity to compete for more than $30 000 in startup funding. The competition consists of a fall semifinals and a winter finals competition. Top student entrepreneurs deliver pitches to judges who are experts in entrepreneurship, angel investing and venture capital.

Cupid's Cup

In 2005, the Dingman Center partnered with Kevin Plank, founder and CEO of Under Armour, to launch Cupid's Cup as a business competition for University of Maryland student startups. After seven successful years, in 2013 the Center and Plank expanded Cupid's Cup to the national stage to attract the nation's top student startups. In its inaugural year as a national competition, the Center received more than 50 applications from 25 universities nationwide. The applicants were put through a rigorous semifinal round of judging where six teams were chosen to pitch in the final competition, which awarded $75 000 in cash prizes. In 2015, the competition received over 200 applications from 90 universities nationwide. Six finalists pitched to an all-star panel of judges including: Plank; ABC Shark Tank's Daymond John; Karen Katz, CEO of Neiman Marcus Group; and Mike Lee, CEO and co-founder of MyFitnessPal. In addition to a competition, Cupid's Cup features an Innovation Showcase where startups from throughout the university demonstrate their products and services and conduct customer discovery. More than a thousand attendees came to Cupid's Cup 2015 and left after an impactful experience.

Social Entrepreneurship

In the 2015–2016 academic year, the Dingman Center expanded its portfolio to include social entrepreneurship. Social entrepreneurship is often described as venture creation for the purpose of solving a social problem. The Center is bolstering its programming to include the Do Good Challenge, an annual competition for social ventures held in partnership with the University of Maryland's School of Public Policy, and the Maryland Social Entrepreneurship Corps, a summer internship program to support small business in Latin America. By streamlining resources around one hub of entrepreneurship, the Dingman Center can help students launch traditional and social ventures.

Innovation and Entrepreneurship Minor

In 2013, recognizing the campus-wide interest in entrepreneurship, the Dingman Center began the journey of creating an Entrepreneurship minor. The curriculum development and approval process was headed by former Dingman Center Academic Director Rajshree Agarwal. The Center is aware of the thirst for knowledge in entrepreneurship from students outside of the Smith School from a variety of disciplines. The minor draws on core principles in business and entrepreneurship to give students across multiple majors and programs of study a broad exposure to the fundamentals that they need to excel in an industry. Regardless of whether the student aspires to be an entrepreneur starting a new company, an innovator working in an existing corporation, or a creator of social value, the minor provides any University of Maryland student with a critical advantage in an otherwise crowded marketplace. This knowledge also helps future entrepreneurs and innovators complement their in-depth expertise within their major field of study by building the entrepreneurial mindsets, skills and relationships invaluable to developing innovative, impactful solutions to today's problems.

In fall 2015, the Innovation and Entrepreneurship minor was launched. In addition to the minor, the Smith School offers nearly 40 entrepreneurship courses to undergraduate and graduate students.

CONTRIBUTIONS TO ENTREPRENEURSHIP RESEARCH

One of the strategic missions of the Dingman Center is to bridge the gap between research and practice. Through the Academic Director, Brent Goldfarb, the Center has been working more closely with faculty to support their research and better connect them to our community.

Smith Entrepreneurship Research Conference

Each year, the Dingman Center supports the Smith Entrepreneurship Research Conference (SERC). The conference is an invitation-only gathering of Ph.D. students and professors who perform research on the topic of entrepreneurship. It is an opportunity for researchers across the world (mainly national but several international participants) to exchange ideas about their work. SERC is also supported by the Department of Management and Organization and the Ewing Marion Kauffman Foundation.

Publications

Rajshree Agarwal, Rudolph P. Lamone Chair and Professor in Entrepreneurship
Rajshree Agarwal has published articles in journals such as *Academy of Management Journal*, *American Economic Review*, *International Journal of Industrial Organization*, *Journal of Industrial Economics*, *Journal of Law and Economics*, *Management Science*, *Review of Economics and Statistics* and *Strategic Management Journal*. She is an associate editor of the *Strategic Entrepreneurship Journal* and the editor of the *SSRN Entrepreneurship and Economics Journal*. Agarwal also serves, or has served, on the editorial board of the *Academy of Management Journal*, *Academy of Management Review*, *Strategic Management Journal* and *Strategic Organization*. She has received research grants from the Kauffman Foundation, the Mellon Foundation, the Marketing Science Institute, the National Science Foundation and the U.S. Department of Agriculture.

Anil K. Gupta, Michael D. Dingman Chair in Strategy and Entrepreneurship
Anil Gupta is the coauthor or coeditor of several books: *Getting China and India Right* (Jossey-Bass/John Wiley, February 2009); *The Quest for Global Dominance: Transforming Global Presence into Global Competitive Advantage* (Jossey-Bass/John Wiley, March 2008 and 2001); *Smart Globalization* (Jossey-Bass/John Wiley, 2003); and *Global Strategy and Organization* (John Wiley, 2003). His newest book, *The Silk Road Rediscovered: How Indian and Chinese Companies Become Globally Stronger by Competing in Each Other's Markets* (Wiley, 2014), was published in 2014. Gupta has published over 70 papers, including several in major journals such as *Academy of Management Journal*, *Academy of Management Review*, *Organization Science*, *Sloan Management Review* and *Strategic Management Journal*.

THE FUTURE IS AS BRIGHT AS A GREAT IDEA

The Dingman Center maximizes the resources of a large state university by working in coordination and partnership with other entrepreneurship initiatives, such as: the Maryland Technology Enterprise Institute, a unit of the A. James Clark School of Engineering; the Career Center; and the Academy for Innovation and Entrepreneurship. Under the leadership of President Wallace Loh, the University of Maryland has made a commitment to being a premier innovation and entrepreneurship institution, and has set an explicit goal of broadening innovation and entrepreneurship to all 37 000 University of Maryland students. In support of this initiative, many new programs have been created across campus, including the Entrepreneurship and Innovation Living and Learning Program, the Academy for Innovation and Entrepreneurship, and the Accelerator.

In the Fall 2015 issue of *TERP* magazine, President Loh stated that the university had been "recognized by *The Princeton Review* for our undergraduate entrepreneurship," and "we will turn imagination to innovation by creating coursework and programs to inspire the next great entrepreneurs."

20. Entrepreneurship at Syracuse University

Alexander McKelvie and John M. Torrens

INTRODUCTION

Syracuse University was an early supporter of entrepreneurship education. In 1993, the Dean of the Whitman School of Management, George Burman, initiated a formalized educational program in Entrepreneurship, including a multiyear endowment to support efforts towards establishing a world-class program. With the help of the Board of Trustees and multiple faculty members, most notably Professor David Wilemon, the Whitman School launched its Entrepreneurship program in the 1994–1995 academic year. This subsequently led to the creation of the Department of Entrepreneurship and Emerging Enterprises, one of the few distinct academic departments solely dedicated to entrepreneurship in the country. Combined with the Falcone Center for Entrepreneurship, responsible for outreach efforts, this is referred to as the Entrepreneurship and Emerging Enterprises program (or the EEE program, as it is more widely known).

The University has remained committed to entrepreneurship and has expanded this focus across the entire Syracuse University campus via a Kauffman grant (in 2007) and a Blackstone Foundation grant (in 2015). Entrepreneurship is a topic that is now embraced in almost every school on Syracuse University's campus. Further, Chancellor Kent Syverud has included entrepreneurship among his four pillars, or areas of focus, for the University.

In this chapter, we provide a synopsis of the EEE program, including its structure, education, research and community outreach. However, the main focus will be on three areas where Syracuse University's approach to entrepreneurship truly excels: 1) the high-quality work that is done at the intersection of education–research–outreach; 2) the University's work with military veterans; and 3) the cross-campus commitment to a collaborative approach to student-centered entrepreneurship.

THE ENTREPRENEURSHIP AND EMERGING ENTERPRISES PROGRAM

The EEE program is housed at the Whitman School of Management and is structured to provide excellence in three areas: education, research and outreach. It is the intersection and mutual support of these three areas that help drive overall program quality and objectives. Impacting over 4500 individuals per year, the Entrepreneurship and Emerging Enterprises program includes both the EEE Department and the Falcone Center for Entrepreneurship. The EEE Department is responsible for the academic components of the program, including teaching and research. The Falcone Center manages the outreach efforts, including the on-campus Couri Hatchery, the South Side Innovation Center, the WISE Women's Business Center, and other related programs. In total, the Falcone Center employs over 10 full-time staff members, while the EEE Department has 13 full-time faculty members. Among these are nine research faculty, including three endowed chairs (the Chris J. Witting Chair, the Bantle Chair in Entrepreneurship and Public Policy, and the Al Berg Chair) and a named professorship (the Barnes professorship). There are also four professors of practice, who bring their real-world entrepreneurial experience to the students through the classroom and mentoring efforts. There are also a number of adjunct faculty members, who generally teach one or two courses per year. They are hired based on their industry experience and teaching ability.

The EEE program offers six different educational degrees, instructing over 2250 students per year. The degrees include an undergraduate major and a minor (only for non-management students), a one-year Master's in Entrepreneurship (MSE), a concentration in the on-campus MBA and online MBA@Syracuse programs, a Certificate of Advanced Studies in Sustainable Enterprise (CASSE, in partnership with Syracuse University's College of Engineering and Computer Science and SUNY's school in Environmental Science and Forestry), and a Ph.D. in Entrepreneurship. The educational programs are consistently ranked among the highest in the United States, including top 20 rankings for both undergraduate and graduate education in the *Bloomberg Businessweek, U.S. News and World Report* and *Princeton Review/Inc. Magazine* rankings.

The EEE program has adopted a view of entrepreneurship that is much more expansive than a singular focus on new venture creation; EEE treats entrepreneurship as a mindset and a way of approaching different business and life challenges. This broad view of entrepreneurship is different compared to what many competing entrepreneurship programs offer. As a consequence of this view, EEE course offerings are organized into four individual tracks (New Venture, Corporate Entrepreneurship, Social Entrepreneurship and Family Business Management). These tracks promote students to understand what skillsets are needed in their chosen future entrepreneurial careers; these skillsets subsequently help drive course selection. Each track includes at least two elective courses that help develop the abilities and mindset necessary for success in that chosen area. The teaching philosophy of the EEE program is around experiential learning, and in each of the tracks students work hands-on for their own startup businesses or with local entrepreneurial firms. This hands-on work also provides the opportunity for synergies across the program's education and outreach offerings; students regularly work with companies that are part of the outreach programs run by the Falcone Center.

As one tangible aspect of the Whitman School's commitment to entrepreneurship education, all School of Management seniors, regardless of major, are required to take an entrepreneurship course as their capstone experience. The course uses new venture creation as the means by which students draw upon and integrate their entire undergraduate education. They do this by demonstrating their mastery of how the various business disciplines work together to form a high-potential new venture. The course requires students to develop a novel concept that is scalable and differentiated enough to attract investment capital of at least $100 000 and achieve revenues of at least $3 million in their fifth year of operations. As part of the course, students conduct rigorous market research and validation to establish feasibility. Students then build out their operating model, marketing plan and financial projections, as part of a complete business plan. The course culminates each semester in a high-pressure, high-excitement competition where up to 65 teams per semester compete based on an executive summary, a 15-minute presentation and a 10-minute Q&A session with a panel of judges that consist of C-level executives, bankers, entrepreneurs, investors and faculty. Pool winners advance to a semi-final round of elevator pitches and a final round the following day where both a complete business plan and presentation are evaluated. Students repeatedly express that this is a transformational experience for them and their careers, as they are offered the opportunity to dig deep into markets and industries, and develop real potential ventures. Further, this experience is often singled out by recruiters as providing Whitman students with a unique competitive advantage over their peers from other schools.

In addition, the EEE program is home to many of the academic thought leaders in the world. Among the nine research faculty members are four editors at the most prolific entrepreneurship journals (*Journal of Business Venturing, Strategic Entrepreneurship Journal, Entrepreneurship Theory and Practice* and *Small Business Economics*). Further, EEE faculty members are on the editorial boards of 21 management and entrepreneurship journals. Combined, they publish over 20 scholarly articles per year, and their research has been profiled in the media such as *NPR*, *Wall Street Journal*, *New York Times*, *Bloomberg Businessweek*, *Inc. Magazine* and *Forbes*. The team includes three winners of the National Federation of Independent Business best doctoral dissertation award. Multiple team members have received best paper awards from the leading entrepreneurship conferences. In 2015, two EEE scholars (Professors Tom Lumpkin and Johan Wiklund) received the Greif Research Impact Award for having the most impactful published entrepreneurship study in 2009, as measured by peer citations.

The development of a critical mass of scholars who are dedicated to the study of entrepreneurship – as opposed to management or marketing scholars who dabble in entrepreneurship – has been central to the productivity of the EEE program. Further, the deliberate strategy of hiring the "best scholar," as opposed to a scholar who happens to work in one specific thematic area, has led to the group possessing expertise in almost every area of entrepreneurship research, including at the individual, team, firm and regional levels of analysis. There are a number of other factors that have led to the high level of research productivity. One of these is the Falcone Distinguished Entrepreneurship Scholar Award, given to a prolific scholar every year. Awardees spend a few days in Syracuse working with EEE faculty and Ph.D. students. Recent winners include Dean Shepherd, Saras Sarasvathy, S. Venkataraman, Ian MacMillan and Michael Frese. A second factor is having an active research paper series. This series includes scholars from outside universities who want to visit and present their work and meet with Ph.D. students, as well as in-house researchers seeking developmental feedback as they prepare their work for journal submission. A third factor is that many members of the EEE team co-author papers with each other – as well as with Ph.D. students. This helps to promote productivity by ensuring that there is teamwork across multiple projects and papers, while also ensuring the development of future scholars. Collaborating is also helpful inasmuch as there is a close-at-hand co-author who can help carry workloads, participate in informal conversations and problem-solving, and provide assistance as occasionally required by schedules and workloads. This success and productivity of the EEE research has helped make Syracuse a sought-after destination for faculty and doctoral students from around the world.

The outreach efforts of the EEE program are run through the Falcone Center for Entrepreneurship. Centered on the mindset of Dream > Believe > Pursue, the Falcone Center provides programming and support to help students and community members successfully create and grow new ventures. The Falcone Center offers programs both to students and to the community at large. Central among the student programs is the Couri Hatchery, a student-centered business incubator located in the Whitman School where over 100 startups are currently operating. Among other services, the Couri Hatchery provides professional mentoring, including legal, accounting, HR, sales and marketing, banking, and technology support. In 2014–2015, Couri Hatchery tenants raised over $3 million in external capital. The D'Aniello internship program offers paid and for-credit internships for students at local entrepreneurial firms needing work on a specific project. There are two main student entrepreneurship competitions run through the Falcone Center. The Panasci Business Plan Competition is a campus-wide student business plan competition where over $45 000 in non-equity prize money is awarded to the top teams whose new venture ideas represent the best potential for success. The Orange Tank Competition is held in conjunction with the Homecoming event in the fall semester, where alumni and student entrepreneurs compete for over $30 000 in prizes.

In terms of community-based programming, there is a focus on particular groups of individuals. The Women Igniting the Spirit of Entrepreneurship (WISE) Women's Business Center, located in the Technology Garden in downtown Syracuse, is an initiative to train and inspire women interested in launching or growing a new business. The WISE Women's Business Center serves over 600 women entrepreneurs per year, whose firms reported over a combined $5 million in revenues. Further, the WISE Symposium, founded in 2002, is a one-day event that includes a variety of seminars and panel discussions offering practical advice covering topics from all aspects of the business world. It includes motivational speeches from local and nationally known successful women entrepreneurs, networking opportunities, and a business expo. Approximately 1000 women attend each year. The South Side Innovation Center (SSIC) is a microenterprise incubator located on the South Side of Syracuse. The SSIC provides office space and equipment to foster the creation of new ventures and help existing businesses grow. It is running at full capacity with 27 tenant companies and works with over 350 entrepreneurs and aspiring entrepreneurs per year through its programming. All in all, the EEE program achieves a high-level impact on three main areas: teaching, research and outreach.

COMMITMENT TO MILITARY VETERANS

Syracuse University has a long history, dating back to World War II and then Chancellor William Pearson Tolley, of supporting military veterans. This commitment to military veterans has also translated to entrepreneurship education. In 2007, EEE faculty member Professor Mike Haynie founded the Entrepreneurship Bootcamp for Veterans with Disabilities (EBV). This flagship program is offered to post-9/11 veterans with service related disabilities. EBV is held annually at Syracuse University and has expanded to a large network of other universities around the country as part of a consortium. The training begins with an online component, followed by a one-week intensive on-site experience, and continuing through an expansive network of mentors. The success of the EBV program led to the creation of a similar bootcamp named EBV-F for the family members and primary caregivers of veterans with disabilities. Over 1200 veterans have graduated from EBV universities since 2007, and over 670 new jobs have been created. Currently, the cohort of EBV graduates is responsible for the creation of more than 180 new small businesses.

A further entrepreneurship educational program, focusing specifically on women veterans, was created in 2010. Veteran Women Igniting the Spirit of Entrepreneurship (V-WISE) is a two-day conference, offered up to three times a year in different cities throughout the United States. Each conference hosts up to 200 female veterans. Choosing from concurrent tracks for startup phase and growth phase companies, attendees learn important tools needed to launch and grow their businesses. So far there have been over 2000 graduates of V-WISE, 65 percent of whom report having started or grown their businesses. Collectively, V-WISE graduates have generated over $41 million in revenue, with 20 percent reporting at least $100 000 in annual revenue.

Since that time, other veteran-focused entrepreneurial activities have been initiated. For instance, the Boots2Business (B2B) program is for active duty service members who are within 12 months of transitioning to civilian life. B2B is part of the military's Transition Assistance Program (TAP). This includes a two-day intensive class at military installations in the United States and abroad, as well as an eight-week online course. Service members learn about small business ownership as a vocational option through modules on opportunity recognition, connecting military service to entrepreneurial success, marketing, financing, market research, operations, business planning, and accessing local resources. Participants complete a feasibility analysis of their concept and readiness before the end of the class. More than 30 000 veterans have participated in B2B programming.

In 2011, and based on the success of entrepreneurship education focused on military veterans and their families, Syracuse University created a university-wide institute: the Institute for Veterans and Military Families (IVMF). IVMF is the first national center to focus on social, economic, educational and policy issues related to veterans and their families. It adopts a multi-disciplinary perspective that includes the arts, business, education, law and others and works closely with industry, government and NGOs to help provide policy and educational support for the veteran community.

CROSS-CAMPUS EFFORTS

The entire Syracuse University campus has embraced an entrepreneurial focus. Some of the expansion beyond the Whitman School of Management occurred following the receipt of the multimillion-dollar grant from the Kauffman Foundation in 2007. This grant was directly purposed to expand entrepreneurship education and research to different various areas of campus. There are strong niche programs in multiple schools, including a Center for Digital Media Entrepreneurship at the Newhouse School of Public Communications, the Janklow Arts Leadership Program at the College of Arts and Sciences, courses and activities related to information technology entrepreneurship at the School of Information Studies, innovative programming in design at the College of Visual and Performing Arts, and a Center for Excellence in Environmental and Energy Innovations hosted by the College of Engineering and Computer Science, to name a few.

As the hub of campus-wide entrepreneurship, the EEE Department works collaboratively with other programs and departments to provide students with a variety of high-impact experiential learning opportunities. The Science and Technology Law Center, housed at the College of Law at Syracuse University, was developed by Ted Hagelin in 1990 in recognition of the need for support services related to technology commercialization and technology transfer. The Center offers support to New York State-based entrepreneurs and innovators in terms of offering intellectual property and regulatory landscape overviews. This work is done by Law students, with faculty oversight. In recent years, students from the EEE program have also assisted in this work by providing market and competitive landscape overviews. The Student Sandbox is a summer incubator program located at the Technology Garden in downtown Syracuse. Through relationships with local businesses and colleges, each summer approximately 30 student businesses receive support and mentoring to help launch and grow their companies.

In 2015, Syracuse University received a multiyear grant from the Blackstone Charitable Foundation as part of the Blackstone Launchpad program. The focus of the grant is to help encourage student engagement in entrepreneurship from different parts of the university campus. The grant will also help increase collaboration between Cornell University, New York University, Syracuse University, University at Albany (SUNY) and University at Buffalo (SUNY). The grant money will be used to develop a physical presence in the Bird Library in the heart of the Syracuse University campus, and to hire staff to help mentor student entrepreneurs.

FINAL THOUGHTS

Syracuse University has a vibrant, student-centered entrepreneurial eco-system that positively impacts thousands of individuals every year. This is accomplished by maintaining a focus on world class research, teaching and community outreach. These programs are driven by an entrepreneurial spirit at the University, with frequent and impactful new innovations being launched on a regular basis. Entrepreneurship at Syracuse University is a collaborative effort within and among the EEE Department, the Falcone Center for Entrepreneurship, the Institute for Veterans and Military Families, and other schools and colleges across the campus.

PART III

Best practice innovations inside and outside the classroom

21. Teaching entrepreneurial foresight

Sam Miller

In the entrepreneurship education space, educators are leading the charge to empower our students with the latest and greatest frameworks (i.e., lean and agile). While approaches like the flipped classroom or getting students outside the building are actively reshaping the entrepreneurial landscape for the better, too often the ideas feeding the process are modest incremental innovations. This chapter demonstrates how entrepreneurial foresight can amplify the idea discovery process, enabling students to spot emerging opportunities and pursue breakthrough innovations that others may overlook.

STRETCHING YOUR COGNITIVE PROXIMITY

Discovery of truly transformative ideas is the brass ring for which aspiring founders strive, yet students struggle to find truly novel ideas. As entrepreneurship educators we strive to stretch the imaginations of our students. Unfortunately, the traditional customer discovery process can actually reinforce the incremental innovation trap, as prospective target customers discuss their dissatisfaction with the status quo (e.g., how many Sony Walkman users would have expressed a need for iTunes?). Thus, innovation often gets constrained by the overpowering gravitational pull of the status quo. Our needs and expectations are shaped by what we know, so our idea space gets bounded in close cognitive proximity to the status quo (Gavetti, 2011). Entrepreneurial foresight helps stretch cognitive proximity beyond core innovation to breakthrough ideas that are then fed into the validation process.

Entrepreneurial foresight leads us to aim for turbulence where breakthrough opportunities can be found. Gavetti (2011) posits that there are three opportunity vectors with the potential to uncover cognitively distant opportunities: enabling technologies, shifting user preferences (think of the emerging perspective regarding asset ownership with millennials, or the desire of baby boomers to start a new career), and societal challenges or constraints (climate change or poverty, for example).

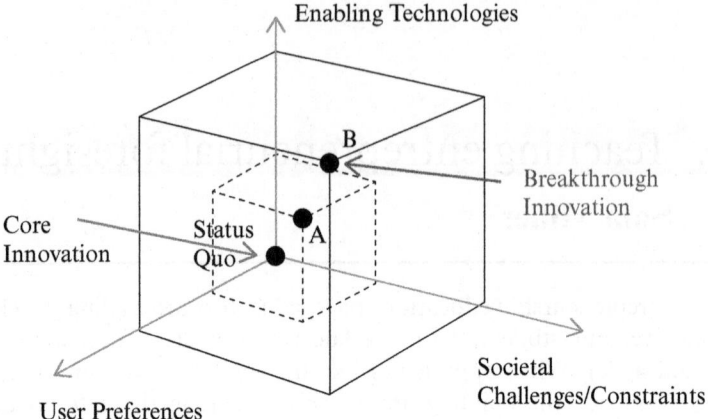

Figure 21.1   Three vectors for uncovering opportunity

Entrepreneurial foresight can enable innovators to stretch their minds and envision a wide range of new and surprising ideas to fill the innovation pipeline with ideas that break the grip of the status quo. The proposed pathway towards these entrepreneurial insights is as follows.

Frame Your Exploration

Framing is an actionable framework that can focus and accelerate the idea generation process. The challenge is to sharpen the focus to enable the entrepreneurs to craft a deeper understanding of what may come next in a particular opportunity space. The framing process begins with one identifying oneself as entrepreneurial, and in this regard I build on identity theory (see Chapter 29 by Duening and Metzger for a full discussion of identity theory). Once this entrepreneurial identity is established, the quest for novel ideas begins. In this space, I have developed a framework I call the "Wheelhouse Assessment." This simple three-step model can help aspiring founders gain a meaningful understanding of how they should focus their exploration:

1. Understand their passion. This is the "Why?" aspect of entrepreneurship. The best way to describe the passion is to challenge the students to define their strategic intent – how do they want to change the world?
2. Assess their core competencies. What are the skills and capabilities that the entrepreneur can put in play? This can be a technical skill such as coding, or it can be a particularly deep knowledge in a sector such as hospitality, retail or professional sports.

3. Define potential gaps and explore the need for potential collaborators. This flexible framework can help sharpen the focus of a team that exists, and can also help clarify needs for potential new partners.

Anticipate the Needs of the Future User

As we work to form hypotheses and conduct experiments to validate our assumptions, we can tend to "push" our status quo perspective onto the future. William Cockayne and his team at Stanford's Foresight and Innovation program refer to this as the "Future User." Using an approach called future telling we can immerse ourselves in non-obvious emerging needs, and "pull" ideas towards the future in a way that overcomes the status quo mindset (Cockayne and Tahvanainen, 2013).

It is important during this stage to leverage the power of creative story telling. Immersive scenarios, done well, create "memories of the future," which can be a powerful way to build empathy with the needs, priorities and aspirations of the future user (De Geus, 2002, p. 21). We use a process called "in-casting" to create a sharp comparison of how the future user's needs and preferences may be distinct from those of the present user.

The second aspect is to push the limits of plausibility. The goal is not to create reliable predictions, but rather to stretch our understanding and imagination – breaking the death grip of the status quo. As futurist Dr. James Dator states in his second law of the future, "Any useful idea about the future must at first sound ridiculous." So we aim to explore for possibilities, not to create reliable predictions.

Mobilize to Get There Early

Once the entrepreneur has visited the future through scenarios and created empathy with the future user, the goal is to activate the ideation process. Given that our exploration has been made intentionally ambiguous, we need an ideation process that fits. Two key considerations are emphasized:

1. Define "opportunity spaces," not particular products. The distinction here is that opportunity spaces have an accuracy expectation that can be described as "probably approximately correct." Yes, that's right – probably approximately correct. This approach enables the entrepreneur to accomplish two key goals: first, to learn, which is to say to sharpen the definition of the emerging need in a way that allows for focused customer discovery; and, second, to evolve, which is to say move from a simple problem–solution understanding towards more

complexity, right in line with the MVP approach to the lean startup process (Valiant, 2013).

2. Unleash the maker instinct. To accomplish this challenge, we have students use Johansen's (2007) foresight tool called "Artifacts from the Future," which helps to cross the bridge from the future back to the present, thus enabling customer discovery and validation activities to be defined and initiated. The key benefit is that it helps to fill the gaps in the unarticulated needs space mentioned earlier.

As mentioned at the beginning of this chapter, the goal is to help students develop a capacity to feed the ideation funnel with insights and concepts that stretch the cognitive proximity of the current idea landscape. Entrepreneurial foresight can be a potent framework to help clarify the fuzzy front end and amplify the ideation process.

REFERENCES

Cockayne, B. and Tahvanainen, A. (2013), *Playbook for Strategic Foresight and Innovation*, Palo Alto, CA: Stanford University.

De Geus, A. (2002), *The Living Company: Habits for Survival in a Turbulent Business Environment*, Boston, MA: Longview.

Gavetti, G. (2011), *The Psychology of Strategic Leadership*, Boston, MA: Harvard Business School Press.

Johansen, B. (2007), *Get There Early: Sensing the Future to Compete in the Present*, San Francisco: Berrett-Koehler.

Valiant, L. (2013), *Probably Approximately Correct: Nature's Algorithms for Learning and Prospering in a Complex World*, New York: Basic Books.

22. Teaching lean: value creation (for students and faculty) in the classroom

Doan Winkel and Jeff Vanevenhoven

The teaching lean idea was born from a need to provide students an authentic experience that better mirrors the process of navigating the uncertainty of entrepreneurship. Entrepreneurship faculty have long debated the most impactful means to facilitate experiential learning. Lean methodology offers a powerful framework to actively engage students in learning entrepreneurship. Launched in 2012, a teaching lean experiment has been evolving at Illinois State University (ISU) via an undergraduate three-credit entrepreneurship course. Through this experience, engaged students develop their entrepreneurial mindset and toolkit.

CONTINUOUS DEPLOYMENT AND PIVOTING

Two tenets of lean startup are continuous deployment and pivoting. This refers to reducing cycle time by releasing all code into production as soon as written and structured corrections designed to test new hypotheses, respectively. In the teaching lean classroom, continuous deployment refers to the teacher giving resources and direction as soon as necessary. This takes constant contact between both parties, requiring students to consistently share their experiences, questions and frustrations. This is accomplished through a messy combination of meetings, G-drive folders, texting, calls and email.

In the teaching lean course framework, pivoting is accomplished through aggregating and responding to students' real-time experiences. Most students progress on a similar path and struggle with fairly consistent obstacles throughout their learning journey. The teacher takes a garbage-can approach by having access to many varied resources. He or she applies appropriate tools when creating assignments, and other learning opportunities on the fly. The teacher "releases" these when students voice questions or concerns.

THE COURSE

The product is the course itself, and the customers are the students, so students' first experiences in this course offer a realistic preview of entrepreneurship. The teacher meets them off-campus where there is significant foot traffic, gives each group 10 $1 bills, and tasks them to legally make as much profit as possible in 30 minutes with no introduction and no instruction. *There is only action*, signaling to the student the course centers around action and that they must own their experiences.

The (Lack of) Structure

Upon debriefing the students' first experience, the teacher engages in customer development to discover students' intentions and previous experience(s) with learning. Through understanding how students have successfully engaged in past learning processes, and their goals for their entrepreneurial journey, the teacher develops the minimum viable product (MVP). The MVP process is used when a product is released before it is finalized and iteratively adapted using customer feedback. The goal is to test hypotheses with user feedback, and begin the learning process as quickly as possible. In this case, the MVP is the first iteration of the course structure; *no structure is developed before actual engagement with students*. The structure is dependent solely on the experience and interests of the students and is unique to each course.

   Students are conditioned to expect structure in their learning experiences, so teachers must quickly establish trust if violating this norm. This is done in the ISU classroom by the teacher explaining to the students that he or she will not ask them to do anything he or she is not willing to do. The teacher takes action, succeeds and fails alongside the students, publicly, *in real time*.

The Experience

Each class session starts with one question from the teacher: *What can I help you with?* Students are encouraged to share their progress, failures and obstacles. Each class is an experiential learning lab. The teacher shares the progress, failures and obstacles faced starting his or her business. It is imperative for teachers to be transparent, as most students will look to their experience as a realistic guide for their journey.

   The teacher is the main resource for the students, sharing experience and recommendations, providing encouragement and feedback, and bringing in subject matter experts in the areas of concern voiced by students. The teacher shares blogs, articles or videos from his or her collection.

After each class, the teacher identifies themes emerging from the students' shared experience, and adjusts the course structure appropriately. This often takes the form of flipped-classroom type videos the teacher produces and shares with the students to offer encouragement and guidance. This, in essence, creates versions 2.0, 3.0 and so forth of the course; the teacher adjusts the roadmap and structure for the course to meet changing needs while maintaining progress towards course objectives.

The Assessment

Assessment is problematic given there are no structured assignments during the course (each student engages in an individualized learning and startup journey). With the spring 2016 semester, the teacher used a pre-test and post-test measuring student perceptions on their progress towards course objectives. Additionally, the teacher encourages students to hand in deliverables throughout the course, and provides feedback and a grade on each deliverable. The teacher informs students these grades are only the teacher's opinion and are not binding, but that the student is responsible for the ultimate course grade through his or her own self-evaluation. At the end of the semester, the teacher asks the students to write a one-page reflective statement. Students are provided the following guidelines:

- *To effectively accomplish course objectives, students need to answer (at least) these questions*:
  - Do people want this?
  - How much will they pay for this?
  - How much does it cost to acquire customers?
  - What is the market size?

- *Specifically, students grade themselves on three questions. Did you*:
  - find early customers and confirm their intent to buy before building?
  - validate your business model with quality data?
  - obtain authentic sales from strangers?

- *Their only choice of grades is A, B or F*:
  - There's no such thing as "almost success" or "almost fail" in real-world entrepreneurship. You either meet (B) or exceed (A) your goal, or you fail at meeting your goal (F).
  - A-level effort means you exceeded expectations, stunned

yourself, became famous. You have no hesitation in answering a thundering "*Yes!*" to those questions above.

- B-level effort means you gave it the old college try, you worked at your business, but blew it off sometimes, had competing priorities, made some progress but could have done (much) more. This means you hesitate or answer "Yes, but . . ." or "No, but . . ." to the questions above.
- Anything less than that is F-level effort. If you never checked in, if you blew off the class for the majority of the semester, if you tried your hardest to figure out how to get by doing as little as possible, you deserve an F.

COURSE OUTCOMES

Entrepreneurship classrooms have become a prominent venue for experimentation. The teaching lean classroom at ISU is a laboratory of extreme experimentation where students take complete ownership of their learning experience, and the teacher guides those journeys. As with any iterative process, it is evolving and bounces between variations of success and failure.

Some students balk at this opportunity, choose not to engage, and complain of the lack of structure and learning. Some students tentatively engage but rely heavily on teacher guidance. Some students grab the opportunity with gusto, engage fully, and emerge more confident in their ability to think and act entrepreneurially and to take ownership of their learning journey. Any student who engages on any level has enhanced his or her ability to recognize and seize opportunities, to mitigate risk, to leverage resources, and to design, build and sell something of value to someone else.

23. Games for the entrepreneurship classroom

Jim Hart

Entrepreneurs are creative individuals, creating products, services, jobs, culture, economic stimulation and opportunities. Entrepreneurship is big-vision creativity. Carl Jung, the famed Swiss psychoanalyst, said, "The creation of something new is not accomplished by the intellect, but by the play instinct, acting from inner necessity. The creative mind plays with the objects it loves" (1970, p. 200). With this in mind, I have developed a series of entrepreneurship games for the classroom that teach hard and soft skills. These games guide students through ideation, primary market research, attracting capital and acquiring resources, and do so through experiential learning. For this piece, "games" are being defined as "activities that challenge, enable interaction with others and are based in 'play.'" It is up to the professor to foster the environment of play within the classroom.

Though these games have been used in a wide range of environments (by myself and others), they are chiefly designed for undergraduate entrepreneurship education. I regularly use them to supplement lectures.

PERSONA IDEATION AND THREE IDEAS

Entrepreneurship typically begins with an idea, addressing a need or problem. However, many entrepreneurs create from what they personally think is interesting, rather than a potential customer, and then try to find a customer base that is also interested in their idea.

Bill Aulet (2013) advocates one should create with a customer in mind, as one increases the likelihood of success in doing so. With this premise, the exercise "Persona ideation and three ideas" was developed.

How to Play

a.   Students are paired (A and B) and asked to interview each other with a series of questions. Examples include "What keeps you up at night?,"

"If I gave you $100, what would you do with it?," "If you could do one thing to make your life a bit easier, what would you do?" and others. In asking these questions, students gain insight into their partner's interests, passions, pain points and problems.

b.   Students then create three original entrepreneurial concepts (products or services – for-profit or nonprofit) specifically for the person they each interviewed (their partner), based on the information each obtained from interviewing the other.

c.   Finally, each person asks his or her partner how many of the ideas, created specifically for that person, he or she 1) dislikes, 2) likes or 3) passionately likes.

Results

Having played this game in a wide array of environments, I have found consistent results. Approximately 95 percent of ideas are at least liked (including liked and passionately liked). Approximately 47 percent are considered "passionately liked," and only 5 percent are not liked at all. In the numerous times I've administered this game, only once has a person not liked any of the ideas created. This said, the partner created only one idea and not three.

As the ideas are created with the interviewed individual's own interests, passions, pain points and so on in mind, there is a higher likelihood the interviewee will like the ideas. Again, this is compared to an idea that is interesting first and foremost to the entrepreneur or creative, but not a pre-defined and specific customer.

MARKET FEEDBACK, SPEED DATING STYLE

How to Play

In this exercise, once students have an entrepreneurial concept, they line up in equally populated rows (either A or B), with each person facing another. In cases of odd numbers, a group of three can be formed. Each student duo has three minutes both to pitch an idea to the other and to receive feedback from the partner (totaling six minutes). Following six minutes, each person on row A moves one seat to the left while row B stays stationary. The person at the end of row A walks to the opposite end of the line. Everyone now sits before someone new. The process then repeats. In the course of an hour-long class, students can gain seven to eight points of peer feedback on their entrepreneurial concepts. At the professor's discretion, discussion can be had.

Benefits

Once a student develops a concept, it is important to gain feedback so as to reduce risk and potentially increase the concept's viability. This exercise or game teaches students about primary market research, risk reduction, adaptation and how engaging others can offer important feedback.

Results

Engaging each other, students might disregard the input entirely. They might discover new information – such as new markets or demographics and/or new revenue streams. As a result of this feedback, students may discover blind spots in their thinking, which can then be addressed, making their concepts stronger and potentially more viable.

THE MARBLE GAME

Canadian Kyle McDonald took a red paperclip and consistently traded up in value. After 14 well-thought-out trades, he went from owning a paper-clip to owning a house. Reading about this remarkable feat, I thought, "That is entrepreneurial wherewithal and I'm going to take that idea into my classroom."

Benefits

Students learn that the initial resources (namely, a marble) have little to nothing to do with their process of acquiring value, outside of being part of their story and serving as a starting point. For most, the marble has no obvious use and serves simply as a shiny object and symbol. The students' story, however, is a major factor in succeeding, as is their approach, sales strategy, passion, and willingness to ask for help. They are urged to utilize their personal network and leverage their own personality.

One couple in my Attracting Capital class recently raised, in three weeks' time, $5000 cash. In any given semester, students typically raise between $1500 and $5000 in assets, including cash – all of which is redistributed to an area nonprofit. This redistribution of assets enables students to do a social good, which has proved popular with my millennial generation students.

How to Play

Pair students into couples and give each couple a marble. In the event of an odd number, one group will have three students. Tell the class each couple has three weeks to amass as much value as possible by trading up. Those who acquire the most value will receive the title of "Champion of the Day" and decide which nonprofit all goods and cash are donated to.

In this three-step game- or exercise-based process, students learn (in an experientially based fashion) how to 1) ideate with a customer in mind, 2) engage in primary market research and 3) attract capital (or assets which can be liquidated). In other words, they learn to create something from nothing (a quintessential entrepreneurial ability) and take the key steps necessary in most entrepreneurs' processes. However, not all students succeed with these games. There are typically some students who try harder than others and typically some who do not try at all. This too serves as a learning opportunity. As is typically the case in real-world entrepreneurship, those who do not boldly act and engage with others (who do not try) do not succeed. Those entrepreneurs who do their best, are willing to try, put themselves out there, adapt, and leverage their own network and resources increase the likelihood of measurable success as entrepreneurs.

REFERENCES

Aulet, B. (2013), Build an end user profile, in *Disciplined Entrepreneurship: 24 Steps to a Successful Startup*, Hoboken, NJ: John Wiley & Sons, pp. 49–56.
Jung, C.G. (1970), The world of values, in *Psychological Reflections*, 2nd edn., ed. J. Jacobi, Princeton, NJ: Princeton University Press, pp. 183–272.

24. A unique student angel investing fund

Sara L. Cochran

Angel investors fund the majority of startups in the United States (Hudson, 2014b) and are referred to as a "hidden hero of the startup and innovation economy" (Hudson, 2014a, para. 1). While the average age of angel investors is currently 57 (Hudson, 2014b), this average age was expected to drop in 2015 (Hudson, 2015). Given angel investments are "critical initiators of startups and job creation" (Verrill and Hudson, 2013), it is important entrepreneurship students learn the fundamentals of angel investing. Because most business students learn best through experiential learning (Kolb, 1984), the University of Missouri developed the Allen Angel Capital Education (AACE) program to teach students the fundamentals of angel investing through a hands-on approach.

AACE is a hands-on class that performs research and invests donated assets in startup companies around Columbia, MO. Through cross-disciplinary collaboration, the team utilize their variety of skills to analyze investments for the possibility of investing their assets alone or as a part of Centennial Investors (CI), an angel network in Columbia, MO. Students cultivate deal flow, perform pre-screening duties, complete due diligence and structure investment contracts. After an equity position is taken, the program monitors portfolio holdings and harvests investments. This course gives students a competitive edge through both developing their strategic thinking skills and facilitating high-caliber network connections outside of their own school.

PROGRAM HISTORY

AACE began in 2009 when two students approached their finance professor about serving as the advisor for an angel investment student club, promising him all he had to do was sign the form. He found the students' energy for the project infectious and instead of forming the club AACE was created as a course.

THE COURSE

AACE is a course offered at both undergraduate and graduate levels. The students in the course make investment decisions that are then turned over to the University. The investments are made as the University of Missouri Board of Curators for the benefit of AACE, which allows the program to leverage the University's balance sheet to be eligible as a qualified investor. The business office and the legal council have official oversight over the AACE investments. However, a member of the class serves as the deal lead for each and communicates with the entrepreneurs.

In order to be considered for the course, students have to apply and be accepted; several applicants are turned away each semester. It is expected that students take the course multiple times, as the deals often span over multiple semesters. The average student completes three semesters. The course is interdisciplinary and multi-level and has seen undergraduates to Ph.D.s from just about every discipline. Typically, the course will include students from engineering, agriculture, journalism, law, psychology, accounting, finance and MBA programs. At the end of each semester, the instructor finds out which students are staying on board and generates a list of gaps to fill and begins the recruiting process targeting students to fill the gaps. The optimal class size is about 19 students so that there are enough persons to get the workload done but not so many that shirking takes place.

Each semester the course begins with the students reading *What Every Angel Investor Wants You to Know* (Cohen and Kador, 2013) and *Fool's Gold? The Truth behind Angel Investing in America* (Shane, 2009). The students are given quizzes over material from the books, and the instructor provides two days of lectures over the basics of angel investing. After that, the course is managed by two student leaders who do everything from scheduling to organizing each class meeting. Each semester, the students go on a trip, either regionally to St. Louis or Kansas City to explore deal flow, or nationally to attend the Angel Capital Association (ACA) National Conference or visit a vibrant investor and entrepreneurial community. The students spend most of the course evaluating deals, making the course very experiential in nature. In order to earn a grade for the course, students are evaluated on their three short papers, their attendance at various community events related to entrepreneurship and investing, and their participation in class.

FUNDING

In the beginning, AACE got $50 000 of a larger grant to the University from the Ewing Marion Kauffman Foundation to support entrepreneurship across campus. AACE also received funding from a local insurance company, the University and various donors, with the name coming from the largest donor, Walker Woodrow Allen. Most of the donations make up the evergreen investment fund; however, University funds are restricted to educational purposes only.

Since its inception, the AACE program has made four investments. One of these startups failed, yet two exits were expected in 2016 that would more than make up for the loss. The fund is evergreen, so the returns from the exits will be reinvested. Because financial success will come with an exit and most exits take at least seven years, other metrics are used to determine the program's success. These include determining if the businesses invested in are still working toward an exit, the job placement of graduates, and the reputation of the fund in the community.

PARTNERSHIP

AACE has a symbiotic relationship with Centennial Investors in Columbia, MO as a dues-paying member. AACE and CI review deals simultaneously, with the AACE students performing due diligence. The turning point of this relationship was when the AACE instructor was asked, "Well, what are the students doing?" In general, the AACE students prove to be more conservative and pass on more deals than the CI members.

BEST PRACTICES

- Enlist an engaged professor to oversee the program, ideally someone already involved with the partner angel group.
- Partner with your local angel group and elicit the strong support of the firm director.
- Engage in cross-disciplinary collaboration and recruit from across campus.
- Blend students from various levels, from undergraduate to Ph.D.
- Use students to lead the course; assign one student to be deal lead and communicate with the entrepreneur.
- Allow students to enroll in the course for multiple semesters.
- Be careful not to abuse students, especially if they are not earning a course credit.
- Pay students for due diligence work if they are not earning a course credit.

- Send out press releases and work with the campus communications office.
- Encourage students to highlight this on their resumes and spread the success stories. Students have received jobs because of this experience.

REFERENCES

Cohen, B.S. and Kador, J. (2013), *What Every Angel Investor Wants You to Know*, New York: McGraw-Hill Education.

Hudson, M. (2014a, November 19), Angels among us – huge impact on Main Street and growing global reach, *Forbes*, retrieved from http://www.forbes.com.

Hudson, M. (2014b), Important things to know about angel investors, Angel Capital Association, retrieved from http://www.angelcapitalassociation.org.

Hudson, M. (2015, January 8), 2015: the year for angel innovation, growth and returns? *Forbes*, retrieved from http://www.forbes.com.

Kolb, D.A. (1984), *Experiential Learning*, Englewood Cliffs, NJ: Prentice Hall.

Shane, S.A. (2009), *Fool's Gold? The Truth behind Angel Investing in America*, New York: Oxford University Press.

Verrill, D. and Hudson, M. (2013, September), Angel investors – critical initiators of startups and job creation, Presented at SEC Advisory Council on Small and Emerging Companies, retrieved from http://www.sec.gov.

25. Teaching entrepreneurial sales skills: a co-curricular approach

Eric Liguori, Birton Cowden and Giles Hertz

INTRODUCTION

Sales drive business and stimulate economic growth to such a large extent that one of every nine Americans works in sales (Grant, 2013). Yet, as a discipline, we fail to properly equip graduates with the sales acumen necessary for entrepreneurial success. While the critical importance of selling is widely accepted by entrepreneurship educators, only 21 percent of AACSB-accredited business schools offer any formal sales training to business students (Fogel et al., 2012). Additionally, the majority of the 21 percent with formal curricula only offer a single class, and often that course is not required for entrepreneurship majors. Thus, it's reasonable to infer that less than 5 percent of entrepreneurship majors are ever exposed to any formal sales training.

SOLD

An Entrepreneurial Sales Skills Bootcamp (SOLD) was established in 2013 to address this deficiency. SOLD is a five-module immersion into professional selling. As of spring 2016, SOLD has been offered at colleges and universities in California, Florida and Massachusetts, and will soon boast over 150 graduates.

Design and Structure

SOLD was designed to offer entrepreneurship students both an introduction to professional selling and a glimpse into a life in sales. A review of contemporary approaches to teaching professional sales led to the development of these five modules contained in the first pilot program conducted in 2013: 1) an overview of sales; 2) prospecting; 3) consumer behavior; 4) penetrating the market; and 5) life in sales. We ran the program weekly for five weeks, with modules 2 and 4 online, and module 5 a seasoned sales professional panel discussion and networking session.

While the pilot feedback was very positive, three themes emerged: 1) the consumer behavior module was ineffective; 2) the e-learning modules were well received (the opposite of what the first author hypothesized given they were crude MVPs); and 3) negotiation was a critical skill that was largely overlooked. Thus, module 3 was changed to negotiation, and the e-learning modules were further refined. Below is a short description of each module:

- Module 1 – overview of the sales process: This module is all about establishing a common language and an understanding of sales; it gets everyone working toward a common goal. Students are exposed to an overview of the sales cycle and sales management systems, different sales strategies and approaches (both direct and indirect), case examples of startup sales approaches, and how to develop a sales strategy for their given organization. We've partnered with Sandler Training's regional offices to conduct this module.
- Module 2 – prospecting: This module focuses on prospect identification and the prospect lifecycle as the prospect progresses through the sales funnel. Specific attention is placed on resources and databases, qualifying leads, and establishing and understanding sales metrics. Students walk away understanding the sales funnel: how to identify potential customers, what resources are available, how to prioritize leads, and the process of attrition of leads, with only some resulting in a sale.
- Module 3 – negotiation: This module begins as an overview to negotiations and best practices, and then quickly pivots into a live learning lab whereby each student participates in a series of experiential exercises beginning with Rowe's (2001) "Two dollar game." Debriefing the learning has proven to be especially critical in this context.
- Module 4 – market penetration: Establishing yourself as a player in the market, especially when you are a young entrepreneur pitching a new startup concept, is difficult. This module covers some case examples of local entrepreneurs who have successfully built reputations and garnered market share despite these obstacles.
- Module 5 – life in sales: We invite five to seven sales professionals to participate in a panel discussion on entrepreneurial sales moderated by a local CEO with "celebrity" status. The panelists are entrepreneurs or sales leads from growth oriented SMEs. The moderator poses the following three questions to the panel:

- How does your organization go about identifying and approaching new customers in the marketplace? What's your process for this?
- Obviously, increasing revenue and profit are key indicators of success, but what other metrics do you use to evaluate the progress and success of your sales pipeline?
- What is the best piece of advice you have for a new startup entrepreneur looking to begin selling to customers?

The panel culminates with an open Q&A session and then networking over light refreshments.

Implementation and Outcomes

SOLD is a part of the Entrepreneurship Education Project (EEP). EEP offers all students who complete the program a formal certificate of completion and eight continuing education units. The certificate option has been appealing to students, and with EEP as the issuing authority university concerns about students receiving an added certificate are minimized. Each module is professionally executed, with much of the content video-recorded.[1] Students are given formal name tents, note cards, speaker bios, pens and notebooks, and instructed to dress in business casual attire. Students are also given supplementary resource materials upon completion of each module, and contemporary sales books are given to each speaker to give away to participants, however they choose. A small fee is charged primarily to ensure students have "skin in the game," even though we typically refund it upon completion.

Delivery of the modules is flexible. In California, it was partially overlapped with a capstone entrepreneurship course and partially co-curricular, and ran weekly for five weeks. In Florida, it is co-curricular and offered as a weekend bootcamp. In Massachusetts, it is run as a five-week required program for freshman entrepreneurship students in their Residential Academic Program. In sum, the structure can be adapted to fit a given university's needs, and it has been well received at the freshman and senior levels.

To date, 98 students have completed SOLD, with about 60 more underway. Outcomes are strong; student feedback has been positive, and, unexpectedly, two students have already received (and accepted) full time sales job offers as a result of module 5's networking component (one for a New York City startup, the other for a corporate sales position with Hershey's). An adapted version of McGee et al.'s (2009) entrepreneurial self-efficacy scale is presently being used, with controls, to assess entrepreneurial sales self-efficacy pre- and post-completion of the program.

In sum, SOLD has proven to be an effective way to expose students to some formal sales topics and to get them thinking more specifically about how to identify, approach and interact with potential customers. We don't contend SOLD is a perfect solution to incorporating formal sales training into our curricula; rather, we recognize it may only be a small bandage on this gaping hole.

NOTE

1. Coleman Foundation support made recording possible. Past video clips can be down-loaded here: http://tinyurl.com/j5k6ol6.

REFERENCES

Fogel, S., Hoffmeister, D., Rocco, R. and Strunk, D.P. (2012), Teaching sales, *Harvard Business Review*, **90**(7), 94–99.
Grant, A.M. (2013), Rethinking the extraverted sales ideal: the ambivert advantage, *Psychological Science*, **24**(6), 1024–1030.
McGee, J.E., Peterson, M., Mueller, S.L. and Sequeira, J.M. (2009), Entrepreneurial self-efficacy: refining the measure, *Entrepreneurship Theory and Practice*, **33**(4), 965–988.
Rowe, M. (2001), The two dollar game, retrieved from http://ocw.mit.edu/courses/sloan-school-of-management/15-667-negotiation-and-conflict-management-spring-2001/lecture-notes/about_game.pdf.

26. Entrepreneurial consulting courses: increasing benefits to students in the new economy

Nathalie Duval-Couetil and Kris Taylor

INTRODUCTION

Consulting courses offered through entrepreneurship education programs can offer great value to both startups and students. Companies get access to low- to no-cost ideas and talent, contributing to their growth and development, while students gain professional experience by diagnosing and addressing the real world challenges faced by entrepreneurs and small enterprises. Goals of consulting courses can be complex and multifaceted – a combination of generating value to the customer in the form of robust market studies and reports, to exposing students to a variety of problem solving, communication, teamwork, and professional skills (Teckchandani and Khanin, 2014). Often housed in business schools, such courses are increasingly valued by accrediting bodies interested in expanding experiential learning for graduates (Doran et al., 2015).

Economic and workforce trends suggest that students in all majors can benefit from experiences that enhance their ability to act as self-employed consultants. Global competition and technological advances have led employers to "disaggregate jobs into specialized tasks," facilitating the growth of part-time and "contingent employment" (Manyika et al., 2011). It is estimated that one in three workers now earn income from work outside the traditional 9–5 job (Edstrom and Ladendorf, 2012), and it is projected that the future competitive success of organizations will hinge on their ability to deploy freelancers, consultants, outsourcing partners and other types of talent (Silverstone et al., 2016).

As a result, contemporary graduates should be prepared to be independent entrepreneurs, as it is likely many will be required to sell their talent, negotiate contracts, evaluate compensation, develop "statements of work," and maintain control over work process and quality (Cappelli and Keller, 2013). Developing these skills is the emphasis of an entrepreneurship consulting course offered through Purdue's cross-campus undergraduate entrepreneurship program.

COURSE OVERVIEW

The Consulting for Emerging Enterprises course is offered as a part of the Certificate in Entrepreneurship and Innovation program, which enrolls over 1000 students per year across 80 majors. The course is organized around two overarching goals pursued in parallel: 1) learning the process and profession of consulting; and 2) executing a consulting project for a local firm. The primary learning objectives for the course include:

- Develop the capacity to think strategically about a small business in a complex and changing environment.
- Create value for a consulting client through tangible deliverables in the form of new methods, processes, systems, products and services.
- Practice leadership and organizational skills by establishing priorities, setting realistic expectations, and completing objectives within a team.
- Demonstrate the ability to work effectively with clients, including building trust, sharing information, learning, and solving problems.
- Learn how to do independent consulting work.

Given the limited number of projects that can be managed and executed successfully, students must apply for one of 16 seats in the course. Students are selected based on their performance in two prior entrepreneurship courses, recommendations from faculty, and their ability to travel to a client site and meet the required time commitment.

Four consulting projects are carried out each semester. Clients represent a mixture of retail, manufacturing, professional, service and non-profit organizations, and there is no cost to participate. They are identified through referrals, local business groups, and the regional Small Business Development Center (SBDC). Selection criteria for clients include: locally owned and operated within 10 miles of campus; established with at least two years of successful operation; between 2 and 250 employees; a strong desire to help entrepreneurially minded students grow; and the ability to provide students with time and support. Each client selects a problem or opportunity on which to focus. In the first phase, students reach agreement on the scope and create an informal contract. Projects have included:

- filling excess manufacturing capacity for a precision machining company;
- evaluating relocation options for a professional services firm;
- researching options for expansion for a biomedical company;
- developing social media strategies for non-profits and retailers;
- conducting market research and evaluating marketing strategy for healthcare clinics, retailers and professional services firms;
- transitioning to a paperless office for a professional services firm;
- assessing customer satisfaction in healthcare services;
- evaluating fund-raising strategies for a non-profit;
- increasing profitability for a retailer and a small manufacturer.

COURSE MATERIALS AND FORMAT

The course meets twice per week. One is a classroom meeting focused on learning the consulting profession, and the other is spent with the client on-site. Two textbooks are used: *Flawless Consulting* (Block, 2011) and *The Trusted Advisor* (Maister et al., 2000). Students learn about the consulting process and profession through reading, lectures, quizzes, presentations, papers and weekly debriefs of their client work. Classroom topics include:

- the roles consultants play;
- establishing relationships and building trust;
- professional and meeting skills;
- contracting;
- secondary market research;
- primary research data collection;
- listening and observing;
- providing client feedback;
- making recommendations;
- identifying and overcoming client resistance;
- consulting ethics;
- choosing consulting as a career.

The consulting engagement utilizes a three-stage model to guide teams as they contract, gather and analyze data, and make recommendations. The model, based on Block (2011), provides a simple and logical framework to guide teams. It structures the consulting engagement as it evolves through the following three phases:

- Phase 1: entry and contracting. The consulting relationship is established with a focus on building trust. A problem statement is discerned, and agreement is reached on the scope, timing and deliverables.
- Phase 2: discovery and dialogue. The problem is defined in more concrete terms through the use of primary and secondary research, as well as questioning and observing. Engaging with the client refines the problem, and examining the facts, ideas and observations yields deeper insights that inform recommendations.
- Phase 3: feedback and the decision to act. Recommendations are distilled from the discovery process and are presented to the client in a way that is meaningful and a springboard to action.

Students sign a confidentiality agreement and define their project and deliverables in an informal contract with the client. Based on the objective(s), students conduct an analysis of the organization and complete pertinent research, ranging across surveys, interviews, visits to competitors and partner organizations, and "secret shopping."

Reports are submitted to the instructor in three phases, and feedback is provided. The first phase is a business overview, using the tools and frameworks learned in previous entrepreneurship classes (e.g., business model canvas). The second phase describes the data collection and analysis processes. The final phase is the students' recommendations. The final deliverable combines all three phases in a report which is presented to the client.

COURSE OUTCOMES

To date, the course has engaged 96 students and 24 client companies from the local business community. All students who participate in the course sit in on client presentations to see the work of their peers and participate in the dialogue that follows. Benefits to students have been multiple. Students have found the course to be a differentiator when applying for jobs with traditional employers as well as consulting firms. Some have been approached about continued consulting or job opportunities with their respective client companies.

Client evaluations have been 100 percent favorable based on formal feedback. Evidence of clients' satisfaction is their willingness to refer others to the program. Evaluation data indicate that value added to clients includes: the interdisciplinary nature of the student consulting teams; their strong interest in entrepreneurship; and the course being led by an experienced independent consultant and entrepreneurship educator who guides students through a rigorous process resulting in useful deliverables. An added benefit to the university is that the experience provides rich connections between students and the business community, particularly with companies unlikely to participate in typical college recruiting activities.

CONCLUSION

Contemporary graduates are entering a job market where the trend away from full-time work and toward contingent workers is likely to continue. Teaching students how they can leverage their education to more autonomously create economic value for clients in a relatively short period of time is a valuable skill. The experience of being comfortable with clients as an independent worker can only enhance a student's resilience and success in the contemporary economy.

REFERENCES

Block, P. (2011), *Flawless Consulting: A Guide to Getting Your Expertise Used*, San Francisco: John Wiley & Sons.
Cappelli, P. and Keller, J.R. (2013), Classifying work in the new economy, *Academy of Management Review*, **38**(4), 575–596.
Doran, M., Sciglimpaglia, D. and Toole, H. (2015), The role of field-based business consulting experiences in AACSB business education: an exploratory survey and study, *Journal of Small Business Strategy*, **12**(1), 8–18.
Edstrom, M. and Ladendorf, M. (2012), Freelance journalists as a flexible workforce in media industries, *Journalism Practice*, **6**(5–6), 711–721.
Maister, D.H., Green, C.H. and Galford, R.M. (2000), *The Trusted Advisor*, New York: Simon & Schuster.
Manyika, J., Lund, S., Auguste, B., Mendonca, L., Welsh, T. and Ramaswamy, S. (2011), *An Economy That Works: Job Creation and America's Future*, retrieved from http://www.mckinsey.com/global-themes/employment-and-growth/an-economy-that-works-for-us-job-creation.
Silverstone, Y., Tambe, H. and Cantrell, S. (2016), *The Rise of the Extended Workforce*, retrieved from https://www.accenture.com/us-en/insight-future-of-hr-rise-extended-workforce.aspx.
Teckchandani, A. and Khanin, D. (2014), The instructor's role in the student consulting process: working with the student team, *Small Business Institute Journal*, **10**(1), 11.

27. University collaboration: the New Jersey state business model competition

Susan Scherreik

New Jersey's entrepreneurship center directors at 11 universities are engaged in an innovative and highly collaborative project: U Pitch NJ, a statewide collegiate business model competition launched at Rutgers University on April 15, 2016. The event kicked off with the CEO of the NJ Economic Development Authority delivering a keynote address to some 150 students, faculty members, alumni, entrepreneurs and venture capitalists. The event was deemed a success, and planning is underway for next year's contest at Princeton University.

Why U Pitch NJ? We believe that linking and leveraging our resources in a statewide competition can reap myriad benefits. First, we feel that showcasing high-quality college startups can raise the profile of our entrepreneurship education programs and brand us as a source of new business development and job creation. We also believe that sponsoring a statewide competition can enrich the entrepreneurship experience for our students and provide them with a powerful forum for recognition. Lastly, we believe that this format is well suited to a densely populated, geographically small state that strives for a sense of its own identity. Indeed, we hope that this competition will help raise awareness that New Jersey – home to Bell Labs and Thomas Edison – is a vibrant place for innovation.

So how does a group of diverse public and private universities – ranging in size from 1400 students to over 66 000 students – pull this off? By taking a grassroots approach that allows us to be nimble and flexible despite operating within bureaucratic organizations. Our first step was to form the New Jersey Coalition of Collegiate Entrepreneurship Directors in response to the frustration we felt at meeting each other at USASBE and GCEC conferences, yet rarely seeing each other at home. At a Coalition brainstorming session, the idea of a statewide competition emerged. As the founding director of the Seton Hall University Center for Entrepreneurial Studies, I volunteered to chair the U Pitch NJ planning committee.

We allowed ample time for planning (18 months), held conference calls or meetings every six to eight weeks (with written summaries distributed to keep all informed), created committees to handle specific tasks, and set up an information sharing site. Above all, we carefully strived to achieve a group dynamic that enabled one member of the group to be the leader who ensured tasks were accomplished (myself), while stressing that all members of the group had an equal say in the creation of the competition. We needed to trust each other, accept doable results rather than strive for perfection, and see the process as fun, exciting and important. With these goals accomplished, our collaboration was marked by pleasant cooperation and few disagreements.

Being a self-selected group of motivated universities helped. With limited time and resources, we felt that conducting a campaign to formally invite every university in New Jersey to participate was beyond our scope. If our launch was successful, we reasoned, others would eagerly become involved in the future. That said, every institution that found us through word of mouth was welcomed. Listed alphabetically, the participating institutions were Drew University, Fairleigh Dickinson University, Montclair State University, New Jersey Institute of Technology, Princeton University, Rider University, Rutgers University, Saint Peter's University, Seton Hall University, Stevens Institute of Technology, and William Paterson University. Additionally, prominent non-profit groups we work with joined our planning effort, which broadened support. These include the NJ Technology Council, the NJ Business Incubation Network, and TechLaunch, a private investor accelerator.

Our biggest challenge involved funding. So that we would not have to rely on securing grants or on outside fund-raising – uncertain and time-consuming options – we asked each university to chip in $500 for cash prizes and event expenses. No participating university, however, wanted the job of collecting and then distributing the funds. Our solution: I asked an alumnus who is a partner in an accounting firm to donate his firm's services. A bank checking account was created for us, and the process worked smoothly, albeit requiring much paperwork to accommodate various university payment procedures.

We devised simple contest rules that would accommodate differences in our programs. We stressed that our focus would be on undergraduates, but allowed universities to select student teams that could mix undergraduates and graduate students because one of the university programs did so in their courses. Many of us choose as student teams the winners of internal business model competitions, but each university had leeway to select its team however it wished. A week ahead of the competition, judges received each team's one-page executive summary. The student teams were evaluated on these summaries, plus their seven-minute oral presentations at the competition itself.

We debated how to select judges, wondering whether we should skip alumni from our universities to avoid the appearance of conflicts of interest. Ultimately, we decided that, above all else, our judges should be prominent New Jersey entrepreneurs. If judges were also alumni of our universities, their affiliations would demonstrate that the state's universities produced successful entrepreneurs, we reasoned. It turned out that several of the judges held undergraduate and graduate academic degrees from two or more of our institutions. In addition, we found that it was a plus to provide our judges with detailed judging criteria with numeric rating grids to guide evaluations. (A committee developed the judging materials.)

Another goal was to give student teams meaningful feedback outside of the judging, and provide networking opportunities for attendees. So we started the event with a pizza party in an exhibition area. The student teams each had a display table with posters and other information about its startup, with business cards or other contact information.

Rutgers was the venue for the competition because it is the state university and centrally located. (The event will rotate among universities.) We scheduled U Pitch NJ from 1 p.m. to 5 p.m. on a Friday. The competition ran an hour longer than anticipated because of the student networking event. Going forward, we may turn U Pitch NJ into an all-day event because we believe every university team deserves equal time, with no preliminary round eliminations. The good news: the event was so engaging that the time flew by, and we believe that a longer event will be as successful.

The next step? We plan on holding a post-mortem meeting to solicit feedback to improve the process. Simply agreeing in advance to hold a post-mortem paved the way for a smooth competition. In the days leading up to U Pitch NJ, a few issues arose but were quickly resolved because we could point to the post-mortem meeting as the proper forum to air concerns.

As one of the judges enthusiastically said to me during the proceedings, "This is a really necessary and important event for the universities to be doing!" All participants have signed on for next year, and we will now begin to invite our colleagues not yet involved. We entrepreneurship center directors bring much to the table, and contests like U Pitch NJ show that we can lead the way in entrepreneurial education innovation. Our bricks-and-mortar institutions provide valuable opportunities and resources, including vibrant alumni networks that connect students with mentors and investors. By cooperating with each other, we leverage our resources to expand our states' entrepreneurial eco-systems.

28. CUNY's STEM Virtual Enterprise program

Christoph Winkler, Stuart A. Schulman and Edgar E. Troudt

The Virtual Enterprise (VE) program at the City University of New York (CUNY) gives students from a variety of educational levels and academic disciplines the opportunity to practice entrepreneurship in a safe learning environment. VE is deeply rooted in experiential learning principles (Kolb, 1984) where students identify, build and launch a business in an online marketplace that connects students from across the globe.

Over the years, the VE program has expanded beyond traditional business programs into science, technology, engineering and math (STEM) disciplines, with support from the National Science Foundation's (NSF) Advanced Technological Education (ATE) program.[1] In order to illustrate the evolution of this innovative entrepreneurship education simulation program, this chapter provides an overview of the main program components of a VE, its curricular adaptations within a STEM context, and an overview of useful resources to help support entrepreneurship education in STEM programs through the CUNY Institute for Virtual Enterprise (IVE).

THE VIRTUAL ENTERPRISE AT A GLANCE

Entrepreneurial learning in a VE is an intrinsically social process that is composed of three program components: an experiential learning pedagogy, a virtual economy, and a social network:

- *Experiential learning pedagogy.* Students in a VE work in teams of three to six students to identify an opportunity and build a viable business model for their idea. They are engaged in a series of ideation cycles in order to derive feedback about their ideas through pitches, market research, and peer and expert feedback. Once students have completed their business model they launch their business within a simulated marketplace, the IVE MarketMaker (CUNY IVE, 2015).

- *Virtual economy.* The IVE MarketMaker is the technological backbone of the VE and is composed of a bank (often as an investment fund), an e-commerce platform, a virtual credit card system and a stock market. During a VE experience students are able to pitch their businesses online by uploading elevator pitch videos, securing funding, building the company website and online storefront, and managing the overall operations and finances. Given that this is an online learning environment, products or services are not real, and funding and sales within the virtual economy are simulated through its own virtual currency.
- *Social network.* Learning within a VE is not limited to the classroom. VEs connect students and businesses through their business websites, enabling students to seek social feedback about their business through Facebook likes and comments. In addition, IVE is organizing a series of online trading days (CUNY IVE, 2015) where participating students can present their businesses to one another. These events are highly interactive and utilize online presentation tools that connect between 35 and 50 student teams across the globe.

When considering the implementation of these three interconnected program components, it is important to note that VE is not a stand-alone curriculum. Instead, VE should be seen as a customizable entrepreneurship education method or tool that can be offered as a *freestanding course* or *infused into any existing course* of any content discipline (e.g., business, art, science).

THE STEM VIRTUAL ENTERPRISE

Our team at IVE has received several NSF grants to develop a nationally replicable and scalable model for technician education that aims to promote innovation and entrepreneurship within a STEM workforce (e.g., Winkler and Troudt, 2008). This work started within the academic fields of information technology (IT) and biotechnology and resulted in the development of two types of course formats.

The first course, *ve^{it}-Careers*, was designed to help early IT students explore the range of IT-related jobs within a VE simulation course. In that course, students are asked to research different jobs within the IT field, create job descriptions for these jobs and ultimately solve technical problems in the corresponding departments as part of a VE simulation experience. The second course was developed for both IT (*ve^{it}-Capstone*) and biotechnology (*ve^{biotech}-Capstone*). It was designed to give advanced IT and biotech students the opportunity to apply their technical skills within a simulated business context. Analogous to the case of a traditional VE, students identify a business problem and develop technology (e.g., DNA collection kit) in order to solve that problem. Subsequently, students are able to pitch for funding and participate in the virtual economy by setting up their online stores and trading their virtual products online and during IVE's online trading days.

Building on this work, IVE has partners with several STEM programs across the United States and helped support adaptations of VE within those respective programs. Our experience has shown that the development of a stand-alone course was often competing with other curricular requirements. As a result, we found the infusion into an existing STEM course to be the most effective one (e.g., Winkler et al., 2015).

GETTING STARTED WITH STEM VE

In order to better serve our growing community, our team at IVE developed a support network that offers both face-to-face faculty development opportunities and online resources. During the Annual Innovation and Entrepreneurship in STEM Entrepreneurship Education Conference (Schulman et al., 2014), participants were offered an immersive and hands-on experience in adapting VE to their own STEM courses or programs. An essential component of the conference is the development of a draft curriculum and associated course evaluation metrics based on an action research framework (Winkler, 2014). To access support material, recordings from the conference, and online webinars visit www.ive.cuny.edu/STEM.

Most recently, IVE is in the process of completing a multi-year project to document entrepreneurship education in STEM (Schulman et al., 2012). The series follows five different VE settings: 1) a business classroom that simulates STEM-related enterprises using VE; 2) a STEM classroom that applies the discipline in a simulated business using VE; 3) a contract research organization where a college serves the small bio-manufacturing needs of the community; 4) a high-school robotics classroom that acts as a business to fund its research venture; and 5) a pitch competition where students ideate and pitch STEM-related businesses. The series covers various concepts that instructors and students may face in such simulations. It is meant both as a learning tool for students and as professional development for STEM instructors. To access the series and learn more about CUNY's STEM VE program visit www.ive.cuny.edu/STEM.

NOTE

1. This material is based upon work supported by the National Science Foundation under Grant Nos. DUE-0802365, DUE-1205031 and DUE-1446976. Any opinions, findings, conclusions or recommendations expressed in this material are those of the authors and do not necessarily reflect the views of the National Science Foundation.

REFERENCES

CUNY IVE (2015), The MarketMaker, retrieved from http://www.ivefinancial. com.

Kolb, D.A. (1984), *Experiential Learning: Experience as the Source of Learning and Development*, Englewood Cliffs, NJ: Prentice Hall.

Schulman, S.A., Troudt, E.E. and Winkler, C. (2012), Student entrepreneurs: a reality-based video series following the STEM Virtual Enterprise, National Science Foundation (Grant No. DUE-1205031).

Schulman, S.A., Winkler, C. and Troudt, E.E. (2014), Conference on the STEM Intrapreneurship and Entrepreneurship Education Spectrum, National Science Foundation (Grant No. DUE-1446976).

Winkler, C. (2014), Toward a dynamic understanding of entrepreneurship education research across the campus – social cognition and action research, *Entrepreneurship Research Journal*, 4(1), 1–25.

Winkler, C. and Troudt, E.E. (2008), Enhancing soft and entrepreneurial skills training for two-year college technicians using a contextualized business simulation program, National Science Foundation (Grant No. DUE-0802365).

Winkler, C., Schweikert, C., Troudt, E.E. and Schulman, S.A. (2015), Infusing business and entrepreneurship education into a computer science curriculum – a case study of the STEM Virtual Enterprise, *Journal of Business and Entrepreneurship*, 27(1), 1–21.

29. UCCS Entrepreneurial Identity Project

Thomas N. Duening and Matthew L. Metzger

The Entrepreneurial Identity Project (EIP) at the University of Colorado Colorado Springs (UCCS) is focused on helping entrepreneurship students develop their entrepreneurial identity. This work is based on a perceived gap between the aspirations of entrepreneurship education and its actual outcomes. That is, entrepreneurship educators traditionally, and rightly, strive to create entrepreneurs. However, if students don't start ventures while they are still in college there is little direct evidence for educators to determine if that goal has been achieved. Thus there is often a gap between educators' aspirations and abilities to measure long-term effects of their entrepreneurship curricula.

We posit that entrepreneurship educators, in addition to striving to create entrepreneurs, should strive to assist students in the internalization of the virtues and character strengths associated with entrepreneurial identity. We believe there is a distinct *something that it is like* to be an entrepreneur. The scholarly literature that informs our classroom interventions and research is centered on identity theory. Identity theory seeks to understand how individuals construct and negotiate a personal work-centered identity. Identity refers to "the conception of the self reflexively and discursively understood by the self" (Kuhn and Nelson, 2006). Identity theory is concerned with questions such as "Who am I?" and "How should I act?" (Cerulo, 1997). Indeed, some scholars have noted that identification with a social category is *necessary* to call forth human action. Foote (1951, p. 19) said: "Doubt of identity, or confusion where it does not cause complete disorientation, certainly drains action of its meaning, and thus limits mobilization of organic correlates of emotion, drive, and energy which constitute the introspectively-sensed 'push' of motivated action." Thus, confusion about one's identity – certainly a commonplace at the age of most undergraduates – not only may cause a sense of disorientation, but also inhibits focused action.

A key distinction in the identity theory literature is that between *identification* and *internalization*. Individuals may identify with a particular social category without necessarily internalizing the category's norms and values (Hogg and Turner, 1987). Social identification helps individuals answer the question "Who are you?" Distinctively, internalization reflects the extent to which the individual incorporates and acts on the values, attitudes and virtues of the referent social identity. It helps the individual answer the question "What should I do next?"

ENTREPRENEURIAL IDENTITY

We base our definition of entrepreneurial identity on the concept of "virtue." Importantly, we distinguish virtue from mindset. Many entrepreneur programs focus on creating an entrepreneurial mindset. We believe that each term is operationalized by the way it is measured. To measure a mindset requires testing a subject and assessing the responses against a pre-established template (Haynie et al., 2010). To measure a virtue, by way of contrast, requires observing how one actually behaves in the world. Since internalization of an identity answers the question "What should I do next?," we believe virtues and their action-in-the-world measurement criteria are best suited as targets for entrepreneurial identity.

We define virtue as "consistent action in the world." What this means is that to be considered virtuous one must be consistent in practicing the virtue. Consider that one would not be considered to be honest if one were honest only occasionally. The notion of "action in the world" connotes that one's practice of a virtue affects others. That is, one would not be considered as honest if there was no one else to make that assessment.

Some of our work on virtues is derived from the scholarly literature on positive psychology. Significantly, in this literature virtues represent character strengths (i.e., trait-like attributes that are at least partially malleable) and are substantively different from personality traits (i.e., inherited attributes that are unchanging). In fact, one definition explicitly specifies that a virtue is "an *acquired* human quality the possession and exercise of which tends to enable us to achieve those goods which are internal to practices" (MacIntyre, 2000, p. 191, emphasis added).

We propose (Duening and Metzger, 2014) that the virtues associated with the social category entrepreneur include: 1) commitment to value creation; 2) deference to the market's judgment of value; 3) respect for private property and contractual obligations; and 4) resilience in the event of failure.

CLASSROOM INTERVENTIONS

The classroom interventions that we currently have deployed in the Principles of Entrepreneurship course (ENTP 3000, a junior level course) are based on the entrepreneurial virtues noted in the section above. After a thorough introduction to the entrepreneurial virtues, students are asked to undertake assignments that require them to step into the world of the entrepreneur and try on the virtues as one tries on a new jacket. Throughout the semester we begin each class session by discussing how well the virtues are "fitting." There is no pressure to conform, only a continual reminder to experiment and compare how it feels to act on the entrepreneurial virtues with their previous life.

The main deliverable for the course requires students to use the semester to explore and internalize the four entrepreneurial virtues. This is an individual project that culminates in a self-reflective essay on how practicing the virtues has affected their life. The individual project description reads as follows:

Entrepreneurial virtues internalization project

You are to write a *seven-page* paper discussing what you experienced by applying the four entrepreneurial virtues in your daily life throughout this semester. Your paper should address:

- How you practiced creating value for others during the semester
- What talents you have that you think can be leveraged for a business venture
- How resilient you are
- How well you are able to live up to obligations you make to others

The responses that we have been receiving to these exercises indicate that students understand both that they are internalizing and reifying the entrepreneurial virtues and that they find the experience rewarding. Student responses indicate that they have embraced the identity development process, which is explicitly discussed in class as a goal of the project prior to its assignment. Below are just a few representative responses we received to the project from the fall 2015 class:

- *STUDENT #1:* "To me one of the most important entrepreneurial virtues that we learned this semester was the creation of value for others. I think, of everything I learned and got from this class, this is the one that stuck out the most to me and that I found to be one of the most important things that I learned."

- *STUDENT #2:* "The virtues that I have learned are something that will be with me every day and I'll know that creating value is something I can do every day."
- *STUDENT #3:* "My overall experience from applying the entrepreneur virtues to my daily life over this semester can be summed up by saying that creating value for others and living life with virtues improves your quality of life."
- *STUDENT #4:* "The most important piece of knowledge I gained from UCCS's Entrepreneurship 3000 class is that not all learning is done in a classroom with my nose in a textbook. To really become an entrepreneur, one must be willing to try new things despite the risks and not give up on their goals . . . Through the practice of value creation I learned a lot about myself. I was able to directly identify the things that mean the most to me along with the skills I possess."

These are just several responses from the fall 2015 undergraduate cohort (total student count 64). In the spring 2016 semester the Entrepreneurial Identity Project involved more than 110 students, including 46 MBA students. We anticipate following up with consenting students for several years after they graduate to determine whether the entrepreneurial virtues have been internalized and continue to play a role in their lives. Our belief is that students who identify themselves as entrepreneurs when they graduate – *note*: *whether or not* they have started a venture by that time – are more likely one day to start a venture. In addition, we hypothesize that they also will be more resilient to venture failure and to try multiple times before succeeding or seeking more traditional career paths.

REFERENCES

Cerulo, K. (1997), Identity construction: new issues, new directions, *Annual Review of Sociology*, **23**, 385–409.

Duening, T.N. and Metzger, M.M. (2014), The entrepreneurial method: moral virtues as the foundation of entrepreneurial expertise, *American Journal of Entrepreneurship*, **7**(1), 78–101.

Foote, N.N. (1951), Identification as the basis for a theory of motivation, *American Sociological Review*, **16**(1), 14–21.

Haynie, J.M., Shepherd, D.A., Mosakowski, E. and Earley, P.C. (2010), A situated metacognitive model of the entrepreneurial mindset, *Journal of Business Venturing*, **25**(2), 217–229.

Hogg, M.A. and Turner, J.C. (1987), Social identity and conformity: a theory of referent informational influence, in W. Doise and S. Moscovici (eds.), *Current Issues in European Social Psychology*, Vol. 2, Cambridge, UK: Cambridge University Press, pp. 139–182.

Kuhn, T. and Nelson, N. (2006), Reengineering identity: a case study of multiplicity and duality in organizational identification, *Management Communication Quarterly*, **16**(1), 5–38.

MacIntyre, A. (2000), *After Virtue: A Study in Moral Theory*, London: Duckworth.

30. The Campus-linked Accelerator Program in Canada

Francine Schlosser, Margaret Cichosz-Grzyb, Martin Croteau, Donovan Dill, Valerie Fox and Annette Markvoort

DEVELOPING A PROVINCE-WIDE YOUTH ACCELERATION AND INNOVATION STRATEGY

There is an interesting innovation policy experiment underway at academic institutions in Ontario, Canada. Ontario's universities and community colleges, once focused almost exclusively on research and teaching, are now leading the charge on supporting youth entrepreneurship. A myriad of new initiatives are emerging on Ontario campuses, including outreach campaigns, experiential learning opportunities, mentorship programs and startup accelerators.

In Canada, universities conduct a disproportionately large percentage of total research and development when compared to universities in other industrialized nations. However, Canada has struggled to commercialize the results of this academic research. Key stakeholders in Canadian business, government and academia have recognized that improving Canada's entrepreneurial culture is critical to becoming more globally competitive, and that Canada's academic institutions must be an important part of the solution (Institute for Competitiveness and Prosperity, 2012).

In recognition of this, Ontario's provincial government has been making significant investments in regional networks to support entrepreneurship for over 15 years. In 2001, Ontario created a network of Small Business Centres to help local businesses. In 2009, they took the next step by creating Regional Innovation Centres that help build highly scalable technology-based businesses.

Many of the millennial generation are not content with the idea of a traditional job and view entrepreneurship as a tool to build the life they want for themselves and to change the world (Fromm, 2015). Recognizing the need to better support young entrepreneurs, Ontario has recently added significant investments in campus entrepreneurship activities to its innovation strategy. These investments are managed by the Ontario Centres of Excellence (OCE), an organization with a long track record of bridging the gap between academia and the private sector. OCE's role is to help integrate academic institutions into Ontario's growing entrepreneurship ecosystem and, consequently, to help embed entrepreneurship within the culture and mandate of Ontario's universities and colleges.

CAMPUS-LINKED ACCELERATORS

The Campus-linked Accelerator (CLA) was introduced to scale (grow) campus-linked entrepreneurship capacity by funding those post-secondary institutions with proven experience and existing commitments to entrepreneurship capacity, and campus-linked entrepreneurship activities and/or capacity and success in supporting youth-led entrepreneurship (Ontario Centres of Excellence, 2015). The CLAs were meant to create, improve and sustain a culture of entrepreneurship among students and youth in their regions, and to integrate these entrepreneurial activities with investors, industry and other stakeholders in their region (Ontario Centres of Excellence, 2016). Ten post-secondary institutions in Ontario were funded by the provincial government to expand their activities related to entrepreneurial exposure and awareness, education, lean startup, commercialization and incubation.

This policy capitalized on institutions that were already set up with research capacities, learning environments and teachers, thus reducing pressure on program budgets to cover dearth costs (for example, lab environments, and technology). By introducing entrepreneurship as a discrete outlet within the institutions, the government could optimize academic funding to match with new economic realities. Additionally, this created recruitment opportunities in the catchment areas, providing a reason for non-students to engage with the campus and take advantage of other opportunities.

Today, building on the original 10 CLAs, a network of 42 universities and colleges in Ontario is undertaking entrepreneurship activities on campuses. These academic institutions are further linked to Ontario's Small Business Enterprise Centres and Regional Innovation Centres to form the Ontario Network of Entrepreneurs (ONE). With over 100 member organizations working together to help Ontario entrepreneurs, the ONE is among the largest collaborative networks of entrepreneurship support organizations in the world.

The budget for this initiative has reflected its strategic importance within the province of Ontario's innovation agenda. A total of $25 million over two years was allocated in Ontario's 2013 budget as part of its Youth

Jobs Strategy. In 2015, funding was renewed, with a further $13.8 million over two years. In the second round of funding, the province initiated an even more cohesive strategy, encouraging collaboration between academic institutions within the same community, and even greater integration of universities and colleges within their regional entrepreneurship ecosystem.

INSTITUTIONAL DIFFERENTIATION

Each institution has interpreted and introduced entrepreneurship programming that mirrors its own culture and strengths. For example, the ACCEL program at Centennial College relies upon a deeply experienced team of professionals for mentoring. In contrast, the University of Windsor's EPICentre has been built from the bottom up through the active collaboration and engagement of faculty members in all disciplines. The DMZ at Ryerson University, one of the top three incubators in the world, was built on the university's strategic programming in digital media and technology, and so grew from the "Digital Media Zone" to encompass other zones of expertise. The location of the campus has also impacted the development of individualized CLA initiatives. The University of Windsor, located across the Detroit River from Detroit, works with Detroit and other Michigan-based incubation and acceleration to develop cross-border entrepreneurial opportunities.

INSTITUTIONAL VALUE OF ENTREPRENEURSHIP

Although each institution must report on standard metrics imposed by the Ontario Centres of Excellence to allow for a collective evaluation of the CLA program, the interpretation of success is also allowed to vary according to the objectives and milestones set by each institution. This creates a better integration with the different capabilities and competencies based on institutional size, location and research strengths.

These institutions share a similar value on entrepreneurship at the executive levels. For example, at the University of Windsor and Ryerson University, entrepreneurship and career preparation are embedded within each institution's strategic plan. Top-down support from the President's Office is essential to sustain multi-disciplinary entrepreneurship on campus. Fanshawe College provides tangible support by earmarking internal entrepreneurship funding based on enrollment, to the tune of $1.50 per student per semester from student services fees.

SHARING BEST PRACTICES

The Ontario Centres of Excellence administer and coordinate the initiative, by collecting and disseminating best practices among the participating institutions. To this end, a shared "CampusStart" portal has been introduced, and institutions are encouraged to share success stories on this. They also hold quarterly meetings of the CLAs, and discuss best practices and problem solutions.

REGIONAL INTEGRATION

The policy has encouraged the larger CLAs to build collaborative relationships with the local entrepreneurship ecosystem, including taking leadership positions in formalized regional support networks, cross-pollinating advisory boards, and becoming members of the boards of directors for the Regional Innovation Centres, Economic Development Agencies and Chambers of Commerce.

CONCLUSION

The Campus-linked Accelerator Program provides an example of a deliberate government policy to develop and connect a treasure-trove of highly innovative youth to scalable economic enterprise development.

REFERENCES

Fromm, J. (2015), Millennials in the workplace: they don't need trophies but they want reinforcement, *Forbes*, retrieved January 30, 2016 from http://www.forbes.com/sites/jefffromm/2015/11/06/millennials-in-the-workplace-they-dont-need-trophies-but-they-want-reinforcement/#6960222e5127.
Institute for Competitiveness and Prosperity (2012), *Small Business, Entrepreneurship, and Innovation*, Working Paper 15, February, Toronto: Institute for Competitiveness and Prosperity.
Ontario Centres of Excellence (2015), retrieved December 29, 2015 from http://www.oce-ontario.org/programs/entrepreneurship-programs/CLAs.
Ontario Centres of Excellence (2016), retrieved March 7, 2016 from http://www.oce-ontario.org/programs/entrepreneurship-programs/CLAs#sthash.X1Z8FVef.dpuf.

31. Social media – a powerful tool for entrepreneurship students

Gene Poor and Kirk Kern

Over the last decade social media has evolved into a very powerful two-way marketing tool for engaging customers, building relationships, sharing information, networking, and increasing sales. Entrepreneurs now have the power to leverage the consumer voice through social media's interactive and integrated components, from marketing, advertising and public relations to customer service and product or service development (Qualman, 2013).

In North America 74 percent of adults use social media, including 49 percent of the 65-plus population (Pew Research Center, 2014). Additionally, social media induced sales were expected to grow from $20 billion in 2014 to more than $30 billion in 2015 (Statista, 2016). Analysts predict social media's rapid evolution will be so disruptive it will result in a significant change in how we live and, specifically, how entrepreneurs carry on commerce by 2017. Yet despite 10–15 years of development, social media is still in its infancy, and these platforms are still in a state of flux. While it is difficult to track and follow given new platforms continue to surface, there are some dominant platforms: Facebook, Twitter, YouTube, Instagram, LinkedIn, Google+ and Pinterest.

The use of social media at Bowling Green State University (BGSU) is best represented by four distinct phases. Each of these phases has had key elements and events that led to a substantial social media movement among students, faculty and administration.

PHASE ONE – BIRTH OF ENTREPRENEURSHIP AND EARLY SOCIAL MEDIA

Gene Poor arrived at BGSU in 2003 and added website development and blogging to the curriculum. Entrepreneurship students purchased their domain name, built and branded their website and business, and blogged their expertise. Ultimately the entrepreneurship minor evolved into a five-course sequence of compatible majors across campus.

PHASE TWO – EXPANSION OF SOCIAL MEDIA (2012)

The BGSU College of Business hired a non-academic Dean (Ray Braun) who recognized the power of social media as well as appointed Kirk Kern as Director of the Dallas-Hamilton Center for Entrepreneurial Leadership. Braun and Kern welcomed Erik Qualman, an internationally recognized expert on social media, to BGSU's campus in spring of 2013. He demonstrated the power of social media during his keynote speech by addressing how a word-of-mouth marketing message can erupt into a "world-of-mouth" volcano.

Inspired by the positive reaction to Qualman's message by the conference attendees, Braun, Kern and Poor became committed to revamping the curriculum to include teaching the importance of "social media" in all entrepreneurship courses. The trio developed a system called Integrated Social Media Strategy (ISMS), the notion that all social media efforts have a planned, logical direction that ultimately leads the audience to an appropriate website. Buried in the ISMS message is the notion of finding an appropriate social voice that encourages audience interaction, builds relationships, and generates desired goals and results. The ISMS became the marketing framework for all five entrepreneurial courses.

PHASE THREE – TOTAL SOCIAL MEDIA IMMERSION

Braun and Kern co-created the "Hatch™" in the spring of 2013. This 10-week program is open to all students and includes a website, a Facebook presence and a Twitter account as mechanisms to generate participation. At the beginning of each spring semester, the selected participants are paired with an alumni mentor who helps hone their business idea into a provocative presentation using Instagram, YouTube and Vine. In April, the students pitch their proposals to five alumni, who question them and can invest their own money into the students' venture. To make the event even more compelling, outside investors can use Twitter to tweet their interests in either partnering with a student venture or funding a venture that was not funded by any of the alumni.

The 2015 Hatch™ was held in front of a live audience of 3500 people. It was also streamed via the Internet to 68 alumni watch parties throughout the USA and Europe. Social media platforms drove this entire event.

PHASE FOUR – EXAMPLES OF STUDENT SUCCESS

ESHP 2040 Introduction to Entrepreneurship

Once students in the introductory course saw how social media could be used successfully in entrepreneurship, the movement began to grow. Paul H. is a classic example: he is a huge fan of Instagram and was cognizant of the platform's image quality over quantity requirements. As a hobby, he began experimenting with stop-motion animation and became an expert at creating unique 15-second videos. He posted a few stop-motion videos on Instagram that illustrated the correct way of tying a tie, folding clothes and packing a suitcase. A clothing company saw a few of his Instagram shots and hired him to make short trial commercials, which were extremely successful, and an ongoing collaborative entrepreneurial business was born!

ESHP 3040 Entrepreneurial Creativity

In the Entrepreneurial Creativity course, Pinterest is required for collecting inspirational ideas about starting new ventures. One student, Kristen, uses Pinterest to find ideas and to showcase her products. She has over 40 000 niche followers who subscribe to her website blog. She has a channel on YouTube with dozens of Vblogs and is progressively moving toward a network. All of these efforts allow her to cross-sell her ideas on Amazon and similar sites.

ESHP 3140 The Sell

This is an entrepreneurial marketing course that incorporates ISMS for marketing research, branding and product launch as a class project for a veteran businessman who developed a new dry rub seasoning mix. He used Facebook to reach 347 self-proclaimed grilling devotees to understand their buying habits. Armed with knowledge about customers from researching Facebook and Twitter, and a minimal $2000 budget, the students designed an ISMS driven soft launch of the client's product. Finally, they suggested using Periscope to broadcast at the upcoming area rib-off to entice attendees to sample this new product. The client agreed to launch the product in 2016 – all because of the power of social media.

ESHP 3240 The Prelaunch

This entrepreneurial marketing course helps students gain confidence about launching their products. Elsa V., ESHP student and a 2015 Hatch participant, has created a new enterprise called "Pieces of Me." Her unique concept is designed to take a customer's personality and turn it into a wearable work of art. A specialized and patented algorithm creates an exclusive icon pattern based on the unique characteristics of the customer. The customer can then purchase customized products that display this distinctive pattern. This venture from customer input to product output is entirely dependent on social media. Elsa has leveraged and used Pinterest, Twitter, Facebook and Instagram both to launch her business and to gain customers.

LOOKING FORWARD

We have made great strides using media, but we're still learning. Each social media platform evokes its own unique message. What content or story works on one platform may not work on another. It takes an incredible amount of effort to figure out how best to use social media. Unlike the case for traditional marketing media that give nearly instant feedback, it takes a long time to see if social media offers a payback, but if you're not playing the game there will be no payback!

REFERENCES

Pew Research Center (2014), Social media update 2014, retrieved from http://www.pewinternet.org/2015/01/09/social-media-update-2014/.

Qualman, E. (2013), *Socialnomics: How Social Economics Transforms the Way We Live and Do Business*, Hoboken, NJ: John Wiley & Sons.

Statista (2016, January), Worldwide social commerce revenue from 2011 to 2015, retrieved from http://www.statista.com/statistics/251391/worldwide-social-commerce-revenue-forecast/.

Index